Days of the Lord
THE LITURGICAL YEAR

Days of the Lord
THE LITURGICAL YEAR

Volume 3.

Easter Triduum / Easter Season

THE LITURGICAL PRESS
Collegeville, Minnesota

The English translation of Volume 3 of this series is by Greg LaNave and Donald Molloy. The original French text of *Days of the Lord* (*Jours du Seigneur*, Brepols: Publications de Saint-André, 1988) was written by the authors of the *Missel dominical de l'assemblée* and *Missel de l'assemblée pour la semaine* under the direction of Robert Gantoy and Romain Swaeles, Benedictines of Saint-André de Clerlande.

ACKNOWLEDGMENTS
Excerpts from the English translation of *Lectionary for Mass* © 1969, International Committee on English in the Liturgy, Inc. (ICEL); excerpts from the English translation of *The Rite of Holy Week* © 1972, ICEL; excerpts from the English translation of *The Roman Missal* © 1973, ICEL; excerpts from the English translation of *Documents on the Liturgy, 1963–1979: Conciliar, Papal, and Curial Texts* © 1982, ICEL. All rights reserved.

Scripture selections are taken from the New American Bible *Lectionary for Mass*, © 1970 by the Confraternity of Christian Doctrine, Washington, D.C., and are used by license of said copyright owner. All rights reserved. No part of the New American Bible *Lectionary for Mass* may be reproduced in any form without written permission from the copyright owner.

Scripture quotations are from the *New American Bible with Revised New Testament*, © 1986 Confraternity of Christian Doctrine. The text of the Old Testament in *The New American Bible with Revised New Testament* was published in *The New American Bible*, © 1970 Confraternity of Christian Doctrine. Other quotations, as indicated, are from *The Jerusalem Bible*, © 1966 by Darton, Longman & Todd, Ltd. and Doubleday & Company, Inc.

Cover design by Monica Bokinskie.

LIBRARY OF CONGRESS CATALOGING-IN-PUBLICATION DATA

(Revised for vol. 3)

Days of the Lord.

Translation of: Jours du Seigneur.
Includes bibliographical references.
Contents: v. 1. Season of Advent. Season of Christmas/Epiphany — v. 3. Easter and the Easter season — v. 6. Ordinary time, Year C.
1. Church year. 2. Catholic Church—Liturgy.
BX1970.J67313 1990   263'.9   90-22253
ISBN 0-8146-1899-5 (v. 1)   ISBN 0-8146-1904-5 (v. 6)
ISBN 0-8146-1900-2 (v. 2)
ISBN 0-8146-1901-0 (v. 3)
ISBN 0-8146-1902-9 (v. 4)

Contents

The Easter Triduum 1

Chrism Mass: Sacramentally Marked with the Anointing
of Christ 6

Holy Thursday: The Last Supper 14

Good Friday: The Lord's Passion 23

The Easter Celebrations 37
Easter Vigil: Christ Is Risen! 39
The Liturgy of Light 41
The Liturgy of the Word 42
The Liturgy of Baptism................................ 63
Easter Sunday: The Last Day of the Easter Triduum 67

The Fifty Days of Easter 77

Second Sunday of Easter 84
Years A, B, C: Paschal Faith 85
Year A: The Church—Paschal Community 91
Year B: Community, Faith, and Hope 97
Year C: The Presence of Christ in the Community 103

Third Sunday of Easter 107
Year A: Raised According to Scripture, Recognized
in the Breaking of the Bread...................... 107
Year B: He Is Living In Our Midst 116
Year C: Church of the Resurrected and Witness
of the Apostles 124

Fourth Sunday of Easter 133
Year A: The Paschal Exodus in the Wake of Christ 133
Year B: Children of God Under the Staff of Christ 140
Year C: The Great Multitude Gathered by
the True Shepherd................................ 147

Fifth Sunday of Easter 153
   Year A: The Risen Jesus—the Way and the Truth
         and the Life—the Cornerstone 153
   Year B: Live On in Me and Bear Fruit! 162
   Year C: "A Little While . . . Now . . . Soon" 170

Sixth Sunday of Easter 178
   Year A: The Spirit—Presence of the Lord 178
   Year B: The Love of the Lord Fills the Universe 184
   Year C: The Church of the Risen Lord and the Life
         of the Spirit 193

The Ascension of the Lord 203
   Years A, B, C: You Will Be My Witnesses to the
         End of the World 205
   Year A: Christ Raised to Heaven, Present in the Church 210
   Year B: Christ Raised to Heaven, and the Church—
         His Body 216
   Year C: Christ, Our Hope, Raised to Heaven 221

Seventh Sunday of Easter 227
   Year A: Thanksgiving Prayer of Christ and the Church 226
   Year B: The Lord Dwells with His Own 233
   Year C: Behold Christ, Standing at the Right Hand
         of God...240

Pentecost 249
   Vigil Mass: Drawing Life from the
         Wellspring of the Spirit 251
   Sunday Mass—Pentecost 268
   Years A, B, C: The Spirit Makes One People of All
         Nations 270
   Year A: Gift of the Risen Christ and Spirit for
         the Common Good 275
   Year B: Witnesses of Christ with the Holy Spirit 281
   Year C: The Spirit of the Father in the Lord's Prayer 287
   Everyday Pentecost 293

From Bethlehem to Emmaus 297

Notes...305

The Easter Triduum

At first, all those who became disciples of Christ through the apostles at Pentecost went regularly to the Temple. At the same time, they gathered in various homes to break bread in memory of the Lord, who had told them to do so on the eve of his passion (Acts 2:46). As they began to form distinctive communities,[1] they ceased to attend the Temple (in Jerusalem) and the synagogal offices[2] (outside of Jerusalem): they met among themselves, "[devoting] themselves to the teaching of the apostles and to the communal life, to the breaking of bread and to the prayers" (Acts 2:42).

The Day of the Lord—Weekly Passover

The Christians regularly came together on "the first day of the week." The gathering took place in the evening,[3] and could last quite late into the night. Such was the case at Troas, in the Roman province of Asia, when the community came together with Paul (who was staying there during his third missionary journey):

> On the first day of the week when we gathered to break bread, Paul spoke to them because he was going to leave on the next day, and he kept on speaking until midnight. . . . and a young man named Eutychus who was sitting on the window-sill was sinking into a deep sleep as Paul talked on and on. Once overcome by sleep, he fell from the third story and when he was picked up, he was dead. Paul went down, threw himself upon him, and said as he embraced, "Don't be alarmed; there is life in him." Then he returned upstairs, broke the bread, and ate; after a long conversation that lasted until daybreak, he departed (Acts 20:7, 9-11).

This account, with its happy ending—that all present "were immeasurably comforted," notes the editor (Acts 20:12)—tells us much about the Christian assembly at the time.

"The first day of the week" is not merely a reference to the day after the sabbath, the seventh day of the week according to the biblical account of creation (Gen 1:1–2:3). In the New Testament, the term has a "theological" significance. It evokes the day—the first of the week—when Christ was raised from the dead[4] and appeared to the disciples.[5] Very early on, observance of "the Lord's day" (Rev 1:10) expressed the Christian faith in the Lord's resurrection. The disciples gathered to hear the "memoirs"

1

of the apostles and the writings of the prophets, "to break bread and give thanks."[6] This was the weekly Passover, "the original feast day,"[7] the core of the liturgical year that grew up around it.[8]

Weekly Celebration and Yearly Passover

The early Church celebrated only a weekly commemoration of "the Lord's day," as a memorial of the resurrection. But wouldn't a yearly celebration of the resurrection have held a special distinction from the Jewish Passover celebrated during the week beginning with the fourteenth day of Nisan?[9] Paul says as much when he writes to the Corinthians: "For our paschal lamb, Christ, has been sacrificed. Therefore let us celebrate the feast, not with the old yeast, the yeast of malice and wickedness, but with the unleavened bread of sincerity and truth" (1 Cor 5:7b-8).

Nevertheless, we can be sure that the early Church did not, at the beginning, have a distinct celebration of a Christian Passover. It began to appear, in some Churches, at the beginning of the second century and at Rome at the end of the century. The question as to how its date should be determined produced a lively controversy in the latter years of the century. The Asian Churches celebrated it on the fourteenth of Nisan. At Rome, and elsewhere, it took place on the following Sunday. Actually, the controversy nearly led to a schism, though it subsided after Pope Victor ordered all the Churches to celebrate the Christian Passover on the Sunday following the fourteenth of Nisan.[10]

The Holy Triduum in Early Times

If there was disagreement over when Easter should be celebrated, never was it suggested that Christ's death should be separated from his resurrection: it was unanimously agreed that the two together made up the paschal mystery. How could it have been otherwise, when the faith said that Christ had suffered, died, was buried, and rose again on the third day, as he had clearly,[11] or not so clearly, foretold? The annual celebration of Easter readily incorporated these features, based as they were on Scripture and faith. Even before there was a "Holy Thursday" or the setting-aside of one day for the commemoration of Christ's death, there was a kind of "Holy Triduum": Friday, Saturday, and Sunday. The first two days, commemorating Christ's death and burial, were days of fasting, penance, and meditation, giving way finally to paschal joy. Ambrose (339–397) speaks of this in a letter to the bishop of Emilia—the region of Parma and Modena, in Italy—regarding Easter and its celebration.

> We must observe both the days of the passion and the resurrection, so that there may be a day of woe and a day of joy, a fast-day and a feast-day . . . This is the holy Triduum . . . during which Christ suffered, was buried and rose again; concerning which he said: "Destroy this temple, and in three days I will raise it up."[12]

Augustine (354–430), baptized by Ambrose in Milan on Easter night in 387, says much the same in the ringing conclusion to a sermon given on the eighth day of Easter.

> The Word suffered his flesh to hang on a tree,
> the Word suffered his flesh to be pinioned by nails,
> the Word suffered his flesh to be pierced by a lance,
> the Word suffered his flesh to be put into a tomb,
> the Word has raised his flesh, appeared in it to his disciples, allowed them to touch him.
> They touch, they cry: "My Lord and my God?"
> Behold the Day that the Lord has made.[13]

We see evidence of a liturgy for Good Friday and the Mass of the Lord's @ 600 Supper in Rome in the seventh century; they were imposed in all the Western Churches, superseding local custom. Thereafter, the Holy Triduum began on Holy Thursday, and each day had its own specific liturgy.

The Missal and Breviary of Pius V

The liturgical configuration of these "three holy days" arose from the combination or interlacing of a bewildering array of customs and traditions; the results were sometimes barely coherent.[14] A veritable mosaic of liturgies was in use, though they all shared a number of common elements. It was always the same mystery that was celebrated, under the authority of the bishops, who were the ones who published the liturgical books. Even so, the variety of liturgical practices increased the possibility of deviations in the celebration of the mystery. Finally, the Council of Trent authorized the pope to promulgate a breviary and missal that would be used, to the exclusion of all others, in the whole Roman Church. These were promulgated by Pius V (1566–1572) in 1568 and 1570, respectively.[15]

This reform established Holy Thursday, Good Friday, and Holy Saturday as the days of the "Holy Triduum," with major liturgies in the morning, since Pius V forbade the celebration of Mass or Communion after noon. Such was the situation until 1951.[16] In that year, Pius XII (1939–1958) 1951 authorized the celebration of the Easter Vigil during the night of Holy Saturday. In 1955, the same pope published a new *Ordo* for Holy Week that allowed evening celebrations on Holy Thursday and Good Friday: this reform set a pattern for Vatican II.

The Easter Triduum Today

What was previously known as the Holy Triduum or, more recently, "the three holy days," is now called the Easter Triduum.[17] It "begins with the evening Mass of the Lord's Supper, reaches its high point in the Easter Vigil, and closes with evening prayer on Easter Sunday."[18] The Missal makes provision for the following: "Evening Mass of the Lord's Supper" on Holy Thursday; on Good Friday, "the celebration of the Lord's passion," "in the afternoon, about three o'clock, unless pastoral reasons suggest a later hour"; on Holy Saturday night, "the Easter Vigil"; and Mass on the "Sunday of the resurrection."[19]

In parallel fashion, the Liturgy of the Hours for Easter Triduum was altered to fit this framework.[20] Till noon on Holy Thursday, the Office of Lent is still used, and there is no office for Vespers or Compline.[21] Good Friday contains the offices of readings and morning (Lauds) and daytime prayer. The same is true for Holy Saturday, though it has an evening prayer (Vespers), since the Vigil takes place at night. This is a significant enough change from what was done in the past. There is no more "Tenebrae," a very popular office for which many composers created grand musical "responses."[22]

The institution of the liturgies of the Easter Triduum has also had an effect on local customs. If the Way of the Cross on Good Friday is still popular in parishes that celebrate the liturgy of the passion at the end of the day, the *Stabat Mater* and the great "Sermon of the Passion," which were used in many churches have, for the same reason, fallen into disuse.[23] Nevertheless, we must be grateful for the reforms of the Easter Triduum that came from Vatican II, i.e., celebrations in the vernacular and at appropriate times of day.

The major liturgies of Holy Thursday, Good Friday, and Holy Saturday reflect this. The celebration of the Last Supper and the passion at times when most people are able to attend leads to a participation that is "full, active, and conscious." "The Passion of Our Lord Jesus Christ According to John," the "general intercessions" and the "veneration of the cross," are very powerful moments on Good Friday. In the past, early morning liturgies on Holy Saturday were, for the most part, very poorly attended. Now, even if the congregation does not fill the church, the Vigil has become a truly paschal celebration. Each of these liturgies is spiritually alive; they teach not in words (i.e., in sermons) but in actions: they lead to an active celebration in the mystery. On Holy Thursday, after the Mass and transferral of the Blessed Sacrament, everyone is invited to join in adoration; and many people join in reading the "farewell discourses" (John 14-17).[24] The atmosphere of meditation carries on from this first liturgy till the celebration on Good Friday. Finally, the mood of silent waiting on Holy Saturday gives way to the joyful alleluias that spring forth on Easter night, the shouts that endlessly proclaim our Easter faith: "Christ is risen! He is truly risen!"

However, in order to fully appreciate and experience the wondrous depth of the mystery of the Easter Triduum, the faithful must make a firm effort to free themselves from the worldly preoccupations that are sources of distraction. The lifestyles of the secular world clash with the serious reflection demanded during these holy days; however, we know that it is well worth the effort to try to be *in* the world but not *of* the world, especially during the Triduum. This is the paradoxical duty of every Christian today, as it has always been.

> Do not conform yourselves to this age. . . (Rom 12:2).

> We have not received the spirit of the world but the spirit that is from God, so that we may understand the things freely given us by God (1 Cor 2:12).

> If you died with Christ to the elemental powers of the world, why do you submit to regulations as if you were still living in the world? (Col 2:20)

Chrism Mass

Sacramentally Marked
with the Anointing of Christ

Since the Easter Triduum does not begin until the evening of Holy Thursday, the rest of the day belongs to the season of Lent, which has no specific final liturgy.[1] The office is the same as it has been throughout the season.[2] Yet the Missal contains a distinctive Mass, the "Chrism Mass," for this day. It is a "ritual"[3] Mass that is concelebrated with the bishop presiding; every priest in the diocese is invited, and those who do participate renew their sacerdotal promises.

It is admittedly difficult to gather the people and clergy together with the bishop on Holy Thursday morning for the Chrism Mass. Therefore, the Missal says that it may be celebrated on Monday, Tuesday, or Wednesday of Holy Week instead.[4] Even so, it is typically very poorly attended, even by the priests.[5] It belongs neither to the Easter Triduum nor to Lent.[6] Yet it points to the celebration of the sacraments of baptism, confirmation, ordination, and anointing of the sick, whose paschal character is thus highlighted.

The text of the liturgy for this Mass strongly affirms the priestly nature of the people of God, among whom ordained priests have a special ministry. At the same time, the role of the bishop in the diocesan Church is highlighted: he is the one who ordains the priests and gives them their assignments; but, and equally important, he is the primary dispenser of the sacraments—especially baptism and confirmation—since, even when he does not celebrate them personally, the holy chrism that he has consecrated must be used.[7] So we have some matter for reflection, meditation, and prayer at the threshold of the Easter Triduum.[8]

The Church of Christ, a Priestly People
The present Chrism Mass is devoted to the consecration of the holy chrism[9] and, therefore, the anointing that Christians have sacramentally received, allowing them to participate in the fullness of the spirit that Jesus received at his very conception.[10] Consecrated by the Holy Spirit, Jesus

has been made, by God, "Christ and Lord." In him, we are consecrated to be "faithful witnesses in the world to the salvation Christ won for all mankind."[11]

It would be worthwhile to note the readings in the Liturgy of the Word for this Mass. We begin with the famous oracle of Isaiah (61:1-3, 6, 8-9). Isaiah begins by speaking about himself as the Messenger of God, after his investiture:

> The Spirit of the Lord GOD is upon me,
>   because the LORD has anointed me . . .

Then he turns to the people to whom the Lord's Anointed One is sent:

> You yourselves shall be named priests of
>   the LORD,
> ministers of our God you shall be called.

The Gospel recounts Jesus' first preaching, at Nazareth (Luke 4:16-21). After reading the part of Isaiah that is used in this Mass, closing the scroll and handing it to an assistant, Jesus sat down. "And the eyes of all in the synagogue looked intently at him. He said to them, 'Today this scripture passage is fulfilled in your hearing.' "

The prophecy is fulfilled *in* Jesus, but also *for* those to whom he is sent: the poor, the imprisoned, the blind, and the oppressed, to whom he proclaims "a year of favor from the LORD."

Ever since the beginning, Christian faith has been assured that Jesus Christ, "who loves us," "made us a kingdom, priests to his God and Father," as we read in the first chapter of the Book of Revelation, which forms the second reading for the Chrism Mass (Rev 1:5-8).[12]

The preface proclaims this as well:

> By your Holy Spirit you anointed your only Son
> High Priest of the new and eternal covenant.
> With wisdom and love you have planned
> that this one priesthood should continue in the Church.
> Christ gives the dignity of a royal priesthood
> to the people he has made his own.

Recalling the divine manifestation (theophany) that took place after Jesus' baptism, the consecratory prayer of the chrism continues:

> By his suffering, dying, and rising to life
> he saved the human race.
> He sent your Spirit to fill the Church
> with every gift needed to complete your
> saving work.

From that time forward, through the sign of
holy chrism,
you dispense your life and love to men.
By anointing them with the Spirit,
you strengthen all who have been reborn in
baptism.
Through that anointing
you transform them into the likeness of
Christ your Son
and give them a share
in his royal, priestly, and prophetic work.[13]

Among the Priestly People, Some Are Ordained

In the strongest sense of the term, there is only one Priest—Jesus Christ,
the one, perfect and eternal mediator between God and humanity, who
came to reconcile us all to his Father, the acceptable sacrifice for our salvation, forever present in the people he gathers and sanctifies, particularly through the sacraments, through the Eucharist of which he is the
principal celebrant by means of the Spirit. Otherwise, all of our rites would
be void of meaning and therefore powerless. Strictly speaking, whoever
the minister—Peter or Judas—it is Christ who baptizes, grants forgiveness of sins, and ordains some to be priests among his "priestly people."
"Was Paul crucified for you? Or were you baptized in the name of Paul?"
(1 Cor 1:13). Therefore, the common priesthood of the faithful and the
ministerial priesthood—whatever the differences between them—share
in the one priesthood of Christ and, in a certain sense, share in a common ordination.[14] Likewise, between the Christian people and their priests
is a definite solidarity and reciprocal obligation. This is expressed very
clearly in the renewal of the priest's vows that takes place during the
Chrism Mass—after the Liturgy of the Word—and in what the bishop says
to the faithful.

The ordained priesthood is a position of service to the whole Church,
to which not all are called, but which those who are called must exercise
with charity. Priests are the stewards of God's mysteries in the proclamation of the Word and the celebration of the Eucharist and the other
sacraments. They must keep their eyes fixed on Christ, the sovereign
Priest, in order to faithfully carry out their ministry.

For priests to be what they ought is a matter of vital importance for
the Church. Thus the faithful must pray earnestly for them and for the
bishop, the head of the local Church,[15] giving thanks to the Father who

wishes "that this one priesthood [of Christ] should continue in the Church."

> Christ gives the dignity of a royal priesthood
> to the people he has made his own.
> From these, with a brother's love,
> he chooses men to share his sacred ministry
> by the laying on of hands.

> He appoints them to renew in his name
> the sacrifice of our redemption
> as they set before your family his paschal meal.
> He calls them to lead your holy people in love,
> nourish them by your word,
> and strengthen them through the sacraments.

> Father, they are to give their lives in your service
> and for the salvation of your people
> as they strive to grow in the likeness of Christ
> and honor you by their courageous witness
> of faith and love.[16]

The True Nature of the Church Mirrored in a Liturgy

Vatican II said that the liturgy, especially the Eucharist, is the highest manifestation of the Church's true nature.[17] This is emphatically the case with the Chrism Mass, a liturgy celebrated once a year in every diocese.[18]

The Church cannot be encompassed by one definition;[19] this was well understood by Vatican II. The council said that "the inner nature of the Church was now to be made known to us through various images,"[20] especially "sheepfold," "field of God," "edifice, house, family of God," "the New Jerusalem," "mystical body of Christ," people of God. None of these images, all drawn from Scripture, express the whole reality, though they all point to it: each one must be incorporated into the complete "definition." What the Church is, is more perceived or "shown in itself" than defined.[21] In the Chrism Mass we can see some of these elements.

The diocese is the local Church, not a mere territorial,[22] administrative, or pastoral[23] division of the universal Church.[24] In itself, it is an ecclesial unity that lacks nothing. The bishop, as such, is a "sacrament," i.e., a visible and efficacious sign of Christ the "High Priest, Good Shepherd, the teacher and servant of all," which is expressed when we say that he "is a genuine sign."[25] He is such by means of his sacramental ordination. Through him, the Christian people in the diocese have every sacrament: he consecrates the holy chrism, he ordains priests, every Eucharist is celebrated in communion with him; as the minister of charity in the local Church, he is in communion with the other bishops—the other local Churches—and with the pope, who presides in charity over the communion of all the Churches, the *Catholica* that is unified in its diversity.

This is what is mirrored in the Chrism Mass: the bishop, priests, deacons, and faithful of a local Church are gathered for the blessing of the holy oils and the chrism that is needed, in this ecclesial unity, for baptism and confirmation, the anointing of the sick and dying, and the ordination of the priests who dispense the sacraments.

The Chrism Mass focuses attention on the fact that the celebration of every Eucharist,[26] indeed every sacrament, is related to the bishop's ministry, and that all preaching of the Word, under its multitude of forms, comes from him.[27] This dependence vis-à-vis the bishop is not first, and certainly not foremost, of a juridical order, but is rather mystical and sacramental, because in the Church everything comes from the Head, Christ, for whom the bishop is instituted as ''a genuine sign'' in his episcopal ordination. The liturgy of the Chrism Mass does not state this: it ''reveals'' it. Everything about the Church essentially belongs to the sacramental order, the order of the visible that is rooted in and expresses an invisible reality. It is the mystical body of Christ.

In every sacramental liturgy, whether it is concelebrated with many priests in a large assembly or by only one with a handful of the faithful, the bishop is present[28] and, through him, the whole local Church in communion with the other Churches and the universal Church.

Christian Sacraments, Paschal Celebrations

The focus of the Chrism Mass is still the blessing of the holy oils and the chrism. At first, it occurred on Holy Thursday because these things were needed for the baptisms on Easter Vigil. There is no longer the same need for this. Yet the Church has maintained the practice, which reminds us that it is ''from the paschal mystery of the passion, death, and resurrection of Christ'' that ''all sacraments and sacramentals draw their power.''[29] In the context of a solemn liturgy, in a humble village church, or in the quiet intimacy of a sickroom, the celebration of a sacrament is always a paschal celebration.

This is why, from now on, all the sacraments are to take place in the context of a ''ritual Mass.''[30] They are all ''linked with the holy Eucharist and directed toward it. For the most blessed Eucharist contains the

Church's entire spiritual wealth, that is, Christ Himself, our Passover and living bread. Through His very flesh, made vital and vitalizing by the Holy Spirit, He offers life to men. They are thereby invited and led to offer themselves, their labors, and all created things together with Him."[31]

Sacramental Anointing for the Mission

As the mystical body of Christ, the Church was born on Pentecost, when Peter preached to the crowds and the first believers were baptized (Acts 2:14-47). From that moment on, the community of newly baptized disciples, on whom the Spirit had descended, took on a missionary character. The sacraments—especially baptism and the anointing of the Spirit—make the Church a missionary community;[32] every Christian, through baptism, is required to take on this mission.

> For this the Church was founded: that by spreading the kingdom of Christ everywhere for the glory of God the Father, she might bring all men to share in Christ's saving redemption; and that through them the whole world might in actual fact be brought into relationship with Him. All activity of the Mystical Body directed to the attainment of this goal is called the apostolate, and the Church carries it on in various ways through all her members. For by its very nature the Christian vocation is also a vocation to the apostolate. No part of the structure of a living body is merely passive, but each has a share in the functions as well as in the life of the body. So, too, in the body of Christ, which is the Church, the whole body, "according to the functioning in due measure of each single part, derives its increase" (Eph 4:16). Indeed, so intimately are the parts linked and interrelated in this body (cf. Eph. 4:16) that the member who fails to make his proper contribution to the development of the Church must be said to be useful neither to the Church nor to himself.[33]

There is, to be sure, "diversity of service but unity of purpose." But everyone "shares in the priestly, prophetic, and royal office of Christ and therefore have their own role to play in the mission of the whole People of God in the Church and in the world."[34] Vatican II insisted on this point.

> The laity derive the right and duty with respect to the apostolate from their union with Christ their Head. Incorporated into Christ's Mystical Body through baptism and strengthened by the power of the Holy Spirit through confirmation, they are assigned to the apostolate by the Lord himself. They are consecrated into a royal priesthood and a holy people (cf. 1 Pet 2:4-10) in order that they may offer spiritual sacrifices through everything they do, and may witness to Christ throughout the world. For their part, the sacraments, especially the most holy Eucharist, communicate and nourish that charity which is the soul of the entire apostolate.[35]

On all Christians therefore is laid the splendid burden of working to make the divine message of salvation known and accepted by all men throughout the world.

For the exercise of this apostolate, the Holy Spirit who sanctifies the People of God through the ministry and the sacraments gives to the faithful special gifts as well (cf. 1 Cor 12:7), "allotting to everyone according as he will" (1 Cor 12:11). Thus may the individual, "according to the gift that each has received, administer it to one another" and become "good stewards of the manifold grace of God" (1 Pet 4:10), and build up thereby the whole body in charity (cf. Eph 4:16). From the reception of these charisms or gifts, including those that are less dramatic, there arise for each believer the right and duty to use them in the Church and in the world for the good of mankind and for the upbuilding of the Church. In so doing, believers need to enjoy the freedom of the Holy Spirit who "breathes where he wills" (John 3:8). At the same time, they must act in communion with their brothers in Christ, especially with their pastors. The latter must make a judgment about the true nature and proper use of these gifts, not in order to extinguish the Spirit, but to test all things and hold fast to what is good (cf. 1 Thess 5:12, 19, 21).[36]

As the liturgy constantly reminds us, we must pray that the sacraments sanctify us and enable us to grow into the "spiritual man." But perhaps we too often forget the need to pray, as the Chrism Mass teaches us, that they may renew in us "the image of Christ's goodness."[37]

Father,
by the power of the Holy Spirit
you anointed your only Son Messiah and Lord of creation;
you have given us a share in his consecration
to priestly service in your Church.
Help us to be faithful witnesses in the world
to the salvation Christ won for all mankind.[38]

Few of us ever participate in the Chrism Mass.[39] Nevertheless, what happens there concerns the whole local Church and each of its members: priests, deacons, religious, and laity. Each of them has been marked with holy oil and chrism at baptism, confirmation, and some at ordination. Each of them participates, at least from time to time, in a sacramental celebration that makes use of the blessed oils and the holy chrism consecrated by the bishop during the Chrism Mass. These sacramental anointings may often appear to be simple rites of scant importance; nevertheless, their value comes from the very nature of each Christian and the whole people of God.

Every member of the priestly people is consecrated by an anointing that allows for a sacramental participation—that is, a real one, through signs—

in the anointing of Christ, eternal Priest, Head of the Church, his mystical body and the temple of the Holy Spirit in which each baptized person is a living stone (1 Pet 2:5).[40]

The unity of the Church is fundamentally of a sacramental or mystical order. Its cement (so to speak) is Christ's grace, which binds together all the living stones. Each local Church is a sacramental unity formed by the anointing of the priests and baptized laity with the chrism consecrated by the bishop, who himself has been marked by it in his episcopal ordination, celebrated in communion with the college of bishops in unity with the pope, the servant and guarantor of unity for the whole Church.

But let us not forget: this anointing makes the Church a priestly people in which everyone has the duty to proclaim the gospel, in accordance with the sacraments one has received, as well as one's vocation, grace, and charisms.

Holy Thursday

The Last Supper

The Easter Triduum opens with a Mass that seems to be in no way distinguishable from any ordinary Mass.[1] Nevertheless, it has its own special character, seen first of all in the time of its celebration. Every Eucharist is a memorial of the supper Jesus shared with his disciples "before he was given up to death, a death he freely accepted,"[2] "the day before he suffered to save us and all men."[3] At this Mass we add that this occurred "today": not that the liturgy is meant to be regarded as an "anniversary," but because the Lord's passion is celebrated the next day. "Today," then, in the context of the Easter Triduum, is "the night he was betrayed."[4]

Yet this celebration is not an attempt to recreate the atmosphere of the upper room and the emotions of the apostles as they gathered around Jesus. On that night, they no doubt understood Jesus' words and deeds only imperfectly. The fact that they were celebrating a farewell supper must have been a source of great sadness and bewilderment to them (John 16:18). Understanding could only have come as they reflected on it in the light of the events of the following days, and the paschal faith and experience of a Church that gradually learned to follow where Jesus had shown the way. The Gospels' and Paul's accounts show how this is reflected in the early liturgy.[5]

We cannot understand it today in abstraction from that tradition which, as Paul says, is "received from the Lord" (1 Cor 11:23) and passed down through centuries of faith, theological reflection, and the life of worship. Moreover, the "institution narrative," which is at the heart of the Eucharistic Prayer, is not an "objective" or "neutral" recapitulation of a historical event that we regularly recall. Nor is it an attempt to reach back from our celebration today to "the night Jesus was betrayed" so as to make them magically coincide.

Jesus is spoken of in the third person, which indicates that he is physically absent. The verbs are in the past tense: he took bread; gave it to his disciples; likewise with the cup. Nothing that is said suggests that we are mimicking the Last Supper. However, in the context of the lit-

urgy, this story actualizes Jesus' words and deeds. When the priest says "This is my body," "This is my blood," these words of Jesus effect, here and now, what they express. In this sense, there is no difference between one Mass and another: Holy Thursday has no special symbolic or sacramental status. Rather, it is exemplary because it explains more clearly the fundamental link between what Jesus did "before he was given up to death, a death he freely accepted" and what we do every time we celebrate the Eucharist in memory of him, till he comes again.

The various intertwining themes of the Lord's Supper are seen more clearly and powerfully when it is celebrated at the beginning of the Easter Triduum. Likewise, we know that the Eucharist is the sacrament of the Lord's presence during his absence: it increases our hunger for his coming; only on that day will we be truly filled. "Come, Lord Jesus, come!" A proper appreciation of this does not demand that we pretend we are present at the Last Supper, twenty centuries ago. Never is the liturgy to be understood as a historical reconstruction. It does not turn back the tide of history; it does not ignore all that has happened since the time of the events we commemorate; it does not locate us in the past. In the present-day of salvation history, the liturgy is the reactualization of crucial events. It does not make the historical occurrences themselves present: in a very real sense, they belong irrevocably to the past. Nevertheless, they can be effective here and now because their power comes from God and because Christ has enabled his Church to enact them sacramentally, i.e., through efficacious signs.[6] This is why and how we truly proclaim: "On the night he was betrayed, he took bread and gave you thanks and praise. He broke the bread, gave it to his disciples and said: 'Take this, all of you, and eat it: this is my body which will be given up for you.'"[7]

The Ancient Rite of Passover

These rites and symbolic actions are not haphazard inventions: they are deeply rooted in Semitic ancestral culture and its religious rites. They grew slowly out of various (not necessarily religious) customs and gained more and more significance as the rest of the culture grew and added new structures to replace or augment the old. Such was the case with the rites of the Old Testament, especially Passover, and the Christian rites that came from them, especially the Eucharist. One can understand nothing about the Eucharist—could it have any meaning?[8]—if one ignores the tradition within which Jesus celebrated the Last Supper[9]: the Jewish Passover of his time was itself rooted in ancient custom.

The nomadic Semites had a feast that they celebrated the night of the first full moon of spring, when they were about to lead their flocks to summer pastures. With the unleavened bread of the Bedouins, and some desert herbs, they ate a roasted lamb from the flock. This "migration" was a very important occasion, and very dangerous. To ward off these dangers, they marked their tent-pegs with the blood of the lamb.[10] Connection with the Exodus gave this old rite a new meaning: Passover was celebrated as a memorial of God's intervention on his people's behalf and an expression of hope in the Messiah's coming. The ritual, which became codified in great detail, was divided into two distinct rites: unleavened bread, and the sacrifice of the paschal lamb, spoken of in the text from Exodus we read today (Exod 12:1-8, 11-14).[11]

The Church could hardly celebrate the Last Supper without proclaiming this passage. On the one hand, it is the basic text for the Passover rite as it was celebrated in Jesus' day. It tells us what he must have done on the eve of his own sacrifice for our salvation. On the other hand, Christian tradition has seen the sacrifice of the paschal lamb as a prefiguring of the sacrifice of the one of whom John the Baptist said: "Behold, the Lamb of God, who takes away the sin of the world" (John 1:29), a formula repeated in every Eucharist.

> There was much proclaimed by the prophets about the mystery of the Passover: that mystery is Christ . . .
>
> For the sake of suffering humanity he came down from heaven to earth, clothed himself in that humanity in the Virgin's womb, and was born a man. Having then a body capable of suffering, he took the pain of fallen man upon himself; he triumphed over the diseases of soul and body that were its cause, and by his Spirit, which was incapable of dying, he dealt man's destroyer, death, a fatal blow.
>
> He was led forth like a lamb; he was slaughtered like a sheep. He ransomed us from our servitude to the world, as he had ransomed Israel from the land of Egypt; he freed us from our slavery to the devil, as he had freed Israel from the hand of Pharaoh. He sealed our souls with his own Spirit, and the members of our body with his own blood.
>
> He is the One who covered death with shame and cast the devil into mourning, as Moses cast Pharaoh into mourning. He is the One who smote sin and robbed iniquity of offspring, as Moses robbed the Egyptians of their offspring. He is the One who brought us out of slavery into freedom, out of darkness into light, out of death into life, out of tyranny into an eternal kingdom; who made us a new priesthood, a people chosen to be his own for ever. He is the Passover that is our salvation.[12]

Certain elements of the ancient rite are particularly significant for us. Unleavened bread was the food of nomads: they had no time to let the dough rise.[13] Likewise, "bitter herbs" were those found in the desert. The Eucharist is the Passover of believers who have no permanent dwelling-place on this earth (Heb 13:14). They are a nomadic people, and the Eucharist is their bread for the journey.

The Passover could not be eaten alone: it was shared among a family or between neighbors. Not only because it was a whole lamb that must have been eaten, but because one is saved in community, by belonging to the people of God.

The celebration took place at night, at the beginning of a journey. This was because the flock slept during the night and one had to be ready to leave at dawn. The Passover ritual gives new meaning to these rather incidental facts. "Since the dough they had brought out of Egypt was not leavened, they baked it into unleavened loaves. They had been rushed out of Egypt and had no opportunity even to prepare food for the journey" (Exod 12:39). It also adds: "This was a night of vigil for the Lord, as he led them out of the land of Egypt; so on this same night all the Israelites must keep a vigil for the Lord throughout their generations" (Exod 12:42). Later, retelling the story of the Exodus, the sages will dwell on the fact that the people's deliverance occurred during the night (Wis 18:5-19). The gospel will take up the theme: the Lord will return unexpectedly, at night; one must be awake to greet him (Luke 12:35-40; 1 Pet 1:13). This expectation of the Lord's coming will mark the celebration of the Christian Passover, especially at the beginning: will not Christ return on Easter night? In any case, the Eucharist, celebrated "until he comes" (1 Cor 11:26), points to the Lord's return; and it is this hope that vivifies the Church. Such is the effect also of the tradition of nocturnal prayer, which many monks keep in the middle of the night or before dawn.

Finally, the ancient Passover included the rite of marking doorposts and lintels with blood. Blood is frequently synonymous with life itself; the spilling of blood means death. To pour out one's blood for someone is to offer one's life. We sometimes speak of "blood brothers," those who have intermingled their blood and thus have a special bond. From all this comes the redemptive power of blood, first in the Old Testament,[14] then in the New.[15] The immolation of a victim can be an act of adoring God, the source and master of life, or an expiatory sacrifice.[16] But in either case, the life offered to God returns, purified, to humanity: hence the sprinkling of the people with the victim's blood. The sacrifice is thus part of a process that must be understood as a whole: it is not required to satisfy a bloodthirsty god. The blood of the paschal victim on the doorposts and lintel of a home signifies that therein dwell people whose lives God has promised to save.

The ancient rites are not fully effective; hence they must be repeated. What they express imperfectly, Christ has accomplished once and for all in the sacrifice of his life. Sinless, he gave himself up for the sins of the whole world, rendering to God the perfect worship of a humanity completely reconciled with its creator and Father. Resurrected, he is the eternal Priest through whom, with whom, and in whom all honor and glory are given to God for ever and ever.

His blood does not mark the doorposts of our homes: we drink it under the sign of wine, the blood of the vine. His glorified flesh is our food in the sacrament of bread broken and shared. Every Eucharist celebrates the passover of the Lord, in which we partake in joy and thanksgiving.

> *Our blessing-cup is a communion with the blood of Christ.*
>
> How shall I make a return to the LORD
>   for all the good he has done for me?
> The cup of salvation I will take up,
>   and I will call upon the name of the LORD.
>
> Precious in the eyes of the LORD
>   is the death of his faithful ones.
> O LORD, I am your servant;
>   I am your servant, the son of your handmaid;
>   you have loosed my bonds.
> To you I will offer sacrifice of thanksgiving,
>   and I will call upon the name of the LORD.
> My vows to the LORD I will pay
>   in the presence of all his people.
> (Ps 116:12-13, 15, 16, 17-18)

The Eucharist: Tradition from the Lord

Each of the Gospels gives an account of the Last Supper within the larger context of the passion.[17] None of them attempt to give a complete account: consequently, we can hardly make an exact reconstruction of the supper, with all Jesus' words and actions. Yet as different as these accounts are,[18] they are certainly not contradictory. This is simply explained by the fact that each of the evangelists drew on earlier oral traditions[19] but incorporated them with an eye to his own specific interests: though inspired, the evangelists were still authors. The same goes for the account of the institution of the Eucharist.[20]

Paul's admonition to the Corinthians regarding the flaws in their assembly led him to remind them of what he had ''delivered'' to them, "the tradition" that he himself had "received from the Lord [Jerusalem Bible]." It is quite right that we read this most precious testimony during our celebration on Holy Thursday (1 Cor 11:23-26).

Paul reminds the Corinthians what he passed on to them: he calls it—even in A.D. 57—"the tradition I received from the Lord." It is the hieratic account of the Last Supper, such as it has come down to us today in the Eucharist. We do just what the first Christians did, "in memory" of the Lord. Centuries have passed since then, but through the Eucharist, the same sacramental rite they observed, we are, like them, contemporaries of Christ, whose body we share and whose cup we drink. Each time, we share in "the new covenant" proclaimed by the prophet (Jer 31:31-34) and instituted by Christ. We communicate in the redemptive sacrifice of the "Suffering Servant" (Isa 53:10-12).[21] At the same time, the Eucharist, celebrated "until he comes," is an expectation of the Lord's glorious return. Thus it is at the center of the mystery of the Church and of faith; indeed, it is the mystery of Church and faith. The way the community or Church celebrates it brings judgment on itself. Likewise, because it forms the Church, the Eucharist reveals to each and every community what it is and what it must become as it celebrates "the mystery of faith."

Jesus—Master and Lord—as Servant

The Gospel for this day is John's account of what Jesus did at the Last Supper: "Before the feast of the Passover, Jesus knew that his hour had come to pass from this world to the Father. He loved his own in the world and he loved them to the end" (John 13:1-15).

The solemnity of this opening cannot help but catch our attention. It sets the tone immediately for the extraordinary character of what follows. We are urged from the very first to listen carefully to the account of Jesus' washing the disciples' feet, and it is hinted that this is a good deal more important than a mere example of Jesus acting in an unexpected manner.[22] To be sure, one can draw a lesson about humility and service from Jesus' example, but we should not imagine that we have understood the story so quickly. The scene of the washing of feet is first and foremost a "revelation in action" whose meaning is not immediately apparent. "What I am doing, you do not understand now, but you will understand later." Jesus' remark to Peter is an invitation to the Christian today to meditate on this passage in the light of Easter and Eucharistic faith.

Unlike the other evangelists and Paul, John gives no account of the institution of the Eucharist; nevertheless, Eucharistic themes abound in his

Gospel. In fact, one often has the very strong feeling that John has transcribed something he preached in a Eucharistic liturgy.[23] Such is the case here. At least, the Mass of Holy Thursday is the best context for understanding the story of the washing of the feet.[24]

"Before the feast of Passover . . ." Remembering what Jesus did at the Last Supper, one expects John to recount the institution of the Eucharist. Instead, we read the story of the washing of the feet, a solemn rite enacted by Jesus: he "rose from supper and took off his outer garments. He took a towel and tied it around his waist. Then he poured water into a basin and began to wash the disciples' feet and dry them with the towel around his waist." How could one not be astonished and intrigued by this: "What does it mean?"[25] Peter reacts with his customary alacrity: "Master, are you going to wash my feet? . . . You will never wash my feet." He will not allow the Lord to humble himself[26]: he does not understand that the action has a hidden meaning. Jesus' response—"Unless I wash you, you will have no inheritance with me"—leads him to think of it as an act of purification[27]: "Master, then not only my feet, but my hands and head as well." But the meaning of Jesus' action goes beyond this.

"As I have done for you, you should also do"
Washing their feet during a supper he took with them "before the feast of Passover," Jesus showed his disciples what they must do: "I have given you a model to follow." *Now*, we can understand it, for we have seen how he loved his own "till the end," even dying for them, so that they might have a "share with him," in his inheritance, after he passes "from this world to his Father."[28] This is a "revelation in action" of the mystery of God, of Jesus and his passover.

"God is love" (1 John 4:8, 16). This is not an abstract definition, but a very concrete one, for: "The way we came to know love was that he laid down his life for us" (1 John 3:16). He has done this freely and knowingly, for he wished to serve his own, though he was "Teacher and Lord." This is what appears concretely in the washing of his disciples' feet just before he was to pass from this world to his Father, even when he knew that he was about to be betrayed.

It is also "a model": "Love one another as I have loved you." "Let us love not in word or speech but in deed and truth." John will admonish us (1 John 3:18). "As" he has loved us: "We [too] ought to lay down our lives for our brothers" (1 John 3:16). To die for them? There have always been and will always be some Christians for whom "to lay down one's life for one's brother" means precisely this. But every disciple of the Lord must live for others, knowing that jealousy to guard one's life for one's own sake is to lose it, whereas "whoever hates his life in this world will preserve it for eternal life" (John 12:25). To understand and accept this, we must look to Jesus' "model": he goes before us to the Father, without leaving us to our own devices on the paschal road.

The "Sign" of the Washing of Feet and the Sacrament of the Eucharist

Although John does not use the word here, the washing of feet can be understood as one of the "signs" that stake out the Fourth Gospel,[29] and a "sign" of the passion.[30] Thus we see that Jesus removes not only his clothes but his very self, taking on "the form of a slave" (Phil 2:7). And it is thus, John insists, that he appears as the "Teacher and Lord" who draws all to himself (John 12:32).

Jesus performed this "sign" during the Last Supper, just before his passion. John does not say so, but his hearers, especially when they celebrate Holy Thursday, understand that this was when the Eucharist was instituted. With this in mind, we can see how the "sign" of the washing of feet complements what Paul and the Synoptics say about the "institution of the Eucharist": it is the sacrament both of the love of God and Christ and of the bond of charity between Christians. The fact that the liturgy for Holy Thursday contains Paul's "institution account" and John's "washing of feet" supports this connection.

The annual celebration of the Last Supper at the beginning of the Easter Triduum is an invitation to deepen one's awareness of what the Eucharist is and what it demands as the sacrament of the Passover and the new covenant.

> At the Last Supper, on the night when He was betrayed, our Savior instituted the Eucharistic Sacrifice of His Body and Blood. He did this in order to perpetuate the sacrifice of the Cross throughout the centuries until he should come again, and so to entrust to His beloved spouse, the Church, a memorial of His death and resurrection: a sacrament of love, a sign of unity, a bond of charity, a paschal banquet in which Christ is consumed, the mind is filled with grace, and a pledge of future glory is given us.[31]

The liturgy of Holy Thursday ends with a procession to the place of Eucharistic reservation, where it is kept till the next day. There is no Office of Vespers. The Church keeps silent vigil in adoration, meditation, prayer, and thanksgiving. On Good Friday, we will hear the Passion of Our Lord Jesus Christ According to John (John 18:1-19:42). To prolong today's celebration and to prepare for tomorrow's, one would do well to read slowly, alone or in a group, chapters 13-17 of John's Gospel, where one can feel the beating of Christ's burning heart as he speaks to his disciples one last time. At the end of the supper, "When [Judas] had left" (John 13:31), he confides his greatest testament and revelation to the disciples.

> The upper room
> is full of light.
> Christ in the midst of the apostles
> tells us of the Father;
> his voice leads us
> to the threshold of the Kingdom.
>
> Here is the table
> where the Church begins;
> today the Lord shares with us
> the bread of the covenant;
> he puts into our hands
> the sign of the Passover.
>
> Our hearts are amazed
> and desire better to understand,
> but it is the Word who speaks;
> Jesus asks us:
> "How will you measure
> the love I give you?"
>
> A fire burns him
> and draws him from his brethren.
> His passion now consumes him;
> the Master rises:
> already the nightly exodus
> is accomplished.
> Who wants to follow him
> to the garden of darkness?
> Where in the night will be the disciples
> of the man of sorrow?
> Jesus is alone
> at the time of sacrifice.[32]

Good Friday

The Lord's Passion

Let us welcome with a free heart the glory of the cross that shines over the world. Let our eyes, enlightened by the Spirit of truth, pierce through to the meaning of the Lord's saying by which he announced the imminence of his passion: "Now is the time of judgment on this world; now the ruler of this world will be driven out. And when I am lifted from the earth, I will draw everyone to myself" (John 12:31-32).

O wondrous power of the cross! O inexpressible glory of the passion! In it the world's judgment and the crucified's victory appear in full light! Yes, Lord, you have drawn all to yourself! When you stretched your hands all day long toward a rebellious people, the whole world understood that it must give glory to your majesty. You have drawn all to yourself, Lord, for the veil of the temple was torn, the Holy of Holies was left open, the figure gave way to reality, prophecy to fulfillment, Law to gospel. You have drawn all to yourself, Lord, for the piety of all nations celebrates everywhere in full view the mystery that previously was veiled under signs in one temple in Judea.

Your cross, O Christ, is the source of every blessing and grace.[1]

When Pope Leo the Great preached this sermon on the Wednesday after Palm Sunday, after having read Luke's account of the passion, there was still no particular liturgy for Good Friday in Rome.[2] Even so, this passage is a wonderful testimony to the way the Christian tradition thinks of the cross: as a manifestation of the glory, the redemptive power, the sovereign majesty of the Lord. "Source of every blessing and grace," it is contemplated by Christians in the bright light of Easter. Gathered around it, they do not weep over a corpse: they adore the conqueror of death. To be sure, they do not minimize Christ's sufferings, but they speak of them without sadness. Despite its somber atmosphere, Good Friday is not a day of mourning,[3] but a celebration, a thanksgiving for the infinite love God showed the world through his Son's passion.

Beginning on Holy Thursday evening, the Church dwells in meditation. "God did not spare his own Son, but gave him up to suffer for our sake." "Jesus Christ loved us, and poured out his own blood for us to wash away our sins." "We worship your cross, O Lord, and we praise and glorify your holy resurrection, for the wood of the cross has brought joy to the world.''[4] "We worship you, O Christ, and we praise you, because by your cross you have redeemed the world.''[5]

Into this period of meditation comes the liturgy of Good Friday, very smoothly. It begins with silent prayer, at the end of which the priest speaks to God in the name of the assembly.

> Lord,
> by the suffering of Christ your Son
> you have saved us all from the death
> we inherited from sinful Adam.
> By the law of nature
> we have borne the likeness of his manhood.
> May the sanctifying power of grace
> help us to put on the likeness of our Lord
> in heaven
> who lives and reigns for ever and ever.

The celebration has four parts: the Liturgy of the Word, with John's account of the passion; the general intercessions; the veneration of the cross; and Communion, using the bread consecrated the day before.

My Servant Shall Be Exalted; He Will Justify Many

Good Friday presents us with a truly exemplary Liturgy of the Word. Both the Old and New Testament readings have been chosen according to their relationship to the Gospel, as is the case when solemnities or feasts are celebrated on Sundays,[6] and they both prepare us very well for the reading of the Passion. First comes the prophetic text known as the "Fourth Song of the Servant of Yahweh" (Isa 52:13–53:12).[7]

When one reads a passage like this in the Bible, one naturally wonders who the prophet had in mind: who could this Servant be? The Christian tradition has long answered this question unequivocally, "Jesus"; he is the only one who perfectly fits Isaiah's image.[8] The description of the servant matches that of the Lord and some elements of his passion. Isaiah's text gains all the more meaning when one reads it slowly and with an eye to Christ on the cross. "He was spurned and avoided by men," "yet it was our infirmities that he bore, our sufferings that he endured . . . he was pierced for our offenses, crushed for our sins . . . by his stripes we were healed . . . though he was harshly treated, he submitted and opened not his mouth; like a lamb led to the slaughter . . . he was cut off from the land of the living . . . a grave was assigned to him among the wicked and a burial place with evildoers . . . a new tomb where no one had ever been laid" in a garden (John 19:41), "though he had done no wrong." He is "the servant of the Lord" like no one before or since.

More importantly, as proclaimed on Good Friday, this text is an indication of how we should read John's account of the passion. In fact, by virtue of its very realistic vision of the tragic fate of the servant of God, this "song" highlights by contrast the happy outcome of what happens and the glory that belongs to the one who seemed to have been made nothing.

"See, my servant shall prosper, he shall be raised high and greatly exalted." "So marred was his look beyond that of man, and his appearance beyond that of mortals." "We thought of him as stricken, as one smitten by God and afflicted." No! "He gives his life as an offering for sin."[9] "Through his suffering, my servant shall justify many." "Because of his affliction he shall see the light in fullness of days." "So shall he startle many nations," "those who have not been told shall see" what they could not have imagined: "the man of suffering" became, through his sacrifice, the leader of many sinners redeemed by the death of the Just Man.[10]

Isaiah's oracle ends with a vision of peace, serenity, and hope.[11] After the reading comes a psalm of confident praise, not a song of mourning or despair.

Into your hands I commend my spirit.

In you, O LORD, I take refuge;
  let me never be put to shame.
In your justice rescue me.

Into your hands I commend my spirit;
  you will redeem me, O LORD, O faithful God.

For all my foes I am an object of reproach,
  a laughingstock of my neighbors, and
  a dread to my friends;
  they who see me abroad flee from me.
I am forgotten like the unremembered dead;
  I am like a dish that is broken.

But my trust is in you, O LORD;
  I say, "You are my God."
In your hands is my destiny; rescue me
  from the clutches of my enemies and my
    persecutors.
Let your face shine upon your servant;
  save me in your kindness.

Take courage and be stouthearted,
   all you who hope in the LORD.
(Ps 31:2, 6, 12-13, 15-16, 17, 25)

Jesus, Son of God, Our High Priest

The second reading is like the right-hand panel of a triptych, with the Gospel in the middle. Isaiah tells us of a mysterious "servant of God" who, through his suffering, will save many and be glorified by God. Now, a Christian author tells us of the dignity of one whose name we now know and of the mystery of his obedience to the Father: "Jesus, the Son of God" (Heb 4:14-16; 5:7-9).[12]

"Let us hold fast to our confession." Jesus is the Son of God. His work—the passion—can only be understood in light of the resurrection. By his death he has torn apart the veil that separated the world and the sanctuary "in the heavens" where God dwells. He is the high priest of his own sacrifice, the perfect sacrifice that is ever before his Father, since he dwells eternally in his presence. He is, "in the heavens," the eternal and definitive Passover.

But he has not thrown off his human condition. He is eternally the crucified Christ, marked with the wounds of his passion, glorious though they may be. He "was tempted in every way that we are," even in the face of death, a scandal for reason and faith: "My God, my God, why have you forsaken me?" (Ps 22:2).[13] Yet he "never sinned": "Father, into your hands I commend my spirit" (Luke 23:46).[14] The indelible mark of his own trial makes Jesus a high priest who can sympathize with weakness. He enables us with confidence to "approach the throne of grace to receive mercy and favor and to find help in the time of need."

Christ's Prayer, Granted By God

Death is a scandal for human reason; it tends to lead to a radical pessimism: "For the lot of man and of beast is one lot, the one dies as well as the other. Both have the same life-breath, and man has no advantage over the beast; but all is vanity" (Eccl 3:19). But if this is the case, what must we say about the death of one whom God himself acknowledges to be just, his own Son? How did Jesus regard his own death? True man, he trembled at the thought of death; perfect man, and not an impervious hero, he felt the anguish and horror of it more than anyone.

> He stumbled. He fell like anyone else. He felt weariness. For him, too, stones were hard and wooden beams heavy. He sweated while he worked.

He sweated human blood at Gethsemane, and so it poured forth when he was struck with a lance on Calvary. A chemical analysis would have proved this. With human nerves he suffered the symptoms of a human death, the thirst of a bleeding man, the terrible immobility of the cross. His lungs gave one last breath, as all the dying do.

With a human soul he felt the grief of seeing his deeds overthrown by men, the shame of a decisive defeat, the laughter of the people, head-shaking, the ridicule of the final hours, everything he had already tasted in the dregs of the chalice, a stone's throw from slumber . . . His mother wept at his feet.

He was forsaken by his Father, abandoned by God, submitted to the barrenness of absolute destitution: a cross on the cross, death within death.

All this is the earthly reality. He was made vulnerable, mortal, recognized only slowly. Never will I contemplate sufficiently the abyss of the blessed humanity of my God.[15]

"In the days when he was in the flesh, he offered up prayers and supplications with loud cries and tears to God, who was able to save him from death." Does his prayer conflict with God's silence? No, this cannot be: "He was heard because of his reverence." Indeed, "troubled" at the thought of the kind of death he would suffer, he exclaimed: " 'Yet what should I say? Father, save me from this hour? But it was for this purpose that I came to this hour. Father, glorify your name.' Then a voice came from heaven: 'I have glorified it, and will glorify it again' " (John 12:27-28).

Such are the data of faith, which must be held concurrently, even though our reason cannot resolve their apparent contradictions. "Son though he was, he learned obedience from what he suffered" which, in order to be complete, must include total self-renunciation, even to the point of giving his life. "When perfected, he became the source of eternal salvation for all who obey him." To the wise, death, especially that of the just man, remains a mystery, for there is no reasonable solution to it. But the believer accepts it in faith as he contemplates Christ. "[He became] obedient to death, even death on a cross," in order to vanquish death and lead us all to life.

The cross of Christ is a sign not of death but of the good news—the gospel—of life, hope, and the guarantee of eternal life.

Today sees our Lord Jesus Christ on the cross; we celebrate, so that we may understand that the cross is a celebration, a solemn, spiritual feast. Before, the cross was synonymous with condemnation; now it is an object of honor. Before, a symbol of death; now, the means of salvation. It has been the source of countless blessings for us: it has delivered us from error, it has shone on us when we were in darkness. We were vanquished, yet it reconciles us with God. We were foes, yet it has regained God's friendship for us. We were estranged, yet it has brought us back to him . . . We have discovered a wellspring.[16]

"Whoever loves his life loses it, and whoever hates his life in this world will preserve it for eternal life" (John 12:25).

These first two readings are an excellent preparation for the Passion According to John.[17] Let us keep them in mind while we listen to the Gospel, which we acclaim by saying: "Glory to you, O Lord!"[18]

The Passion of the Lord According to John

More than the others, John's account of the passion is remarkably dense, theologically (John 18:1–19:42):

A Believer's Testimony to Faith. The mysterious "hour" that is alluded to throughout John's Gospel, its focal point, is the Lord's passion.[19] It is the supreme "sign" that is the end and summary of all the others.

In his presentation of the mystery of Jesus' incarnation and mission,[20] John writes: "He came to what was his own, but his own people did not accept him" (John 1:11). The decisive "hour" of the cross, for which the Son of God became man, is that of his glorification.[21] Through his passover from this world to the Father (John 13:1), he brings to an end the work for which he came into the world (John 19:28): thus, "It is finished" (John 19:30). The cross manifests the Father's love (John 12:16; 13:32) and the world's judgment (John 17:12-16). Christ's glory, cloaked in his flesh and partly revealed in the "signs," appears now in full light.[22] Jesus' cross is the throne of the witness to the truth.[23] From the death of the Son of God springs life[24] for all those who will lift their eyes to the crucified, pierced by a soldier's lance (John 19:37).

Themes that have appeared throughout his Gospel rise up again in John's account of the passion. The announcements, hidden signs and symbolic sayings that adorn his text are fully realized here. Theology and history are united. His account contains all the attention to detail that comes from an eyewitness: "His testimony is true. He knows that he is speaking the truth" (John 19:35). But, most importantly, John points his readers to the deepest level of meaning: "so that you also may [come to] believe" (John 19:35).

With Full Knowledge. The first thing that strikes one is Jesus' calm and unshakable freedom. He does not submit to events: he is fully cognizant of them. Far from being taken by surprise, he sees things coming and thus can control them. He knows that his "hour" has come (John 13:1) when he will be handed over (John 13:11); he knows "everything that was going to happen to him" (John 18:4). Such knowledge does not endow him with a kind of fatalistic courage, such as we see and admire in people when they are faced with something inevitable. For Jesus, this is "the cup the Father has given him," which he will not refuse (John 18:11).

Notice the arrest scene. Jesus confronts the soldiers and guards who have come to arrest him: " 'Whom are you looking for?' They answered him, 'Jesus the Nazorean.' He said to them, 'I am [he].' " Such calm determination and self-control is not lost on the soldiers: they step back and fall to the ground: Jesus has to take matters into his own hands so that they will carry out their orders (John 18:4-8). For now the "hour" has come, as it had not that day when the guards went away, not having dared to arrest him, as they had been told to do (John 7:44-52). But in the process of giving himself up, before letting himself be bound, Jesus gives them a command: "If you are looking for me, let these men go." The soldiers obey him, threatening none of the disciples, not even Peter, who had struck Malchus, the high priest's servant, with a sword, severing his ear. Jesus rebukes him for his violence: "Put your sword into its scabbard" (John 18:8-11). Undoubtedly, he is in command.

Even Pilate, an unscrupulous man who despised the Jews,[25] is troubled by him. One would have expected him to be in charge, cowing the accused with his authority to grant or withhold mercy; instead, Jesus has the upper hand. Pilate wants to release him; he grows more and more fearful as he questions him. It is out of fear that he finally hands him over to his accusers (John 18:28–19:16). Finally, Jesus is his own master, even on the cross. He "handed over the spirit," (John 19:25-30).

What a contrast with the behavior of the disciples! They witness events uncomprehendingly. Peter, admittedly, follows Jesus to the high priest's house. But he denies that he is a disciple of "this man," and that he had been "in the garden with him" (John 18:15-18, 25-27).

After Jesus' death, it is Joseph of Arimathea, not one of those closest to Jesus but "secretly a disciple of Jesus for fear of the Jews," who is bold enough to ask for the body. With Nicodemus, the man who had first come to Jesus at night (John 3:1-21), he buries Jesus in a tomb (John 19:38-42).

Jesus' Kingship. Pilate questions Jesus closely about his kingship. "Are you the King of the Jews?" The title is ambiguous, for Pilate uses it in the sense of a temporal power that might oppose Caesar (John 18:33; 19:12). Jesus does not deny his kingship, but he explains how it must be understood. "My kingdom does not belong to this world . . . my kingdom is not here. . . . For this I was born and for this I came into the world, to testify to the truth" (John 18:35-37).

The evangelist notes that these words trouble Pilate, who "became even more afraid" when he was told that Jesus "made himself the Son of God" (John 19:7-8). The soldiers, on the other hand, take them as an excuse to mock Jesus with the trappings of majesty. They put a crown of thorns on his head, they dress him up in a purple cloak, slapping his face in a cruel mockery of an act of homage (John 19:1-3). Pilate, when he regains his self-control, then pretends to take Jesus' kingship seriously, as a way to humiliate the Jews, who persist in putting him into an impossible situation (John 19:4-5, 19-22).

John records these facts for our benefit. Yes, Jesus is a king. But this appears at the very "hour" of the passion, which is also the hour when we will show the authenticity of our faith, adoring Christ crowned with thorns.

The Mysteries of Calvary. After Pilate hands Jesus over to his accusers, the evangelist mentions many details that are either explicitly or implicitly symbolic.

Jesus goes to Calvary on the eve of the sabbath, which was the most important day of Passover, just as the paschal lamb is being sacrificed in the Temple (John 19:14, 31). Like a new Isaac (Gen 22:6), he carries the wood for his own sacrifice (John 19:17), of which it seems that he himself is the high priest, as is suggested by his seamless robe (Rev 1:13).

At the place of crucifixion, he can be seen by many; moreover, the inscription Pilate has placed on the cross is written in Hebrew, Latin, and Greek (John 19:20); in other words, all people can thus behold the one who is lifted on the cross (John 12:32). Before handing over his spirit, he turns to his mother, the new Eve and mother of believers (Gen 3:20), and the disciple whom he loved (John 19:26-27), the truthful witness. The body of the new Adam is put in a tomb—a new tomb—in a garden, the new Eden (Gen 2:8)?

The Lord's death fulfills Scripture (John 19:28), bringing to an end the work for which he was sent (John 4:34): to manifest to all people the name of his Father, who gave everything to him (John 17:6-7).

Christian tradition has seen the blood and water that flowed from the lance wound (John 19:34) as the source of the sacraments.

My mouth opens to the stream
of sacred Blood flowing from your side,
like the child at the breast
who draws to himself his mother's bosom,

So that I may drink the joy
and exult in the Holy Spirit,
and relish the taste of the Cup,
the immaculate Love of unmixed Wine.[26]

Jesus Appeals to His Disciples' Witness. When the high priest asks him about his disciples and his teaching, Jesus responds: "Ask those who heard me what I said to them; they know what I said" (John 18:19-23).

He has left us his teaching, which comes to us in all the works of the New Testament, so that we may proclaim it to every nation, speaking not only in words but in deeds, the language that no one can misconstrue. What people say about Jesus Christ (Matt 16:13-15) depends on what we say about him, the testimony we give both individually and in the Church.[27]

If our testimony lacks conviction, it is most often because it does not see clearly enough that Jesus' passion is his supreme revelation, that his kingdom is not of this world. Even so, our faith proclaims that the Messiah must suffer in order to enter his glory and accomplish our salvation.

Do not go into the garden,
Oh! Jesus,
Do not go into the garden
before the dawn!
If I do not go into the garden
in the dead of night,
who will lead you to the sunrise
of Paradise?
I will go into the garden
in the dead of night.

Do not let them bind your hands,
Oh! Jesus,
do not let them bind your hands
without a word!
If I do not let them bind my hands
like a thief,
who will break open the prisons
in which you languish?
I will let them bind my hands
like a thief.

Do not hang on the cross,
Oh! Jesus,
do not hang on the cross
till you die!
If I do not hang on the cross
like a bird,
who will protect you from
the flames of hell?
I will hang on the cross
like a bird.

Do not let your heart be pierced,
Oh! Jesus,
do not let your heart be pierced
by your executioners!
If I do not let my heart be pierced
like a ripe fruit,
from whom will you drink the blood and water
that will heal you?
I will let my heart be pierced
like a ripe fruit.

Do not go into the tomb,
Oh! Jesus,
do not go into the tomb
that they have dug!
If I do not go into the tomb
like a grain of wheat,
who will lift from your coffins
your lifeless bodies?
I will go into the tomb
to sleep there.

Christ has gone into the garden, Alleluia.
Christ has let them bind his hands, Alleluia.
Christ has willingly suffered the cross, Alleluia.
Christ has let his heart be pierced, Alleluia.
Christ has slept in the tomb, Alleluia.[28]

Though we do not sing "alleluia" till the Vigil, it swells in each of our
hearts and the whole Church when, under John's guidance, we meditate on the passion of the Lord. Never should we forget or underesti-
mate the sufferings Jesus went through on the cross. But we must
contemplate him on the cross as the glorious victor over Satan (John
12:31), over sin and death. The gibbet has become the tree of life. The
arms of the Lord stretched out "between heaven and earth" are "the
everlasting sign of the covenant" that the Father has made with human-

ity through the Son.[29] "So let us confidently approach the throne of grace to receive mercy and to find grace for timely help" (Heb 4:16: Second Reading).

The General Intercessions

After the reading of the Passion, the liturgy continues with a set of general intercessions. Since 1969[30] we have become used to these kinds of petitions, both in the Sunday Eucharist and the Liturgy of the Hours; nevertheless, Good Friday is still the model for all to follow. It can claim the greatest antiquity.[31]

In this prayer, "the people, exercising their priestly function, intercede for all humanity"[32]: it is not simply a petition for everyone's personal needs, though such an aspect is both legitimate and necessary, but a true liturgical act.[33] It is performed by the whole assembly, each member having a place in it. One might call it "concelebrated prayer." The celebrant introduces and concludes it; the intentions are proclaimed by the deacon, cantor, or other appointed member of the congregation; and the whole assembly joins in with a common invocation or a time of silence.[34] Thus, the prayer's structure is quite dynamic: it includes an active participation on everyone's part. Finally, it reminds the assembly—however small it may be—of one of its essential functions: to pray for the whole world, and not just for itself; to express its sense of belonging to the universal Church.

This prayer, as said on Good Friday, is exemplary in two respects. First in its structure. The deacon—or someone else—states each intention, which is followed by a moment of silence that allows all those present to interiorize it, to make it their own. The celebrant then says a relatively developed prayer, to which everyone assents with "Amen" or an acclamation. Second, it is genuinely universal, since one prays in turn for the Church, the pope, the clergy and laity of the Church, the catechumens who will be baptized during the Easter Vigil, Christian unity, the Jews, those who do not believe in Jesus Christ, those who do not believe in God, public officials, and people in special need. Entering into this prayer is not difficult. Moreover, it teaches us something about all personal prayer in the liturgy. Sometimes there are situations that legitimately demand, so to speak, particular intentions. But even so, "specific" Christian prayer is never entirely self-centered, concerned only with its own needs and problems; it must always be open to the universal.[35] We pray "as the Lord taught us," who suffered his passion for us all, so that the reign of God might come. Christian prayer is fundamentally missionary. It is often called "the breath of the soul." This is appropriate, as long as the breath has the rhythm of the Church and the Spirit. Our confidence in prayer comes from Jesus, because our prayer takes its power from his intercession with the Father. He is "at the right hand of God and intercedes for us" (Rom 8:34), who "is always able to save those who approach God through him, since he lives forever to make intercession for them" (Heb 7:25).

The Veneration of the Cross. The general intercessions are followed by the veneration of the cross, a rite that originated in Jerusalem with the discovery of the cross in 326, during a journey to the Holy Land by Helena, mother of the emperor Constantine (c. 247–330).[36] The veneration of the cross is a high point of the Good Friday liturgy today: it expresses the Church's faith in and gratitude to Christ who turned the wood of an instrument of torture into the means of redemption and the sign of God's infinite love. The cross stands as an irresistible call to love God who has loved us so well. Again, the veneration of the cross is a reminder that Christ's death and resurrection are the two parts of the one paschal mystery. One need only listen to the chants that accompany the rite.

> This is the wood of the cross,
> on which hung the Savior of the world.

> We worship you, Lord,
> we venerate your cross,
> we praise your resurrection.
> Through the cross you brought joy to the world.

After the rather austere first two sections of the liturgy, these songs ring with a joy that foreshadows the breaking forth of the "alleluia" on Easter night.

The "Reproaches"—"My people, what have I done to you? How have I offended you? Answer me!"—inspire an appeal to God's mercy with overtones of praise.

> Holy is God!
> Holy and strong!
> Holy immortal One,
> have mercy on us!

And the rite ends with a hymn.[37]

> O Cross, more worthy than cedar,
> on you the life of the world was nailed,

on you Christ has triumphed:
death has destroyed death!

Glory to you, Jesus, Savior,
your cross gives us life!

Behold the tree of life
where the new Adam offers his blood
to gather all people into one Body:
Come, let us adore!

Behold the tree of life
where the savior of the world holds out his hands
to embrace us all, in his forgiveness:
Come, let us adore!

Behold the tree of life
where the Father's beloved
opens the gates of the kingdom:
Come, let us adore!

Behold the tree of life
where love cries that it is forsaken
to give hope to all the unloved:
Come, let us adore!

Behold the tree of life
where the Son of Man gives the Spirit
while breathing his last within the Father's hands:
Come, let us adore!

Behold the tree of life
where the light of the world shines in the darkness
in order to accomplish the Passover of the universe:
Come, let us adore!

Behold the tree of life
where Jesus gives us his mother,
the new Eve of a redeemed world:
Come, let us adore!

Behold the tree of life
where the innocent man bears our sins
in order to reconcile earth and heaven:
Come, let us adore![38]

Communion. Good Friday's liturgy ends with Communion, using bread consecrated the day before. It takes place in great simplicity. After the community's "Our Father" and the priest's prayer "Deliver us, Lord, from every evil," and the usual acclamation "For the kingdom, the power

. . . ,'' the priest says a prayer and gives a blessing. Both speak of resurrection.

> Almighty and eternal God,
> you have restored us to life
> by the triumphant death and resurrection of Christ . . .

> Lord,
> send down your abundant blessing
> upon your people who have devoutly recalled
> the death of your Son
> in the sure hope of resurrection.

Within all the churches devoid of the Eucharistic presence and with their altars stripped, there falls a deep silence. It will only be broken, the next day, during the celebration of the Liturgy of the Hours, in the calm waiting for the Lord's resurrection, meditating on his mysterious descent to the dead, bringing them the good news of their deliverance.

> Something strange is happening—there is a great silence on earth today, a great silence and stillness. The whole earth keeps silence because the King is asleep. The earth trembled and is still because God has fallen asleep in the flesh and he has raised up all who have slept ever since the world began. God has died in the flesh and hell trembles with fear.
>
> He has gone to search for our first parent, as for a lost sheep. Greatly desiring to visit those who live in darkness and in the shadow of death, he has gone to free from sorrow the captives Adam and Eve, he who is both God and the son of Eve. The Lord approached them bearing the cross, the weapon that had won him the victory. At the sight of him Adam, the first man he had created, struck his breast in terror and cried out to everyone: "My Lord be with you all." Christ answered him: "And with your spirit." He took him by the hand and raised him up, saying: "Awake, O sleeper, and rise from the dead, and Christ will give you light."
>
> I am your God, who for your sake have become your son. Out of love for you and for your descendants I now by my own authority command all who are held in bondage to come forth, all who are in darkness to be enlightened, all who are sleeping to arise. I order you, O sleeper, to awake. I did not create you to be held a prisoner in hell. Rise from the dead, for I am the life of the dead. Rise up, work of my hands, you who were created in my image. Rise, let us leave this place, for you are in me and I am in you; together we form only one person and we cannot be separated.
>
> For your sake I, your God, became your son; I, the Lord, took the form of a slave; I, whose home is above the heavens, descended to the earth and beneath the earth. For your sake, for the sake of man, I became like a man without help, free among the dead. For the sake of you, who left a garden, I was betrayed to the Jews in a garden, and I was crucified in a garden.[39]

The Easter Celebrations

The Easter Triduum finds its center in the vigil on Holy Saturday night.[1] This third of the holy days is, in terms of its liturgy, the greatest of all the Days of the Lord. It begins with Vespers on Saturday, when the Church expresses its impatience to see the rising of the morning sun.

> Shine now, flashes of Easter,
> glinting in the morrow's dawn,
> herald the returning bridegroom
> who rouses all on his way.
> The night cannot hold
> the body inflamed with the desire
> to begin a new age.
>
> The earth breaks open when he stands,
> as in the past when God gave him
> his Spirit, his breath, a voice
> in the garden of Genesis.
> The flesh of his flesh is named:
> the wound in his side
> is open so that a people might find birth
> in it.
>
> Behold the hour of God's hastening,
> with his hand he overshadows the waters,
> he draws from them a new world,
> life abounding everywhere!
> Where then is God's tomb?
> Death is dead under the eyes
> of those who will believe in his grace.[2]

The main liturgy occurs at night, and the Triduum ends, after Mass on Easter Sunday, with Vespers that night.

> Whom do you seek as evening falls,
> with hearts lit by inward fire?
> Where are you going
> with heads bowed?
> To the day promised
> to those who will have welcomed
> the light that God makes
> to shine in the darkness.

Should you not be cautious?
The new day which appeared
after Jesus' passover,
it rises:
What will we do if he is not there?
When our light decreases
we know well that it is already
the world's dawn.

And you too, come see him,
but hasten, for it is late!
Each of you will have his share
of grace;
each of you, if you are aware,
and the spirit leads you through his night,
will see the promised day rise:
it is God who is coming.

This is why we flock
to his new creation:
God always does what is good
for man.
He discovers him little by little,
softly he opens our eyes,
for nothing is impossible for God,
since he gives himself.[3]

Easter Vigil

Christ Is Risen!

As far back as we can trace, the Easter Vigil has been celebrated at night. At first it was very plain: an assembly that ended with the breaking of the bread and an *agape*, following a fast of one or more days. As the Roman Easter Vigil developed, it added a baptismal rite, the Office of the *lucenarium*, a blessing of the new fire, and a candlelight procession.[4]

Thus the Vigil became more and more meaningful. At first, the celebration was at night (like the weekly Eucharist) because most of the community could not assemble during the day. However, the evangelists situate the discovery of the tomb "as the first day of the week was dawning" (Matt 28:1), "very early" (Mark 16:2; John 20:1), "at dawn" (Luke 24:1). Again, Jesus is the "light of the world" that came into the world as a "revelation to the Gentiles" (Luke 2:32).

Through baptism, the believer passes from death to life (Col 2:12); ritually and really, he is plunged with Christ into death so as to come to new life with the one who "was raised from the dead by the glory of the Father" (Rom 6:4). Thus is baptism called "illumination"—in Greek, *photismos*—and the baptized, "illuminated."

Today, thanks to electricity, we can have as much light as we want, when we want it. In the past, the lighting of lamps in the evening was a rite: it was generally a joyous occasion, especially when many lamps were lit, as for a banquet, e.g., at the beginning of the sabbath on Friday evening. Christians saw this light that drives away darkness as a symbol of the Christ-light: "Joyful light of the Father's eternal glory, blessed and holy, Jesus Christ!"[5] This rite becomes most solemn in the context of the great night illuminated by the resurrected Christ. This was explained in the solemn proclamation of the Lord's resurrection that was the origin of the *Exultet*.

Finally, since we customarily extinguish all lights on Holy Thursday evening, we must light a new flame in order to celebrate a liturgy at night. This also has been ritualized: the blessing of a new fire and the procession into the Church led by the Easter candle: *Lumen Christi! Deo gratias!*

The evolution of the rite has had some difficult times. Even in the thirteenth century, the liturgy was still not entirely structured; in fact, there had been a general decay in it since the seventh century, most notably in the fact that it was celebrated earlier and earlier in the day on Holy Saturday. When Pope Pius V (1566–1572) reformed the Missal, he forbade the celebration of the Eucharist after midday. Thus on Holy Saturday morning, in churches full of sunlight, with a barely perceptible flame on the Easter candle, was sung "O night truly blessed"! Moreover, very few people were able to attend such a long liturgy on Holy Saturday morning, so it fell into greater and greater insignificance.[6]

The biblical, patristic, theological, and liturgical renewal that began in the 1920s became more and more aware of the unacceptability of this situation and its impoverishment of the Easter celebration. In a decree dated February 9, 1951, Pope Pius XII (1939–1958) authorized the celebration of an Easter Vigil during evening hours on Holy Saturday, the rites being altered to foster greater congregational participation. In 1955, he decreed that this celebration must take place at night.[7]

Currently, we follow the "Missal of Paul VI" (1963–1978), promulgated on April 3, 1969.[8] The celebration has four parts: the blessing of the fire, procession of the Easter candle and chanting of the *Exultet;* the Liturgy of the Word, containing seven readings from the Old Testament,[9] one from Paul's Letter to the Romans (6:3-11), and the Gospel (Matt 28:1-10, Year A; Mark 16:1-8, Year B; Luke 24:1-12, Year C); the baptismal liturgy, which includes at least the blessing of the water and a renewal of baptismal vows; and finally, the Eucharistic liturgy.

> On this night, dear brethren, we celebrate the vigil in honor of the Lord's burial: let us keep watch while he sleeps in our stead. Long before, he announced his passion through the prophecy: "When I lie down in sleep, I awake again, for the Lord sustains me" (Ps 3:6). He calls the Father Lord. Let us watch while he sleeps, so that, through his death, we might live. While he slumbers, we celebrate a vigil, so that, now that he watches for us, we may sleep secure as Christ keeps eternal vigil. For on this same night he rose; it is to see this, that we devote ourselves to the vigil. "He was handed over to death for our sins," hence he sleeps; "and raised up for our justification" (Rom 4:25), hence, in this very night during which he sleeps, we celebrate our vigil, so that we may be assured that he will not sleep during his vigil. We await the hour of his awakening, fearful that, though we await our justification, our hearts may be inclined to sleep. Let us watch then, dear brethren, and pray that we may not be led into temptation.[10]

The Liturgy of Light

Although the spoken word has an important place in the liturgy, it is more fundamentally a matter of symbolism, whether in things or actions. If one comes to it looking for obvious teaching, or with a utilitarian mentality, one is bound to be disappointed. It is essential that one approach it with a receptive attitude, ready to be swept along in a way that appeals both to the mind and the heart, indeed to one's whole being. One must not only listen but gaze with open eyes on the realities present in signs that cannot be fully captured in words. One must also draw in faith what purifies, nourishes, and increases participation in the liturgy.[11] This is the way to participate most perfectly and joyfully in the Easter Vigil.

The ritual of light is neither utilitarian—there are many lights in our churches that are turned off at this time—nor based in folklore. "May the light of Christ, rising in glory, dispel the darkness of our hearts and minds."[12]

The procession led by the elevated Easter candle evokes the journey of God's people, led no more by a bright cloud but by the glorious light of Christ that shines on every person coming into the world (John 1:9), and which draws ever nearer: "Christ our light!—Thanks be to God!"

> Rejoice, heavenly powers! Sing, choirs of angels!
> Exult, all creation around God's throne!
> Jesus Christ, our King, is risen!
> Sound the trumpet of salvation!
>
> Rejoice, O earth, in shining splendor,
> radiant in the brightness of your King!
> Christ has conquered! Glory fills you!
> Darkness vanishes for ever!
>
> Rejoice, O Mother Church! Exult in glory!
> The risen Savior shines upon you!
> Let this place resound with joy,
> echoing the mighty song of all God's people!
>
> My dearest friends, standing with me in this holy light,
> join me in asking God for mercy . . .[13]

In a church lit by tiny flames, kindled from the Easter candle that is placed high for all to see, rises the longest and most lyrical of liturgical thanksgivings.[14] It sings of the "night truly blessed," "when Christians everywhere, washed clean of sin and freed from all defilement, are restored to grace and grow together in holiness"; "when Jesus Christ broke the chains of death and rose triumphant from the grave"; "when heaven is wedded to earth and man is reconciled with God.'' The expressions of an eternal thanksgiving come thick and fast, marked by truly astounding statements: ''O happy fault, O necessary sin of Adam, which gained for us so great a Redeemer!'' And after having declared: ''Accept this Easter candle, a flame divided but undimmed, a pillar of fire that glows to the honor of God,'' the chant ends with a prayer.

> Let it mingle with the lights of heaven
> and continue bravely burning
> to dispel the darkness of this night!

> May the Morning Star that never sets find
> this flame still burning:
> Christ, that Morning Star, who came back
> from the dead,
> and shed his peaceful light on all mankind,
> your Son who lives and reigns for ever and ever.

Listening to this wonderful chant, one can understand why the Easter candle is lit at every baptism; so should it also be obvious why it will still be burning at one's funeral, the passage from death to life, with Christ.

> Christ our Light!
> Thanks be to God!

The Liturgy of the Word

The second part of the celebration is an unusually lengthy Liturgy of the Word, containing multiple readings from the Old Testament.[15] It is appropriate, on this night, that we spend more time than usual listening to the Scriptures, particularly the Old Testament. One must ''begin with Moses and the prophets'' in order to understand ''that the Messiah should suffer these things and enter into his glory'' (Luke 24:26-27). God wants ''to teach us in both the Old and the New Testament to celebrate this passover mystery.''[16] As a matter of fact, the selection of readings is similar in both Eastern and Western Christian tradition, and even corresponds to Jewish tradition.[17]

The first four Old Testament readings recall the ''Four Nights'' of Jewish tradition.

> Four nights have been inscribed in the book of memorials. The *first night* is when God created the world: the world was formless and void and darkness covered the abyss (Gen 1:2). The Word of God was light and shone on it. This is called the first night.

The *second night* was when God appeared to Abraham and Sarah (Gen 17:17) to fulfill what Scripture says: Abraham at one hundred could father a child and Sarah at ninety could bear a child . . . And Isaac was thirty-seven when he was offered on the altar . . .

The *third night* was when God came against the Egyptians in the night (Exod 12:29; Wis 18): his hand destroyed the first-born of Egypt and protected the first-born of Israel in order to fulfill Scripture: "Israel is my son, my first-born" (Exod 4:22). This is called the third night.

The *fourth night* will be when the world comes to an end. The yoke of iron will be smashed and sinful generations destroyed. And Moses will come out of the desert . . .

This is the night of the Passover for the name of the Lord: the night reserved for the salvation of all the generations of Israel.[18]

The three other Old Testament readings have clear baptismal overtones, especially in the context of the Easter Vigil.

The text from the Letter to the Romans (6:3-11) that follows deals with baptism as the passage from death to sin to life for God.

Finally, the Gospel—whether Matthew, Mark or Luke—leads us to the Lord's tomb that, "on the first day of the week," "at dawn," the women will find empty, and where they will receive the first announcement of the resurrection.

The Liturgy of the Word tonight invites us to listen "attentively" and to remind ourselves of the way in which God, our creator, has "saved his people throughout history" and how he, "in the fullness of time, sent his own Son to be our Redeemer."[19] "Today this Scripture passage is fulfilled in your hearing" (Luke 4:21). We pray: "Through this Easter celebration, may God bring to perfection the saving work he has begun in us."[20]

"In the Beginning" Treats of Everything

The experience of what he does for his people leads one to ask: "Who is this God who loves us so?"[21] Such was the question that a wise and faithful Israelite in the sixth or fifth century B.C. asked himself, while meditating on God's lordship over history, most recently seen in the return from the Babylonian Exile. To answer this question, one must look back "to the beginning" of all things (Gen 1:1-2:2).

"God created the heavens and the earth." He made man and woman "in his image, after his likeness." He told them to "fill the earth and subdue it." This is God's first revelatory act, which must be remembered whenever one tries to understand the world. He who wrote what became the first page of the Bible[22] is the "prophet of the past,"[23] to which one must constantly look in order to understand the present. With this "beginning," the author paints a great fresco that is both easy to grasp and of a great theological—or even mystical—depth, remarkable in such a well-ordered and easily remembered story.[24] He knows the ancient Babylonian myths about the creation of the world, and uses them to a certain point, stripping them of their disturbing anthropomorphism and the dualistic framework of a struggle between the principles of good and evil. The God of Genesis creates with a word: "God said . . . and so it happened." His Word will play a key role in sacred history, demonstrating his creative power and initiative.[25] Likewise with his breath, and with water and light.

Everything God has created is "good," "very good"; the word of God will become flesh in his Son Jesus Christ, the light coming into the world (John 1:9-14) who, as perfect image of the Father,[26] will make a new creation by water and the Spirit, and will enable us to discover the image of God according to which we have been created.[27] The human being is placed at the summit in the temple of creation: all humanity has value in God's eyes. He can never forget them.

> Why, man, do you value yourself so little when you are worth so much in God's eyes? Why do you seek the matter from which you come and not the meaning of your existence? The whole world you see around you, was it not built for you? For you, the light drives back the darkness that surrounds you, it rules night and measures day. For you, the heavens shine with the light of sun, moon, and stars. For you, the earth is bedecked with flowers, forests, and fruits. For you was created such a bewildering array of living beings in field, stream, and air.[28]

The dignity of man and woman that comes to them from God is the basis of their inalienable and sacred rights, as well as their duties and responsibilities.[29] God has made them "little less than the angels" (Ps 8:6); they participate in his universal kingship. There is no image of God that can rival the one the creator himself has made.[30] Nothing can nullify God's first blessing over the human couple: neither their faithlessness, nor the corruption of a world contaminated with violence, nor the upheaval of the Exile. This blessing "in the beginning" runs through the whole story of the patriarchs in the Book of Genesis; it hangs over the stages of the covenant. It is weighted with the wonders to come.

> Behold the night,
> the great night of beginnings,
> when nothing exists but Love,
> a Love that takes shape:

separating land and water,
God prepared the Earth
like a cradle, where he would come one day.[31]

Listening to the beautiful poem of creation at the Easter Vigil, the Christian eye turns to Christ, "the image of the invisible God, the firstborn of all creation. For in him were created all things in heaven and on earth" (Col 1:15-16). "In the beginning, God created the heavens and the earth" said Genesis. "In the beginning was the Word, and the Word was with God, and the Word was God. He was in the beginning with God. All things came to be through him, and without him nothing came to be," proclaims John (1:1, 3). In and through Jesus Christ comes the decisive victory of order over chaos, light over darkness: "What came to be through him was life, and this life was the light of the human race; the light shines in the darkness, and the darkness has not overcome it" (John 1:4-5). Contemplating the risen Lord, "we saw his glory" (John 1:14). Participating in his paschal mystery, "all of us . . . are being transformed into the same image from glory to glory" by his Spirit (2 Cor 3:18). Through him, God, who worked wonders in creating humanity, has done something "still more wonderful" in redeeming it.[32] Let us give thanks to God. May he send his Spirit to renew the face of the earth. "Let us allow Christ to paint his image in us. Let us not be the painters of strange images!"[33]

LORD, *send forth your Spirit, and renew the face of the earth.*

Bless the LORD, O my soul!
   O LORD my God, you are great indeed!
You are clothed with majesty and glory,
   robed in light as with a cloak.

You fixed the earth upon its foundations,
   not to be moved forever;
With the ocean, as with a garment, you covered it;
   above the mountains the waters stood.

You send forth springs into the watercourses
   that wind among the mountains. . .
Beside them the birds of heaven dwell;
   from among the branches they send forth their song.

You water the mountains from your palace;
   the earth is replete with the fruit of your works.
You raise grass for the cattle,
   and vegetation for men's use,
Producing bread from the earth.

How manifold are your works, O LORD!
In wisdom you have wrought them all—
the earth is full of your creatures . . .
Bless the LORD, O my soul! (Ps 104:1-2a, 5-6, 10, 12, 13-14, 24, 35c)

Or:

Of the kindness of the LORD the earth is full.

For upright is the word of the LORD,
  and all his works are trustworthy.
He loves justice and right;
  of the kindness of the LORD the earth is full.

By the word of the LORD the heavens were made;
  by the breath of his mouth all their host.
He gathers the waters of the sea as in a flask;
  in cellars he confines the deep.

Happy the nation whose God is the LORD,
  the people he has chosen for his own inheritance.
From heaven the LORD looks down;
  he sees all mankind.

Our soul waits for the LORD,
  who is our help and our shield,
May your kindness, O LORD, be upon us
  who have put our hope in you.
(Ps 33:4-5, 6-7, 12-13, 20, 22)[34]

Abraham's Test

The story of Abraham's test, when God told him to sacrifice his only son, Isaac, seems quite shocking today, even when one knows that Isaac will not end up being sacrificed. Never should someone be asked to demonstrate his or her fidelity by murder; a father cannot be asked to kill his son, even if one knows—as the father does not—that he will be stopped at the last moment.[35] Any willingness to commit murder must be condemned. Obedience to whoever ordered it is no excuse.[36] However, the New Testament occasionally refers to Abraham's sacrifice of Isaac;[37] it was a popular theme of early Christian iconography.[38] And since the liturgy includes it here, we must pay close attention to the text. Thus we find it to be a story full of meaning, both within its context and as read in our liturgy (Gen 22:1-18).[39]

It all begins with an unforeseen divine initiative: "The Lord said to Abram: 'Go forth from the land of your kinsfolk and from your father's house to a land that I will show you. I will make of you a great nation, and I will bless you; I will make your name great, so that you will be a blessing. I will bless those who bless you and curse those who curse you. All the communities of the earth shall find blessing in you' " (Gen 12:1-3). The promise is difficult to reconcile with human judgment: leaving to go one knows not where, abandoning a secure home in order to become "a great nation"! And yet, "Abram went." What the Lord has said, Abram thinks, he will do. Shortly thereafter, the promise is further defined: "Look up at the sky and count the stars, if you can. Just so shall your descendants be" (Gen 15:5). Abraham has no child; he and his wife Sarah are already old. But the Lord makes this covenant with him: "To your descendants I give this land" (Gen 15:18). Again, Abraham is forced to believe that this will happen, since God says so. Sarah suggests that her husband should assure himself of a son through Hagar, her Egyptian slave. "Perhaps I will have sons through her" (Gen 18:1-2). But no, it is Sarah who must bear Abraham the child of the promise. And since God said it, so it happened: Sarah conceived in her old age and gave birth to a son, Isaac (Gen 21:1-8). From his calling to Isaac's birth, the story of Abraham is a set of promises for which the only assurance is the Lord's word. What God asks of him now must be seen in this context. Abraham is called to give the supreme proof of his faith. What happens is not merely tragic and baffling, concerning only him. His test reveals that the fulfillment of the promises of salvation is guaranteed, from the moment that God speaks them; nothing can hinder the realization of God's word.[40] At the same time, this episode reminds Christians of what God will accomplish in his Son.

When God proclaimed to a young daughter of Israel that she would bear a son to whom the Lord would give the throne of David and whose reign would be without end, Mary said to the angel: "May it be done to me according to your word" (Luke 1:26-38). Joseph, likewise, did "as the angel of the Lord had commanded him": he took Mary into his home, though she was already with child (Matt 1:18-25).

When Jesus began to preach with unparalleled authority and worked signs and wonders never before seen, the crowds followed him enthusiastically, thinking that he would soon institute the kingdom of the promise. His closest disciples, who had left everything to follow him, thought that they could count on having a seat near him then (Matt 20:20-28). His last entrance into Jerusalem seemed to everyone there like a triumphal march. How could he be betrayed, suffer, and die? Peter said, "God forbid, Lord! No such thing shall ever happen to you" (Matt 16:21-22). But thus it happened, because God had said so through the prophets and the whole of Scripture (Luke 24:25-27). And the sacrifice of this Son is carried out.

> Behold the night,
> the strange night on the hill,
> and nothing exists but the Body,
> the Body wounded with thorns:
> Through the crucifixion,
> God makes as fertile as an orchard
> the earth where he plants death.[41]

The Christian tradition has always known that what is mysteriously prefigured in Abraham's action is realized in Christ. The Fathers loved to point out particularly significant details.

> Isaac carrying the wood for the holocaust is a figure of Christ who "carried the cross by himself" (John 19:17); however, it is the priest's office to carry the wood for the holocaust; Christ is therefore both priest and victim. The same is indicated in the following: "The two walked on together." Abraham, who performs the sacrifice, bears the fire and the knife; Isaac, however does not walk behind him, but with him, showing that he also fulfills a priestly function.
> Isaac, Scripture continues, says to his father Abraham: "Father!"—Imagine the temptation presented by the son's voice. Imagine how the voice of a son who is about to be sacrificed would move his father's heart. But Abraham's inflexible faith does not prevent him from responding affectionately: "Yes, son."—Here are the fire and the wood, says Isaac, but where is the sheep for the holocaust? Abraham responds: "Son, God himself will provide the sheep for the holocaust."
> Abraham's response, both correct and prudent, strikes me. I do not know what he was thinking of, for he refers not to the present but the future when he says: "God will provide." His son asks about the present, he speaks about the future. So the Lord himself will provide the sheep in the person of Christ.[42]

We know well that Jesus is the Lamb that God has kept in reserve, the Son of the promise accomplished once for all through his death and resurrection. His death too was a test for faith: the apostles did not come through it easily. His resurrection was only acknowledged slowly by the first witnesses: the Spirit was needed to make them understand every passage "that referred to him in all the Scriptures" (Luke 24:27). May we, like Abraham, the father of believers, and the vast number of witnesses around us, hope against all hope in Jesus Christ, the Son whose sacrifice conquered death!

Keep me safe, O God; you are my hope.

O Lord, my allotted portion and my cup,
    you it is who hold fast my lot . . .
I set the Lord ever before me;
    with him at my right hand I shall not be disturbed.

Therefore my heart is glad and my soul rejoices,
    my body, too, abides in confidence;
Because you will not abandon my soul to the nether world,
    nor will you suffer your faithful one to undergo corruption.

You will show me the path to life,
    fullness of joys in your presence,
    the delights at your right hand forever.
(Ps 16:5, 8, 9-10, 11)

When Israel Left Egypt

It is impossible to celebrate Passover without reading the account of that memorable night when God, by his power, freed his people from their oppressors. The Exodus from Egypt is the first great event in the collective memory of the people of God. It is the preeminent reference for establishing the meaning of their existence and reawakening their hope; they celebrate it faithfully from generation to generation. A rabbi of the Middle Ages said, not without reason, that this story should be at the beginning of the Bible: it is the foundational event (Exod 14:15–15:1).[43]

What exactly happened? What is the historical basis for this great story, which at several points is reminiscent of the story of creation?[44] Historians and critics are concerned with such things;[45] this is their *métier;* they are devoted to answering such questions despite the lack of certainty that is inherent in the work. But however "demythologized" the story may thus become, the historical fact, in the religious memory of a people, has taken on, in the course of the centuries, the status of an event. It is recognized as an important intervention of the divine. Isn't this the truth that must concern us?[46] If "the epic is history heard at the doors of legend,"[47] one could say that the epic story of the passage of the Red Sea is history, read with the eyes of faith, that recalls a particularly special intervention of God on behalf of his people. It will be evoked in one form or another, succinctly or with great elaboration, at critical moments in salvation history.

> Afterward I led you out of Egypt, and when you reached the sea, the Egyptians pursued your fathers to the Red Sea with chariots and horsemen. Because they cried out to the Lord, he put darkness between your people and

the Egyptians, upon whom he brought the sea so that it engulfed them (Josh 24:6-7).

This is the Passover celebrated each year, the ritual meal of unleavened bread and the paschal lamb whose meaning the father of the family explains to his children.[48] Jesus alluded to it throughout his ministry. It is at the center of the Last Supper, the new Passover banquet, and Jesus' discourses after the meal (John 13–17). John structures Jesus's ministry around three Passover feasts.[49] He presents the Lord as the true paschal lamb, whose sacrifice on the cross ushers in the new exodus, which leads to the Father.[50] In the apostolic letters (1 Cor 5:7) and the Book of Revelation (14:1), the Church acclaims "Christ our Passover." And ever since Paul (1 Cor 10:1-2), it has regarded the passage of the Red Sea as an image of baptism. All these themes are echoed when, at the Easter Vigil, the story of the Exodus is proclaimed in our assemblies. We follow Christ, the bright cloud who enables us to overcome obstacles that seemed insurmountable.

> Behold the night,
> the blessed, bright night,
> and nothing exists but Jesus,
> Jesus in whom everything finds its end:
> breaking open our tombs,
> God would lead to a new day
> the earth that saw his defeat.[51]
>
> This is the night when Christians everywhere,
> washed clean of sin
> and freed from all defilement,
> are restored to grace and grow together in
> holiness (*Exultet*).

What he did previously for one people, God now does for the salvation of every nation.[52] In thanksgiving, the Christian assembly can make the canticle of Moses its own, singing of Christ's victory that delivers us from slavery to sin and death.

> *Let us sing to the* Lord;
> *he has covered himself in glory.*
>
> I will sing to the Lord, for he is gloriously triumphant;
>   horse and chariot he has cast into the sea.
> My strength and my courage is the Lord,
>   and he has been my savior.
> He is my God, I praise him;
>   the God of my father, I extol him.

The LORD is a warrior,
LORD is his name!
Pharaoh's chariots and army he hurled into the sea;
   the elite of his officers were submerged in the Red Sea.

The flood waters covered them,
   they sank into the depths like a stone.
Your right hand, O LORD, magnificent in power,
   your right hand, O LORD, has shattered the enemy. . . .

And you brought them in and planted them
   on the mountain of your inheritance—
the place where you made your seat, O LORD,
   the sanctuary, O LORD, which your hands established.

The LORD shall reign forever and ever.
(Exod 15:1-2, 3-4, 5-6, 17-18)

A Limitless Happiness

The fourth great stage of salvation history—the "fourth night" when the light will shine—is announced by a "word of the Lord," given through his prophet in what is known as "the Book of Consolation" (Isa 54:5-14).[53]

God himself is the speaker. With infinite tenderness, he comes to his people and, in tones of wondrous kindness, whispers in its ear: "He who has become your husband is your Maker; his name is the Lord of hosts; your redeemer is the Holy One of Israel, called God of all the earth," who has created and recreated you without end.

God is joined to his people with a bond of love that nothing can destroy. Yes, there will be hard times, when the covenant seems to be forsaken and God himself appears as a party to the rupture. But no; his love is stronger, and forces him to make the first step: "The Lord calls you back"; "for a moment I hid my face from you; but with enduring love I take pity on you." "For his anger lasts but a moment; a lifetime, his good will" (Ps 30:6). After the flood, God promised never again to cover the earth with water (Gen 9:11). Now he swears no longer to be angry or to utter threats. "In his tenderness" he swears an oath: "Though the mountains leave their place and the hills be shaken, my love shall never leave you nor my covenant of peace be shaken." "Where sin increased, grace overflowed all the more" Paul will say (Rom 5:20).

Then comes a striking address to Jerusalem. "O afflicted one, storm-battered and unconsoled, I lay your pavements in carnelians, and your foundations in sapphires; I will make your battlements of rubies, your gates of carbuncles, and all your walls of precious stones. In justice shall you be established, far from the fear of oppression, where destruction cannot come near you." Jerusalem's glory is like that of a mother whose children are her jewels.[54] "All your sons shall be taught by the LORD" (Isa 54:13) by the Spirit that he will put in them (Ezek 36:27).

Today is this word of God fulfilled.

> *I will praise you, LORD, for you have rescued me.*
>
> I will extol you, O LORD for you drew me clear
>   and did not let my enemies rejoice over me. . . .
>
> O LORD, you brought me up from the nether world;
>   you preserved me from among those going down into the pit.
> Sing praise to the LORD, you his faithful ones,
>   and give thanks to his holy name.
> For his anger lasts but a moment;
>   a lifetime, his good will.
> At nightfall, weeping enters in,
>   but with the dawn, rejoicing. . . .
>
> "Hear O LORD, and have pity on me;
>   O LORD, be my helper."
> You changed my mourning into dancing . . .
>   O LORD, my God, forever will I give you thanks.
> (Ps 30:2, 4, 5-6, 11-12a, 13b)

Come, Listen, and You Will Live

Each great stage of salvation history turns the Christian's eye toward Christ, the beginning and end of all things. The first four readings of the Easter Vigil offer this mystery for our contemplation in faith. The three prophetic oracles that follow urge us to continue this reflection, contemplating, so to speak, in a more immediate fashion, and in a sacramental perspective, the work accomplished by Christ.

First comes the conclusion to "the Book of Consolation" (Isa 55:1-11).[55]

The hour has come to quench one's thirst, to be fed with "rich fare," to "seek the LORD while he may be found." This is offered to all, even those with no money: invitations to the Lord's table are extended gratuitously. There one can receive the pardon and salvation that give life.

What is striking in this text is the importance given to the Word, in accord with the significance it has throughout the "Book of Consolation," especially in the calling of the prophet. There is no grand spectacle: "A voice says, 'Cry out!' " The prophet asks: "What shall I cry out?" And the voice responds: "Though the grass withers and the flower wilts, the word of our God stands forever" (Isa 40:6, 8). God's Word is the centerpiece of the book's sixteen chapters. It is the initiator; from it comes salvation. It does what it says. These themes, which are developed throughout the "Book of Consolation," are succinctly reprised in its conclusion: "Listen, that you may have life. . . . The word that goes forth from my mouth shall not return to me void, but shall do my will, achieving the end for which I sent it."

Christians cannot help but think of what John's Gospel says: "In the beginning was the Word, and the Word was with God . . . And the Word became flesh and made his dwelling among us" (John 1:1, 14). They remember that, just before the passion, Jesus declared: "I came from the Father and have come into the world. Now I am leaving the world and going back to the Father" (John 16:28), and that his last words were "It is finished" (John 19:30). Having fulfilled his mission, Jesus, the Word of God, returned to the Father from whom he came.

We know now that we may quench our thirst by turning toward him.

> *With joy you will draw water*
> *at the fountain of salvation . . .*

> God indeed is my savior;
>   I am confident and unafraid.
> My strength and my courage is the LORD,
>   and he has been my savior.

> With joy you will draw water
>   at the fountain of salvation.

> Give thanks to the LORD, acclaim his name;
>   among the nations make known his deeds,
>   proclaim how exalted is his name.

> Sing praise to the LORD for his glorious achievement;
>   let this be known throughout all the earth.
> Shout with exultation, O city of Zion,
>   for great in your midst
>   is the Holy One of Israel!
> (Isa 12:2-3, 4bcde, 5-6)

Come to Wisdom!

The preceding reading suggested a meditation on the Word that has resounded in the world. Now comes a hymn to the Wisdom that "has appeared on earth and moved among men" (Bar 3:9-15, 32–4:4)

The evil in and around oneself can be explained by only one thing: straying from God's paths, wandering far from the source of Wisdom. It must be admitted that true wisdom is beyond human capacity. Some people do become great thinkers. But the very diversity of their philosophies of life, frequently at variance with each other, means that they cannot be fully satisfactory: sooner or later, one realizes that these thoughts—however sublime—are not true knowledge. One's hunger remains for a clear and certain vision of the deepest truth. Wisdom, then, does not belong to this world: so how may one gain access to its treasures? God alone knows: he created all things, and thus knows the secret of each. Does this mean that the search for wisdom is doomed to failure? No, for it is revealed to us. Thus, the search that was full of despair becomes joyous, and our eyes finally contemplate the light.

> My own wings did not suffice: but my mind was struck by a shining light that fulfilled my desire. For the highest fantasy there is not enough breath; but already my desire and will were turned, like a wheel that is moved regularly, by the Love that moves the sun and the other stars.[56]

"The book of the precepts of God, the law that endures forever," is the communication of the Wisdom of the Lord, source of truth and life that must not be abandoned, and to which one must return after going astray. The Law is God's manifestation and presence on the earth. But Christ, "full of grace and truth" (John 1:14) is himself "the wisdom of God" (1 Cor 1:24), "the way and the truth and the life" (John 14:6). In him, God has spoken to us (Heb 1:2). Through baptism, we are "within the law of Christ" (1 Cor 9:21).

> LORD, *you have the words of everlasting life.*
>
> The law of the LORD is perfect,
>   refreshing of the soul;
> The decree of the LORD is trustworthy,
>   giving wisdom to the simple.
>
> The precepts of the LORD are right,
>   rejoicing the heart;
> The command of the LORD is clear,
>   enlightening the eye;
>
> The fear of the LORD is pure,
>   enduring forever;
> The ordinances of the LORD are true,
>   all of them just;
>
> They are more precious than gold,
>   than a heap of purest gold;
> Sweeter also than syrup
>   or honey from the comb.
> (Ps 19:8, 9, 10, 11)

"I will put my Spirit into you"

The last of the seven Old Testament readings comes from the Book of Ezekiel, where the prophet repeats what the Lord said to him (Ezek 36:16-28).

God speaks of what has happened: the sin, crimes, and idolatry of the people who angered him and resulted in their exile. The corruption was scarcely believable[57]: one need look no further for the cause of exile. But the nations did not understand this. They said mockingly: "Where is your God? So much for his omnipotence!"

The Lord could not be unmoved on hearing these blasphemies.[58] God says: "I will prove the holiness of my great name . . . The nations shall know that I am the Lord . . . when in their sight I prove my holiness through you." This is the guarantee of salvation, for no one can demand the Lord's intervention on the basis of one's own merits. He will act; but in such a way and to an extent that no one could imagine.

He will gather his scattered people. Though this does refer to the earthly gathering of the people from exile, that is only one part of God's plan: it prefigures the full realization contemplated by the visionary of the Book of Revelation.

> After this I had a vision of a great multitude, which no one could count, from every nation, race, people, and tongue. They stood before the throne and before the Lamb, wearing white robes and holding palm branches in their hands. They cried out in a loud voice:
> "Salvation is from our God, who is seated on the throne,
> and from the Lamb" (Rev 7:9-10).[59]

This gathering will not happen unless the people are cleansed of the stains of idolatry, and this can only be done by God. Thus Ezekiel speaks of a rite of washing with water, through the mediation of which comes God's sanctifying power.[60] It reaches the very heart of the person, who is created anew: the "stony heart" is replaced by a "natural heart." God will put his Spirit in his new creatures to regenerate them.

Again, on hearing such an oracle, the Christian cannot help but think of the wondrous realization of the promises in Jesus Christ and the regeneration that happens in baptism. Christ is "mediator of a new covenant."[61] Baptism, a second birth in water and the Spirit (John 3:1-8), makes us new creatures.[62]

> As the hind longs for the running waters,
> so my soul longs for you, my God.

Athirst is my soul for God, the living God.
  When shall I go and behold the face of God?

Those times I recall,
  now that I pour out my soul within me,
When I went with the throng
  and led them in procession to the house of God,
Amid loud cries of joy and thanksgiving,
  with the multitude keeping festival.

Send forth your light and your fidelity;
  they shall lead me on
And bring me to your holy mountain,
  to your dwelling place.

Then will I go in to the altar of God,
  the God of my gladness and joy;
Then will I give you thanks upon the harp,
  O God, my God!
(Ps 42:3, 5; 43:3, 4)

Or:

A clean heart create for me, O God.

A clean heart create for me, O God,
  and a steadfast spirit renew within me.
Cast me not out from your presence,
  and your holy spirit take not from me.

Give me back the joy of your salvation,
  and a willing spirit sustain in me.
I will teach transgressors your ways,
  and sinners shall return to you.

For you are not pleased with sacrifices;
  should I offer a holocaust, you would not accept it.
My sacrifice, O God, is a contrite spirit;
  a heart contrite and humbled, O God,
    you will not spurn.
(Ps 51:12-13, 14-15, 18-19)[63]

Baptism, Death to Sin for New Life

After all these Old Testament readings, the liturgy contains a passage
from the Letter to the Romans, where Paul connects Christian baptism
to Christ's death and resurrection (Rom 6:3-11).[64]

"We know that Christ, raised from the dead, dies no more; death no
longer has power over him. As to his death, he died to sin once and for
all; as to his life, he lives for God." But we also know: "Our old self was
ucified with him so that our sinful body might be done away with, that

we might no longer be in slavery to sin." We are "dead to sin living for God in Christ Jesus." How could one make any clearer the fact that human fate is concretely bound up with Christ's death and resurrection, that Christ not only died but rose again for all people? This is what Christians "know" with the certainty that comes from faith.

But they must not forget— this is also an article of faith—that they have a share in Christ's passover through baptism. Paul, to remind them of this, speaks of the baptismal rite, which in his day involved total immersion in water. The person being baptized experienced a sense of suffocation followed by a return to life on coming out of the water.[65] However, this baptismal death-resurrection, real though it may be, is but a sacramental pledge of our Passover to come, when we will pass from death to "a like resurrection "

> Paul shows us clearly how birth through baptism is a figure of resurrection after death. This will be realized for us by the power of the Spirit . . .
> Our earthly body, as long as the soul is present, enjoys a peaceful life; so too will it receive eternal, incorruptible life by the power of the Spirit.
> This is the birth given to us in baptism, which is the figure of our resurrection: we receive its grace through the same Spirit, but in the manner and measure of a pledge. We will receive it in full when we will be truly raised and incorruptibility will be given us.[66]

In the meantime, we can and must lead "a new life," in conformity to what we already are: dead to sin, living for God with Christ. Thus we can, even today, proclaim: "I shall not die, but live, and declare the works of the Lord."

The exceptionally long but correspondingly rich Liturgy of the Word culminates with the proclamation of the Gospel of the resurrection, preceded by a triple Alleluia and the traditional singing of three couplets of Psalm 118.[67]

> *Alleluia. Alleluia. Alleluia.*
>
> Give thanks to the Lord, for he is good,
>   for his mercy endures forever.
> Let the house of Israel say,
>   "His mercy endures forever."
>
> The joyful shout of victory
>   in the tents of the just:
> "The right hand of the Lord has struck with power:
>   the right hand of the Lord is exalted."
> I shall not die, but live,
>   and declare the works of the Lord.

> The stone which the builders rejected
>   has become the cornerstone.
> By the LORD has this been done;
>   it is wonderful in our eyes.
> (Ps 118:1-2, 15-16a, 17, 22-23)

The Gospel reading is not the same every year, but rather comes successively from Matthew (Year A), Mark (Year B), and Luke (Year C), while John is read on Easter morning.[68]

The Lord's resurrection is the central mystery of faith. No one view of it will perceive its fullness. The evangelists focus on particular aspects, in such a way that their presentations are quite distinct; they highlight a variety of things that affect salvation history for the community and the individual. We must not try to reduce these different accounts to one version under the pretext of discovering exactly what happened. Rather, we must take the story as it comes from Matthew, Mark, Luke, and John and let them lead us in a contemplation of the mystery;[69] this is what the liturgy invites us to do.

Christ's Resurrection and the New Age

Matthew sees Christ's resurrection as the inauguration of a new age that is a prelude to the end of time (Matt 28:1-10—Year A).

His account is the most detailed, the most theologically elaborate, and the most "liturgical" (thanks to its hieratic nature). He notes that two women in particular, "Mary Magdalene and the other Mary" were at Jesus' burial and saw Joseph of Arimathea roll "a huge stone across the entrance to the tomb"; he tells how guards were placed to keep watch at the tomb, after the stone had been sealed (Matt 27:55-66).[70] It seems that the end of the story has come. But the evangelist knows that this is not so. He recounts these details so that the reader may remember them when reading what follows. The story of the resurrection begins with the two women, who had witnessed the burial and the placing of the guard, coming to the tomb.

"After the sabbath, as the first day of the week was dawning, Mary Magdalene came with the other Mary" and must have found the situation as they had left it when they came to visit Jesus' tomb. But then some extraordinary things happened. First, "a great earthquake," which Jesus had spoken of as the forerunner to his coming (Matt 24:7), like the one that took place at the moment of his death, when the graves opened and 'the bodies of many saints who had fallen asleep were raised" (Matt

27:52). Like the soldiers stationed at the cross (Matt 27:54), those who guarded the tomb were struck with fear: they "became like dead men." "An angel of the Lord descended from heaven, approached, rolled back the stone, and sat upon it. His appearance was like lightning . . ."

Now, despite his use of the standard trappings of biblical apocalypse, Matthew's account is really non-hysterical. He doesn't tell us these things to satisfy our curiosity, but so that we might understand that the resurrection ushers in a new world, the end of time: "The first day of the week." He wants us to understand that the omnipotent, invisible God is at work; without these signs, there would have been nothing to see, as is hinted in the *Exultet:* "Most blessed of all nights, chosen by God to see Christ rising from the dead."[71]

Unlike the deathly frightened guards, the women hear the angel's message: "Do not be afraid! I know that you are seeking Jesus the crucified. He is not here, for he has been raised, just as he said."[72] This is the simple but powerful Easter message, such as it will be proclaimed from apostolic times on.[73] The resurrection depends directly on faith in Jesus' word.

The angel adds: "Come and see the place where he lay. Then go quickly and tell his disciples, 'He has been raised from the dead, and he is going before you to Galilee; there you will see him.' " This also, Jesus had announced and promised (Matt 26:32). It is an important message. They must go and tell it quickly. Thus the women hurry to bring the disciples the news. They are "fearful" certainly, but also "overjoyed."

"And behold, Jesus met them on their way and greeted them."[74] He reassures them: "Do not be afraid!" Then he repeats the command to go and tell the disciples—whom he calls "my brothers"—to go to Galilee, where "they will see me."

The rendezvous with the risen Christ in Galilee is very important. It is there that the disciples will show their faith in him: they fall down in homage, despite their previous doubts. In a wonderful climactic scene, which has an undeniably hieratic character, they are sent forth: "All power in heaven and on earth has been given to me. Go, therefore, and make disciples of all nations, baptizing them in the name of the Father, and of the Son, and of the holy Spirit, teaching them to observe all that I have commanded you. And behold, I am with you always, until the end of the age" (Matt 28:18-20).

This is the conclusion of Matthew's Gospel. The hieratism and sobriety of Matthew's account of the resurrection give it a definite liturgical flavor. As in the liturgy, the women do homage before Jesus. In a that the Christian reader cannot understand, the evangelist reminds us that the Lord's resurrection is essentially a matter of faith. It would be fruitless to try to find "proofs" in the Gospel that would attest to the truth of the resurrection in a way that would withstand historical scrutiny.[75] Easter faith rests on the truthful testimony of those who saw the risen Christ.[76] Moreover, this faith has left indelible marks on human history ever since that "first day of the week" when the announcement of the resurrection was received and passed on by witnesses who were wholly unprepared for this mission.

> May your tongue proclaim these things, woman,
>   and explain them to the sons of the kingdom
>   who wait for me to awaken; me, the Living One.
>   Go quickly, Mary, gather my disciples.
>   In you I have a loud trumpet:
>   play a song of peace to the fearful ears of my hidden friends,
>   waken them all from sleep,
>   so that they may come to meet me
>   and light their torches.
>   Go and say: "The bridegroom is awake, coming out of the tomb,
>   leaving nothing within.
>   Dispel your mortal grief, apostles, for he is risen
>   who offers fallen man the resurrection."[77]

The Enigma of the Empty Tomb

Mark's account of the resurrection ends very abruptly; thus it must be read all the more attentively (Mark 16:1-9—Year B).[78]

The evangelist mentions the haste with which Mary Magdalene, Mary, the mother of James, and Salome prepare to anoint and perfume Jesus' body. "When the sabbath was over,"[79] using the little time left in the day, they go to buy aromatic spices. Thus having all they need, they can go to the tomb the next day, very early, just after sunrise. On the way, they speak of their chief concern: "Who will roll back the stone for us from the entrance to the tomb?" But on arriving, they see that the stone, a huge one, has been rolled away. Perhaps relieved by this fact, they enter the tomb but are then seized with fear: a young man clothed in white is there, "sitting on the right side." He says to them: "Do not be amazed! You seek Jesus of Nazareth, the crucified. He has been raised; he is not here. Behold, the place where they laid him. But go and tell his disciples and Peter, 'He is going before you to Galilee; there you will see him, as e told you.' " This is the same Easter message that one finds in Mat-w and Luke. But Mark's account ends rather unexpectedly: "then they went out and fled from the tomb, seized with trembling and bewilderment. They said nothing to anyone, for they were afraid.'' What does this mean?

Mark knows well enough that the women did not take long to go to the disciples, as they were told to do. He himself saw and heard the apostles proclaim the Lord's resurrection, first in Jerusalem and soon thereafter throughout the nations. He would not have written his Gospel if he had not participated in this mission, perhaps even with Paul and Barnabas,[80] then with Peter, whose teaching he recounts. But by leaving us with the empty tomb, doesn't Mark want us to understand that each of us must write the conclusion, continuing the story received from the women who heard the angel's message, that each of us must receive, in faith, the announcement of the resurrection and bear the good news to others, that each of us must go to Galilee to ''see'' the Lord?

> Who are these women, paralyzed with fear? They are you and I! They are all Christians entrusted with a message as stupendous as that of the resurrection and who dare not speak it. And why do they not dare to speak it? Because one cannot proclaim it without undergoing a kind of death: the death to self of the one who must renounce all goods in order to follow Christ (Mark 10:21); the death of a Christian martyr in times of persecution and trouble (Mark 8:34); the death of the convinced preacher whose word is fire and burns him who pronounces it. The human being resists this death with all his strength. So the women keep silent, like the disciples who fled at their master's arrest.[81]

By leaving us before the empty tomb, Mark invites us to seek the risen Christ elsewhere, wherever he shows himself—in the Church, in the liturgy, or in secular life. Having found him where he says we shall, we must go forth and speak without fear, telling everyone we meet: ''He has been raised.''[82]

''Remember What He Said''

Luke wrote a two-part work: the Gospel and the Acts of the Apostles. The Lord's resurrection is both summit and center. Everything, by Luke's account, seems to take place in one day and one place, Jerusalem[83]: the finding of the empty tomb, the angel's announcement of the resurrection, the disciples' disbelief, the appearance of the risen Christ to verify that he is alive, the sending forth of the disciples with the promise of the Spirit, and, finally, the ascension. This is clearly a literary device.[8]

Before beginning his second book—the apostles' preaching and the li of the Church—Luke thus summarizes the earlier events. Thus we find his story colored by his own concerns and genius (Luke 24:1-12).

Like the three other evangelists, Luke reports the discovery of the empty tomb "at daybreak on the first day of the week" by the women "bringing the spices they had prepared." They find "the stone rolled away from the tomb," they enter and verify that Jesus' body is no longer there. Two angels appear to them. One is reminded of Luke's predilection for angels: they appear in the annunciations to Zechariah, Mary, and the shepherds, and at Jesus' agony.[85]

The women are humble—"they bowed their faces to the ground"— and deeply troubled, like Mary at the annunciation (Luke 1:29). At the prompting of the heavenly messengers, they remember what Jesus had said when he was still in Galilee (Luke 9:22), and they go readily to tell "all these things to the eleven and to all the others." Only then does Luke give their names: "Mary Magdalene, Joanna, and Mary the mother of James."

That everything should happen at Jerusalem is not surprising, coming from Luke. In addition, both in his Gospel and in Acts, women play a large role: discreetly, but none the less authentically, showing great devotion and openness to the Word of God.[86] Like Mary (Luke 2:19), these women come to the tomb mindful of the words that have been spoken to them. So must all believers be attentive listeners to the Word, especially that pronounced by the Lord, for there is the foundation of faith, especially faith in the resurrection that is its keystone and gives meaning to our lives. "When you are in the night, like these women, Luke tells us, when you no longer know what to do, your head bent toward the cold stone of the tomb, remember the words that Jesus said when he preached on the earth: there you will find meaning for your life and discover your mission to others."[87]

At the same time the evangelist teaches that a search for Jesus' mortal body is pointless. The only thing that matters is "the Living" who is near "the Living God"[88] and who, because of his new state, is also mysteriously but truly present in our midst through his Word and Bread.

> O night of matchless splendor!
> death could not keep in its grasp
> the only Son.
> Jesus throws off the shroud
> and emerges victorious:
> Christ is risen!

But it happens in secret,
and only God knows
the moment
when life triumphs.

Someone near the cross did not doubt;
until today the woman has borne alone
the world's hope.
Her faith anticipates the hour
and knows already:
Christ is risen!

But it happens in secret
and only God knows
the joy
with which Mary trembles.

Jesus, light of the world, dwell in us!
Why seek in the empty tomb
another sign?
Love rises singing
from the heart's depths:
Christ is risen!

But it happens in secret
and only God knows
the fire
that awakens today.[89]

The Liturgy of Baptism

After a very long Liturgy of the Word, the Easter Vigil contains a Liturgy of Baptism. It may have one of two forms, depending on whether the water is blessed for a baptism that will occur during the liturgy or within the Easter season. But, even if there is no baptism, the community is asked to renew its baptismal promises after being sprinkled with the holy water. One might say that Easter night is the anniversary of every Christian's baptism.

The blessing of the baptismal water evokes the moments in salvation history where water played a special role: in the beginning, when the Spirit of God gifted it with sanctifying power; in the flood, where it prefigured death to sins and the birth of justice; in the passing of the Red Sea, presaging Jesus' baptism; in the water and blood flowing from Christ's pierced side, on the cross; and in the sending of the disciples to teach all nations and baptize them in the name of the Father, and the Son, and of the Holy Spirit.

Father, look now with love upon your Church,
and unseal for her the fountain of baptism.
By the power of the Holy Spirit
give to the water of this font
the grace of your Son.
You created man in your own likeness:
cleanse him from sin in a new birth of innocence
by water and the Spirit.[90]

Lord our God,
this night your people keep prayerful vigil.
Be with us as we recall the wonder of our creation
and the greater wonder of our redemption.
Bless this water: it makes the seed to grow,
it refreshes us and makes us clean.
You have made of it a servant of your loving kindness:
through water you set your people free,
and quenched their thirst in the desert.
With water the prophets announced a new covenant
that you would make with man.
By water, made holy by Christ in the Jordan,
you made our sinful nature new
in the bath that gives rebirth.
Let this water remind us of our baptism;
let us share the joys of our brothers
who are baptized this Easter.[91]

These prayers are especially meaningful when one retains in mind and heart all that was proclaimed during the Liturgy of the Word. Baptism is a simple rite, but extremely significant. A paschal rite, it allows one to participate in all the wonders that God has done throughout the ages. It is a great blessing that each year we can reawaken our awareness of this first sacrament of Christian initiation with our brothers and sisters, renewing with them our baptismal profession: There is "one Lord, one faith, one baptism; one God and Father of all . . ." (Eph 4:5-6).

God, the all-powerful Father of our Lord Jesus Christ,
has given us a new birth by water and the Holy Spirit,
and forgiven all our sins.
May he also keep us faithful to our Lord Jesus Christ
for ever and ever.[92]

"Christ is risen! He is truly risen!" This cry that is raised on Easter night echoes from age to age and, in each annual celebration, from one Christian assembly to another. It is prolonged in endless alleluias that heaven earth join in singing, with overflowing joy.

The Eucharistic Prayer shows this every Sunday and every day. But on this night, when we have heard of all that God has done "since the beginning," one can see better than ever that it is the song of the whole creation, where the endless praise of heaven is joined to that of earth.

> Father, all-powerful and ever-living God,
> we do well always and everywhere to give
> you thanks
> through Jesus Christ our Lord.
> We praise you with greater joy than ever
> on this Easter night,
> when Christ became our paschal sacrifice.[93]

> O Night clearer
> than day
> Night when love
> comes from the tomb
> Night that frees
> Jesus from the snare
> Night more shining
> than snow
> Night more burning
> than flames
> *O night clearer*
> *than day*

> O night sweeter
> than heaven
> Night of wakefulness
> for all the Body
> Night when the breath
> fills the earth
> Night that glitters
> with light
> Night of the victory
> that kills death
> *O night sweeter*
> *than heaven*

> O night greater
> than peace
> Night that clouds
> the hidden world
> Night when grace
> shines in glory
> Night that draws
> our history

Night that pours off
the impure heart
O night greater
than peace

O night stronger
than time
Night of the Living
over the universe
Night of speech
for all silence
Night when the Church
comes to birth
Night of living water
after the frost
O night stronger
than time.[94]

The Last Day
of the Easter Triduum

Light of the world, O Jesus,
Although we have never seen
Your open tomb,
Whence comes this light among us,
This feast among feasts,
If not from you, the risen one?

When someone we meet says to us:
Where is your Christ today
And his miracle?
We respond: whence comes the Spirit
That turns us toward his Passover,
If not from him?

Our hearts burn
When your love descends
And whispers to us:
Love has come, the day will come
In the hearts of all creatures,
And the Lord will appear.

And if someone says to us: Now
Show us a worthy sign
Beyond yourselves!
The sign is that at his return
We must do what he loves
In order to testify that he is love.[1]

The liturgy for Easter Sunday—the last day of the Easter Triduum—is
peaceful and serene. One interiorizes and meditates on the good news
proclaimed with more exuberance during the night: "The splendor of
Christ risen from the dead has shone on the people redeemed by his
blood"; "Our Redeemer has risen from the tomb"; "The Lord is risen
as he promised."[2] Celebrated in this atmosphere, the Eucharistic thanksgiving on Easter Sunday has a joyful tone which is not really containe

but which rather springs from hearts penetrated with light and wonder, expressed best with simple words.

> The Lord has indeed risen, alleluia.
> Glory and kingship be his forever and ever.[3]

At the same time, the Church turns to God to ask him for the resurrection of his Son to produce "today" the fruit of renewal: "Let us look not beyond our lives for him: he will join us on our own paths."[4]

> God our Father,
> by raising Christ your Son
> you conquered the power of death
> and opened for us the way to eternal life.
> Let our celebration today
> raise us up and renew our lives
> by the Spirit that is within us.[5]

At the Source of Apostolic Preaching and Faith

From Easter Sunday to the end of the Easter season, the first reading for the liturgy will be taken from the Book of Acts.[6] Today's passage tells how the apostles, charged by God with this mission, proclaimed Christ's resurrection "to the people," witnessing to what they had seen and heard. Peter's *Credo*, which expresses the faith of the first Christian community after Pentecost, has been faithfully passed down to us through the living tradition of the Church.[7] One finds a clear echo of it in the "Apostles' Creed," still recited today (Acts 10:34a, 37-43).[8]

Jesus' actions "all over Judea, beginning in Galilee after the baptism that John preached" took place publicly. Like many other people— whether enthusiastic, suspicious, or hostile—a centurion of the Roman army would certainly have heard the news. Doubtlessly, he would have been aware of Jesus' reputation: "He went about doing good and healing all those oppressed by the devil." But the pagan officer had something more important to learn, and Peter revealed it to him. If Jesus of Nazareth did such things, it was because God had anointed him with the Holy Spirit and power and "was with him." To see that Jesus' works are signs, and to recognize by these signs who he truly is, one needs light from above. Peter could not forget what Jesus once told him: "Flesh and blood has not revealed [to you that I am the Messiah, the Son of the living God], but my heavenly Father" (Matt 16:16-17). This light is transmitted by prophecy: Scripture (interpreted by the Spirit), an apostle's preaching, a believer's testimony.

The centurion of Caesarea would have heard of Jesus of Nazareth's death on the cross and the terror of the officer in charge of the execution (Matt 27:54), perhaps even those things that happened at the tomb. But he could not know the good news of the resurrection: Peter was sent to announce it to him by swearing that with others, "chosen beforehand by God," he saw the risen Christ, and ate and drank with him. This is the testimony of faith. Peter himself, along with the other witnesses, was at first troubled by the discovery of the empty tomb, not knowing what to think, supposing the women's words to be "nonsense" (Luke 24:11-12). For him to pass from doubt and perplexity to faith, the Lord had to appear to the apostles, explain the Scriptures to them, and remind them of what he had said (Luke 24:13-35).

Our faith in the resurrection rests on the testimony of the apostles, transmitted in and through the Church; those who have received it must make it known to others: "The Lord has truly been raised and has appeared to Simon" (Luke 24:34).

But Easter is not an ending. It is the summit of salvation history and gives it its definitive orientation; it continues now and shall continue until the end. Today, everyone who believes in the risen Lord "has forgiveness of sins." Tomorrow, Christ the conqueror of death will appear as "judge of the living and the dead."

This is, in all its fullness, the mystery celebrated by the Church.

This is the day the LORD has made;
let us be glad and rejoice in it.

Give thanks to the LORD, for he is good,
    for his mercy endures forever.
Let the house of Israel say,
    "His mercy endures forever."

The joyful shout of victory
    in the tents of the just:
    "The right hand of the LORD has struck with power:
    the right hand of the LORD is exalted."

I shall not die, but live,
    and declare the works of the LORD.

The stone which the builders rejected
    has become the cornerstone.
By the LORD has this been done;
    it is wonderful in our eyes.
(Ps 118:1-2, 15-16a, 17, 22-23)

Raised with Christ to Live with Him

The second reading can be either one of two very short but very dense Easter catecheses of Paul's. The first is addressed to the Christian community at Colossae (Col 3:1-4).

This passage contains neither argument nor explanation, but only simple and strong affirmations. "If then you were raised with Christ, seek what is above, where Christ is seated at the right hand of God." We can understand this since we have heard the apostle proclaim, during the Vigil, that, through baptism, we are "living for God in Jesus Christ" (Rom 6:11).

"Think of what is above, not of what is on earth." Who would deny the value of such an exhortation? Now, Paul is not thinking only of the demands of the Christian moral life; his meaning is more generally applicable. Christians live in a world where they are endlessly bombarded with theories, philosophies, and religious doctrines that lead them away from the original paths by claiming to know a sure way of obtaining salvation. Sometimes they can be quite seductive, in part because of the way they are presented (i.e., as lofty, mystical paths). Their seductiveness is heightened by an integration of genuine Christian elements. And they flatter the not uncommon human taste for feeling superior—through superior knowledge or belonging to a group of initiates—with the added allure of the exotic. The highest realities, Paul says, are found in Christ in God's presence.[9]

The apostle says that what we have already "died with Christ," and remain still "hidden with Christ in God." But the day will come when the truth of all things will be revealed: "When Christ your life appears, then you too will appear with him in glory." The path of the Christian life is an unbroken following of the mystery of Christ.

> We do not want a religion that is "outside of life." Very well. But what is life? It must be taken in its entirety. What life would be worthy of our love and concern if it did not lead to eternal life? We want an "incarnate" religion: well enough. We want it to be completely under the sign of the incarnation. Let us not be halfway logical, but follow the path of the incarnation to its end. Let us not disrupt the rhythm of the Christian mysteries that are joined together in word and action. The Word of God, becoming incarnate, performs the first act of an unbreakable series, which runs through death, resurrection, and ascension. Incarnated into the fullness of human life, our religion, in order to be faithful to Christ, must plant the cross in it, so as to introduce the life-giving death without which there is no glorious resurrection. But, since we are so incurably carnal, the Lord's resur-

rection itself stood in danger of being misunderstood. Thus the ascension follows the resurrection, making the meaning of the latter unmistakable and forcing us to look upwards, beyond the terrestrial horizon where everything belongs to man's natural state. Thus the lesson of the ascension does not contradict the lesson of the incarnation: it prolongs and deepens it. It does not place us below or outside of human life: it obliges us to take it on fully while aiming beyond.[10]

Christian life is animated by the tension between what we already are and what is still invisible, though present, in us. We must actively take on the challenge of becoming what we should be; otherwise, we fall into a state worse than that from which we were freed by baptism.

> Take care not to be trapped, after having said: "We reject Satan. Christ, make us one with you!" The sinner was made naked, because he had sinned. Here, the baptized is made naked for his deliverance. The former's glory was removed; the latter puts off the old man as easily as removing a cloak. He is anointed like an athlete before the contest. At the same time he is born, not, like the first, little by little, but all at once. He is anointed, not only on his head, like the priests in the old days, but more abundantly. The priest's head, right ear, and hand received anointing to urge him to obedience and good works; this man is anointed all over. For he comes not only to be taught but to fight as he is lifted to the dignity of a new creature.[11]

Celebrating the New Passover, Purified of the Old Leaven

The other option for the second reading comes from another letter of Paul's. The liturgical context in which it is read gives this very short text general applicability (1 Cor 5:6b-8).[12]

"Do you not know that a little yeast leavens all the dough?" This saying is a proverb. Jesus used it to teach that if the kingdom had modest beginnings, it contains the seed of great growth.[13] But the Gospels also speak of another way of regarding leaven: as an agent of corruption, putrefaction, and decay.[14] It is in this sense that Paul speaks of it here, calling to mind what is done on the Vigil of Passover. Not only does the celebration take place with unleavened bread, but all leaven and leavened bread must be removed from the house.[15] "Clear out the old yeast," says Paul, in order that you yourselves may become "a fresh batch of dough," Passover bread made of "sincerity and truth." Elsewhere, the apostle speaks of putting off the old man and his deeds, for he has been nailed to the cross with Christ.[16] This is what always happens in baptism, through which we become, with the Lord, Easter people. But Easter, a feast marked by the celebration of baptism and the renewal of baptismal promises, is also tied to paschal communion. "Become what you are: the body of Christ," Augustine said to the communicants. What Paul says in this passage from the First Letter to the Corinthians applies equally well to participation in the Eucharist in which we become, each time, "unleavened bread."

> Thus we celebrate in a proper manner the Passover of the Lord with the unleavened bread of purity and truth, while, having once rejected the leaven of ancient evil, the new creature drinks and eats of the Lord himself. Participation in the Body and Blood of Christ does nothing else than make us enter into what we take and carry everywhere, in spirit and flesh, the one in whom we are dead, in whom we have been buried, in whom we are raised, as the apostle says: "After all, you have died! Your life is hidden now with Christ in God."[17]

"Christ our Passover has been sacrificed." We must prepare to participate in the eternal Passover when he comes again, by celebrating, purified of the old leaven, the Eucharistic sacrament of the definitive Passover.

> Christians, to the Paschal Victim
> Offer your thankful praises!
> A Lamb the sheep redeems: Christ, who only
> is sinless,
> Reconciles sinners to the Father.
> Death and life have contended in that
> combat stupendous:
> The Prince of life, who died, reigns immortal.
>
> Speak, Mary, declaring
> What you saw, wayfaring.
> "The tomb of Christ, who is living,
> The glory of Jesus' resurrection;
> Bright angels attesting,
> The shroud and napkin resting.
> Yes, Christ my hope is arisen:
> To Galilee he goes before you."
>
> Christ indeed from death is risen, our new
> life obtaining.
> Have mercy, victor King, ever reigning!
> Amen. Alleluia.

See and Believe

After having heard the other evangelists,[18] we now read John's account of the finding of the empty tomb "on the first day of the week . . . early in the morning" (John 20:1-9).[19]

John deals more quickly than the others with the discovery by Mary Magdalene and her companions.[20] Their first thought is that Jesus' body has been taken away and put they know not where. The evangelist says that Mary Magdalene hurried right away to tell this to Peter and "to the other disciple whom Jesus loved," an expression that refers to John himself. Right away this suggests that the apostles, with Peter at their head, are the proper witnesses of the resurrection (Acts 10:41: First Reading).

"So Peter and the other disciple went out and came to the tomb. They both ran, but the other disciple ran faster than Peter and arrived at the tomb first." However, he does not enter, but waits for Peter and lets him go in first, recognizing his primacy.

Bending down, he can see "the burial cloths there." Peter, entering the tomb dug out of the hillside, sees both this and that "the cloth that had covered his head" is there, "not with the burial cloths but rolled up in a separate place." Clearly, the body has not been stolen. The empty tomb, which itself proves nothing, is thus clearly to be seen as a sign that hints at what has happened. John goes immediately from the appearance of the sign to faith in the reality it points to: "He saw and believed."

This is a wonderful formula. Certain things—water changed to wine as at Cana, cures, lance thrusts into a dead body, an empty tomb with shroud and veil neatly rolled up—everyone can see these things. To recognize them as "signs" requires an understanding informed by faith. It is attained when one sees and confesses the supernatural reality that God has wished to reveal to human eyes without dazzling them with too sudden and strong a light.[21] John, more than anyone else, has developed this theology of signs that are indispensable for faith but do not coerce it.

John wants us to understand the interaction between "signs" and Scripture. The latter allows one to understand the signs that in turn lead to an understanding of Scripture. If the disciples had not "known" through Scripture[22] that Jesus must rise from the dead, the empty tomb would have remained an unsolved puzzle. But, conversely, the "sign" of the empty tomb led them to a full knowledge of Scripture. Such is always the case.[23]

Finally, this Gospel offers a reflection on the complementary nature of love and authority in the Church. This question must be dealt with very carefully, and today's Gospel is a valuable guide. "The disciple whom Jesus loved" arrives at the tomb first, but he gives way to Peter, the leader of the apostles, not arrogating any right to himself, from the fact that he believed immediately.[24] The true saints, despite their profound conviction, rooted in a particular "vision" or "revelation," have never tried to overthrow those who have been given authority in the Church.[25]

> In the Church, love always moves more quickly than ministry. It senses more quickly what needs to be done, and it throws itself into the work zealously. Ministry, even when it moves as quickly as possible, cannot overtake love . . . Love consists in generosity; in this way it is more rapid . . . But love is not entirely reckless. The two run well together. Love stays in contact with ministry and is at its disposal, but it is the latter that keeps it in good shape.[26]

The Lord's resurrection is the supreme blessing for all believers. Every man and woman—each according to grace, charism, and ministry—must announce it to the whole world.

> At the dawn of the new day, who seeks you?
> Empty is the tomb where Jesus lay!
>   Alleluia! alleluia!
> Run to the land of the living:
> you will see him as he promised!
>   Alleluia! alleluia!
> The beloved Son has risen in glory!
>   Alleluia! alleluia!
> Proclaim it to the whole world!
>
> Christ is living, alleluia!
> We live again in his joy!
>
> My heart and my flesh cry for joy, alleluia!
> You have turned my sorrow to laughter.
>
> I come to you with festive songs, alleluia!
> You have opened for me the road of life.
>
> Freed, I am born again in your light, alleluia!
> Your love is stronger than death.
>
> You are my Lord and my God, alleluia!
> You lead me to the wellsprings of peace.[27]

The Easter Triduum ends with the evening office on Easter, when we recall the story of the road to Emmaus.[28]

> Jesus, who has made my heart burn
> with the words of Scripture,
> does not let their wounds
> heal in me:
> My mind turns inward,
> My feet point outward,

So that the fire of your blessing
May come to others!

The table where you wished to be seated,
For the breaking which reveals you,
I see again: it gleams
with you, the only Master!
May I go out into the evening
Where too many of my people are without the news,
And, bearing your name in me,
Make you known!

Their eyes have never found you
You no longer enter their inn,
And each says: "Where will I go
If God abandons me?"
But your springtime sap
Has roused my thirsty vines,
So that I may be this stranger
Burning with Easter![29]

How can we close the Easter Triduum without looking to her whom the Easter gospels never mention, the Virgin Mary? John is careful to note her presence near the cross with Mary, the wife of Clopas, and Mary Magdalene (John 19:25). Before handing over his spirit to God, Jesus confided his mother to "the disciple whom he loved" and "from that hour the disciple took her into his home" (John 19:26-27). How could she not have known of the discovery of the empty tomb and John's running there after Mary Magdalene's message? Why would she herself not have been in the garden? We ought not to try to fill in the evangelists' silence by supposing, e.g., that she received her own announcement of the resurrection, she believed on hearing the message, the risen Christ appeared to her first, etc. Mary, the model of the disciple who kept the Word and meditated on it in her heart,[30] who was at Cana when Jesus first spoke of his "hour" (John 2:4), must have been attentive to the other "signs" worked by her Son and understood them in the light of the Scriptures. Why should we trouble her meditation and silence when the evangelists, particularly John, have respected them? We will find her again in Jerusalem, in the upper room with the apostles and some women, waiting, seated in prayer, for the coming of the Spirit (Acts 1:12-14). After this, Scripture never speaks of her again. Chosen to bear the savior, in the disciples' midst at the Church's birth, she was the humble handmaiden of the Lord. On Easter evening we salute her and join her to the joy of all believers.

Regina caeli, laetare.

Queen of heaven, rejoice, Alleluia!
For the Lord whom you were worthy to bear, Alleluia!
Has risen as he said, Alleluia!
Pray for us to God, Alleluia!

The Fifty Days of Easter

The Easter season is, except for Ordinary Time, the longest liturgical season and, more importantly, it is different from the rest. Advent has a dual focus: the solemnities at Christmas and Christ's second coming at the end of time.[1] Lent is a preparation for the yearly celebration of Easter.[2] Ordinary Time forms an integrated whole; moreover, it runs from the Baptism of the Lord till Ash Wednesday, and from the Monday after Pentecost till the Saturday before the First Sunday of Advent.[3] The Easter season, on the other hand, is not a preparation for a solemnity but a prolongation of that just celebrated.

> The fifty days from Easter Sunday to Pentecost are celebrated in joyful exultation as one feast day, or better as one "great Sunday."
> These above all others are the days for the singing of the *Alleluia*.
> The Sundays of this season rank as the paschal Sundays and, after Easter Sunday itself, are called the Second, Third, Fourth, Fifth, Sixth and Seventh Sundays of Easter. The period of fifty sacred days ends on Pentecost Sunday.
> The first eight days of the Easter season make up the octave of Easter and are celebrated as solemnities of the Lord.[4]

Seven Weeks from Easter to Pentecost

Easter Sunday is both "the first day of the week" and the eighth day after Saturday. The solemnity celebrated "on the first day" extends throughout Easter Week[5] as well as the following Sundays: in the *Roman Missal Revised by Decree of the Second Vatican Council* and promulgated by Paul VI, these Sundays are called Sundays *of* Easter, not *after* Easter. This apparently slight difference is very meaningful. Each of these successive Sundays is a celebration of the solemnity of Easter: this is the underlying unity of the Easter season. Each day of this season is said to be celebrated "as one feast day, or better as one 'great Sunday.'"

One must realize that this is not to be understood literally. The liturgical reform promulgated in 1969 would be unbearably burdensome if it presented to us today the unattainable ideal of an Easter feast fifty days long! Who could celebrate it thus? Not even religious communities would find it possible. Perhaps a few self-sufficient hermits could manage it, but even this is doubtful. Nevertheless, what the *General Norms for the Liturgical Year* say must be taken seriously, for it is an opportune reminder of the way one must live the Sundays of Easter and also those of Ordinary Time.

The seven Sundays of Easter very clearly celebrate the paschal mystery under one or another of its aspects, as found in the biblical readings: if this is understood, how could one not become more fully aware of the fact that every "ordinary" Sunday is the weekly celebration of the Passover?

The Biblical Readings

All the biblical readings during the Easter season, both for the Mass[6] (Sundays and Weekdays) and the Office, are taken from the New Testament. On Sunday, the first reading always comes from the Acts of the Apostles;[7] the second reading comes from either the First Letter of Peter (Year A),[8] the First Letter of John (Year B),[9] or the Book of Revelation (Year C);[10] and the Gospel readings are all from John, except for the Third Sunday in Years A and B.

The Book of the Acts of the Apostles is like the Church's diary from Pentecost to its establishment in Rome.[11] However, it is not the work of a mere scribe who wrote a day-by-day account of the words and deeds of the apostles, especially those of Peter and Paul. Rather, it is the testimony of a historian—Luke—who witnessed many of the things reported himself, but has chosen to reflect on certain specific events because of their importance, as far as he can tell, for the Church and its future. He sets these events at the distance necessary for reflection. The very same method is used today by men and women who set down, for example, the political or artistic life of their times. They may well produce chronological records, but they do not keep track of every detail of every event in which they have participated. They focus on certain themes; they devote a particular chapter to the memory of someone who has greatly influenced them. Often, they have to include an appendix that sets forth the chronology clearly. The Acts of the Apostles belongs to this literary genre; however, Luke never gives us a clear chronology, and hardly any indications that would allow one to be constructed. Nor has he divided the book into chapters, as is customary today. Exegetes differ on the book's format, as one can see in the different divisions of the text in modern Bibles.[12] But one thing stands out: Luke, influenced as he is by Greek culture, frequently makes use of "intertwining."[13] He does this by using transitions that refer to the past, particularly the origin of the Church in Jerusalem.

Luke tries to underline the significance of everything that happened from the birth of the Church to the formation of the community in Rome. Above all, he tries to show how the Holy Spirit guided the Church's development and expansion into the Gentile world, and how the wonders that occurred came about because the apostles and their "followers," the new converts and the various communities, were obedient to the Spirit. This is precisely the reason why the Acts of the Apostles is as precious a witness for us now as it was then. Circumstances may change; the Church may once again be confronted by unexpected problems. If it is attentive to the Spirit that animates it, if it displays a missionary zeal and audacity, everything, even setbacks and persecutions, will serve the greater glory of the name of the Lord, dead and resurrected, present and active in the midst of his people.

The First Letter of Peter appears to be a circulating pastoral letter—one could call it an "encyclical"—addressed to Christians, "the chosen sojourners of the dispersion in Pontus, Galatia, Cappadocia, Asia, and Bithynia," regions in the north and northwest of present-day Turkey.[14] The author calls himself "Peter, an apostle of Jesus Christ" (1 Pet 1:1). He writes from Rome—"Babylon"—with the help of a secretary named Silvanus,[15] and he is accompanied by someone he calls "Mark, my son" (1 Pet 5:12-13). We know that Mark, Paul's one-time companion, left him (Acts 13:13). According to tradition, he joined Peter and, in his Gospel, provided an echo of Peter's teaching. Finally, we can be certain that this letter was written a little before Nero's persecution in A.D. 64.[16]

The Christians to whom Peter sends this letter are like "sojourners" or "aliens" (1 Pet 1:1; 2:11) in a world that is both intrigued and irritated by their behavior; it is there that they must give an account of their hope, often at the cost of persecution (1 Pet 4:12; 5:9). Far from being beaten down by this, they find it a cause for rejoicing: through their suffering, they share in Christ's glory (1 Pet 1:6-7, 11; 4:13). These are not neophytes to whom Peter is speaking. The many allusions to baptism do not mean that this is a baptismal catechesis; Peter is writing to believers to console and encourage them in the midst of trials.

They live in a world that threatens them on all sides. Their strange conduct leads people to believe that they hate humanity. But they do not try to escape this hostile world. They have better things to do than spend all their time refuting slanderous accusations. God has chosen them in Jesus Christ to bring to this world, which they therefore cannot ignore, the living hope of the kingdom inaugurated by Christ's resurrection, by doing good, responding to curses with blessings, whatever the cost.

Peter, in contrast to Paul, begins by exhorting, encouraging, and consoling; he then briefly reiterates the common faith, above all its central affirmation, the paschal mystery; in imitation of Christ, one must pass through suffering in order to attain glory. Note something else: in the heading of the letter, Peter, surprisingly, does not use the word "Church." One could suppose that he wants to avoid any suggestion that Christian communities are concerned only with themselves.

The First Letter of John, like Peter's letters, belongs to the collection of New Testament writings that have been called, almost since they were written, the "catholic epistles," doubtlessly because most of them are not addressed to particular communities or people, but to the Church as a whole. Although the author does not give his name, the letter's traditional attribution to the apostle John has never been seriously questioned. Indeed, its literary and doctrinal kinship with the Fourth Gospel is immediately apparent.[17]

The author calls his correspondents "my children" (1 John 2:1). Such an affectionate appellation indicates the authority John enjoys with respect to his correspondents. Ancient tradition says that this letter was addressed to the Christians of the province of Asia.

Because of a scarcity of conjunctions, it is difficult to establish the layout of the letter. But the author has that distinctive character found also in the great discourses of the Fourth Gospel. Taking up the same great themes several times in the same order, John develops his thought in the form of a spiral around a central idea: our communion with God through faith and in charity. He expresses this at the beginning and at the end of the letter: "For the life was made visible; we have seen it and testify to it, and proclaim to you the eternal life that was with the Father and was made visible to us" (1 John 1:2); "I write these things to you so that you may know that you have eternal life, you who believe in the name of the Son of God" (1 John 5:13).

Such a result is achieved thanks to the renunciation of sin, to charity, and ecclesial communion (1 John 1:5–4:6). The force of these convictions is not propounded through a logical, linear, deductive argument. Rather one is reminded of waves following one another or of a symphony, whose various themes are stated and restated with an always different orchestration, till at last they are joined all together.

The Revelation of John belongs to a literary genre of which there is no other example in the New Testament.[18] It is both strange and baffling, with its absolutely extraordinary visions; down through the centuries, even till our own day, especially in times of crisis, it has been the object of innumerable commentaries and interpretations.[19]

Despite its decidedly catastrophic nature, the book loudly proclaims a powerful message of hope. If it evokes the present with its many trials, it is in order to tear the veil, to "reveal" (another name for the book is "Apocalypse," which in Greek means "revelation") the aim of history, whose end is hidden in God.[20] In order to do this, the author uses symbolic visions[21] that stir the courage of those who must battle today, letting them see dimly how their struggles lead them toward the final victory. It is a mistake with this kind of literature to be concerned with the precise significance of the details: numbers, dates, names, etc.[22] Instead, one should let oneself be borne along by the breath of faith and hope that runs through the book.

The authors of apocalyptic literature belong to the prophetic tradition. But while the prophets seek to understand the present by looking at the past, the seers who write apocalypses "remember the future."[23] Like long-jumpers, they get a good, long start; coming to the jumping point, they leap as far forward as possible. They know what the future actually holds no more than we do. They can only speak of it in the imagery of extraordinary visions, painting with vivid colors a fantastic picture, using allegorical language. But one thing they do know, which they want to express: God is faithful to his promises; he will act in the future as he has done in the past; he will guide the world and his plan of salvation to their end.

The author of the Book of Revelation describes his mission in the context of a manifestation of Christ ("Christophany"). The book opens with a vision of the Son of Man, who is the risen Jesus (Rev 1:13), head of the Church and lord of history. This first vision functions as a backdrop to the whole book.

The author speaks successively "to the seven churches" in Asia Minor, i.e., to the whole Church, the whole people of God, the believers whom John calls companions, because he is intimately joined with them in Christ Jesus. They share "distress, the kingdom, and the endurance" (Rev 1:9). Their trial is that of Christ oppressed in his members. May they prove their endurance![24]

John says that he was "caught up in spirit on the Lord's day" (Rev

1:10). On the day of Christ's resurrection, or the weekly Passover? Or better yet, does the expression refer to the time when we are definitively marked by the Lord's victory over death, which will be manifested fully when he returns? Whatever the case, this fact must be remembered, for it allows us to be imbued with the paschal atmosphere of the whole letter.

The Gospel According to John, unlike the others, is not read successively during Sunday Mass. Chapter 6 is read almost completely from the Seventeenth to the Twenty-first Sunday of Ordinary Time, Year B. Certain other Sundays at various times in the liturgical year make use of it. But it is during the season of Easter that it is read at greatest length: there are seventeen extracts from it (one occurring three times) in the Lectionary from the Second Sunday of Easter to Pentecost Sunday.[25]

These texts are principally drawn from chapters 13 to 17, commonly called "the last discourse."[26]

In fact, one can distinguish two discourses in these five chapters, which are somewhat repetitive. The first begins after the denunciation of Judas and ends with Jesus' command to leave the room where he had washed his disciples' feet and ate with them (John 13:31–14:31). The second begins with the allegory of the vine and ends with an exhortation to faith and hope (John 15:1–16:33). At the conclusion of these two discourses comes the great "priestly prayer" (John 17:1-26). Speaking to his Father, Jesus, on his way toward the fulfillment of his "hour," clearly reveals the ultimate object of his mission: "so that they may all be one, as you, Father, are in me and I in you . . . [so] that the love with which you loved me may be in them and I in them" (John 17:21, 26).

One would seek in vain for a strict plan in the construction of these chapters. Rather John has here collected some sayings retained by tradition: Luke presents a more sedate echo of them (Luke 22:24-30). By reprising, in the course of his Last Supper, a series of themes begun during the course of his ministry, Jesus has expressed, in a sort of spiritual testament, the paschal import of his sacrifice. The form is reminiscent of the catechesis of the father of the family who, during the Passover meal, explains the meaning of the celebration to his children.[27] John has also drawn on the literary genre of farewell discourses, used, in the Bible, by a famous master before being borne to heaven.[28]

Instead of searching for a central theme—love, for example[29]—one must read and meditate on "the testament of Jesus" by following the meandering trail of his thought. The first discourse begins with Jesus' sayings on the "new commandment" (John 13:31-35). It continues with an exhortation to faith (John 14:1-14), then a development of the need to know Jesus, to dwell in him, to observe his commandments, and ends with his departure and the sending of the Spirit of truth (John 14:15-31).

The second discourse reprises the same themes, but with different harmonies. First comes the allegory of the vine, which shows the vital union between Jesus and those who dwell in him (John 15:1-17). Then come some specifics concerning the role of the Spirit: he will help the community opposed by the "world," to which it must make the Father and his Messenger known; he will sustain it in the battles of faith by revealing how Jesus has already vanquished the power of darkness (John 15:18-16:33).

The great priestly prayer (John 17) evokes Jesus' passion, his resurrection, his continuation in the Church, the union of all believers and their participation in the life of the Trinity.

To say that fifty days of Easter are celebrated as "one feast day, or better one 'great Sunday' "[30] might seem to be hyperbolic. But an overview of the scriptural texts used for the Sundays at this time is sufficient to indicate the importance and richness of this season that is the center and summit of the liturgical year. It is not simply a fifty-day extension of a particularly important feast: it sets the paschal mystery at the heart of Christian life for every celebration of the sacraments and for every Day of the Lord. Christ's resurrection is the primordial object of the faith and hope of the disciples and the Church, their reason for living, the spring from which all else flows.

In order to draw the fruit of this liturgical season, one must allow oneself to be swept along in the dynamic of the successive celebrations. The winding path of the liturgy is a matter for rejoicing, not complaining. Its many detours present the same mystery from different points of view, so that one may contemplate its astounding richness, its countless implications. Time is needed: one cannot take a shortcut through the seven Sundays of Easter.

Second Sunday of Easter

As usual, the first two readings for this Sunday vary according to a three-year cycle, but the Gospel is the same every year (John 20:19-31).

It is fair to say that this portion of John's Gospel is absolutely indispensable. It tells of two appearances of the resurrected, the first taking place in the evening of the day—"the first day of the week"—the empty tomb was discovered, the second "a week later." The two accounts are really one, for the first appearance took place when Thomas, "one of the Twelve," was absent, the second, "a week later," when he was present. But this is not an insignificant detail. Thomas' twofold reaction, first disbelief in his companions' testimony: "We have seen the Lord!," then a personal avowal of faith: "My Lord and my God!," connect these two stories of the only "official," so to speak, appearances of the risen Christ to the apostles.[1] They end with a saying of the Lord that holds true for all believers: "Blessed are those who have not seen and have believed." And finally, this passage is the conclusion of the Fourth Gospel, written so that we might believe and, through faith, that we might have eternal life (John 20:31).[2]

Paschal Faith

As hinted in the Gospel readings on Easter Sunday, John, in writing the final pages of his Gospel, had one very definite goal: to define paschal faith,[3] to show how the "eyes of faith" allow the human eye to perceive hidden truths. This Sunday's Gospel tells all believers how one can believe without having seen with the eyes of flesh, and Jesus' words—"Blessed are those who have not seen and have believed"—assure us that our condition compares anything but unfavorably to that of the first witnesses of the resurrection: like us, not without hesitation and difficulty, they had to go beyond immediate experience, moving from "seeing" to "believing." Eight days after the celebration of Easter, this Gospel acts like an icon to be kept in the forefront of one's awareness throughout the fifty days of Easter (John 20:19-31).

Jesus Came and Stood in Their Midst

The appearance of the resurrected to the disciples "on the evening of the first day of the week" was not unlike the appearance to Mary Magdalene "on the first day of the week . . . early in the morning, while it was still dark" (John 20:11-18).[4] But there were some important differences. Mary saw, in the garden, a man she took for the gardener. He asked her: "Woman, why are you weeping?" He called her by name: "Mary!" and she recognized him: *"Rabbouni!"* It was an unexpected encounter, but not entirely strange. Mary Magdalene thought that the sorrowful events she had witnessed were a nightmare from which she had just been awakened. The Lord corrected her: "Stop holding on to me." The "Master's" death and resurrection were perfectly real, ineffable facts, steps toward a fulfillment: "I have not yet ascended to the Father."

That very evening the disciples found themselves gathered in a locked room, having carefully bolted all the doors. Suddenly "Jesus came and stood before them." Before his disciples had time to react, he said, "Peace be with you." No longer was he a man bound by physical laws. He belonged to no "place." He appeared in a locked room that no one could have entered except by breaking down the doors. He it was, with nailmarks in his hands and the lance wound still visible in his side (John 19:34). But he appeared in a wholly new state, which shall belong to him forever: he is the Living One seated at the right hand of the Father. Transfigured, freed from the constraints of his mortal body, he can appear anywhere: no obstacle, no locked door can prevent him from "coming." As he promised, he did not leave us orphans. He left, but only for our benefit (John 14:18; 16:7). Resurrected, he brought to his own the peace he promised them (John 14:27), which good news the disciples then had to proclaim to all people.

Gift of the Holy Spirit and Forgiveness of Sins

Sending his disciples as the Father had sent him, the risen one breathed on them and gave them the Holy Spirit. Theirs was the mission to bring salvation into the world.

This passage is often called the "Johannine Pentecost," but somewhat inappropriately. According to Acts, at Pentecost the breath of the Spirit gave birth to the Church. Peter's preaching caused a large number of conversions among the pilgrims in Jerusalem: "Parthians, Medes, and Elamites, inhabitants of Mesopotamia, Judea and Cappadocia, Pontus and Asia, Phrygia and Pamphylia, Egypt and the districts of Libya near Cyrene, as well as travelers from Rome, both Jews and converts to Judaism, Cretans and Arabs. . ." About "three thousand" received baptism on that day, the first-fruits of the missionary preaching soon to be carried out everywhere (Acts 2).

Everything is less dramatic in John's Gospel. There is no "noise like a strong driving wind," no fire that separates into tongues of flame and comes to rest on the disciples. At Pentecost, they "began to speak in different tongues, as the Spirit enabled them to proclaim." Here, nothing happened outwardly (cf. Acts 2:2-6). Jesus was there. The disciples stood speechless and "rejoiced when they saw the Lord." Only he was able to do anything: he "breathed on them and said to them, 'Receive the holy Spirit. Whose sins you forgive are forgiven them, and whose sins you retain are retained.'" One couldn't imagine a more solemn, yet serene and gentle, scene. By his presence alone, the risen one awakened his disciples' faith. They had locked themselves in "for fear of the Jews," i.e., those of them who had condemned Jesus: suddenly they found themselves comforted, overflowing with great joy. They "did not yet understand the scripture that [Jesus] had to rise from the dead" (John 20:9): now they saw him before them, and their eyes were opened to faith. After verifying that the tomb where the Lord had been laid was empty, with the shroud lying on the ground and the head-wrapping "rolled up in a separate place" (John 20:5-7), two of them returned home (John 20:10), perplexed: now they heard the risen Christ opening up a new future and imposing a mission on them; it belonged to them to continue the work of salvation undertaken by the Lord in the forgiving of sins.

It is at once so simple and so grand that the evangelist need add nothing. What point would there be in more details? It is not the length of the appearance that matters, but its inexpressible intensity. Why could he have not reported the disciples' reactions? The only things that belong here are silence and adoration.

Nevertheless, contemplation cannot ignore the duty of witnessing. Thomas, one of the Twelve, was not there when Jesus came. When he showed up, the others told him: "We have seen the Lord!" His answer was, "Unless I see the mark of the nails in his hands and put my finger into the nailmarks and put my hand into his side, I will not believe."

"Do not persist in unbelief, but believe"

Of course the evangelist does not tell us this about Thomas to present him as a skeptic, an example to avoid. Nor does he present him as a man who will believe nothing without proofs.[5] On the one hand, the Gospel tells us that every one of the disciples first reacted to the announcement of the resurrection with incredulity or doubt.[6] On the other hand, John specifically says that Jesus showed the disciples his wounds: the stigmata of the passion proved that it was really the crucified who was standing there in their midst. Thomas' request—to probe the nailmarks with his finger and put his hand in Jesus' side—fits very well with this. The episode with Thomas is perfectly integrated into this part of the Gospel.

The appearance "a week later" follows the same pattern as the first, "on the evening of the first day of the week." Once more, despite the locked doors, Jesus came and stood before them. He greeted the disciples in the same way: "Peace be with you." The first time, he took the initiative to show them his hands and side. Now he invited Thomas likewise, by the same signs, to prove that it was he. Having witnessed the resurrection with the others, Thomas must have the same experience, see the same "proofs" as they. In his First Letter, John, who insists on the identity of the Word and Jesus, the reality of the incarnation of the Son of God (John 1:14), writes: This is "what we have heard, what we have seen with our eyes, what we looked upon and touched with our hands [concerning] the word of life" (1 John 1:1). At the end of his Gospel, he proclaims just as strongly the reality of the resurrection, the identity of crucified and resurrected. Faith and grace have given supernatural keenness to the senses of God's chosen witnesses. Thus they could "see" with their eyes and "touch" with their hands the body of the risen Lord. This is why their witness is definite and irrefutable.[7]

Nevertheless, Thomas' character is of particular importance for us. He appears at the hinge between two generations of believers. He belongs to the group of the "chosen witnesses" (Acts 10:41) who saw the risen one and to those who, throughout the ages, have received the faith that comes from the apostles, appropriating it for himself. Like the other first witnesses, Thomas had to pass from doubt to belief. His special experience, reported by the evangelist, reinforces, so to speak, the apostolic witness.

> I am ready to believe what you say, if only
> it may be certain,
> I am ready to open myself completely if you
> will force into this hard heart,
> Harder than an oak stump or firm chestnut
> wood,
> An axe with so strong and deep a blow that
> it must stay there!
> I am even ready to die, but only if
> You die first and all the passion
> And everything it entails be fulfilled and
> if again
> You will rise from the tomb and say to me:
> "Thomas!"
> I am ready to believe in you, Lord, and do
> what you wish,
> If I may for but one moment touch the holes
> in your hands and feet.
> And I will acknowledge you and call you my
> Lord and my God,
> If you will let me touch you and put my
> hand into your heart![8]

"Do not be unbelieving, but believe" is more of an exhortation than a reproach, and the Lord addresses it to each of us. Moreover, John concludes this passage and his whole Gospel[9] by declaring: "Jesus did many other signs in the presence of [his] disciples that are not written in this book. But these are written that you may [come to] believe that Jesus is the Messiah, the Son of God, and that through this belief you may have life in his name.''

''Blessed are those who have not seen and have believed''
However often one has heard it, this last saying of Jesus in John's Gospel, after the accounts of the appearances, is disconcerting. We have difficulty seeing how it can be so: we have such need to verify things ourselves! Sometimes we would rather subject something to an assortment of tests rather than trust our own eyes.[10] But we also sometimes accept someone's testimony on the basis of their word, having no need to see the thing ourselves. The dialectic ''seeing-believing,'' which is so important in John, is not entirely foreign to us.

It is not enough to see in order to believe. The apostles, like us, had to go beyond experience to attain faith in the resurrection; and this, we forget all too easily, was not easy for them. They saw Jesus' suffering, his nailing to the cross, death and burial. That this was he, three days later, would hardly have been obvious. Therefore, it would be unjust to suppose that the apostles' faith had no merit.

In order to believe, one must dispense with clear and certain evidence. The testimony of the apostles allows us to partake in their experience as privileged witnesses and believers, attaining, in their wake, the paschal faith that is able to recognize in the man Jesus, ''crucified under Pontius Pilate,'' ''the only Son, God, who is at the Father's side'' (John 1:16).

Thomas, like the other apostles, believed in the one he saw. We believe without having seen. But the testimony of the Scriptures has been given to us, along with that of witnesses who were not ''slow of heart to believe'' (Luke 24:25), who in their panic and fright ''thought they were seeing a ghost'' (Luke 24:37). Yes, happy are we who can say, like Thomas when he believed: ''My Lord and my God!'' For, if we believe that Christ is living, it is not only because reliable witnesses have seen; however important, indeed essential, their witness may be, what is more crucial is the personal acknowledgment of the risen Lord, an act that transcends all proofs, all logic. Stop being incredulous in order to believe? This is very important, but it is not the necessary conclusion of a ''proof.'' Each of us can enumerate his or her own reasons for believing, but in the end, we must admit that not one of them is the reason for our faith.

> Happy are those who have seen
> the risen one
> and recognized victory
> in his wounds.

But happy are we
who believe without having seen
and, still without seeing him,
love Jesus, our Savior.

Lord, you are living,
we have recognized you,
at the last day we will see you.

Without seeing the fulfillment of the promises
your fathers hailed them from afar.

In the mirror of hope
you contemplate the invisible.

More precious than perishable gold,
your faith gives praise to God![11]

Paschal Faith and Liturgy

The story of the double appearance of the risen Lord to the apostles and the finale to John's Gospel, which we will read later, have a definite, liturgical, and especially Eucharistic flavor.

"The first day of the week," when the Lord appeared to the apostles, is the day when the Christian community comes together to celebrate the Eucharist, sacrament of the Lord's presence during his absence.

"He comes" in the midst of his own, but under "signs" that both reveal and conceal him. Only faith can perceive his presence.

As on the evening of Easter, he brings peace and, with it, forgiveness of sins, joy, and the effusion of the Spirit. The celebration ends with the directive to go out and bring to the world the good news of the resurrection, to witness to it, to show that faith is the source of happiness, the experience of beatitude.

In union with the whole Church
we celebrate that day
when Jesus Christ, our Lord,
rose from the dead in his human body.[12]

Dying you destroyed our death,
rising you restored our life.
Lord Jesus, come in glory.[13]

The Church—Paschal Community

The Christian Community of the Early Days

Paschal faith and the bestowal of the Spirit transformed the apostles. Recently holed up in fear in a house with locked doors, they boldly proclaimed the good news of the resurrection and urged their listeners to become believers, too, and be baptized. Their call was heard by thousands of men and women who constituted the first Christian community, which, as Acts recounts, grew marvelously, first in Jerusalem, then throughout the Gentile world. Three times the author paints scenes that briefly depict the early community. It would be a mistake to regard these so-called "summaries" as "snapshots." They may more profitably be compared to pictures taken at a family reunion, with some people posing stiffly, others relaxed and smiling, but all in their Sunday best. Such pictures, which show the family in all its glory, quickly become treasures; the older generation shows them to the younger, embellishing them somewhat, recounting how happy they were in those days, despite their troubles.Today's liturgy contains the first of these pictures (Acts 2:42-47).[1]

Filled with the Holy Spirit, the apostles announced that God had raised Jesus from the dead (Acts 2:24). The power of their testimony quickly convinced a great number of people to receive baptism and become believers (Acts 2:41). Before going on to deal with Peter's and John's deeds in Jerusalem (Acts 3:1–4:31), Luke briefly states the characteristics of the community of disciples: devotion to the apostles' instruction, communal life, the breaking of the bread, and the prayers. These four were like pillars on which the community rested; the four essential features that identified it, the "four perseverances"[2] that solidified its structure. Without these there would have been lassitude and the negligence that leads to waste and ruin.

The first proclamation of the message—then and now—states the core of faith. But that is not sufficient. Instruction is needed, and not only just to deepen what was initially given. One must learn who Jesus is, what his "resurrection from the dead" means for him and for us, who God is, the Father that Jesus has revealed, how to live like a Christian, etc. This is the labor of catechesis before and after baptism, the never-ending deepening of the faith. The Gospels and the other apostolic writings were written with this end in mind. The Church is forever based on this original ground. To be devoted "to the apostles' instruction" is a question of life or death for every Christian and the Church as a whole. "It is by keeping in communion with the apostles that the faithful are assured of dwelling in communion with the divine persons."[3]

The whole history of the Church and the Christian communities testifies to this. Living and faithful contact with the teaching of the apostles—and more generally with Scripture—is characteristic of periods of Christian and ecclesial vitality. When this fidelity and devotion is lost, Christian ecclesial life is destroyed, the Christian mind quickly takes itself to vague religiosity, or falls back on pagan superstition. By contrast, all Christian and ecclesial renewal is the fruit of renewed attention to the sources of faith: the teaching of the apostles who themselves passed on the teaching of the Lord.

Perseverance in the communal life is the second characteristic of the Christian community, the most outwardly visible. It is a deep unity of spirit that finds very concrete expression: the sharing of goods, each receiving on the basis of need.[4] Thus the solidarity of this community has a different basis than that found between members of other groups, e.g., a circle of friends brought together by a certain affinity. The brothers and sisters of this community do not choose each other. Their communion extends to all; it calls on each member to serve the needs of all, beginning with the poorest, where there can be no question of repayment; to share everything in common, even to go so far as to sell one's property and goods "and divide them among all according to each one's need" (Acts 2:45). Such is the extreme, an expression of fraternal communion that is extremely difficult to fulfill. Is it perhaps a Utopian practice, just barely possible for restricted groups, an idealized picture of the communion that existed in the first Christian community? Perhaps, at least to a certain extent. Nevertheless, such is the ideal that we are bound to try to realize in one way or another. At least, each Christian community must look at itself in this mirror in order to judge its practice and mentality. If there appears to be too great a gulf between the ideal and the reality, the community must undertake together the needed changes, so that it may not become a scandal to itself and others.[5]

Devotion to the breaking of the bread is the third characteristic of the

Christian community, and it is tightly bound up with the former. In Luke's vocabulary, "to break bread" has a very definite meaning. It does not refer to ordinary meals (which are dealt with elsewhere) but the Eucharistic meal. There it is that the Body of Christ is built up, that "communal life" begins, thanks to participation in the one bread broken and the cup shared, the Body and Blood of the risen Christ.[6]

Devotion to the "breaking of the bread," "on the first day of the week"—to the Sunday Eucharist—is much more than a "legal" obligation for Christians: it is a necessity. To stay away purposely, especially for a long time, effects a break with "communal life," "excommunication" in the etymological sense of the term. The possibility of this reunion is the fundamental demand of all Christians, proclaimed and defended in defiance of all contrary authority. To be prevented from joining it by peculiar circumstances—sickness, travel, imprisonment, etc., is a trial.[7] But it is no longer the Lord's Supper that one celebrates if the "breaking of the bread" does not include the sharing of goods "according to each one's need."[8]

Finally comes devotion "to the prayers."[9] The plural here is explained by the fact that at the time, in Jerusalem, the Christian disciples were still attending the Temple for the various "hours" of liturgical prayer.[10] Later, because of the influx of Gentiles into the Church and its spreading outward to the various provinces of the empire, the disciples set up their own prayer gatherings,[11] which, up to a certain point, followed the rhythm and even the form of Jewish practice, especially that of the synagogue.[12] Thus, devotion to the prayers is a characteristic of the community and each disciple. Not to pray—be it only at "special" times—also separates one from the community of believers.[13]

The end of this first "summary" mentions the joy experienced by the community, expressed in its praise. This is typical of Luke, who can be rightly called the evangelist of joy and thanksgiving: the three canticles in his Gospel are still chanted every day by those communities that pray the Liturgy of the Hours.[14]

Luke likewise frequently mentions the radiance of the Christian community and the welcome it found among the people, i.e., the humble people. He will note this attraction for the "simple" even when the community is faced with persecution.[15] Nothing could better show that this radiance comes from the Lord's power: he it is who brings new believers into the community where wonders are done. Even so, it must still rest firmly on the four pillars that make its seat.

Give thanks to the LORD *for he is good,*
for his mercy endures forever.

Let the house of Israel say,
  "His mercy endures forever."
Let the house of Aaron say,
  "His mercy endures forever."
Let those who fear the LORD say,
  "His mercy endures forever."

I was hard pressed and was falling,
  but the LORD helped me.
My strength and my courage is the LORD,
  and he has been my savior.
The joyful shout of victory
  in the tents of the just.

The stone which the builders rejected
  has become the cornerstone.
By the LORD has this been done;
  it is wonderful in our eyes.
This is the day the LORD has made;
  let us be glad and rejoice in it.
(Ps 118:2-4, 13-15ab, 22-24)

In the Hope of Salvation, the Outcome of Faith

The second reading comes from the beginning of the First Letter of Peter (1 Pet 1:3-9).[16]

"Blessed be the God and Father of our Lord Jesus Christ, who in his great mercy gave us a new birth to a living hope through the resurrection of Jesus Christ from the dead, to an inheritance that is imperishable, undefiled, and unfading . . ." The style of this great prayer of blessing for the revelation of salvation in Jesus Christ is reminiscent of that found in Jewish prayers, as well as in the benedictions in Second Corinthians (1:3-7) and Ephesians (1:3-4). From the very first, the author inspires in his readers an aura of prayer, wondering contemplation of the whole of God's plan.

"Praised" or "Blessed" is the first word of Zechariah's *Benedictus* (Luke 1:68) and the "eighteen blessings" of the synagogal liturgy;[17] a wonderful example of a continuous style of praise in the Bible.

At the beginning of the letter, Peter reminds his correspondents that they have been chosen "in the foreknowledge of God the Father, through sanctification by the Spirit, for obedience and sprinkling with the blood of Jesus Christ" (1 Pet 1:1-2). The benediction develops this affirmation.

God, "the Father of Jesus Christ," has already given us new birth through participation in the resurrection of his Son. Baptism leaps to mind. However, though this is not to be excluded, what is really at issue is the wondrous power of the Lord's resurrection, the central object of Christian faith, source and guarantee of our "living hope." For we do not yet possess the promised inheritance "imperishable, undefiled, and unfading" that moths and decay cannot destroy "nor thieves break in and steal" (Matt 6:20). It is "kept" for us by God, "standing ready to be revealed in the last days."

To be sure, Christians face many difficulties: slander (1 Pet 2:12), frequent ill treatment (1 Pet 2:19), sporadic persecutions (1 Pet 3:13-14), and the bleak prospect of the immediate future (1 Pet 4:12-14). The letter's author knows all this perfectly well. But nothing can trouble the believer's hope, whose faith has undergone trial by fire. Perseverance will give glory to God. Joined in praise of Christ who has conquered suffering and death, they will find, in him and with him, their ultimate happiness, which cannot be denied them. The *Benedictus* of Peter and all Christians is also their *Magnificat*. Yes, "for us, the Lord Jesus is this: the source of our own trembling of joy"[18] as he was for Mary and all the poor whom he called "blessed" (Matt 5:3-12).

Written by Peter, this praise reflects a mature and profound meditation on the scandal of the cross by one who, after having first failed in the hour of trial, always sought to walk in the way of the Lord, who has suffered for us (1 Pet 2:21; 5:4).

> As the sun is the joy
> of those who seek the day,
> so my joy is the Lord,
> for he is my sun.
> His rays resurrect me,
> his light drives all darkness from my eye.
>
> Thanks to him I have acquired eyes
> and seen his holy day;
> I have been given ears
> and heard his truth;
> I have been given knowledge
> and trembled with joy.[19]

The Christian assembly that, ever since the beginning, has been held regularly "on the first day of the week," is at the heart of the mystery of faith and the Church. It is itself a mystery, a sacrament, i.e., a visible reality with an invisible dimension. Through signs, it opens the way to the divine, so far as it is possible in this world; it realizes now for every believer, every ecclesial community and the whole Church what will happen fully and definitively at the second coming.

The risen Lord comes to the liturgical assembly that celebrates the mystery of God's salvation accomplished by the death and resurrection of his Son, the gift of the Spirit and the proclamation of the Gospel. We perceive his presence under the form of bread and wine, the sacrament of his Body and Blood that were handed over for us, and in which we all communicate.

Communion in the same bread and cup builds the community of those who profess the same faith and have received the same baptism. They are the Church, in which every member, in community and individually, praises God when they are gathered together, as well as in their daily lives, whose harshest trials cannot shake their deeply rooted joy.

They are already sure of the inheritance that God will give them in heaven.

Community, Faith, and Hope

The Ideal of Holding All Goods in Common

The second "summary" in the Acts of the Apostles focuses on the common possession of goods, which shows just how radical the perfect Christian community must be (Acts 4:32-35).[1]

This practice is an ideal to be kept always in mind and therefore a goad, even if it is not a legal obligation. Luke illustrates this with two examples. The first—edifying—is that of Joseph, "also named by the apostles Barnabas (which is translated 'son of encouragement'), a Levite, a Cypriot by birth, [who] sold a piece of property that he owned, then brought the money and put it at the feet of the apostles" (Acts 4:36-37). The second—scandalous—is that of Ananias and Sapphira. They had some property that they sold in order, so they said, to give the money to the apostles. But, before doing so, they kept back some of the proceeds, though they claimed they had given everything. They lied not to the community but to God; they put the Spirit of the Lord to the test: would he notice their deception? On hearing Peter's rebuke, first Ananias and then his wife fell down and died. It was their fraud that punished them, for the community had laid no obligation on them to sell their property. Having sold it, they were still free to do with the money as they wished, according to Peter (Acts 5:1-11). To give up some of one's wealth, to offer the community a share in one's earnings, and especially to go so far as to give all one possesses has always been and will always be, in the Church's eyes, an freely-made decision. Only the Holy Spirit can suggest it to someone as an inescapable duty, while he also grants the strength to fulfill it joyfully. The same is the case with celibacy freely chosen "for the Kingdom." "God loves a cheerful giver" (2 Cor 9:7).

Nevertheless—as we know perfectly well—money creates formidable barriers between people everywhere, including those within the Christian community: Luke is particularly sensitive to this unjust, not to say sacrilegious fact, that runs counter to the will of God, who created the world and its riches for the enjoyment of all.[2] No one is a proprietor, in the strict sense, even of his or her legitimately owned goods, but merely their manager.

The Book of Acts does not hold up the Christian community as a model for solving the problem of an inequitable distribution of goods through the sharing of wealth. But it is a pointed reminder that there must be a solidarity between rich and poor of such a kind that the surplus of the former is used to help alleviate the poverty of the latter. "There was no needy person among them . . . [for distribution was made] to each according to need." In fact, "if one shares what one has, it is not so that one may become poor, but so that there may be no poor in the community. A community would not be worthy of the name if some of its members lived in plenty while others lacked necessities. Thus the koinonia undertakes the concrete practice of sharing to assure that everyone's needs are met."[3] Christian communities and each of their members must be mindful of the ancient divine precept: "There should be no one of you in need" (Deut 15:4).[4]

> If a brother or sister has nothing to wear and no food for the day, and you say to them, "Goodbye and good luck! Keep warm and well fed," but do not meet their bodily needs, what good is that? So it is with the faith that does nothing in practice. It is thoroughly lifeless. To such a person one might say, "You have faith and I have works—is that it?" Show me your faith without works, and I will show you the faith that underlies my works! (Jas 2:15-18)

Some people have taken the renunciation of property to its extreme. Such was the monk who, owning nothing but a copy of the Gospels, sold it in order to buy some food for the poor, and who said: "I have sold the very word that says: 'Sell what you have and give it to the poor.' "[5] Such examples in the communal life of monks and religious, as well as other communities, cannot solve the problem of poverty in the world. But they do denounce it as scandalous and make us think. They present an image of what a Church or a world where everything was held in common could or might be. At any rate, the Christian attitude toward riches and the duty of sharing them is not based on reasons of justice or political expediency, but the demands of faith. The Christian tradition perpetually repeats, teaches, and preaches this.

> You shall not turn away the needy, but shall share all your wealth with your brother, claiming nothing for yourself; for if you share immortality with him, all the more should you do so in perishable things.[6]

The Fathers took this teaching of the apostolic Church and based on it sometimes harsh exhortations to the rich.

They proclaim themselves masters of the common goods they hoard, because they were the first to own them. If everyone of them kept only what he required for his immediate needs, and if the surplus was given to the poor, wealth and poverty would be abolished . . . You are not a thief? You have taken for your own the goods of which you were supposed to be the caretaker . . . To the hungry belongs the bread you have. To the naked belongs the cloak that is hidden in your trunk. To the footsore, the shoes rotting in your house. To the poor the money you have buried in the earth. How can you oppress so many people that you could help?[7]

This does not mean that all forms of ownership are reprehensible. What the Fathers condemned was the inequitable distribution of goods

The Lord our God has desired that this earth might be the common possession of all, its fruits serving all, but avarice has led to the dividing up of property. Therefore, if you lay claim to something as your own property which was given to the whole human race, and the animals as well, it is right for you to give at least a part of it to the poor. They have the same rights as you; do not refuse them food.[8]

In the beginning God did not create rich and poor. He no more gave the one wealth in abundance than he denied it to the other. On the contrary, to all he gave the same earth to cultivate. If, then, the earth is common to all, how is it that you own so many hectares while your neighbor does not have even the smallest plot of ground? . . .

Suppose even that your ancestors did not steal, that money sprung up from the ground in front of them. What conclusion shall we draw? That these riches are good? Absolutely not. You will say that, at any rate, they are not evil. Perhaps. They are not evil if they do not come from theft, and if you share them with the poor . . . How could it not be sinful to be the sole owner of the Lord's gifts, to enjoy alone the fruit of the common goods? If we can call our own the goods that belong to the Lord of all, so can everyone else, who, like us, are his servants. The things of the Lord are for all.[9]

Still today, many voices are raised in the Church, voices of bishops, priests, lay men and women, to denounce the abuse of hoarded wealth, reminding Christians everywhere of their prophetic duty in this matter. The ideal picture presented by Acts is the reference point to which one must constantly look in evaluating personal and community practice, while praying that the Holy Spirit will give to those who adhere to the faith "one heart and one mind."[10]

Faith, Commandments, Communal Charity

We begin our reading of the First Letter of John during the Easter season with a passage from the last chapter (1 John 5:1-6).[11]

Throughout this letter, the author's thought moves not rectilinearly but in a spiral. Several themes are joined together or rather revolve around a principal theme, a main idea, which here is that of faith.[12] John begins with certain affirmations: faith is the human response to the testimony that God gives to his Son through the Spirit of truth; it expands into love. But of what faith is he speaking, and what is its object?

Faith, John says here, is "to believe that Jesus is the Messiah, the Son of God," as he wrote at the conclusion of his Gospel, which was written so that we might have that faith (John 20:31)[13] by which one is begotten of God, who gives "life in his name" (John 20:31). In other words, one becomes a son in the Son and through him. Thus it is a supernatural faith. But it is not a cold adherence to the truth to which the Spirit gives witness: it contains love for the Father and "the one begotten by him," Jesus Christ his Son. Everything is connected. By his person, words, and deeds, Jesus has revealed the love of God or, as John writes, that "God is love" (1 John 4:8). To love God and to love others as he loves them, is to have a share in the life of God, "to be begotten" of him.

> "Beloved, let us love one another." Why? Because a man tells us to do so? No, "because love is of God." This itself is a beautiful eulogy of love, to say that "it is of God": but he goes further, so let us listen attentively. He said: "love is of God"; he adds: "everyone who loves is begotten of God and has knowledge of God. The man without love has known nothing of God." Why? "For God is love." What more could he say, my brethren? If there was no praise of love throughout this epistle, not the least word of it anywhere in Scripture, and if we had only this word from the mouth of the Holy Spirit—that "God is love"—we would want to ask for nothing more.[14]

John has said; "Whoever does not love a brother whom he has seen cannot love a brother whom he has not seen" (1 John 4:20). There is often a tendency to conclude from this that all love of others is, whether one knows it or not, charity in the Christian sense, or even an implicit love of God. This is not what the author of the letter says. What he says is that one can speak of charity when the love flows from love for God.[15] In other words, to reduce charity to its horizontal dimension is to give it a secularized meaning, to deprive it of its supernatural, vertical dimension.

Even so, it is not enough to say: "I love God!," just as it is not enough to say: "Lord, Lord!" (Matt 7:21). "For love of God is this: that we keep his commandments" (1 John 5:3). Only love with obedience is not illusory. Such was the love Jesus had for his Father, whose will he accomplished. And John adds immediately: "And his commandments are not burdensome." They demand plenty, to be sure. But one cannot call painful or wearisome what has to do with love and expresses it: such things ought to be performed with joy. "The yoke of Christ carries us more than we carry it,"[16] for the commandment always bears with it the grace that will enable it to be accomplished.

Continuing his meditation on faith, John reminds us that it is victory over the world; for through it one is united with Christ who, by his death on the cross, has triumphed over the powers of this world. "For the accuser of our brothers is cast out, who accuses them before our God day and night. They conquered him by the blood of the Lamb and by the word of their testimony" (Rev 12:10-11), those "who keep God's commandments and bear witness to Jesus" (Rev 12:17).[17]

John's contemplative gaze comes to rest on Jesus, the Son of God, object of our faith, warrant of our hope, guarantee of our future glory: "But one soldier thrust his lance into his side, and immediately blood and water flowed out. . . . This happened so that the scripture passage might be fulfilled: 'Not a bone of it will be broken.'[18] And again another passage says[19]: 'They will look upon him whom they have pierced'" (John 19:34-37).

To John's testimony is added that of the Spirit, who inspires faith and confirms it by enlightening the disciples: "And no one can say: 'Jesus is Lord,' except by the holy Spirit" (1 Cor 12:3). When the time had come for Jesus to pass from this world to the Father, he said: " 'When the Advocate comes whom I will send you from my Father, the Spirit of truth that proceeds from the Father, he will testify to me.' " (John 15:26). And also: "He will teach you everything and remind you of all that [I] told you" (John 14:26). He guarantees to the Church the faithful transmission of truth, for "where the Spirit of God is, there is the Church and all its grace. And the Spirit is truth."[20]

Some ways of speaking about the first Christian community might make one think that the early Church experienced a kind of golden age, though an all-too-short one: "Why couldn't we have lived in that blessed time?" The reality is quite different. The Christian community has always been made up of men and women of whom the best stood side by side with the mediocre, and even the worst. Nevertheless, in the fervor of their new conversion, those who adhered to the faith, thanks to the fact that "with power the apostles bore witness to the resurrection of the Lord Jesus," did leave a wonderful example of an ideal community. They were careful that no one in their midst should be in need. Some went so far as to sell property and houses and give the proceeds "to the apostles to be distributed," in order to supply the needs of their poor comrades.

Luke did not paint this picture to amuse our idle fancies, but to reawaken our zeal and stimulate us by placing before our eyes the ideal toward which the Christian community must strive with open hearts and confidence in the possibilities granted by the Spirit. Even today, there are men and women among us who voluntarily give all they own to their brothers and sisters in misery, even becoming themselves the poorest of the poor. Can Christians who have not heard the same call from the Spirit be content with admiring them from afar and offering them a pittance? There is great diversity among vocations and situations, but never can a believer be thought of as the absolute owner of certain goods, nor behave as such, and all people must strive for a just division of wealth.

> God destined the earth and all it contains for all men and all peoples so that all created things would be shared fairly by all mankind under the guidance of justice tempered by charity. No matter what the structures of property are in different peoples, according to various and changing circumstances and adapted to their lawful institutions, we must never lose sight of this universal destination of earthly goods. In his use of things man should regard the external goods he legitimately owns not merely as exclusive to himself but common to others also, in the sense that they can benefit others as well as himself. Therefore every man has the right to possess a sufficient amount of the earth's goods for himself and his family. This has been the opinion of the Fathers and Doctors of the Church, who taught that men are bound to come to the aid of the poor and to do so not merely out of their superfluous goods. When a person is in extreme necessity he has the right to supply himself with what he needs out of the riches of others. Faced with a world today where so many people are suffering form want, the Council asks individuals and governments to remember the saying of the Fathers: "Feed the man dying of hunger, because if you do not feed him you are killing him," and it urges them according to their ability to share and dispose of their goods to help others, above all by giving them aid which will enable them to help and develop themselves.[21]

To act thus is to "keep the commandments" of God, to walk in the truth of the Spirit, to live in faith in Jesus, the Christ, the Son of God, the world's conqueror.

The Presence of the Risen Christ in the Community

From Jesus' Ministry to the Apostles'

The third "summary" of the Acts of the Apostles deals primarily with the actions of the apostles, by whose hands "many signs and wonders were done among the people" (Acts 5:12-16).[1]

From the very beginning of Acts, Luke emphasizes the importance of the apostles' role—Peter's in particular—in the Christian community; it is hardly surprising that it should be made the principal subject of a "summary." On the other hand, one might be surprised, not to say embarrassed, that the focus is on the power of performing miracles: Peter's shadow "falls on" a sick man, and he is suddenly healed! Why this insistence on extraordinary signs, which would not continue? Isn't it rather the apostolic ministry of preaching and presiding over the community that must persevere in the Church? No doubt. The rest of Acts will deal with this very subject. It will tell how the apostles very early on chose men to carry on their ministry, how they established positions in the community with certain duties—deacons, supervisors (bishops), elders—among them, assuring the apostolic succession. But here Luke shows how by certain deeds the apostles continued the mission of Jesus himself.

It was at the Temple that the Lord, surrounded by his disciples, spent the last days of his life teaching; as Luke notes in his Gospel, "And all the people would get up early each morning to listen to him in the temple area" (Luke 21:37-38). It is also at the Temple that the first Christian community gathers and the apostles' preaching meets with great success "enjoying favor with all the people. And every day the Lord added to their number those who were being saved" (Acts 2:47).

The crowds besiege the apostles as they did Jesus, and for the same reasons: from the neighboring villages, they brought their sick and those who were troubled by unclean spirits to be healed; they carried the sick into the streets and laid them on cots and mattresses so that Peter might walk by them. Luke here imitates the tradition when it gives a broad presentation of Jesus' miracles: Coming down the mountain with them, Jesus "stood on a stretch of level ground. A great crowd of his disciples and a large number of the people from all Judea and Jerusalem and the coastal region of Tyre and Sidon came to hear him and be healed of their diseases; and even those who were tormented by unclean spirits were cured. Everyone in the crowd sought to touch him because power came forth from him and healed them all" (Luke 6:17-19).[2]

Finally, Luke puts Peter in the most prominent spot, as he did in the story of the miraculous catch (Luke 5:1-11).[3] Yet he does not ignore the fact that other apostles performed miracles too, particularly Paul (Acts 14:8-10; 20:7-12). But by putting him in the forefront, Luke reminds us that Peter has the preeminent spot in the apostolic college.

Though they continue Jesus' work, neither Peter nor the other apostles pretend to replace the Christ whom they proclaim. It is in his name that the sick are cured (Acts 3:6). They have received the power they wield from the Lord, and they know it. Jesus had sent the Twelve "to proclaim the kingdom of God and to heal [the sick]" (Luke 9:2). The seventy-two exercised this mission during the Lord's lifetime (Luke 10:9); they told him in astonishment: "Lord, even the demons are subject to us because of your name" (Luke 10:17).

As a sign of the coming of the kingdom, the healing of the sick shows that the Lord is always at work in his Church through the ministry of his messengers, at whose head Jesus placed Peter. But they also refer to other cures, other resurrections that are constantly performed in the Church, in the name of the Lord Jesus, for all who believe.

> If we pay attention to Christ's works, more marvelous still, we see how those who believe are raised; if we understand which death is worse, we see how those who sin die. All men fear bodily death, but scarcely the death of the soul. They all struggle to avoid a death that will inevitably come. The man who must die strives not to die, the man who must live eternally hardly troubles himself not to sin. And trying not to die, he strives in vain; he can postpone death, but he cannot escape it. But if he wants not to sin, he need not struggle, and will live eternally.[4]

The First and the Last, the Living

From the Second to the Seventh Sunday of Easter, the Lectionary for Year C contains six passages from the Book of Revelation: today we hear part of the opening vision (Rev 1:9-11a, 12-13, 17-19).[5]

The author introduces himself: "I, John, your brother, who share with you the distress, the kingdom, and the endurance we have in Jesus."

He has been exiled to Patmos, a Greek island in the Aegean Sea, "because [he] proclaimed God's word and gave testimony to Jesus."[6]

The vision occurs "on the Lord's day," when Christians gather together to celebrate the Lord's resurrection. Under the impulse of the Spirit, "a voice as loud as a trumpet" orders John to write in a book that he must send "to the seven churches,"[7] represented by "seven gold lampstands" All this reminds one of the liturgical assembly where the apostolic writings are read.

Among them John sees "one like a son of man, wearing an ankle-length robe, with a gold sash around his chest." A "son of man": the expression comes from the Book of Daniel (chapter 7). Jesus uses it to refer to himself,[8] combining it with the description of the Suffering Servant in Isaiah.[9] It indicates the transcendence of the one who bears the title, and his role as judge on the last day[10]: "the First and the Last" or as John writes elsewhere, "the Alpha and the Omega," "the beginning and the end" (Rev 1:8; 21:6; 22:13).

His clothing recalls Jesus' transfiguration.[11] He appears suddenly, as Jesus did in the resurrection appearances. Like the apostles then, John is frightened: "I fell down at his feet as though dead." And as at the resurrection appearances, the seer hears a message that rids him of his fear: "Do not be afraid."[12]

"I am . . . the one who lives. Once I was dead, but now I am alive forever and ever. I hold the keys to death and the nether world." It is the Lord who is revealed, recognized by paschal faith. His victory over death gives unending life to those who believe in him. His resurrection, attested by those who saw him alive and proclaimed the good news, is the summit of salvation history, the event that determines the present and the "time to come."

> To you, with your unbegotten Father,
> Uncreated, not bound by time, Being-in-itself,
> And with your consubstantial Spirit
> That proceeds from the Father in an
> ineffable manner,
>
> To the one divine nature,
> To your one lordship and to the One who
> exists forever,
> To the Trinity of perfect Persons
> Who perfect creation,
>
> Glory and honor and power,
> And the highest sovereignty,

In the past, present, future,
And for eternity without end.[13]

The apostles, the first witnesses of the Lord's resurrection, were also the first to experience the presence of the risen one in the Christian community. It was given them to accomplish, as had been promised, the very works and signs of Jesus. This earned them hardships and persecutions; but despite this opposition, more and more men and women came to profess their faith in the Lord.

Indeed, the apostles witnessed to what they saw: the Son of Man, the risen Lord who opens the gates of life to all believers.

Their testimony is present among us; we have their writings that we read in assemblies gathered "on the Lord's day," where the resurrected one is present in the sacrament of Word and Eucharist.

Without having seen we believe,
Christ fulfills the promise:
Christ is truly risen,
He is our rebirth.
The spirit of the Son witnesses to it,
Burning desire for the Father.
Alleluia, alleluia,
Christ is our rebirth,

Christ is lifted from the dead
and draws us into his glory:
Christ is exalted in his flesh,
He is our hope.
Why seek among the dead
the living heart of the earth?
Alleluia, alleluia,
Christ is our hope.

We feel this day rise
like a shining sun:
Christ strikes fire in our hearts
The burning love of the Passover.
On our paths may we find the torch
that dispels the night.
Alleluia, alleluia,
The burning love of the Passover.[14]

Raised According to Scripture, Recognized in the Breaking of the Bread

We Are Witnesses to It: God Has Raised Jesus

The liturgy's choice of texts to be read day after day does not favor the search for—or the dream of—a historical reconstruction of the various events in the life of the people of God, the life and ministry of Jesus, the birth and early growth of the Church.[1] The liturgy is a celebration and proclamation of the mystery of salvation as it occurs in our history. Whatever the circumstances of time or place where it is proclaimed, the Scripture text we hear "is fulfilled today."[2] Although it is taken from a discourse on "the day of Pentecost," the first reading, from the Acts of the Apostles, is perfectly at home in the liturgy for the Third Sunday of Easter, because in it Peter proclaims the paschal mystery that we are celebrating (Acts 2:14, 22-28).[3]

Peter's proclamation is very solemn: he stands up "with the Eleven," who are gathered around him. He appears as their spokesperson. He speaks to the inhabitants of Judea and to those people who have traveled to Jerusalem, which is perfectly appropriate: he is in Jerusalem. These people are the first concerned; the events respecting "Jesus the Nazorean" took place in the city where Peter and his hearers now are. But what Peter proclaims this day, in this city, to a specific audience, is a message and a testimony that is valuable for all, especially for us today. We are gathered to listen faithfully to the apostles' teaching, on which our faith is based.

In the Eastern liturgy, after proclaiming the title of the book from which the reading will be taken—e.g., "A reading of the Acts of the Apostles," "the Gospel of John"—the deacon or priest says: "Let us be attentive!"[4]

We know that "Jesus the Nazorean was a man commended to you by God with mighty deeds, wonders, and signs, which God worked through him . . ." (Acts 2:22) when he lived in the midst of his people. All this, handed down to us by "eyewitnesses" (Luke 1:2), has been recounted by the Gospels so that we may understand its meaning. The other apostolic writings witness to the way in which the good news was proclaimed and taught to the first generation of the community. These inspired texts show us that the mystery of Christ and his message very quickly became objects of reflection and were developed with different emphases in response to the catechetical needs of new believers. Placed in particular situations, confronted with specific difficulties and temptations, bearing the burden of their past, they saw themselves constantly called to the grace of baptism and the gift of the Spirit, which pushed them relentlessly forward. Their faith and generosity were thus sustained and stimulated. Faithful to the apostles' teaching, Christians continue, in the Church and under the guidance of the Spirit, to study the Old and New Testaments, which tell us over and over things that we will never fully comprehend.

Jesus, "delivered up by the set plan and foreknowledge of God," was put to death, crucified at the hands of "lawless men" (Acts 2:23). For some, such an ignominious end proved that God was not with him: "He saved others; he cannot save himself . . . He trusted in God; let him deliver him now if he wants him. For he said, 'I am the Son of God' " (Matt 27:42-43). For others, even today, Jesus' fate makes him an all too common type of man, and no more: the type that undertakes an action that should attract everyone's approval; instead, they awaken a hostility that leads them to a tragic death. But it is a cruel test for those who had put their hope in him: this man was "a prophet mighty in deed and word before God and all the people; . . . chief priests and rulers both handed him over to a sentence of death and crucified him. But we were hoping that he would be the one to redeem Israel" (Luke 24:19-21).[5] So one asks: "How could God have abandoned him so?"; "He went about doing good and healing all those oppressed by the devil, for God was with him" (Acts 10:38); "Can the divine omnipotence be held in check by death?"

These questions and others like them are all the more troubling when one remembers God's intervention on behalf of those he loved, whom he did not abandon, even when everything seemed lost: Joseph, Moses, the Suffering Servant, a persecuted sage, etc.[6] Wouldn't God do even more than this for his own Son?

This is precisely what happened, as faith proclaims: "God raised him up, releasing him from the throes of death, because it was impossible for him to be held by it." He was raised "in fulfillment of the Scriptures," the creed says. Peter thus alludes to Psalm 16. When we say it, we express our hope: God will not abandon us to death; the corruption of our flesh will not endure forever; we will pass from death to life; God's presence—the sight of his face—will fill us with joy. When Christ says it, it becomes the *Magnificat* of the resurrected one, for whom this hope has become a reality. Yes, Jesus has known death. He was laid in the tomb, but he escaped corruption. Such is God's doing, the fruit of his intervention.[7] Brought into the Temple of the divine glory, Christ has been filled with joy.

Peter continues, in a friendly but frank tone: "One can confidently say to you about the patriarch David that he died and was buried, and his tomb is in our midst to this day. But since he was a prophet and knew that God had sworn an oath to him that he would set one of his descendants upon his throne, he foresaw and spoke of the resurrection of the Messiah, that neither was he abandoned to the netherworld nor did his flesh see corruption. God raised this Jesus . . ." (Acts 2:29-32).

The reading ends with the evocation of the mission of the apostles and, after them, the Church and each believer: to testify to Christ's resurrection, glorification, and sending of the Spirit. In faith and hope, each believer can personally appropriate Psalm 16, which is most meaningful when read in the assembly of a Sunday of Easter.

> *You will show me the path to life.*
>
> Keep me, O God, for in you I take refuge;
>   I say to the LORD, "My LORD are you."
>
> O Lord, my allotted portion and my cup,
>   you it is who hold fast my lot.
>
> I bless the LORD who counsels me;
>   even in the night my heart exhorts me.
> I set the LORD ever before me;
>   with him at my right hand I shall not be disturbed.
>
> Therefore my heart is glad and my soul rejoices,
>   my body, too, abides in confidence;
> Because you will not abandon my soul to the nether world,
>   nor will you suffer your faithful one to undergo corruption.
>
> You will show me the path to life,
>   fullness of joys in your presence,
>   the delights at your right hand forever.
> (Ps 16:1-2a, 5, 7-8, 9-10, 11)

Freed from a Futile Life by the Blood of Christ

For the Christian, everything—especially the demands of moral life—flows from paschal faith and the hope based on Christ's passover. We are reminded of this by the passage from the First Letter of Peter we read this Sunday (1 Pet 1:17-21).[8]

"Now if you invoke as Father him who judges impartially according to each one's works, conduct yourselves with reverence during the time of your sojourning, realizing that you were ransomed from your futile conduct;" "with reverence" denotes the general attitude of the believer, the filial respect for the Father that demonstrates obedience to his will: indeed, how could one not do everything to please him?[9] Yesterday, we led a futile way of life, traveling without hope.[10] Now, we know that we are marching toward the place of final rest, salvation, our "redemption" (Eph 4:30). But this is not all: we have been freed "with the precious blood of Christ as of a spotless unblemished lamb." The oracles of the second part of Isaiah (40–55) have found their realization. The prophet announced that God himself would be the guarantee of the liberation of his people, who would not be redeemed for money (Isa 52:3), but by the sacrifice of a Servant, who was likened to a lamb led to the slaughter (Isa 53:7). Like the sacrificial lamb of the passover (Exod 12:5), Jesus is spotless and unblemished, bearing the sin of the world.[11] "He was known before the foundation of the world but revealed in the final time for you," for he has always had the salvation of the faithful in mind. One also thinks of the sacrifice of Isaac, when Abraham said: "Son, God himself will provide the sheep for the holocaust" (Gen 22:8).[12] In fact, Christian tradition, even in the ancient iconography of the catacombs, regarded Isaac, for whom God substituted a lamb, as a figure of Christ. In any case, for the letter's author, what was said to happen in the future has appeared with Jesus, who has brought all the ancient promises and prophecies to their fulfillment.

This is why he says that the times in which we are living are "the final time." Jesus' coming and his paschal sacrifice have inaugurated the last stage of history; however, it is not yet "the end." Thus it becomes very important to put one's faith and hope in God and his Son, to live "with reverence" in order to share in the glory that is promised us, the glory of the risen Lord.

> The imagery has passed away; the reality has come. The lamb gives place to God, the sheep gives place to a man, and the man is Christ, who fills the whole of creation. The sacrifice of the lamb, the celebration of the Passover, and the prescriptions of the Law have been fulfilled in Jesus Christ. Under the old Law, and still more under the new dispensation, everything pointed toward him.[13]

Jesus' Passover and the Scriptures

The episode of the pilgrims to Emmaus, which is very important in Luke's Gospel, is a story that can produce strong emotion every time we read it. It touches us directly. It would seem likely that the importance of the apostles' experience, the actual seeing of Christ after the resurrection, is incomparable; that it is impossible to pierce the mystery by means of some "analogous" thing we find in our own experience; that one must simply accept their testimony as true. However, one really is able to identify easily, even spontaneously, with Cleopas and his companion, so close is the path of their faith to ours. And it is clearly to make us understand this that Luke tells this story (Luke 24:13-35).[14]

The event took place on the very day of the Lord's resurrection. Most of the story dwells on what happened on the road from Jerusalem to Emmaus.[15]

The two disciples are returning to their home, no doubt distressed by what has happened to Jesus and disappointed in their expectations. They elaborate on this to a stranger who joins them and asks why they are so sad. Then they add: "Some women from our group . . . have astounded us: they were at the tomb early in the morning and did not find his body; they came back and reported that they had indeed seen a vision of angels who announced that he was alive. Then some of those with us went to the tomb and found things just as the women had described, but him they did not see."

Luke tells us right away that this stranger is Jesus. But neither Cleopas nor his companion recognizes him. "Their eyes were prevented from recognizing him." Haunted by images of the death of the prophet in whom they had believed, they can see nothing else. Only one thing surprises them: that the stranger does not share their feelings and is ignorant as to their cause. "Are you the only visitor to Jerusalem who does not know of the things that have taken place there in these days?" They don't even seem surprised to hear him say: "Oh, how foolish you are! How slow of heart to believe all that the prophets spoke! Was it not necessary that the Messiah should suffer these things and enter into his glory?" Without asking him who he is, they listen when "beginning with Moses and all the prophets, he interpreted to them what referred to him in all the scriptures." There is nothing remarkable in this. When one experiences great grief, one listens, without bothering about the speaker's identity, to anyone who knows how to speak to one's heart. And one tries to prolong the encounter. "Stay with us, for it is nearly evening and the day is almost over."

One never tires of reading and rereading this story, where Luke's charm, his psychological finesse, and storytelling power all appear to great advantage. It is important, however, that these qualities are used to serve his purpose, which is instruction. Indeed, one can see here the traditional elements of the Easter message as it is presented in the Acts of the Apostles, the second half of Luke's work.[16] The Scriptures—"beginning with Moses and all the prophets"—make clear "what concerns Jesus."[17] In fact, the Christian reading of the Bible consists in looking for Christ, "the buried treasure in the field of Scripture," a field of which the Christian has become the steward.[18] This does not mean that Scripture provides arguments that prove that Christ is risen. Life does not "demonstrate" but "show" itself. "It was necessary" that Christ suffer the passion in order to enter into his glory: and this is what happened. Scripture allows one to understand the events that concern Jesus; they are the signposts of the road at the end of which one recognizes Christ.

Recognizing Christ in the Breaking of the Bread

The two disciples had listened to a stranger explain at length the Scriptures that dealt with Jesus, whose death was such a blow to them. But when at table they saw him take bread, say the blessing, break it, and give it to them, "their eyes were opened and they recognized him." How could these familiar actions act as such a trigger? Did the disciples remember meals taken with Jesus and his solemn manner of performing the daily table rites? Did they remember what he had once done for the crowd "as the day was drawing to a close" (Luke 9:12)? "Then taking the five loaves and the two fish, and looking up to heaven, he said the blessing over them, broke them, and gave them to the disciples to set before the crowd" (Luke 9:16). Or did they recall the Passover that Jesus had "eagerly desired to eat" with his apostles before he suffered (Luke 22:14)? These questions and others that attempt to probe the workings of the disciples' hearts do not concern us. The Gospel makes no attempt to answer them. However, by the time Luke wrote this story, the disciples were already celebrating the Lord's Supper in their homes (Acts 4:46). Luke's readers know that by breaking bread in their homes, "in memory"[19] of the Lord, they renew, as they were told to do, what Jesus did on Holy Thursday evening. The evangelist is not suggesting that the risen Lord was reenacting the Last Supper at Emmaus, but he obviously does hope that we will make the connection with the Eucharist. Only then will we truly understand this remarkable story, which makes us feel as involved as the book's first audience. Really, their situation was similar to ours;[20] their faith rested on the testimony of Scripture and those who had seen the risen Lord, whom the breaking of the bread reveals as present and active in the midst of those to whom he gives his flesh to eat, the food of eternal life. The road of faith leads to this recognition of the resurrected.

> When is the Lord made known? In the breaking of the bread. This is our certainty: in partaking of the bread, we recognize the Lord. He has chosen to be recognized there, where we who cannot see his flesh nevertheless eat it. Who are you, believers, that sharing the bread comforts you! The Lord's absence is not absence. He whom you do not see is with you. When Jesus spoke to the disciples, they did not believe that he was risen. Their hope did not reawaken: they had lost hope. They walked along, dead, with the Life. And the Life walked with them, without yet being raised in their hearts.

> Do you want to live? Then do as the disciples, and recognize the Lord. The Lord who appeared like a traveler seemed to be going farther, but they were able to detain him. In the sharing of bread, the Lord was made present. Learn where to seek and find the Lord: he is there when you all partake of his flesh.[21]

The account of Jesus' manifestation has strong catechetical and liturgical overtones. It evokes the process of Christian initiation, which begins with the explanation of Scripture and culminates in the admission of the newly baptized to the Eucharistic table. At the same time, one can see—if not the actual outline of a celebration—at least its guiding principle. The proclamation and exposition of Scripture, to which a relatively long time is devoted, leads into the Eucharistic thanksgiving and communion, the summit of the liturgy, which, though shorter in length, are incomparably more dense. The Gospel reading this Sunday highlights the not always clearly perceived link between Word and Eucharist, and the passage from one to the other.

> Remain with us, Lord Jesus,
> you who were the guest at Emmaus;
> throughout the watches of the night,
> resurrected, you lead us.

> Taking bread, you broke it,
> then our eyes recognized you,
> the flickering flame in our heart
> foretells our true happiness.

The time is short, our days are fleeting.
But you prepare your house,
you give a meaning to our desires,
a future to our labors.

You the first of the pilgrims,
the star of the last morning,
awake in us by your love
a great hope in your return.[22]

The Testimony of the Apostles and Disciples

Without taking a moment to revel in their joy, the disciples ''set out at once and returned to Jerusalem where they found gathered together the eleven and those with them.'' Such a step is significant. Luke gives no reasons for this precipitous return to the city the disciples had left only a few hours earlier. One might think that they wanted to share this marvelous encounter with the others. One might also see their return to Jerusalem as a sign of their conversion. They had left the apostles and their companions to go back home, disillusioned; once they had become believers, wouldn't they rush to rejoin them? Such reflections, which are not contradicted by the text, are legitimate. However, the Gospel is content to note what the others told the two on their return to Jerusalem, the place of ''the things that happened to Jesus.'' Keeping to the story, it seems that the apostles and their companions took the word to be true immediately, saying, ''to each other, 'The Lord has truly been raised and has appeared to Simon!' ''

Thus the appearances to the apostles, especially Peter, are brought to the forefront. Luke recounts them briefly enough.[23] But what the story says here shows, if there is a need for such witness, that the faith of every disciple is based on the testimony of the apostles, especially Peter, who had seen the risen Lord. Agreement with this first testimony authenticates our faith. Our own recognition of the Lord, prepared by the hearing of the Scriptures and accomplished in the breaking of the bread, allows us to share in the experience of those who were chosen to be the authoritative witnesses of what they had seen. Authentic faith is apostolic.

Luke continues: ''Then the two recounted what had taken place on the way and how he was made known to them in the breaking of bread.'' Thus ends the story. New believers tell all their companions in the Church how they came to faith. Thus all can return home bearing the good news to others: ''Go in peace to love and serve the Lord. Alleluia, alleluia!''

The liturgy lasts only a short time. There comes a moment when it ends and the assembly takes its leave. Every one returns home, once again taking up daily tasks. Instructed by the Scriptures, revived by their encounter with the Lord in the breaking of the bread, it is with a different step that the familiar paths are trodden. The testimony of the apostles has stirred our faith. Perhaps we will have to confront unforeseen stumbling-blocks, but we know that our life has a goal, that the windings of the road will not leave us befuddled, that our life is our Passover in the wake of the risen Christ, who meets us "on the Lord's day" in order to share with us again the bread of life. What we have seen, what we have heard, and what has been given to us fills our hearts with joy and confidence, the power to speak to the whole world.

> Let us acclaim the word of God.
>
> Let us proclaim the mystery of faith.
>
> Let us give thanks to God.

He Is Living in Our Midst

Christ Rejected, Christ the Savior, the Author of Life
We read this Sunday the passage in Peter's second discourse where he announces the Lord's resurrection (Acts 3:13-15, 17-19).[1]

"The God of Abraham, [the God] of Isaac, and [the God] of Jacob, the God of our ancestors, has glorified his servant Jesus . . ." Jesus' resurrection is the summit toward which salvation history has tended since the beginning, the fulfillment of divine revelation throughout the centuries, the definitive liberation prefigured by the deliverance from Egypt; and the first of the five titles Peter gives to Jesus in this discourse is "servant." This title is particularly meaningful, for it refers to the four great songs in the Book of Consolation,[2] the coming of a persecuted Chosen One whom God will make victorious and who, by his sufferings, will obtain salvation for the nations.

Jesus has been "disowned," and "put to death," he who was "the Holy and Righteous One," "the author of life." To proclaim these titles while recalling the fate suffered by the one who bears them is a profession of faith; it is to confess God's infinite mercy and love as well as the sin of those who have not yet recognized God's messenger. It is also to recognize with thanksgiving the divine power: nothing can prevent it from completing the work of salvation. God knew that the Messiah would suffer. Because of his love for us, he took that risk. But death did not have the final word: "God raised" the broken body of Calvary. This is the good news that the apostles proclaim, to which they testify in the midst of the people.

Speaking to those who had seen what had happened to Jesus, Peter addresses them directly: "You denied the Holy and Righteous One and asked that a murderer be released to you. The author of life you put to death." At this moment, how could he speak otherwise, saying "one" or "they"? This does not mean that the apostle is accusing his hearers of being personally guilty of the death of the "servant of God," "the Holy and Righteous One," "the author of life," "the Messiah." Did not Peter himself deny Jesus? Nor does he make them bear the weight of a collective responsibility. He recalls only the deeds that took place in the city, whose inhabitants were thereby to some extent involved. Peter's apostrophe must make us look at ourselves, making us humble through our recognition of our part in the sin of a violent world where the just continue to be rejected and killed, as was the Just man. We tend to make others—"one," "they"—bear the blame for faults and sins committed by a society, a community, or a Church to which we belong, for better or for worse!

Peter immediately adds: "Now I know, brothers, that you acted out of ignorance, just as your leaders did." Yes, even "your leaders." It would thus be improper to accuse the people of having allowed themselves to be manipulated by wicked leaders. It is sad but true that sometimes—how, we do not know—ignorance and thoughtlessness reach such proportions. The history of all peoples furnishes sad examples of this. Yet no one is cursed with an eternal malediction. How could it be otherwise for the Jewish people, considering their relationship to the merciful God who is faithful to his promises?[3] So Peter's invective ends with a vibrant call: "Repent, therefore, and be converted, that your sins may be wiped away!"[4]

This call is addressed to everyone and particularly today to Christians assembled to celebrate the Lord's passover. This is why we turn toward God to beg his forgiveness and at the same time to sing our song of thanks.

> O LORD, let the light of your countenance shine upon us!
>
> When I call, answer me, O my just God,
>   you who relieve me when I am in distress;
>   Have pity on me, and hear my prayer!
>
> Know that the LORD does wonders for his faithful one;
> the LORD will hear me when I call upon him.
>
> O LORD, let the light of your countenance shine upon us!
> You put gladness in my heart.
>
> As soon as I lie down, I fall peacefully asleep.
> (Ps 4:2, 4, 7b-8a, 9a)

To Know Jesus, the Just Man, Victim for Sins

We continue this Sunday our reading of the First Letter of John (1 John 2:1-5a).[5]

"My children, I am writing this to you so that you may not commit sin." John speaks to his readers like a wise master,[6] but with an overtone of affection, appropriate coming from an elderly leader of the Church.[7] He is particularly careful to put his "children" on their guard against sin,[8] the worst thing that could happen. To commit sin is to fall back into darkness, under the power of the evil and death from which Jesus has freed us. It is to renounce our filial condition to become "children of the devil" (1 John 3:10), to "belong" to him, for he has always been a sinner, and it was in order to destroy his works that the Son of Man appeared (1 John 3:8).

The one who is born of God through Christ (John 1:12) is still vulnerable. What can be done when one falls back into sin? How can one leave it? By turning toward Christ in whom "We have an Advocate with the Father, Jesus Christ the righteous one," infinitely better than the most talented lawyers with all their eloquence and tested dialectical skill, but who can rely on nothing else to obtain clemency from the judge for a client who is guilty of a crime. Christ "is an offering for our sins, and not for our sins only, but for those of the whole world." Jesus does not have to argue attenuating circumstances for our acquittal. He himself is close to God, "our sanctification," "our redemption" (1 Cor 1:30). The sinner who is attached to Christ by the bond of faith is assured of receiving, with pardon, a renewed gift of lost justice. Far from regarding the sin for which Christ is "an offering" once for all in a detached manner, the believer battles with all his might to resist, with God's grace, the renewed attack of the forces of sin and darkness.[9]

> Do not suppose that John means that we may sin with impunity, when he says: "God who is just can be trusted to forgive our sins and cleanse us from every wrong"; nor that men can therefore say: "Let us sin! let us do what we want; Christ purifies us, he is faithful and just, and purifies us from all iniquity." John robs you of this false security and sows the seed of a healthy fear. You are looking for false security? Worry instead! The faithful and just God will forgive our sins, in so far as you are displeased with yourself and try to overcome your imperfections. For what does John say next? "My children, I am writing this to you so that you may not commit sin." Will this be by chance, since, in this life, sin is always sneaking into you? What can we do? Must we despair? Listen: "But if anyone does sin, we have an Advocate with the Father, Jesus Christ the righteous one. He is expiation for our sins."
> He is our advocate. Do what you can not to sin; but if because of the inherent fallibility of this life sin creeps into you, as soon as you see it, regret it, condemn it; having condemned it, you will come before your judge with assurance. In him you have an advocate: do not worry about losing your case, once you have confessed your fault. Sometimes in this life a man

is given an eloquent voice and so is saved; you will have to rely on the Word, and will he not save you? Cry: "We have an Advocate with the Father."[10]

"The way we may be sure that we know him is to keep his commandments." Recourse to this concrete criterion allows one to forsake the illusions and errors that threaten to vitiate our faith.[11] Such dangers occur when one pretends to know God (1 John 2:4), to see him (1 John 3:6), to live in communion with him (1 John 2:3), to live in light (1 John 2:9), without bothering about keeping his commandments.[12] At the root of such errors and illusions is a serious misconception of the reality of the incarnation. Jesus is the Word made flesh (John 1:14). To divide him into the Son of God and the historical Jesus leads to all sorts of aberrations.[13] Whoever keeps the commandments will not fall into this error. Such a person "knows" Jesus, and does not regard the Son of God as an abstraction, but rather lives in union with him; for true mysticism is embodied in that.[14]

"To keep his commandments" has two meanings. First, to reject the lusts of the "flesh," i.e., "sensual lust, enticement for the eye, and a pretentious life, is not from the Father but is from the world. Yet the world and its enticement are passing away" (1 John 2:16-17). Second, "to keep his commandments" is to model one's life on Jesus, "to live [just] as he lived" (1 John 2:6), since he, and he alone, is "the way and the truth and the life" (John 14:6). In sum, whoever keeps God's commandments knows and shows that he or she truly "knows" him. Furthermore, "whoever keeps his word, the love of God is truly perfected in him." This last affirmation is greater still. In so far as one loves God, one also loves neighbor: "If anyone says, 'I love God,' but hates his brother, he is a liar; for whoever does not love a brother whom he has seen cannot love God whom he has not seen" (1 John 4:20). But we can only love one another with true charity because God loves us, in so far as we put to work the love he has poured into our hearts. "God is love, and whoever remains in love remains in God, and God in him."[15]

It Truly Is the Crucified that They Have Seen Alive

This Sunday's Gospel is the continuation of that read for the Third Sunday of Year A. "[The disciples of Emmaus] recounted what had taken place on the way and how he was made known to them in the breaking of the bread. While they were still speaking about this, he stood in their midst . . ." (Luke 24:35-48).

This second part of the story demands as much attention as the first. It recapitulates what the evangelist, after "investigating everything accurately anew . . . [writes it down] in an orderly sequence . . ." (Luke 1:3), regards as having to be remembered of the resurrection appearances.[16] Like the other evangelists, Luke presents the "official" experience of the apostles, who doubtlessly saw the resurrected Jesus, in the framework of one appearance. Every believer can thus give a good account of the reliability of the teachings they have received (Luke 1:4).

It would be pointless to try to discover the actual number of resurrection appearances: clearly, neither the evangelists nor the other apostolic writers bothered much about it.[17] By contrast, the tradition has carefully preserved and passed on the testimony of the "official" appearances, because they primarily deal with the Twelve.[18] With Peter at their head, they are, as a group, the chosen witnesses of the Lord's resurrection and "pillars" of the Church (Gal 2:9) whose mission it is to proclaim and testify to the mystery. This is essential. Throughout the Bible, believers have been a people gathered by God, not a greater or lesser number of individuals: it is in and for a people that God reveals himself. Likewise, Christ's disciples form a community—the Church—united in the faith transmitted by the apostles who were chosen by Jesus and instituted by him as a "college."[19]

The privileged experience of the Twelve means first of all that they truly saw Jesus, and not some phantom or "spirit," the product of their imagination or desire. The appearance of the resurrected surprised them, making them startled and terrified. He had to prove to them many times over that it really was he. Despite this, "they were still incredulous for joy and were amazed." He whom they had seen die was now "in their midst." He showed them his crucified hands and feet, inviting them to touch him: "Touch me and see, because a ghost does not have flesh and bones as I have." At his request, they gave him "a piece of baked fish; he took it and ate it in front of them." One could hardly claim more concretely the identity of the resurrected and the crucified—"It is really I"— and the reality of his body. What is the nature of this body? The Gospels content themselves with saying, with no explanation, that it was not subject to the constraints of mortal bodies, such as that with which Jesus experienced death and burial. Henceforth, Jesus may come and go anywhere he pleases. Paul asks himself about our own resurrection: "With what kind of body will [the dead] come back?" "A spiritual body," he responds (1 Cor 15:35-44). This likewise affirms the identity of the body before and after resurrection, though one can say no more without experience thereof. It is possible to verify that something, a profound and concrete reality, is so, though its full explanation cannot be grasped.[20]

This Is What One Reads in the Scriptures

Doubts that persist, as the evangelist points out, even after the resurrection appearances, are laid to rest decisively by the Scriptures. Luke recalls this in three sentences. Jesus himself, when he was still with the apostles, prepared them for what was going to happen to him: his sufferings, death, and resurrection. These events fulfilled—as they had to—all that "referred to him in all the scripture" "beginning with Moses and all the prophets." To cite these passages would be overly pedantic; they are strewn throughout the Gospels. Here, however, Luke speaks of them generally. Indeed, in the Acts of the Apostles he shows how the apostolic preaching appeals over and over again to the testimony of Scripture. If one would read Luke's Gospel, one should follow it by a reading of Acts. The risen Jesus gave the apostles "understanding of the scriptures." The Church, along with them, receives the same gift in the Spirit. It uses the gift particularly in the ministry of exegetes. "Some strange things come to light when one listens judiciously to the use the New Testament makes of the witnesses of the Old Testament. Many times, one is tempted to wonder if they are being treated fairly. Many of them would undoubtedly have been astonished at being connected with Jesus. Sometimes, of course, we ourselves are regarded as witnesses because of what we have done at one time or another without understanding our relationship with 'the big picture.' The New Testament cites its witnesses at a stroke, not bothering to quote the sacred texts, because its business is not to quote, but to announce the good news."[21]

It is the ending—passion and resurrection—that illuminates the life and person of Jesus.[22] The apostles' preaching shows that all of Scripture—ancient laws, history of God's people,[23] prophetic oracles, and above all the psalter[24]—must be interpreted in the light of the risen Christ.

You Are Now Witnesses to It

During his mortal life, Jesus could not proclaim the kingdom of God beyond the confines of the country where he lived. After his resurrection, though, such bonds are broken. Through the ministry of the apostles, his voice can echo throughout the earth, the good news being proclaimed in every tongue. The forgiveness of sins and the salvation that come from the resurrected can reach all those who believe in him,[25] from one end of the world to the other, even to the end of time. The greatest hopes of the prophets are thus realized.[26] Going out from Jerusalem, the place where the mystery of the incarnation reached its summit with Jesus' passover, and the cradle of the faith, the mission has become universal.

The spreading of the good news is certainly submitted to the law of incarnation that led the Father to send his son in our flesh. The apostles and their successors died one after another. Not so the life acquired by the resurrected: it is passed on from generation to generation. Some Christian communities may break apart or even disappear. Not so the Church of the resurrected. This assurance indicates our responsibility, for each one according to vocation has a share of responsibility in the testimony that Jesus has confided "to the Eleven and the rest of the company," filled with joy by the Lord's coming into their midst.

> Now, brothers, how does the joy of your heart witness to your love for Christ? This is what I think; see if I am right: if you have ever loved Jesus, living, dead, raised to life, on this day when the messages of resurrection are proclaimed over and over in the Church, your heart rejoices within you and says: "It has been told to me; Jesus, my God, is alive!" At this news my spirit, which was so heavy with sorrow, languishing in indifference or ready to fall prey to discouragement, reawakens. The sound of this happy message can even draw wicked men from death. If it were not so, one would have to despair of and shroud in forgetfulness those whom Jesus, coming up from hell, has left in the pit. You will truly know that your spirit has fully recovered its life in Christ, if it can say with conviction: "It is enough for me, if Jesus is alive."
>
> If these words express a deep attachment, how worthy are they of Jesus' friends! So is the pure affection that says: "It is enough for me, if Jesus is alive!" If he lives, I live, for my soul dwells in him; even more, he is my life and everything I need. What can I lack if Jesus is alive? If everything were taken from me, it would not matter, if only Jesus might be alive. Even if he wants me to lose myself, it is enough for me that he lives, even if it is only for himself.[27]

One can never exhaust the wondrous discovery of "the breadth and length and height and depth" (Eph 3:18) of the mystery of Christ's resurrection, source and center of our faith, object of our liturgical celebrations. All of Scripture must be reread to focus its light on the event of Easter and on the person of the resurrected. The inverse is likewise necessary, rereading the whole Bible as the Christ of Easter teaches us how. One can better understand, at any rate, why the Word of the Old Testament is proclaimed in the liturgy. True, during Eastertime all three readings come from the New Testament; however, particularly on this Third Sunday, Peter and the Gospel urge us to be mindful of what "the law of Moses and the prophets and psalms" say about Jesus.

The Lord's resurrection remains a mystery. But the resurrected is present "in the midst" of the world and the Church. The apostles proclaim it, believers witness to it by their faith, conversion, and obedience to the commandments. Each Sunday, the Christian community experiences the grace and joy of coming together to feed and fortify its life by communicating in the Body and Blood of Christ.

Church of the Resurrected and Witness of the Apostles

Witnesses with the Holy Spirit of the Risen Christ

Last Sunday, we read in Acts a general account of the apostles' activity in Jerusalem at the Church's beginning.[1] Today, we read Peter's speech before the Sanhedrin. It is actually the second that the apostles' spokesperson addresses to the members of the high council concerned with the internal government of the Jewish community and religious questions.[2] It is an exemplary, though short, testimony to the apostolic faith in the risen Jesus (Acts 5:27b-32, 40b-41).[3]

As often happens, the interrogation first focuses on the intentions of the preachers, who are suspected of having subversive goals. If they could be convicted of wanting to destabilize the established order and undermine the legitimate authority, it wouldn't be necessary to find some other reason to condemn them.[4] A trial over the profession of doctrines is always longer and more hazardous. "You have filled Jerusalem with your teaching and want to bring this man's blood upon us" (Acts 5:28).

"Peter and the apostles" are careful not to be drawn into this debate.[5] His famous response expresses his unshakable determination, solidly anchored in the certitude of having received from on high a mission which he cannot and must not avoid: "We must obey God rather than men."

This principle is often reprised when one is confronted with a contradiction between a divine commandment and a human precept, and this is entirely legitimate in moral or ethical matters. In Peter's mouth, on the other hand, it is primarily a question of faith, particularly the duty of witnessing that falls to the believer. On a previous occasion he said: "It is impossible for us not to speak about what we have seen and heard" (Acts 4:20). This is precisely the issue: "The God of our ancestors raised Jesus, though you had killed him by hanging him on a tree. God exalted him at his right hand as leader and savior to grant Israel repentance and forgiveness of sins." We have here the expression of the apostles' paschal faith in just a few words.

"The God of our ancestors." This phrase must be recognized, by anyone at all familiar with Acts, as a staple of apostolic preaching: the God of Abraham, Isaac, and Jacob has accomplished, in Jesus, what he proclaimed form the beginning through Moses, the prophets, and all of Scripture. Perhaps we are not sufficiently aware today of this continuity in God's plan, which culminates in Jesus. That would be a genuine impoverishment of the content of Christian faith and our knowledge of the paschal mystery. The Old Testament is still an integral part of Scripture. The God of Jesus—and therefore our God—is that of "our ancestors."[6]

We are accustomed to speak of Christ as dead and risen. Peter says that he was put to death by hanging on a tree. Usually, we only see this as a reminder of Jesus' infamous and tragic death. But there is more here when one remembers what Paul says: "Christ ransomed us from the curse of the law by becoming a curse for us, for it is written, 'Cursed be everyone who hangs on a tree' " (Gal 3:13). This statement is found in Deuteronomy (Deut 21:23). However it may appear at first glance, such a way of speaking refers to a highly religious conception of crime and the responsibility of the one who commits it, the limits of human justice, and the relation between what is done on the earth and the judgment of God who is the creator and the one supreme judge. A crime is not only an act that people cannot tolerate. even more is it sin against God. People may be able to suppress the criminals among them: but the punishment they inflict is not a substitute for the just sentence that comes from the wisdom and justice of God alone. The condemnations of the criminal pronounced here below thus becomes a malediction when the crime is so obvious that one imagines that God will sanction the human sentence.

Now, Peter says that Jesus, put to death by hanging on a tree, has been "exalted" by God who has made him leader and savior. "Leader" not in a political sense, but because he is the Prince of the life that he communicates to his own (Acts 3:15). "Savior," a title which in the Bible belongs to God.[7] According to its definition—"the Lord saves" (Matt 1:21)—Jesus' name is the only one "by which we are to be saved" (Acts 4:12).[8] What a turnaround! Jesus, "accursed," has been glorified by God! Condemned by human judgment, God has made him our Savior; he brings conversion and forgiveness of sins! This is an unfathomable mystery.

"We are witnesses of these things, as is the holy Spirit that God has given to those who obey him." The Spirit's testimony is linked to the apostles. This second witness is, to be sure, invisible. However, the transformation of frightened disciples into fearless announcers of Jesus' resurrection is very visible. "But if [their purpose or activity] comes from God, you will not be able to destroy them," said Gamaliel, one of the members of the Sanhedrin (Acts 5:39).

Released after being scourged, the apostles "left the presence of the Sanhedrin, rejoicing that they had been found worthy to suffer dishonor for the sake of the name." Nothing and no one can stop them from preaching: "We must obey God rather than men." When one proclaims the gospel of the resurrection, one may suffer "even to the point of [wearing] chains, like a criminal. But the word of God is not chained" (2 Tim 2:9). The apostles and the long line of witnesses after them have borne everything "for the sake of those who are chosen, so that they too may obtain the salvation that is in Christ Jesus, together with eternal glory" (2 Tim 2:10). In celebrating the Lord's passover, each Christian assembly prays and gives thanks by making its own, with Christ, the words of a psalm that expresses the faith and confident determination of those who are witnesses, with the Holy Spirit, of the one whom God has exalted by making him the Savior.

> *I will extol you, O LORD for you drew me clear.*
>
> I will extol you, O LORD, for you drew me clear
> and did not let my enemies rejoice over me.
>
> O LORD, you brought me up from the nether world;
> you preserved me from among those going down into the pit.
>
> Sing praise to the LORD, you his faithful ones,
> and give thanks to his holy name.
> For his anger lasts but a moment;
> a lifetime, his good will.
> At nightfall, weeping enters in,
> but with the dawn, rejoicing.
>
> Hear, O LORD, and have pity on me;
> O LORD, be my helper.
>
> You changed my mourning into dancing;
> O LORD, my God, forever will I give you thanks.
> (Ps 30:2, 4, 5-6, 11-12a, 13b)

Honor and Glory to the Lamb that Was Slain

In a vision, the author of the Book of Revelation contemplated the glory the risen Lord enjoys near God. One can only speak of it in images, as prophets and mystics always do. John is one of them. What he saw[9] was like a great heavenly liturgy that celebrated the triumph of "the Lamb that was slain," solemnly enthroned near God (Rev 5:11-14).

In Revelation, "the Lamb that was slain" denotes Christ.[10] It recalls the fourth song of the Servant in Isaiah (Isa 53:7): "Though he was harshly treated, he submitted and opened not his mouth; like a lamb led to the slaughter or a sheep before the shearers, he was silent and opened not his mouth. Oppressed and condemned, he was taken away, and who would have thought any more of his destiny? He was cut off from the land of the living, and smitten for the sin of his people" (Isa 53:7-8). This was the text that the Ethiopian, the high official of Queen Candace, was reading in his carriage when Philip joined him on "the road that goes down from Jerusalem to Gaza." "Philip opened his mouth and, beginning with this scripture passage, he proclaimed Jesus to him" (Acts 8:26-40). Although scarcely mentioned in the New Testament outside of the Book of Revelation, the image of the sacrificial lamb must have been a familiar one in apostolic catechesis.[11] John himself, in his Gospel, readily alludes to the paschal lamb when he speaks of Jesus' passion.[12] Clearly, it is the crucified who is the focus of the triumphal liturgy contemplated by the seer.

As in the vision in Daniel (7:10), a whole court surrounds the throne of God: "many angels . . . and the living creatures and the elders.[13] They were countless in number and they cried out in a loud voice: 'Worthy is the Lamb that was slain to receive power and riches, wisdom and strength, honor and glory and blessing.' Then I heard every creature in heaven and on earth and under the earth and in the sea, everything in the universe, cry out: 'To the One who sits on the throne, and to the Lamb be blessing and honor, glory and might, forever and ever.'" This great acclamation of praise—the "doxology"—of the whole universe associates the Lord Jesus—"the Lamb that was slain"—to the glory that belongs to God. The Amen of "the four living creatures"—reminiscent of the four mysterious "living creatures" of Ezekiel (1:4-28)—tells how this praise is earned. "Yes, it is right and good!" "And the elders fell down and worshiped."

Reading this passage from Revelation, filled with so many liturgical reminders, turns our eyes and attention to the liturgies of this world, "as we wait in joyful hope for the coming of our Savior, Jesus Christ."

> For the kingdom,
> the power and the glory are yours,
> now and forever.[14]

The Appearance of Jesus on the Seashore

This Sunday, we read the greater portion of the last chapter of John's Gospel, which is reckoned to be a later addition, written either by the author of the Gospel himself or, more likely, one of his disciples.[15] Whatever the case may be, the canonicity of this finale to the Fourth Gospel has never been challenged.[16] Moreover, the story of Jesus' appearance on the shore of the sea of Tiberias has considerable significance (John 21:1-19).

The story mentions seven disciples: Simon Peter, who is the foremost in place and action; Thomas; Nathanael of Cana in Galilee; the sons of Zebedee, i.e., James and John; and two others whose names are not given. Simon Peter decides to go fishing. The others accompany him in the boat. They fish all night, but catch nothing.

One can sense, in the somewhat commonplace nature of these details, a possible meaning to which the author wants to awaken his reader by suggesting certain questions. Would the disciples around Simon Peter really be simply returning to their former way of life, as if, after Easter, they had lost hope in the future, as if they thought that the story had come to an end? We can be sure that the author of this appendix to the Fourth Gospel did not write it without reading what had happened before: Jesus' appearance to the disciples, "on the first day of the week," when he gave the Spirit to the apostles and established their mission; the appearance "a week later," with the beautiful profession by Thomas, one of the seven mentioned here (John 20:19-29).[17] Therefore it falls to us to understand the import the author intended in this "appendix."

Clearly, it is not a matter of recognizing the resurrected again. John—the disciple Jesus loved—does not hesitate when he hears the voice tell them to throw their net off the starboard side: "It is the Lord!" Peter doesn't doubt his companion's exclamation for a second: he immediately jumps into the water and swims back to shore, leaving the others to bring back the boat and the heavily weighted net. Besides, the reader is told from the very first: "When it was already dawn, Jesus was standing on the shore; but the disciples did not realize it was Jesus." In the dim light of early morning and a hundred yards from land, there is nothing surprising about this. But, when they came near him, "none of the disciples dared to ask him, 'Who are you?' because they realized was the Lord." The whole focus of the story is first the catch, then what happened on the shore: the meal prepared by Jesus for his disciples, and his dialogue with Peter.

The Miraculous Catch as a ''Sign'' of the Church

The Fourth Gospel typically situates its action at Jerusalem. However, some of the ''signs'' do occur in Galilee: the calling of Philip, originally from Bethsaida in Galilee like Andrew and Peter, and of Nathanael, also a Galilean (John 1:43-51); Jesus' first ''sign'' at Cana in Galilee (John 2:1-12); the healing of an official's son, again at Cana (John 4:43-54); the ''sign'' of the multiplication of loaves on the shore of the sea of Tiberias, the walking on the water and the great discourse on the bread of life in the synagogue of Capernaum in Galilee (John 6:1-71). The fact that the story of the miraculous catch belongs to this line of Galilean memories recorded by John ought to strike us. Most of these episodes deal with the disciples' faith; they are ''signs,'' i.e., acts which point to something beyond themselves. The miraculous catch is one of these. The anonymous author of this story has clearly understood very well—interiorized, one could say—the way John reads what others call miracles, and how he sees them as ''signs.''

He emphasizes the contrast between the work to which the disciples betook themselves all night and the enormous, sudden catch when they threw the net ''over the right side,'' as Jesus had told them to do. The editor insists: there were only large fish, and yet the net was not broken; the fish numbered one hundred fifty-three! This last detail is certainly not given by chance, for its own sake. What the number symbolizes, we are not sure.[18] At the very least, it suggests an abundance: one could not want, or even imagine, a greater catch. Again, to see this catch as a ''sign'' of the Church hauling a multitude of believers to the shore is certainly not arbitrary, especially considering what follows.[19]

The ''Sign'' of the Meal Prepared by Jesus

''When they climbed out on shore, they saw a charcoal fire with fish on it and bread. 'Bring some of the fish you just caught,' Jesus told them.'' When Peter hauled the net to dry ground, Jesus said to them: ''Come, have breakfast.'' Then, ''he took the bread and gave it to them, and in like manner the fish.''

This scene is simple and natural, full of humanity and delicacy. If one studies it for very long, however, one gets the feeling that it signifies a greater reality, a ''mystery.'' The story cannot be seen simply as a manifestation of Jesus' kind ministrations, preparing his disciples, who were weary after a hard night, some refreshment.

Some ancient commentators saw the fish laid on the coals as a symbol of Christ: *Piscis assus, Christus passus*—"The broiled fish is the suffering Christ."[20]

> What does the broiled fish signify to us, if not the very mediator of God and suffering men? He has deigned to be hidden in the waters of the human race, he has wished to be caught in the net of our death, and in his passion, he has been, so to speak, broiled on the fire of tribulation.[21]

The connection is suggestive, even if one cannot say that the author attaches any symbolic meaning to the broiled fish. It would be even more difficult to speak about the bread. But when Jesus fed the crowd on the edge of the sea of Tiberias, he also gave them bread and fish, and after all had eaten their fill, there were twelve baskets left over of the fragments of bread (John 6:1-15). This "sign" was an announcement of the Eucharist. The author certainly means to call this to mind. In any case, the Christian of today who knows the Gospels cannot help but make these connections while reflecting on such a suggestive passage, especially when it is read during the Eucharistic celebration. We know that it is the Lord who has set the table and invites us: "Happy are those who are called to his supper." He gives himself to be the food of those he gathers: "The Body and Blood of Christ—Amen."

The Pastoral Ministry of Peter Under the "Sign" of Love

Throughout the story of this marvelous catch, Peter is discreetly placed in the forefront. He is the first named of the seven, as he is in the lists of the apostles.[22] His desire to go fishing draws the others along. When John sees that it is the Lord who speaks to them from the shore, it is to Peter that he speaks. Peter throws himself into the water and reaches the Lord before the others. When Jesus asks that the newly caught fish be brought to him, Peter hurries to drag the net to the ground by himself, though seven of them on the water could barely handle it. He even manages to do this without breaking the net.[23] After the meal on the shore, Peter appears alone with Jesus, for a solemn dialogue recounted in detail: "Simon, son of John, do you love me more than these?"; "Simon, son of John, do you love me?"; "Simon, son of John, do you love me?" This three-fold interrogation with its growing insistence provokes Peter's firm response: "Yes, Lord, you know that I love you." Yet Peter is hurt by this insistence, which must strongly recall his triple denial in the high priest's house[24]: "Lord, you know everything; you know that I love you." Jesus has not forgotten Peter's tears at the hour of the cockcrow;[25] one look was enough to make the disciple realize, sorrowfully, what he had done (Luke 22:61). By insisting in this manner, Jesus certainly does not intend to open a wound that must still be tender, even after the healing of repentance and forgiveness. To the three-fold profession of love that he has called for, Jesus responds with a thrice-repeated solemn investiture: "Feed my lambs"; "Tend my sheep"; "Feed my sheep." To the apostle whose love he knows, the resurrected, the good shepherd who has given his life for the sheep (John 10:11-14), confides the care of his flock. As the faithful steward of the owner to whom he is bound by the bond of love, Peter will have to defend the sheep from wolves and thieves, make the flock enter and leave by the gate, seek the lost so that there may be only one flock and one shepherd (John 10:1-18, 27-30).[26] Peter's ministry in the Church occurs under the "sign" of love, for the unity of all in charity.[27]

> Jesus is concerned with whether Peter loves him; not whether he acknowl-edges his doctrine; not whether he has the desire to become a fisherman again, but whether there is affection in his heart . . . What Jesus wanted was to make Peter say that he loved him. O Jesus, will it please you so if someone says that he loves you? Really? And will you ask this of me? Oh! how I long for you to ask me and to be sure that you ask me! But I wander: for if there is one thing certain, it is that you always want my love, that you ask me for my love, and ask it I give it to you.[28]

Peter, on the eve of the passion, with a generous heart but not without some temerity, declared to Jesus: "I will lay down my life for you!" Jesus responded that Peter would "follow later" (John 13:36-37). The Lord had to go first so that the other disciples, with Peter at their head, could fol-low the same paschal road. " 'Amen, Amen, I say to you, when you were younger, you used to dress yourself and go where you wanted; but when you grow old, you will stretch out your hands, and someone else will dress you and lead you where you do not want to go.' He said this sig-nifying by what kind of death he would glorify God. And when he had said this, he said to him, 'Follow me.' "

On our entrance into the Church in baptism, we were marked with the sign of the cross.[29] Peter's ministry and the remainder of his days will all be under this sign[30] of the love that God has manifested to us through his Son. May he make us able to say in our turn, even after denying him: "Lord, you know everything. You know that I love you."

At the heart of the liturgy this Sunday is the mystery of the Church living in the tension between the salvation acquired by the Lord's death and resurrection and the celebration in heaven of the fully manifested victory of the Lamb that was slain.

Today is the time of witness and preaching from which no one and nothing can turn us: "We must obey God rather than men."

This is the time of toil, when one sometimes works a full night with no result. Nevertheless, the Lord is present on the shore. If he intervenes, one will be astounded at the size of the catch. One will see, at the dawn of the new day, the "great multitude, which no one could count, from every nation, race, people, and tongue . . . [standing] before the throne and before the Lamb . . ." (Rev 7:9).

This is the time when only one thing matters: to follow Christ, each according to his or her vocation. In the Church, there must be no other emulation than that of the love of God and of his Christ, of communal charity.

> Peter turned and saw the disciple following whom Jesus loved, the one who had also reclined upon his chest during the supper and had said, "Master, who is the one who will betray you?" When Peter saw him, he said to Jesus, "Lord, what about him?" Jesus said to him, "What if I want him to remain until I come? What concern is it of yours? You follow me." (John 21:20-22).[31]

We have in common the Scriptures and the true testimony of the Gospels, which draw for us the way and reveal to us the end toward which we are going with the Church and all believers.

> The Church recognizes two kinds of life as having been commended to her by God. One is a life of faith, the other a life of vision; one is a life passed on pilgrimage in time, the other in a dwelling place in eternity; one is a life of toil, the other of repose; one is spent on the road, the other in our homeland; one is active, involving labor, the other contemplative, the reward of labor.
>
> The first kind of life is symbolized by the apostle Peter, the second by John. All of the first life is lived in this world, and it will come to an end with this world. The second life will be imperfect till the end of this world, but it will have no end in the next world.[32]

In the liturgy, we remember the death and resurrection of Christ, we give thanks for what he has done among us, for us, and through us, we receive the pledge of eternal glory.

The Paschal Exodus in the Wake of Christ

God Has Delivered Up Jesus, Who Was Crucified Lord and Christ
The five discourses of Peter reported in the Acts of the Apostles and read during the Sundays of Easter might appear a bit dull, since they all very nearly say the same thing.[1] It would be a mistake to complain about this repetition. Each of these discourses is an announcement of Jesus' resurrection expressed in certain standard phrases: "Christ is risen! He is truly risen!"[2] No one should grow weary of hearing them over and over during those Sundays that celebrate the feast of Easter.[3] We know that it is impossible to keep great news to oneself. Consider this: When news concerns several persons, a whole group, a crowd, each person tries to outdo the others in shouting aloud with joy, such as the repeated alleluias of the paschal liturgies.[4] To repeat the same news to oneself or others helps it to be accepted and interiorized. To hear the proclamation of the resurrection over and over during the Sundays of Easter is essential to our faith, which needs to be strengthened by the witness of others' faith, particularly the apostles'. The paschal liturgies give us this gift. Therefore we must welcome and be attentive to this new proclamation of Easter (Acts 2:14a, 36-41).[5]

"This man, delivered up by the set plan and foreknowledge of God, you killed. . . ." This way of expressing Jesus' exaltation into God's glory is inspired by Psalm 110:1-2: "The Lord said to my Lord: 'Sit at my right hand till I make your enemies your footstool.' The scepter of your power the Lord will stretch forth from Zion: 'Rule in the midst of your enemies.' "[6] The first announcements of the resurrection are often embellished, in Peter's discourses, by citations from the psalms. It is a way of saying that the event has fulfilled the prophetic oracles[7] or even that Jesus must suffer the passion in order to enter into glory: Moses, the prophets, and the psalms have said so (Luke 24:27). Along with some of the great prophetic texts, the psalms were doubtlessly very familiar to the apostles' listeners. In any case, the use made of them in this discourse authenticates and renews our Christian reading of some of the psalms.

As often happens in such cases, the apostle addresses his audience directly, with a kind of needless aggressiveness: This man whom "you killed." We must not misunderstand the import behind such a saying. What the apostle wants is to cause his hearers to feel personally concerned with what is a message, and not simply a bit of information to which one might remain neutral.[8] This he accomplishes. Peter's audience does not think of itself as being unjustly accused. Rather they were "cut to the heart . . . they asked Peter and the other apostles, 'What are we to do, my brothers?' Peter [said] to them, 'Repent and be baptized, every one of you, in the name of Jesus Christ for the forgiveness of your sins; and you will receive the gift of the holy Spirit.' " As opposed to the feeling of guilt, which focuses on oneself and one's sins, conversion opens to forgiveness and the freedom that comes from it. This call to conversion always accompanies the proclamation of the good news.

Baptism is said to occur "in the name of Jesus Christ" because it involves a profession of faith in the one whom God has made Lord and Christ by raising him from the dead. The reference is not to the formula used in the administering of the sacrament. Moreover, the clearly affirmed link between baptism and the gift of the Spirit leaves the question of ritual open.[9] Instead, it is important to note what Peter then says: "For the promise was made to you and to your children[10] and to all those far off, whomever the Lord our God will call." The universality of salvation, which Luke insists upon and of which he will be a witness by accompanying Paul in his missionary journeys, also belongs to the first announcement of the good news.[11] Luke never misses an opportunity to evoke joyfully, as he does here, the wonderful extension of the Gospel.[12] How can we not marvel at it in our turn? We are witnesses to it as well, since in the centuries following, we have benefited by the promise. Even today we can see that certain peoples who were but recently pagans have benefited by it.

> *The LORD is my shepherd; I shall not want.*

The LORD is my shepherd; I shall not want.
 In verdant pastures he gives me repose;
Beside restful waters he leads me;
 he refreshes my soul.
 He guides me in right paths for his name's sake.
Even though I walk in the dark valley
 I fear no evil; for you are at my side

> With your rod and your staff
>   that give me courage.
>
> You spread the table before me
>   in the sight of my foes;
> You anoint my head with oil;
>   my cup overflows.
>
> Only goodness and kindness follow me
>   all the days of my life;
> And I shall dwell in the house of the LORD
>   for years to come.
> (Ps 23:1-3a, 3b-4, 5, 6)

In the Footsteps of the Shepherd Who Watches Over Us

When they speak to the Christians, the apostles do not only say: "God has made Jesus Lord and Christ, reform your lives." Reminding the baptized of their profession of faith, they exhort them to follow the footsteps of the resurrected, to live the life opened to them by Christ's passover, which they have received in baptism.[13] For the most part, the apostolic letters, sent to specific Churches or groups of Churches,[14] have been written to respond to the needs of their first recipients; nevertheless, they retain an undeniable value for today. This is particularly the case with the passage from the First Letter of Peter that we read today (1 Pet 2:20b-25).[15]

We confess that Jesus has suffered though he "committed no sin" and "no deceit was found in his mouth"; nor did he compromise, in any manner whatever, with what is hollow, fake, or opposed to the God of truth.[16] We proclaim that he has suffered for us, "that you should follow in his footsteps . . . By his wounds you have been healed." Yes, Jesus is the servant spoken of by Isaiah, as the apostle suggests: let us here recall this great text.

> He was spurned and avoided by men,
>   a man of suffering, accustomed to infirmity,
> One of those from whom men hide their faces,
>   spurned, and we held him in no esteem.
>
> Yet it was our infirmities that he bore,
>   our sufferings that he endured,
> While we thought of him as stricken,
>   as one smitten by God and afflicted.
> But he was pierced for our offenses,
>   crushed for our sins,
> Upon him was the chastisement that makes us whole,
>   by his stripes we were healed.

We had all gone astray like sheep,
   each following his own way;
But the Lord laid upon him
   the guilt of us all.
Though he was harshly treated, he submitted
   and opened not his mouth;
Like a lamb led to the slaughter
   or a sheep before the shearers,
   he was silent and opened not his mouth.
Oppressed and condemned, he was taken away,
   and who would have thought any more of his destiny?
When he was cut off from the land of the living,
   and smitten for the sin of his people,
A grave was assigned him among the wicked
   and burial place with evildoers,
Though he had done no wrong
   nor spoken any falsehood.
[But the LORD was pleased
   to crush him in infirmity.]
If he gives his life as an offering for sin,
   he shall see his descendants in a long life,
   and the will of the LORD shall be accomplished through him.
(Isa 53:3-10)

We have not "spurned" him or "held him in no esteem," for we have joined ourselves to him. We know that he has not been "stricken, smitten by God and afflicted," but that God has "exalted him" and has made him "Lord and Messiah" (Acts 2:33, 36). This is our faith. But the apostle's intent is neither to remind us of this interpretation nor to give it official warrant. He says: "But if you are patient when you suffer for doing what is good, this is a grace before God. For to this you have been called, because Christ also suffered for you, leaving you an example that you should follow in his footsteps."

To do "what is good," not to commit sin, not to give heed to deceit, even if such conduct costs us unjust persecutions, is a "grace before God." For it is thus that we proclaim, not with words but in deeds, that he is God, the God of truth. We walk according to his will, like Christ, without straying down the paths of "deceit" that those fools follow who say in their hearts: "There is no God" (Ps 53:2). The Christian is not called to suffer, but to remain united with God whatever the cost, to find joy in him. "To die to sin" never occurs without painful renunciations, whatever they may be. But this death is a Passover. "He handed himself over to the one who judges justly." Christ's "example" is our guarantee.

Let me tell you how I came to know him.
I had heard many speak of him,
but had paid no attention.

Each day he sent me presents, and I never
thanked him.

Often he seemed to want my friendship, but
I ignored him.

I was homeless and miserable and hungry;
every moment I was in peril: he offered me
shelter, comfort, food; he guarded me from
all danger: but I was always ungrateful.

Finally, he met me on the road, and with
tears in his eyes, he entreated me, saying:
"Come and dwell with me."

Let me tell you how he treats me now:
He provides all my needs,
He gives me more than I dare ask;
He anticipates all my desires,
He urges me to ask for more;
He never reminds me of my past ingratitude.
Never does he reproach me for my past
foolishness . . .

Let me tell you what I think of him.
He is as good as he is great,
He loves me with a love both ardent and
true,
He is as bounteous with promises as
faithful to keeping them;
He is as jealous of my affection as worthy
of retaining it.

In everything, I am his debtor, but he
wants me to call him "My Friend."[17]

"Ransomed from your futile conduct" (1 Pet 1:18), because we were "astray like sheep," we "have returned to the shepherd and guardian of [our] souls." Sacrificial lamb who "bore our sins in his body on the cross," Christ has become, through his resurrection, "the shepherd" of our souls.

Jesus, Shepherd, Gate of the Sheepfold
Some of Jesus' more enigmatic sayings become clear when read in light of the resurrection and paschal faith.[18] Only then is it understood that they are revelatory sayings concerning Jesus' person and mission, in them-

selves and for us, though their meaning was at first hidden. This is particularly the case with Jesus' discourse that contains the image of the good shepherd, the beginning of which we read today (John 10:1-10).[19]

Addressed originally to the Pharisees, today these words of revelation concern those who question the necessity of going to God through Jesus, those who would doubt the incomparable character of his mission, those who by their manner of speaking or acting would wish to take his place.[20] If the Church wants Christians gathered for the liturgy to hear this text, it is not to remind them of Jesus' controversies with his opponents, or the way certain Pharisees regarded him, but so that we might believe that Jesus is the Messiah, the Son of God, and thus have life in his name (John 20:31).[21]

Jesus is the legitimate shepherd of the flock. He does not break into the sheepfold, but enters by the gate. The gatekeeper opens it for him. The sheep hear his voice and follow him without hesitation when he comes to lead them out. "But they will not follow a stranger; they will run away from him, because they do not recognize the voice of strangers." One could hardly express this more simply and concretely.[22]

He also says that he enters the sheepfold to lead out all his sheep. There may be nothing remarkable in this: why should the shepherd open the gate of the sheepfold, if not to lead out the sheep? But one cannot help but think of another "going out" of "all the sheep": the Exodus led by Moses, God's messenger.[23] At any rate, Jesus, aware of the limits of his sayings and the doubts that their enigmatic character might foster,[24] goes on to say explicitly: "I am the gate for the sheep."

At first glance, one might well be startled by the lack of coherence between successive images: "the shepherd" becomes "the gate"! But there is an undeniable continuity of conception. It is not enough to understand that Jesus is the shepherd sent by God—like Moses—to lead out his sheep. He is also their "gate" and the only sure way out of the sheepfold. Whoever before or after him pretends to fill this role is an impostor, a thief disguised as the shepherd in order to "steal and slaughter and destroy."

This is a harsh, firm condemnation of the "false prophets, who come to you in sheep's clothing, but underneath are ravenous wolves" (Matt 7:15). It is entirely understandable coming from Jesus, who came so that we "might have life and have it more abundantly."[25] Even so, this condemnation is joined to a promise spoken to all: "Whoever enters through me will be saved, and will come in and go out and find pasture." The false shepherds are also called to conversion, to find the way to salvation for which Jesus is the gate. The sheep already gathered under his staff know that they owe this to the shepherd's love. They accept that he allows them to come and go freely in their pasture while he seeks the lost. They look for his return and come running as soon as they see him, to rejoice with him and welcome in joy the one he bears back on his shoulders (Matt 18:12-14; Luke 15:3-7).

Jesus has passed the gate of death to enter into glory: "God has made him Lord and Messiah." To proclaim his resurrection is to recognize that he is the guide in whose footsteps we must follow in order to have life, and to have it more fully. He marches at the head of the ransomed people, leading them on the road of their paschal exodus.

This shepherd, whose face is worn by suffering but also shines with light, leads us confidently on difficult paths. He watches that nothing unfortunate may happen to us. If the mist sometimes obscures our vision, his voice continues to lead us in the right direction.

> My brothers, we say every day: "We are his people, the sheep of his flock." We also say: "We are lost, we have strayed far from your ways, like lost sheep"; never forgetting that on the one hand we are sinners, while on the other hand Christ is our guide and our guardian. He is "the way and the truth and the life" (John 14:6). He is a light for our road, a lantern for our paths. He is our shepherd, and the sheep know his voice. If we are his sheep, we will listen to him, recognizing and obeying him. Let us be sure to follow when he goes before us; "He walks ahead of them, and the sheep follow him, because they recognize his voice." Let us not receive his grace in vain. When God called Samuel, he responded: "Speak, for your servant is listening" (1 Sam 3:10). When Christ called him, St. Paul "was not disobedient to the heavenly vision" (Acts 26:19). May we long to hear his voice; let us pray that he may give us attentive ears and a heart of goodwill.[26]

Children of God
Under the Staff of Christ

Jesus, the Stone Rejected, Has Become the Cornerstone
"Having died on the cross, Jesus rose on the third day." Such is the Easter message untiringly proclaimed by the apostles and, after them, the Church;[1] such is the faith constantly reaffirmed by all Christians when they say the Creed. For many centuries, unbelievers spoke of it with the indifference and cold objectivity of Festus, the Roman procurator of Judea (from 52 to ca. 60): "The Christians claim that a certain Jesus, who died, is alive."[2] Whatever one thinks of this faith, there seems to be nothing subversive about it today. As for the Christians themselves, a not unlikely result of saying the Apostles' Creed and hearing their testimony is the dulling of their attention. It might even be totally relaxed during the season of Easter when they hear successive announcements of the resurrection that all say the same thing: "Christ is risen." But shouldn't the Sundays of Easter all vie in proclaiming this? The regular reprise of the paschal message and the proclamation of the mystery celebrated during these fifty days help make them penetrate more deeply into us and strengthen our faith. The reminder of the various circumstances in which the apostles gave their testimony is a stimulating example: all occasions are appropriate for announcing the Lord's resurrection; the duty to do so cannot be shirked. Finally, one must acknowledge that since the beginning, the presentation of the same news has taken various forms, which lead to later catechesis. Thus today we have Peter's discourse at his first arraignment before the Sanhedrin (Acts 4:8-12).[3]

Peter and John are asked about the lame man who begged at "the Beautiful Gate" of the Temple: "By what power or by what name have you done this?" (Acts 3:1-26). Peter makes a declaration that responds to the question but is aimed at a larger audience than the members of the council: "You and all the people of Israel should know . . . ." Peter speaks with such force, assurance, and concern with being heard far and near because he is "filled with the holy Spirit," the Spirit of Pentecost who carries the voices of the gospel's preachers everywhere.[4]

It was done "in the name of Jesus Christ the Nazorean whom you crucified,[5] whom God raised from the dead." The "name" of Jesus, i.e., his person,[6] saves whoever invokes it[7] because God, by raising him, has made Jesus Lord.

He is the "stone rejected by you, the builders, which has become the cornerstone" (Ps 118:22). This is not just a forceful and often quoted scriptural image. All of Psalm 118 has a messianic meaning. It was used in this way in the Temple liturgy; it may even have been composed for it. One of the six psalms of the so-called *Hallel*[8] collection, most famous for being sung during the Passover meal, it was used by Jesus at the Last Supper.[9] Verse 22 is cited in the parable of the murderous vineyard workers, which is an announcement of the passion and resurrection of Christ, the Son sent by God (Luke 20:15-18). In addition, Acts and the First Letter of Peter (2:7-8) interpret it as applying to Christ.

Such use indicates the need to reread the Scriptures that witness to Christ and help us to better understand his paschal mystery.[10] The Christian cannot neglect this duty by merely running through the Old Testament every now and then, looking for apologetic material. The way the Church and many Christians each day make use of the psalms is an exemplary guide. This collection of one hundred and fifty inspired poems presents a palette of almost all the literary genres of the Bible. Especially notable are the "historical" psalms. In the events of the past, especially the most significant of them—creation, Exodus, etc.—the inspired poet recognizes God's initiative and action, the manifestation of his sovereign strength, his fidelity. Such meditation casts light on the present when the believer is confronted with questions and doubts, joys and pains. The believer's eye can dimly glimpse the future, which God has promised to realize by sending a savior: this is the subject of the "messianic" psalms. By appropriating all these psalms, the Church and the Christian prolong the authors' meditation, prayer, and thanksgiving in the light of the fulfillment of Jesus Christ and his mystery. This is why one can say that the whole psalter speaks of Christ, prophetically proclaiming him, giving testimony to him. Thus the prayer of the psalms becomes that of the Lord and the Church, his Body.[11]

> *The stone which the builders rejected has*
> *become the cornerstone.*

Give thanks to the LORD, for he is good,
    for his mercy endures forever.

It is better to take refuge in the LORD
    than to trust in man.
It is better to take refuge in the LORD
    than to trust in princes.

I will give thanks to you, for you have answered me
    and have been my savior.
The stone which the builders rejected
    has become the cornerstone.
By the LORD has this been done;
    it is wonderful in our eyes.

Blessed is he who comes in the name of the LORD;
    we bless you from the house of the LORD.

You are my God, and I give thanks to you;
    O my God, I extol you.
Give thanks to the LORD, for he is good;
    for his kindness endures forever.
(Ps 118:1, 8-9, 21-23, 26, 28-29)

Children of God from This Moment

The love of God that is revealed throughout salvation history, proclaimed endlessly in song by the psalms,[12] has reached its summit with the sending of the Son into the world. To be aware of this—to "see" it—it is enough to think of what the Father has made of us: children of God (1 John 3:1-2).[13]

The Word became flesh and entered the world so that "those that did accept him he gave power to become children of God . . . those who believe in his name, who were born not by natural generation nor by human choice nor by a man's decision but of God." (John 1:12-13). This is "what we are." It is so extraordinary and unexpected that nothing more can be said. One can only let one's heart overflow with joy by constantly repeating what we could never have imagined: "We are God's children."

One question immediately comes to mind: "How is it that the world does not recognize us for what we are?" We quickly respond: "The answer is close at hand. Our way of living hides what we are." This is true; however, John does not first look here, but to a deeper explanation: "The reason the world does not know us is that it did not know him" (1 John 3:1). To be sure, "no one has ever seen God. The only Son, God, who is at the Father's side, has revealed him" (John 1:18); by his death and resurrection he has revealed that "God is love" (1 John 4:8). Therefore faith, and faith alone, allows one to recognize that God loves us. The "world" is completely incapable of this in so far as it remains in darkness (John 1:9-10). If it has not "seen" that Christ was the Light, how could it see that Light enlightens the disciples (John 15:18)? John remembers Jesus' prayer: "Righteous Father, the world also does not know you, but I know you, and they know that you sent me. I made known to them your name and I will make it known, that the love with which you loved me may be in them and I in them." (John 17:25-26).

Nevertheless, it is true that believers must deepen what they already know through tradition and baptism, and progress in the faith that is their assurance till that day when what they are will be clearly seen. It is in seeing "God as he is" that revelation will become brightest. "In this world, we give ourselves, with God's help, the eyes and heart that a final transfiguration will make into organs of a power of adoration and of a capacity for bliss—both unique to each of us."[14]

Contemplation of what we are already is not to be confused with an idle wait for the final manifestation. "Everyone who has this hope based on him makes himself pure, as he is pure" (1 John 3:3). Christian morality flows from theology.

> This is our life: to do while desiring. Now, a holy desire exerts us so much more if we have freed our desires from love of the world. We have already said: empty completely what is to be filled. The good must fill our soul, driving out the evil. Suppose God wants to fill you with honey: if you are full of vinegar, where will the honey go? The contents of the vessel must be poured out: the vessel itself must be cleaned; it must be purified, no matter how much scrubbing it takes, in order for it to properly receive this mysterious reality. We cannot give this reality its true name, whether we name it gold or wine; whatever name we pretend to give to what cannot be named, its name is God. And, when we say "God," what are we saying? Is it only to these two syllables[15] that we aspire? Everything we can say falls short of the reality: let us strain toward him, so that, when he comes, he may fill us. For "we will be like him, when we will see him as he is."[16]

Jesus, the Good Shepherd Sent by the Father

Love is not demonstrated theoretically; it shows itself, and it can be tested by its manifestations. Because it is anything but an abstraction, it cannot be satisfied with definitions, discursive arguments, dissertations. The best way to speak of it is in terms of analogies, comparisons from one's experience of it. How much more is this the case when it is a question of the love of God and Christ! Indeed, Jesus speaks of love in precisely this language of parables and allegories.[17] He has shown wonderful skill by choosing ordinary and suggestive images, perhaps particularly when he says: ''I am the good shepherd'' (John 10:11-18).

He first distinguishes himself from the ''hired hand, who is not a shepherd and whose sheep are not his own, [who] sees a wolf coming and leaves the sheep and runs away''; what does it matter to him if the wolf seizes and scatters the sheep? ''He has no concern for the sheep,'' for they do not belong to him. Jesus says of himself: ''I am the good shepherd.'' This much is clear: the true shepherd knows his sheep, and they know him.[18] Notice, though, that he goes beyond simile. He does not say, ''I am like a good shepherd,'' but ''I am *the* good shepherd.'' His knowledge of the sheep does not come from observing them and noting their distinctive characteristics. It is wholly of a different order, a transcendent one: ''I know [my sheep] and mine know me, just as the Father knows me and I know the Father.''

Jesus has stopped speaking in parables and allegories. Like God in his solemn revelations, he says: ''I am''; this means that he acts and will act in conformity to what he is.[19]

''I will lay down my life for the sheep'': not figuratively, but by freely dying on a cross: ''No one takes it from me, but I lay it down on my own. I have power to lay it down, and power to take it up again.'' This is not like a shepherd who fights the wolf to the death. Such action is certainly heroic, but the sheep that are saved or at least allowed to escape are left with no guide, wandering, easy prey now that they are deprived of their defender. The death of Jesus, ''the good shepherd,'' is not a defeat. By ''taking up'' his life again, he will instead increase his flock, leading those as well who are not of this sheepfold, and making them all into ''one flock'' of which he will be the ''one shepherd.'' He fulfills God's work, as the prophet said: ''Like a shepherd he feeds his flock'' (Isa 40:11).[20] He appears as the true David chosen to be the shepherd of Jacob, the people of God, of Israel, his inheritance (Ps 78:70-72): ''My servant David shall be prince over them, and there shall be one shepherd for them all; they shall live by my statutes and carefully observe my decrees'' (Ezek 37:24).

Finally, Jesus ''the good shepherd'' reveals the source of obedience to God and the bond that it establishes with him: ''This is why the Father loves me, because I lay down my life in order to take it up again''; ''This command I have received from my Father.'' These words bring us to the heart of the love relationship between the Father and his Son. God's commandment is the expression of his love for the Son and the sheep he has given him. To let oneself be guided by "the good shepherd" is to love him, and with him and like him, to love the Father.

> Ask yourselves whether you belong to his flock, whether you know him, whether the light of his truth shines in your minds. I assure you that it is not by faith that you will come to know him, but by love; not by mere conviction, but by action. John the evangelist is my authority for this statement. He tells us that "anyone who claims to know God without keeping his commandments is a liar."
>
> Consequently, the Lord immediately adds: "As the Father knows me and I know the Father; and I lay down my life for my sheep." Clearly he means that laying down his life for his sheep gives evidence of his knowledge of the Father and the Father's knowledge of him. In other words, by the love with which he dies for his sheep he shows how greatly he loves his Father.[21]

Jesus, the Christ, has become, by his death and resurrection, the "cornerstone" on which God, "in this, the final age" (Heb 1:2), has built the edifice planned since the beginning, whose levels he had laid from all eternity. Down through the centuries, he prepared hearts and minds, he nourished human desire and hope for the salvation with which the house would be built. He gave his prophets the ability to foresee, albeit dimly, the majesty and the characteristics of the Servant chosen to gather, in this house not built by human hands, the countless multitude of the redeemed.

As always, though, what God's love has done surpasses all hope. He has sent his Son who, though he was put to death, was raised up by the divine power, being made Savior and Shepherd without whom there is no salvation.

This shepherd who has given his life for his sheep continues his work in the world. He raises his voice so that those who are lost may hear his call and come together to form one flock led by one pastor, in whose presence they can find rest and life.

> Brothers, let us set out for these pastures where we shall keep joyful festival with so many of our fellow citizens. May the thought of their happiness urge us on! Let us stir up our hearts, rekindle our faith, and long eagerly for what heaven has in store for us. To love thus is to be already on our way. No matter what obstacles we encounter, we must not allow them to turn us aside from the joy of that heavenly feast. Anyone who is determined to reach his destination is not deterred by the roughness of the road that leads to it. Nor must we allow the pleasure of success to seduce us, or we shall be like a foolish traveler who is so distracted by the pleasant meadows through which he is passing that he forgets where he is going.[22]

The liturgy is the image—the sacrament—of this gathering around Christ who gathers his own, nourishes them with his flesh and blood, leads them in the Father's paths, and speaks to them of other sheep who are not yet of this fold.

> The shepherd,
> with his familiar voice, cries:
> "A new earth!"
>
> He has crossed the ravines of death,
> we leap toward the source of living water.
>
> Shepherd who frees us,
> eternal love!
>
> The lost sheep,
> I go to seek out.
>
> The sick sheep,
> I carry in my arms.
>
> The scattered sheep,
> I gather around me.
>
> The sheep of my flock,
> I lead to my mountain.[23]

The Great Multitude Gathered by the True Shepherd

The Gentiles Welcome the Good News of Christ

Since the Church's beginning, the good news of the resurrection of Christ has been welcomed by Gentiles who have been converted and baptized. At first this was due to peculiar circumstances or because the initiative of the Holy Spirit forced the apostles' hand.[1] It was at Antioch of Pisidia, during Paul and Barnabas' visit, that the evangelization of the Gentiles really began in force.[2] The episode interests us directly since we belong to the line of Gentiles toward whom the apostles are turned. Moreover, the widening of the early mission contains a teaching that is always good to remember (Acts 13:14, 43-52).

As they usually did, the apostles, on arriving in Antioch of Pisidia, called on the Jewish community of the city and spoke to them in the synagogue on the sabbath.[3] Paul never varied from this custom.[4] His preaching had considerable success.[5] "After the congregation had dispersed, many Jews and worshipers who were converts to Judaism followed Paul and Barnabas," who were even invited to return the following sabbath. Meanwhile, Paul and Barnabas were not idle: they encouraged the first converts "to remain faithful to the grace of God." So, "the following sabbath, almost the whole city gathered to hear the word of the Lord." This undoubtedly means that all the Jews were there as well as many others who had heard of these two preachers. But some took offense at this success, and "with violent abuse contradicted what Paul said." "Both Paul and Barnabas spoke out boldly and said, 'It was necessary that the word of God be spoken to you first, but since you reject it and condemn yourselves as unworthy of eternal life, we now turn to the Gentiles.'" In other circumstances, one might talk about seeking a more favorable audience. But such is not the point here: "For so the Lord has commanded us, 'I have made you a light to the Gentiles, that you may be an instrument of salvation to the ends of the earth.'"

The apostles quoted freely, even a verse, according to the Greek translation of the Bible, of the second Song of the Servant in Isaiah (49:1-7). There, it is to God's messenger—the Savior—that the "Lord's command" is addressed. One can understand, then, that the apostles were evoking the universal mission of Christ with the help of this prophetic text: "It is too little, he says, for you to be my servant, to raise up the tribes of Jacob, and restore the survivors of Israel; I will make you a light to the nations, that my salvation may reach to the ends of the earth" (Isa 49:6). This is also a commandment for the apostles. To be sure, only Christ is "a light to the nations." Nevertheless, it is only thanks to the apostles' witness and preaching that the light will actually shine. Jesus said to them: ". . . and you will be my witnesses in Jerusalem, throughout Judea and Samaria, and to the ends of the earth" (Acts 1:8).

The preaching of the gospel to the Gentiles is not therefore a kind of historical accident; it did not happen because the Jews refused to listen, as though if they had, the good news of Christ would not have been proclaimed to the nations. The extension of salvation to the Gentiles is part of God's plan, as the oracle of Isaiah solemnly declares: "All mankind shall see the glory of the Lord" (Isa 40:6).[6] When he appeared before King Agrippa, Paul concluded his plea thus: ". . . I stand here testifying to small and great alike, saying nothing different from what the prophets and Moses foretold, that the Messiah must suffer and that, as the first to rise from the dead, he would proclaim light both to our people and to the Gentiles" (Acts 26:22-23). Therefore, though it was the reaction of some members of the synagogue at Antioch that provided an impetus for Paul and Barnabas to turn toward the Gentiles, that was not the cause of the evangelization of the nations. Nor can this be taken as an argument for the rejection of the Jews;[7] Paul's behavior does not set a precedent for any such thing. Fully aware that God never repents of his promises, Paul would continue to speak to his fellow Jews.[8] The fact that many of them actually refused to listen haunted him till the end of his life.[9] At Antioch of Pisidia, he was forced to leave the area. But he left there some disciples "filled with joy and the holy Spirit," among whom were converted Gentiles.

Quite often since that time, the apostles would have to shake the dust from their feet on leaving an area, even one already Christianized, where the people refused to listen to them. At the same time, Churches filled with the Spirit have been born elsewhere. The episode at Antioch must therefore be read as applying to the present. In giving thanks to God for his universal love, we pray that he may keep us from being deaf to his call and the words of the apostles.

We are his people, the flock he tends.

Sing joyfully to the LORD, all you lands;
    serve the LORD with gladness;
    come before him with joyful song.

Know that the LORD is God;
    he made us, his we are;
    his people, the flock he tends.

. . . for he is good:
    the LORD, whose kindness endures forever,
    and his faithfulness to all generations.
(Ps 100:1-2, 3, 5)

A Great Multitude Surrounding the Lamb

The author of the Book of Revelation is a seer whose eye of faith, brightened by the Scriptures, penetrates to the deep reality and the meaning of events. His gaze does not only carry further than others, so that it reveals in the mists of the future what is not yet. He sees dimensions of things that are beyond normal human vision. His description of what he sees makes use of images and words taken from common speech and transposed into an unusual context. In particular, one finds here visions of celestial liturgies that are like partly opened windows gazing upon the divine mystery at work in human history, which does not yet appear clearly on this earth. It is the first of these liturgical visions that we see in the reading this Sunday (Rev 7:9, 14b-17).[10]

The picture painted by John is read without difficulty, like a representational painting that is free from more or less strange allegorical elements and symbolic figures whose meaning is more or less obscure. The throne and the lamb are familiar images. Around them is "a great multitude, which no one could count, from every nation, race, people, and tongue . . . wearing white robes and holding palm branches in their hands." An explanation is even provided. An elder tells where they come from, why they are there, and where they are preparing to go: "to springs of life-giving water." One must pause here, for in its simplicity, this picture displays a mystery.

God—"the throne"—and the risen Christ—"the Lamb"—occupy center stage in their glory. "The great multitude" is that of the elect, countless as the stars of heaven, and the descendants of Abraham, the father of believers (Gen 15:5). It is composed of people belonging to all the nations and cultures of the whole earth. Their stance—"standing"; their clothing—"white." "Standing" is the posture of prayer;[11] "white robes" evokes those one puts on for the liturgy, removing the clothes of daily life so as not to distinguish one person from another.[12] All those who make up this crowd carry "palm branches in their hands" as if to participate in a triumphal procession: one automatically thinks of Jesus' entry into Jerusalem[13] and our own Palm Sunday processions.[14] In fact, it is a procession that is being prepared, but it must wait until all are gathered. We are at the threshold of the sanctuary: it is a liturgy of gathering, of "station."[15] The atmosphere is one of meditation and a certain impatience that comes not from nervousness but from a barely contained joy, waiting for the signal that will mark the beginning of the great liturgy. All will then begin to march and sing to the sound of instruments.

Guessing the question that can perhaps be read in the seer's eyes, one of the elders says: "These are the ones who have survived the time of great distress." The "time of great distress" is not only martyrdom, since all have undergone it, but the last and greatest trial through which all the baptized must pass to follow Christ in his passover. John remembers what the Lord said, and his vision reminds us of it: "Behold, the hour is coming and has arrived when each of you will be scattered to his own home and you will leave me alone. But I am not alone, because the Father is with me. I have told you this so that you might have peace in me. In the world you will have trouble, but take courage, I have conquered the world" (John 16:32-33).

The whiteness of everyone's garments is also given an explanation: "They have washed their robes and made them white in the blood of the Lamb." This is what happens when at baptism one is plunged into the death of the Lord in order to be born to new life, cleansed of all defilement. Such purification enables one to participate in worship: "For this reason they stand before God's throne and worship him day and night in his temple." The Book of Revelation begins with this "benediction" of Christ (doxology), the first born of the dead: "To him who loves us and has freed us from our sins by his blood, who has made us into a kingdom, priests for his God and Father, to him be glory and power forever [and ever]" (Rev 1:5-6).[16] Thus, all of the people of God participate together in the priestly office.[17] All are called one day to enter into the sanctuary of God's presence.[18]

This vision also brings to our attention the significance of our own liturgy. It is said that it realizes the work of salvation continued by the

Church,[19] that it is "the summit toward which the activity of the Church is directed."[20] Careful thought concerning what the liturgy is in itself, what it implies, will verify these claims. But one must also consider the relationship between the terrestrial and the heavenly liturgies, which reflection occurs less frequently than the Second Vatican Council wished.

> In the earthly liturgy we take part in a foretaste of that heavenly liturgy which is celebrated in the Holy City of Jerusalem toward which we journey as pilgrims, where Christ is sitting at the right hand of God, Minister of the holies and of the true tabernacle. With all the warriors of the heavenly army we sing a hymn of glory to the Lord; venerating the memory of the saints, we hope for some part and fellowship with them; we eagerly await the Saviour, Our Lord Jesus Christ, until he our life shall appear and we too will appear with him in glory.[21]

Each liturgical celebration is circumscribed by time and space; it unfolds here and now.[22] However, it is not focused upon itself. It goes beyond, to the lives of Christians and the Church, even to the heavenly Jerusalem. The totality of liturgies forms a dynamic unity in Christian life and the Church, centered on the end of history, when all liturgy will be fulfilled. The people of God are a nomadic people, journeying toward the Promised Land. In the various stages of their exodus, they celebrate liturgies in tents that are constantly taken down and set up again. A day will come when there will be only one liturgy in the tent of God, where all will assemble, "from every nation, race, people and tongue."[23]

The elder ends with telling the seer that the Lamb will lead the elect "to springs of life-giving water." John knows well those sayings of Jesus that he placed in chapter 10 of his Gospel. We have heard them. Jesus is the shepherd because he has been the sacrificial lamb; he was handed over to the sacrifice in order to lead his own to God, to whose right hand he has been exalted by his resurrection. So there is nothing incomprehensible about calling him both shepherd and lamb in the same breath.[24]

The vision also ends with an evocation of the tension between what we have already—salvation—and its manifestation when "God will wipe away every tear from their eyes."

The Sheep of the Good Shepherd Will Never Perish
The finale of the discourse on the good shepherd returns succinctly to the bond that unites the sheep and their intimate union with the one who leads them. But it is not a mere repetition of what we already know. As a matter of fact, with the last sentence we reach a high point in Jesus' revelation of himself and his relation to the Father (John 10:27-30).[25]

Four verbs express the relationship between the shepherd and his sheep: they "hear" his voice and "follow" him; he "knows" them, he gives them "eternal life." "To hear" is to recognize the authority and importance of the speaker's words; it is to enter into communion with him, to put oneself under his guidance, to "follow" him, to attach oneself to him, to become his disciple. When the speaker is Jesus, the Word of God made flesh, all this has a specially strong, indeed unique, significance. For his part, Jesus alone can say that he "knows" his disciples and "gives life," as Peter exclaimed to him: "Master, to whom shall we go? You have the words of eternal life. We have come to believe and are convinced that you are the Holy One of God" (John 6:68-69).

To those who are thus attached to him, Jesus gives solemn assurance that "they shall never perish," that "no one shall snatch them out of his hand." He is no hired hand, but the Son. He received his mission from the Father and will lose none of those entrusted to his care.[26] Nothing happened to the disciples during Jesus' passion. At his arrest, Jesus took care that no harm would befall them: "If you are looking for me, let these men go" (John 18:8). This perfect security assured to the disciples comes not only from the solicitude and devotion of their shepherd: "The Father and I are one." Rather, Jesus can assure his own of complete protection because he enjoys the same power as God. Even so, the intentioned indeterminateness of this formula suggests a still deeper mystery of unity, that of the Word who was near God, who is God and is made flesh (John 1:1, 14).[27] In a very personal style, Jesus says what he elsewhere affirms in other words: "So that they may be one, as we are one" (John 17:22); "I am in the Father and the Father is in me" (John 10:38; 14:11).[28]

Neither "flesh and Blood" (Matt 16:17) nor knowledge nor even theology can give access to this mystery. Only the faith that joins itself to the Lord can dimly see what this saying truly means: "The Father and I are one."

> May the God of peace . . . who "chose David, his servant, and took him from the sheepfolds" (Ps 78:70), the smallest and youngest of Jesse's sons (1 Sam 17:14), . . . shepherd of shepherd and guide of guides, . . . be presented a splendid flock, without defect, worthy of the heavenly sheepfold, the dwelling-place of the blessed, in the splendor of the saints, so that we may all together, sheep and shepherd, sing his glory in his temple, in Christ Jesus, our Lord, to whom be glory forever and ever. Amen.[29]

The Risen Jesus—the Way and the Truth and the Life— the Cornerstone

New Ministries for New Situations

When it is small and homogenous, a community can get by with a loose organization, modeled on those that have been tried elsewhere. But when its membership grows, especially when they come from different viewpoints, e.g., culturally or linguistically, the old systems will no longer suffice: the community's new look demands that they be adapted, or that others be invented. Acts tells us that this is what happened quite early on in the Church at Jerusalem, with its growing number of disciples, including a large group of ones who spoke Greek (Acts 6:1-7).

These last, who came from outside Palestine, attended synagogues where the Bible was read in Greek.[1] Others, more numerous, attended synagogues where Scripture was read following the Aramean translation of the Targums.[2] The difference in language created communication problems between the two groups. Even more significant, perhaps, were the differences in culture and thought that undoubtedly fostered mutual mistrust between those who had always lived in that country and the others, the children of immigrants. Membership in separate synagogues made their coexistence easier. But when conversion to the new "Way" (Acts 9:2) brought the followers of the two traditions into one Christian community, problems quickly arose. They came to a head in the question of the daily distribution of alms. The Hellenists (Greek speakers) complained that their widows were given less.[3] The apostles did not dispute the ground of these recriminations. They saw that they could no longer spend their time dividing the common goods. That would lead them to "neglect the word of God to serve at table," which would not be right. They therefore called the disciples together and made the Hellenists a proposition: "Brothers, select from among you seven reputable men, filled with the Spirit and wisdom, whom we shall appoint to this task, whereas we shall devote ourselves to prayer and to the ministry of the word." Thus a question of a material order produced a new organization of the community. The solution was adopted unanimously. Seven Greek-speaking believers were thus presented to the apostles: Stephen, Philip, Prochorus, Nicanor, Timon, Parmenas and Nicholas of Antioch, "a convert to Judaism."

Nothing is said about the "Hebrew speakers." Those of them—undoubtedly seven in number as in the synagogal organization—charged with waiting on the tables of the whole community, retained their position. From that point on, though, they were only responsible for their own, while seven others took responsibility for those who spoke Greek. Yet there was no schism in the community. The apostles took charge, instituting seven members to "serve at table"; they, like the others, remained under the apostles' jurisdiction. One may wonder, though, of what exactly this "waiting," this "diaconate"[4] consisted? Was it limited to the joint administration of the common property and its equitable division between the two groups, distinguished by language? The ostensible origin of this "service" might lead one to think so. Note, however, that this new organization was instituted with a certain solemnity: the apostles "prayed and laid hands on them," a sign of investiture though not an ordination rite, at least as we commonly understand the term.

So one commonly speaks of the institution, by the apostles, of the first seven "deacons" or at least of the first seven "deacons" who spoke Greek. On the one hand, it does not seem that they entered an already existing "order." On the other hand, their own assignment from the apostles did not invalidate that of those who were previously charged with the daily distribution of alms for the poor. Nevertheless, on this occasion the apostles endowed the community with a new structure, a "service" adapted to the situation created by the growing number of those who spoke Greek. This "first" would be followed by others. Very quickly, the Seven—as they were called—came to assist the apostles in their preaching and became, without being confused with the elders of the community,[5] missionaries and evangelizers.[6] They imparted to their group, more outward-looking by language and culture than the Hebrews, a remarkable missionary zeal.[7] The occasion of their preaching outside the country was the persecution suffered by the Church at Jerusalem. The Greek speakers were the most affected by it, doubtlessly because of their understanding of the Jewish religion, and more generally their relation to God and the Mosaic Law, which distinguished them from the others.[8]

These were the circumstances (of a surprisingly materialistic turn) that led the apostles to institute a particular ''diaconate'' to forestall a breaking of the community. They responded to the needs—the ''demands''— expressed by the people; they submitted a concrete proposal to the whole community; those who spoke Greek chose the Seven, whom they presented to the apostles. The expansion of the mandate conferred on some members of the community occurred as time went by, and again as circumstances dictated. Clear distinctions between various orders were eventually established. ''It is dangerous to predict, especially the future,'' says a Chinese proverb. How much more is this true when the future is in the hands of the Holy Spirit, who guides the Church patiently, but not passively. So, for example, the Church's history has seen monks leave their monasteries to evangelize pagan countries, where they have founded new monasteries that in their turn have become centers of evangelization. Today, some lay men and women, without being ordained, are given a mandate by their bishop for various pastoral tasks, which not long ago were confined to priests. The immediate reason for this is the dwindling number of clergy. Even so, these innovations testify to the traditional initiative of the Spirit who is the force behind the Church's action and reflection, driving it constantly to be innovative in the service of the gospel.[9] ''We must devote ourselves joyously and fearlessly to the task demanded by our age, following the road which the Church has traveled for twenty centuries.''[10]

> Lord, let your mercy be on us,
> as we place our trust in you.
>
> Exult, you just, in the LORD;
>   praise from the upright is fitting.
> Give thanks to the LORD on the harp;
>   with the ten-stringed lyre chant his praises.
>
> For upright is the word of the LORD,
>   and all his works are trustworthy.
> He loves justice and right;
>   of the kindness of the LORD the earth is full.
>
> But see, the eyes of the LORD are upon those who fear him,
>   upon thsoe who hope for his kindness,
> To deliver them from death
>   and preserve them in spite of famine.
> (Ps 33:1-2, 4-5, 18-19)

Draw Near to the Lord Jesus, the Living Stone

In order to evoke Christ's passover and the Christian's participation in this mystery, the First Letter of Peter uses a somewhat unusual image: "Come to [Jesus Christ], a living stone, rejected by human beings but chosen and precious in the sight of God." After the initial surprise, this ancient apostolic catechesis proves to be of an unexpected doctrinal and spiritual richness (1 Pet 2:4-9).

The development of Christian dogma, theology, and reflection, which are echoed in catechesis, preaching, and especially liturgy, has increased the understanding and expression of the paschal mystery of Christ in which we share.[11] This integral development is an undoubted and invaluable progression: it has been beneficial for the Christian faith and life of every generation, down to us today.[12] Unfortunately, it may happen that a discourse on a truth of faith—on the paschal mystery—can wander on the paths of intellectual speculation or at least seem very abstract. Therefore, one must bridge the gap between the enunciation of doctrine and the life of believers. In an age when theological reflection was still in its infancy, the faith was expressed more concretely, with the help of images from biblical tradition, images that seem quite bold to us.[13] Such, for example, is the image of Christ as the "cornerstone" on whom the Church solidly rests, "a spiritual house" of which believers are "the living stones."

One psalm verse is embedded in Christian memory. It is quoted in the parable of the murderous vineyard workers[14]: "The stone which the builders rejected has become the cornerstone. By the Lord has this been done; it is wonderful in our eyes" (Ps 118:22-23). Jesus himself thus announced, very openly, that death, far from negating or ending his mission, would manifest the Father's love for his resurrected Son: he would become "a stone that has been tested, a precious cornerstone as a sure foundation," set by God (Isa 28:16). Nor have Christians forgotten Jesus' saying about the temple of his body which would be raised in three days (John 2:19-21). After Easter, all of Jesus' mysterious sayings become clear. Thus, when he was first brought before the Sanhedrin, Peter appealed to Psalm 118 to say that Jesus is the stone that was rejected, and had become the cornerstone (Acts 4:11).[15] Lastly, the New Testament—especially Revelation—speaks of the Church as a "spiritual house."[16]

Put into this familiar context, what is said in the First Letter of Peter becomes clear. We confess that Jesus is alive; he is the only one "under heaven given to the human race by which we are to be saved" (Acts 4:12);

we are, through him and with him, alive. On him is built the Church of the living God, and we are integral parts of the construction. Whoever is not firmly fixed, cemented into this edifice and to Christ "the cornerstone" cannot hold: such a person is a useless stone, and thus absolutely rejected. There is no shame or disappointment, no death for the one who believes in the Lord and obeys him. Even more, faith in Christ makes believers "a chosen race, a royal priesthood, a holy nation, a people he claims for his own." No longer is it a matter of a promise— "You shall be" (Exod 19:6)—but of its realization today: "You are."

The titles of "chosen race" and "a people God claims for his own" define the image of the "spiritual house": it has no material connotation. The "living stones" are people. This "nation," this "people" of which they are a part has been gathered by God. They owe their unity to him. They are "holy," that is, sanctified, because Christ is their head.

The appellation "holy priesthood," "royal priesthood" has sometimes been taken to mean that every baptized person is in fact a priest, in our common understanding of the term. Certainly, for some centuries, the Catholic Church has avoided insisting on the priestly character of all the baptized. Today, with certain controversies being toned down, the "common priesthood of the faithful" has once again taken its rightful place in the Church's doctrine. There is a real participation in the unique priesthood of Christ. This has important consequences for participation in the sacraments, particularly the Eucharist, for prayer, and for the duties of the laity in the apostolate. Distinct from that of ordained priests, the "common priesthood of the faithful" allows for a better understanding of the nature and function of the ministerial priesthood within the priestly people, as well as the indispensable complementarity of both.[17] Peter is clearly speaking of the proclamation of the gospel that falls to all. Actually, today perhaps more than ever, the spreading of the good news demands that all believers take on responsibility for it, according to individual vocations and charisms. It is just as great a mistake, for the very same reasons, to ignore the evangelizing ministry of the laity as of the priesthood.[18]

> "You are a chosen race, a royal priesthood." This praise was given long ago by Moses to the ancient people of God, and now the apostle Peter rightly gives it to the Gentiles, since they have come to believe in Christ who, as the cornerstone, has brought the nations together in the salvation that belonged to Israel.
>
> Peter calls them "a chosen race" because of their faith, to distinguish them from those who by refusing to accept the living stone have themselves been

rejected. They are "a royal priesthood" because they are united to the body of Christ, the supreme king and true priest. As sovereign he grants them his kingdom, and as high priest he washes away their sins by the offering of his blood. Peter says they are "a royal priesthood"; they must always remember to hope for an everlasting kingdom and to offer to God the sacrifice of a blameless life.[19]

"I am the way and the truth and the life"

All of Jesus' sayings—some more than others—reveal their full meaning when they are read during Eastertime.[20] This is especially the case with regard to the "Last Discourse," the beginning of which we read today (John 14:1-12).[21]

When "his hour had come to pass from this world to the Father," Jesus, knowing how his departure would trouble his disciples in all ages, left us this saying: "Do not let your hearts be troubled. You have faith in God; have faith also in me. In my Father's house there are many dwelling places; if there were not, would I have told you that I am going to prepare a place for you? And if I go and prepare a place for you, I will come back again and take you to myself, so that where I am you also may be. Where [I] am going, you know the way."

We have often heard and meditated on these words. But Thomas' objection never ceases to haunt us: "Master, we do not know where you are going; how can we know the way?" We know that Christ has been raised to the heavens, to the right hand of the Father; these ways of speaking express both our faith and our inability to designate more concretely this transcendent place where the Lord of glory dwells, where he prepares a place for us. Like Thomas, we want to know more about it and learn the way to it, which cannot be drawn on a map.

Jesus' response frees us from useless efforts and flights of imagination: "I am the way and the truth and the life. No one comes to the Father except through me." The way, the truth, and the life is a Person, Jesus himself! Our ways can disappear or become obsolete. Jesus the way is always accessible and leads infallibly to the end. In him, the humanity whose Head he is has traveled the road—the Passover—that goes from this earth to the eternal dwelling-places. This is why he is not only the guide but the way, as well as the truth and the life. Everything hangs together. Our question here receives an unexpected response: without pretending to explain away the mystery, it sheds a light on it that beyond all hope satisfies our spiritual intelligence and, one might say, reassures us. It is pointless to toil to find the secret road: it is revealed to us in the person of Jesus, who adds: "If you know me, then you will also know my Father." We might be content with such a promise that sharpens our desire to know the Father one day, But Jesus brings us back to the present: "From now on you do know him and have seen him."

What does this mean? Philip anticipates our question. No one has ever seen God (John 1:18; 6:46); so how can Jesus speak in this manner, which evokes a theophany, like that experienced by Moses?[22] Is the hour come when the psalmist's prayer will be answered: "Athirst is my soul for God, the living God. When shall I go and behold the face of God" (Ps 42:3)?

Again, Jesus brings us back to reality: "Whoever has seen me has seen the Father." To doubt this would be to misunderstand who Jesus is, his intimate union with the Father who, through and in the Son, speaks and fulfills his own works. These testify that the Son is in the Father and that the Father dwells in him. What the believers will do—the same works as Jesus—will also be a testimony. For they will perform these works—and even greater—because the Lord has returned to the Father.

> This, then, is the universal way of salvation, that is, granted to all nations by divine mercy, such that whatever men know it or come to know of it, none of them can or ought to say: "Why now?" "Why so late?" For the plan of he who procures it for us is not grasped by our intelligence . . . This, I say, is the universal way of salvation for all believers, in accord with what the faithful Abraham heard from the divine oracle: "In your descendants all the nations of the earth shall find blessing" (Gen 22:18) . . . This is the universal way of which a holy prophecy said: "May God have pity on us and bless us; may he let his face shine upon us. So may your way be known upon earth; among all nations, your salvation" (Ps 66:2-3) . . . This is the universal way which long before had been announced: "In days to come, the mountain of the Lord's house shall be established as the highest mountain and raised above the hills. All nations shall stream toward it; many peoples shall come and say: 'Come, let us climb the Lord's mountain, to the house of the God of Jacob, that he may instruct us in his ways, and we may walk in his paths.' For from Zion shall go forth instruction, and the word of the Lord from Jerusalem" (Isa 2:2-3). It is not the way of only one people but of all the nations: the law of the Lord and his word do not dwell in Zion and Jerusalem; they are spread throughout the universe . . . This is the universal way of the soul's deliverance![23]

The community of believers—the Church—is a reality both visible and invisible, human and divine, or, if one prefers, mystical. A simple definition will not serve, therefore, to express its whole reality adequately: such an attempt will rather almost fatally cause one of its dimensions to stand out, to the detriment of the others, though they are indissolubly bound together. Even though the Church appears analogous to some human groups, it is so crucially distinct from them that to make the comparison part of the Church's definition will unfailingly end up producing serious ambiguities.[24] As with many other realities of the same order, it is better to speak of the Church with the help of images, for "the inner nature of the Church is now made known to us in various images."[25] Taken from Scripture, the terms "building of God" and "holy temple" have the advantage of expressing very concretely the double dimension (visible and invisible, human and divine) of the Church founded on Christ, animated by his masterwork—the Holy Spirit, the role of its members, who both work to build this edifice and are themselves its "living stones" firmly bound one to another and to the cornerstone.

> Often, too, the Church is called the building of God (1 Cor 3:9). The Lord compared himself to the stone which the builders rejected, but which was made into the cornerstone (Matt 21:42; cf. Acts 4:11; 1 Pet 2:7; Ps 118:22). On this foundation the Church is built by the apostles (cf. 1 Cor 3:11) and from it the Church receives solidity and unity. This edifice has many names to describe it: the house of God in which his family dwells; the household of God in the Spirit (Eph 2:19, 22); the dwelling-place of God among men (Rev 21:3); and, especially, the holy temple. This temple, symbolized in places of worship built out of stone, is praised by the Fathers and, not without reason, is compared in the liturgy to the Holy City, the New Jerusalem. As living stones we here on earth are built into it (1 Pet 2:5). It is this holy city that is seen by John as it comes down out of heaven from God when the world is made anew, prepared like a bride adorned for her husband (Rev 21:1f).[26]

Jesus himself used images to reveal the mystery of his person, his passover and the mission that he will carry out till the end of time on our behalf. In him, the invisible God has taken human form. He is, for all people, from generation to generation, "the way and the truth and the life." In leaving this world to go to the Father near whom "there are many dwelling places," he has entrusted his followers with the responsibility of continuing the work whose foundations he has laid. The "house of God," his "people" will never cease to grow. Come from more and more diverse backgrounds, all must find their place in peace and joy. This concern led the apostolic Church to institute seven Greek speakers to serve the tables of their community. In its human structure, the Church always needs reforms. "Every renewal of the Church essentially consists in an increase of fidelity to her own calling. Undoubtedly this explains the dynamism of the movement toward unity. Christ summons the Church, as she goes her pilgrim way, to that continual reformation of which she always has need, insofar as she is an institution of men here on earth. Consequently, if in various times and circumstances there have been deficiencies in moral conduct or in Church discipline, or even in the way that Church teaching has been formulated—to be carefully distinguished from the deposit of faith itself—these should be set right at the opportune moment and in the proper way.''[27]

The Church must ''impart an ever-increasing vigor to the Christian life of the faithful; adapt more closely to the needs of our age those institutions which are subject to change; foster whatever can promote union among all who believe in Christ; strengthen whatever can help to call all mankind into the Church's fold.''[28]

Though enunciated with regard to the liturgy, this principle can be applied to all areas of ecclesial life. It involves submission, in faith, to the Holy Spirit who moves the Church to renew itself, to become young again, to be born again.[29] Thus is it wholly faithful to the tradition that forces it onward. ''I solemnly assure you, the man who has faith in me will do the works I do, and greater far than these. Why? Because I go to the Father.''

Live On in Me and Bear Fruit!

The Difficult Beginnings of the Convert Saul's Apostolate

Luke's account of the early days of the Church is punctuated by three short summaries that emphasize the Christian community's prodigious growth.[1] "The word of God continued to spread" occurs several times, like a refrain,[2] and Luke, the universalist, confirms with evident satisfaction that the new converts came from all ranks of society (Acts 5:14), even the priestly caste (Acts 6:7). But the most unexpected conversion was that of Saul, the fearful persecuter[3] who, under the name of Paul,[4] became the apostle to the nations; the Acts of the Apostles describes his missionary journeys and activities at length.[5] Before coming to this point, however, Luke, as he customarily does, interrupts the story to paint a quick picture wherein one sees how Paul was welcomed into the Christian community and began his apostolate. In this "summary," he recalls in particular the difficulties and persecutions encountered by Paul throughout his ministry, as well as the unwavering assurance of his preaching. This "snapshot" inspires one to read the detailed accounts of the apostle's missionary journeys.[6] But what Luke says here very briefly is worth pausing over, for it contains an important teaching (Acts 9:26-31).[7]

God's initiatives are disconcerting. When Paul tried to contact the community of disciples and join it, he ran into mistrust and suspicion. They could not believe that this man who was famous for his zeal, his rage, even his frenzy (Gal 1:13-14), who pursued and persecuted the community "even to foreign cities" (Acts 26:11) had undergone conversion. Far from welcoming him with open arms, they closed their doors to him, for "they were all afraid of him." This reaction is completely understandable. That it was mistaken in this case does not cast doubt on the legitimacy and even the necessity of testing new converts to be sure of the seriousness of their conversion and the purity of their intention when they demand entrance into the community.[8]

One disciple—Barnabas[9]—acted as Paul's guarantor and sponsor. He himself "was a good man, filled with the holy Spirit and faith" (Acts 11:24). He would present Paul to the apostles. Sent to Antioch by the Jerusalem Church, he would go to Tarsus to join Paul in his apostolate

(Acts 11:22-26).[10] Barnabas, therefore, was the one who introduced Paul to the apostolic ministry. This fact is worth remembering. It was not simply a matter of being acquainted with a newcomer called to exercise a certain responsibility. The intervention of the Spirit (who always intervenes in a calling) does not bypass human mediation, rendering it obsolete. It is pointless to speculate on what Paul would have done if he had continued to move about "freely" in Jerusalem and express himself "boldly in the name of Jesus." In reality, Paul was, so to speak, flung into the apostolate at Barnabas' call. Both were "sent forth by the holy Spirit," but given their charge by the "prophets and teachers" at Antioch who laid their hands on them (Acts 13:1-4). When their preaching at Antioch aroused a controversy, Paul and Barnabas went to Jerusalem to give an account of their conduct and put the question "to the apostles and presbyters" (Acts 15.1-35). Such submission to the Church is an essential criterion of discernment: the Spirit never allows anyone to be free from the constraints imposed by those in authority.[11]

Luke does not forget to mention, even in this brief account, the violent hostility with which Paul met from the Greek-speaking Jews, those who shared his own background and whose cause he had but lately espoused.[12] Such is often the case; indeed, Jesus warned his disciples of it. Luke, like the other evangelists, reports Jesus as saying: "From now on a household of five will be divided, three against two and two against three" (Luke 12:52); "If anyone comes to me without hating his father and mother, wife and children, brothers and sisters, and even his own life, he cannot be my disciple" (Luke 14:26). Choosing the service of Christ is never without such ruptures, even if they are not always so dramatic. At the very least, one must agree to certain renunciations.

Did Paul's forced departure quiet things down? In any case, "the Church throughout all Judea, Galilee, and Samaria was at peace. It was being built up and walked in the fear of the Lord, and with the consolation of the holy Spirit [it grew in numbers]."

At the end of such readings, we always feel a thanksgiving rising in our hearts, a thanksgiving for what the Lord has done and continues to do among us, in his Church.

In the midst of the assembly I will praise you.

. . . I will fulfill my vows before those who fear him.
The lowly shall eat their fill;
   they who seek the LORD shall praise him:
"May your hearts be ever merry!"

All the ends of the earth
  shall remember and turn to the Lord;
All the families of the nations
  shall bow down before him.

To him alone shall bow down
  all who sleep in the earth;
Before him shall bend
  all who go down into the dust.
And to him my soul shall live;
  my descendants shall serve him.
Let the coming generation be told of the LORD
  that they may proclaim to a people yet to be born
  the justice he has shown.
(Ps 22:26b-27, 28, 30, 31-32)

God's Life in Us, Our Life in God

The diversity of charisms, personal vocations, and life situations in the Church produces an array of spiritualities that are so many ways of seeking God in the light of the gospel. Some of these paths cross each other, run parallel, or even join up for a certain distance. This does not mean that they cannot be distinguished;[13] but even so, all of them are roads to faith, following Christ, with the goal of living in communion with God (1 John 3:18-24).

There is one sure means of verifying that one is on a right path: unconditional and boundless fraternal charity. John, more than anyone else, insists on this point: "[Jesus] laid down his life for us; so we ought to lay down our lives for our brothers" (1 John 3:16). This demand might appear unrealistic or limited to those who are actually willing to die for others. Nothing of the sort. "Children, let us love not in word or speech but in deed and truth." This is God's commandment, the one from which all others flow, of which all others are interpretations. It has an unlimited field of application; at any moment, in any situation, it determines what must or must not be done; it admits no exceptions or excuses; it is the standard by which everything is judged, especially the reality of communion with God.

To agonize over the rumblings of one's conscience serves no purpose other than to torment one with sterile remorse. True regret for transgressions does not focus on oneself but turns toward God who, as he pardons us, gives us the true humility we need to move on. "Lord, you know everything; you know that I love you" (John 21:17). Yes, he knows everything. He is much more merciful than we are toward ourselves. He loves us more than we love ourselves. He knows that with his grace we are capable of infinitely more than we had dared dream.

> "If our conscience charges us," that is to say, if it accuses us inwardly, because we have not acted with the intention we should have had, "God is greater than our hearts and all is known to him." You hide the depths of your heart from men; hide it from God, if you can! How could you hide from him, the one to whom a sinner with a fearful or repentant heart once said: "Where can I go from your spirit? from your presence where can I flee?" He wanted to know where he could go to escape God's judgment, and he couldn't find out. Where is God not present? "If I go up to the heavens, you are there; if I sink to the nether world, you are present there." Where to go? where to flee?
>   Flee toward him while confessing, not while trying to hide; you cannot hide from him, but you can confess your faults to him. Say to him: "You are my refuge"; and nourish in yourself the love that alone leads to life.[14]

Fidelity to the commandments is the concrete criterion which verifies that one belongs to the truth and may have a peaceful heart before God, since one dwells in him. There is more: God himself dwells in us by the Spirit whom he has given us. We live in God because God lives in us! The good that we do does not come from ourselves but from the Spirit who is present and active in us. It verifies that we truly are children of God. Thus, since we do not know how to pray as we ought, "the Spirit too comes to the aid of our weakness," and "intercedes with inexpressible groanings" (Rom 8:26). This is why "whatever you ask in my name, I will do," as Jesus promised us.[15] Also, we are able to love as God who is Love (1 John 4:8, 16) because his love has been poured out into our hearts (Rom 5.5).

> If, then, you want to know whether you have received the Spirit, question your heart: ask yourself if you would not have the sacrament without the virtues of the sacrament. Ask your heart: if you find love for your brother there, be at peace. Love would not be found there if the Holy Spirit were not present, for Paul tells us: "The love of God has been poured out in our hearts through the Holy Spirit who has been given to us."[16]

The Vine, the Vinegrower, and the Branches

"Remain in me" is one of the key phrases of John's vocabulary.[17] In its strongest sense, it expresses the bond that unites the Father and the Son,[18] the Son and the Spirit.[19] The same verb refers to the relation instituted between God and the one who keeps the faith and the commandments,[20] between Jesus and his disciples.[21] One of the passages that expresses it most strongly and suggestively is the one we read today (John 15:1-8).

"I am the true vine and my Father is the vinegrower." This form of speech is that used in the great revelations: "I am the bread of life" (John 6:35), "the living bread" (John 6:51); "I am the gate" (John 10:9); "I am the good shepherd" (John 10:14); "I am the way and the truth and the life" (John 14:6).

The Old Testament speaks readily of the chosen people as the vine planted by God. The object of his love and care, it should produce the fruits of justice and holiness. Unfortunately, it has often disappointed God. He has had to intervene to save the healthy shoots from corruption and use them to rebuild his domain. For he so loves his vine that the prospect of having to destroy it fills him with deep sadness, as revealed in this piteous elegy, inspired by God's tenderness.

> Let me now sing of my friend,
>   my friend's song concerning his vineyard.
> My friend had a vineyard
>   on a fertile hillside;
> He spaded it, cleared it of stones,
>   and planted the choicest vines;
> Within it he built a watchtower,
>   and hewed out a wine press.
> Then he looked for the crop of grapes,
>   but what it yielded was wild grapes.
>
> Now, inhabitants of Jerusalem and men of Judah,
>   judge between me and my vineyard:
> What more was there to do for my vineyard
>   that I had not done?
> Why, when I looked for the crop of grapes,
>   did it bring forth wild grapes?
> Now, I will let you know
>   what I mean to do to my vineyard:
> Take away its hedge, give it to grazing,
>   break through its wall, let it be trampled!
> Yes, I will make it a ruin:
>   it shall not be pruned or hoed,
>   but overgrown with thorns and briers;
> I will command the clouds
>   not to send rain upon it.
> The vineyard of the LORD of hosts is the house of Israel,
>   and the men of Judah are his cherished plant;
> He looked for judgment, but see, bloodshed!
>   for justice, but hark, the outcry!
> (Isa 5:1-7)[22]

Matthew's Gospel contains three parables in which Jesus uses this traditional image of the vine to denote the kingdom of God.[23] At the hour of the final revelation, given to his disciples when he was about to pass from this world to his Father, he identified himself—"I am"—as the "true vine."[24] This is a suggestive image. Normally one speaks of a good vinestock or quality shoots. Jesus, rather, is the "true" vine, who absolutely cannot deceive. He possesses a unique quality, transcendent, like no one before or since; it is impossible to conceive of a substitute for him. If therefore there are found some dry branches that bear no fruit, they must be cut off. They are good for nothing if not for the fire. Clearly, Jesus knew what vineyard workers do. "Look at what they do," he says to us. "My Father, the vinegrower, does the same in the vineyard he has planted, which he cultivates with care."[25]

The vineyard owner prunes the good branches so that they will produce more fruit. Dead wood is cut down, gathered, and laid aside to be burned. Likewise those branches that for one reason or another are more or less separated from the stock: there is no chance that they will revive and be laden with grapes. On the other hand, those branches firmly attached to the stock will bear blossoms and fruit in season. A sick vine in any season presents a spectacle of desolation and death, whereas barren branches of a healthy, well-pruned vine offer hope of a good harvest.

"Remain in me as I remain in you." The image gives way to the reality. It is the word of the Lord that trims the vine. It is the welcome reception of Jesus' words that testifies to and guarantees the disciple's fidelity. This fidelity must be constant, for it is a perpetual source of judgment (John 12:31).

> On the part of those who come to the vine, their union with him depends upon a deliberate act of the will; on his part, the union is effected by grace. Because we had good will, we made the act of faith that brought us to Christ, and received from him the dignity of adoptive sonship that made us his own kinsmen, according to the words of Saint Paul: "He who is joined to the Lord is one spirit with him."
>
> From Christ and in Christ, we have been reborn through the Spirit in order to bear the fruit of life; not the fruit of our old, sinful life but the fruit of a new life founded upon our faith in him and our love for him. Like branches growing from a vine, we now draw our life from Christ, and we cling to his holy commandment in order to preserve this life.[26]

The vineyard owner is proud of his vines that bear much fruit. Likewise, the fruitfulness of the Christian life united to Christ gives glory and witness to God; it preaches by action. Jesus was not content with teaching in words. He performed many "signs" that revealed him to all as God's messenger, validated his teaching, and gave glory to his Father.[27] Individual Christians and the Church must bear themselves this same way so that the world may believe and God may be glorified. Without works, faith is dead; the mere profession of it is worthless (Jas 2:14). Instead of leading to God, it points away from him. A good tree is known by its fruits.[28] The Father cannot allow withered branches to cast doubt on the quality of the vine, i.e., the holiness of his Son and the gospel. He "trims" us constantly so that we may bear more fruit while renewing our faithfulness day after day. He strengthens us at the tables of the Word and the Bread, sharing the cup of the fruit of the vine, "wine of eternal salvation."[29]

> The Father's vine
> has borne its fruit,
> a fruit of glory and life.
> Through all the earth
> it spreads its branches,
> branches devoted
> to the Father's praise.
>
> Lord Jesus,
> in you we live!
> As the Father has loved me,
> so I have loved you.
>
> You have received my Word,
> already are you purified.
>
> All that you ask in my name,
> believe that you will receive.[30]

"When the hour had come for him to pass from this world to the Father," Jesus spoke at length with his disciples, gathered with him to celebrate the Last Supper that he had "eagerly desired" (Luke 22:15) to eat with them. This farewell discourse looks to the future, not the past. Jesus does not tell them what he has been or has done for them: he reveals what he is and what he will evermore do for them; he unveils the secret of life that his resurrection opens to them. First they must know that by their faith they are intimately bound to him like branches to the vinestock and that they will thus bear the fruits of eternal life for the glory of the Father.[31]

When believers thus remain in Christ, when his life runs thus in the members of the Church, their share in the truth is made clear. They are "signs" of God and his Christ in the world. Their hearts swell, they welcome joyfully and unhesitatingly all those who are in their turn grafted onto the Father's vine, no matter from where they come, even if they were recently persecutors of the Church.

> In these Easter days,
> Lord God,
> your vine receives new sap.
> Hold the branches to the vine:
> thus will charity make us live
> one for another
> in the one who died and rose for us,
> Jesus, the Christ, our Lord.[32]

"A Little While . . .
Now . . . Soon"

Universal Ministry and Local Churches

The Acts of the Apostles can be read from various points of view, like every writing of its genre. For example, one can follow Paul on his missionary journeys,[1] stopping with him in the various cities he passes. Or, one could be more interested in the apostle himself: his preaching, his way of proclaiming the gospel.[2] From these and other readings, one can draw certain lessons that are applicable to the Church's and various Christian communities' present situation. The brief account of Paul and Barnabas' return to Antioch of Syria at the end of their first journey is particularly interesting: it shows how the apostle organized local Churches and kept watch over them (Acts 14:21b-27).[3]

"In each Church," Paul and Barnabas appointed "presbyters"; this was the form of organization used by Jewish communities of the Diaspora.[4] Since it had been tested, the two missionaries readily adopted it.[5] It was they, not the community, who chose people to hold authority in the local Churches, men who had "put their faith" in the Lord, i.e., who had persevered in faith. It was also they who established these men in their ministry. This institution was accompanied by prayers and fasts, according to the Church's custom whenever an important decision needed to be made for the future of the faith or the Church's mission.[6] But the way in which Luke speaks of the institution of the presbyters evokes an ordination. "It would hardly conform to the spirit of the New Testament to speak of a 'consecration' of those who were especially entrusted to the Lord in the exercise of the responsibility that would fall to them. But one should not hesitate to speak of it as an 'ordination' that gives the presbyters an 'order,' a special place, in the community over which they must watch, like shepherds over their sheep."[7] Each local Church was thus granted its own organization.

Even so, the apostles did not abandon them to themselves, but continued to care for them. So Paul and Barnabas returned to these communities. "They strengthened the spirits of the disciples and exhorted them to persevere in the faith," especially when they were faced with trials.[8] As Jesus had commanded Peter, Paul never worked only for the awakening of faith; he was also concerned with "strengthening his brothers" (Luke 22:32). He did this both by sending his disciples[9] and by writing to the Churches.[10] Such ongoing solicitude for the communities he had founded was his destiny (1 Thess 3:3), the ministry he had to continue to exercise. Notice the double ministry: the apostles gave the Churches they had founded their own caretakers; at the same time, and without usurpation, the apostles kept watch over these foundations, visiting them, sending them letters, and even imposing their authority when necessary.[11] In time, this double ministry became more clearly structured. The bishop of Rome would preside in charity over all the Churches: very early on he was given universal authority, which nonetheless did not suppress the authority of the local bishops. Intermediate jurisdictions were established, nearly always in conjunction with the extension of evangelization to the far-flung reaches of the world. Some, in the West, are present only in historical record.[12] Others, in the East, are still in place.[13] And recently, new forms of ministry over the local Churches have been established.[14]

We cannot presume to know what the future holds, for under the guidance of the Spirit, the Church will never cease to adapt itself and create new forms to respond to circumstances of time, place, language, and culture, becoming more and more catholic and universal.[15] "Let us give thanks for all that the Spirit has already begun to bring about in our Church. Our response to present-day challenges must be profound and radical. This is an urgent task. No one can stand to one side and indulge in skepticism: the first communities were not born in that way."[16]

> *I will bless your name forever and ever.*
>
> The LORD is gracious and merciful,
>   slow to anger and of great kindness.
> The LORD is good to all
>   and compassionate toward all his works.
>
> Let all your works give you thanks, O LORD,
>   and let your faithful ones bless you.
> Let them discourse of the glory of your kingdom
>   and speak of your might.
> Making known to men your might
>   and the glorious splendor of your kingdom.

Your kingdom is a kingdom for all ages,
  and your dominion endures through all generations.
(Ps 145:8-9, 10-11, 12-13ab)

New Heaven, New Earth

The Gospel and Revelation of John are among the last writings of the New Testament.[17] The Gospel was written at a time when and in a place where the growth of new ideas and doctrines, and their conflict, endangered one's ability to have a proper conception of the mystery of Jesus; at least, they were troublesome for the Christians.[18] This context stimulated the profound theological reflection that characterizes the fourth evangelist. The Book of Revelation, on the other hand, is the fruit of the author's lengthy meditation, his spiritual and mystical experience. At the end of the book, he shares with his readers the vision of "the holy city, a new Jerusalem," that he had been allowed to contemplate. Today we read the beginning of this final revelation (Rev 21:1-5a).[19]

"Then I saw a new heaven and a new earth. The former heaven and the former earth had passed away, and the sea was no more." The appearance, the dawning of a fresh, new world is at the core of all the hope expressed in the cries of suffering and embattled people, in the songs of poets and lovers, in the prayers of believers and mystics. This hope runs throughout the Bible, especially arising from the agonizing experience of the Exile. It upheld and inspired the strength of the exiles, and was endlessly renewed by the exhortations of the prophets, whose eyes could see through the darkness.[20] But whatever the clairvoyance and the boldness of their pictures, the prophets imagined the future while looking to the past, albeit an idealized one. Their prayers appealed to and proclaimed, at best, a more beautiful restoration, wondrously more beautiful and perfect than the best previous realizations, even of the first creation.

In Revelation, John goes a good deal further. He "sees" a universe, a world, that is completely new. "The former heaven and the former earth," which won the admiration of the author of Genesis (1:31), have disappeared. With them has disappeared the battleground where good and evil and light and darkness fought each other, where the ancient serpent tried to destroy humanity. Likewise, "the sea was no more," the formidable abyss, symbol of all dangers (Ps 69:3), replete with evil power (Rev 13:1; 17:1), whose depth evokes the depth of hell (Jonah 2:6-7).[21] During the Exodus, it was opened to let the people pursued by Pharaoh's army, pass through (Exod 14:21-29). Now, the whole universe opens for "the holy city, a new Jerusalem," the dwelling place of God and those who shall be "his people." "There shall be no more death or mourning, wailing or pain": death itself has disappeared with "the old order." This city is not made by human hands: it descends from heaven, "as a bride adorned for her husband." "The one who sat on the throne said: 'Behold, I make all things new.'"

A great and exalted vision that peremptorily contradicts the words of the despondent sage: "What has been, that will be: what has been done, that will be done. Nothing is new under the sun. Even the thing of which we say, 'See, this is new!' has already existed in the ages that preceded us" (Eccl 1:9-10). Qoheleth is right in so far as he considers only what corresponds to his experience. John the mystic has "seen" beyond. It is not of only one thing, but everything that he can say: "See, this is new!"

Such is God. He created the heavens and the earth, the whole world of creatures "good, very good."[22] This creation manifests his wisdom, power, and love.[23] All creatures, in the heavens, on the earth, and in the sea, proclaim his glory: "He established them forever and ever; he gave them a duty which shall not pass away" (Ps 148:6); "Bless the Lord, all you works of the Lord, praise and exalt him above all forever" (Dan 3:57).[24] The creator did not err in this work. Whatever disorder human sin brought into it, even if our foolishness made it unlivable, God's plan would not be changed. For one man has ransomed all and will lead creation to its goal, whatever may happen. Moreover, Jesus, who shared in our human condition even unto death, draws us toward "the holy city, a new Jerusalem," which is "prepared" near God, and in which the resurrected will be enthroned. John's vision proclaims this faith and hope; however, at the same time, it reaffirms the value of the "former heaven and the former earth" where we still live. It reminds us of what is at stake in our present life and the grace that subsists in this world, which will pass away in order to bring to birth "a new heaven and a new earth."

> Whoever will passionately love Jesus, hidden in the forces that make the earth grow, him the earth will lift up, like a mother, in her huge arms, and allow him to contemplate the face of God . . .
> Whoever will have passionately loved Jesus hidden in the forces that make the earth die, him the earth will clasp, while she weakens, in her huge arms, and with her, he will reawaken in the bosom of God.[25]

"As I have loved you, so you also should love one another"

Unlike most people, Jesus was not caught off guard by his death: it was constantly before his eyes, and he freely gave himself up to it when the "hour" had come. He was in control of himself till the very moment when he handed over his spirit. This is why, before his death, he wanted to gather his disciples for one last supper when, in leisurely fashion, he could speak to them heart to heart. Today we read the beginning of this testament (John 13:31-33a, 34-35).[26]

"Now is the Son of Man glorified, and God is glorified in him. [If God is glorified in him,] God will also glorify him in himself, and he will glorify him at once." The style of this initial declaration is reminiscent of a liturgical proclamation. At least, it expresses the Church's faith very well. It also fits with the other sayings of Jesus reported in John's Gospel, where the Lord's passion is always bound up with his glory. Although deeply troubled by the prospect of his death, Jesus wanted freely to say: "Yet what should I say—Father, save me from this hour? But it was for this purpose that I came to this hour. Father glorify your name." This prayer was immediately granted: "Then a voice came from heaven: 'I have glorified it and will glorify it again'" (John 12:27-28). When Jesus speaks "now," during the Last Supper, the passion had begun, for Judas had left to "do quickly" what he had decided (John 13:27). "The hour has come for the Son of Man to be glorified" (John 12:23).

Only faith can perceive this mystery. The cross remains a frightful scandal, or at least an obstacle, if Jesus is not recognized as the Son of God who was near him "in the beginning," through whom "all things came to be," who once "made his dwelling among us," "and we saw his glory: the glory as of the Father's only Son, full of grace and truth" (John 1:1-14). Jesus' glory was veiled during his earthly life, but not totally obscured. Following John, we learn to see in the "signs" that Jesus performed some manifestation of his glory.[27] After all the others, his resurrection is the "sign" that manifests the glory he had in the Father's presence "before the foundation of the world" (John 17:5, 24), to which he has been exalted forevermore. Our Eucharistic celebrations perpetuate, till he returns, what Jesus did in the course of the last supper he took with his disciples.

Next he says: "My children, I will be with you only a little while longer." There is nothing strange about this, given the circumstances. On the contrary, a formula like this is altogether customary for addressing one's own for the last time. However, the attentive reader of John's Gospel will remember that at the various times when Jesus mentioned his departure, he said: "Where I go you cannot come."[28] To follow him into his Father's house, his disciples must wait for the day when he will come to seek them out: then they will be wholly reunited with him (John

14:2-3). Jesus, though, will not leave them orphaned: the Spirit will bring them peace and the assurance that he is alive (John 14:15-31). What he says "now" thus deals with the intermediate time, the time in which we live.

"I give you a new commandment: love one another. As I have loved you, so you also should love one another." One might legitimately wonder how this "new" commandment differs from the prescription of love for neighbor that is found in the Law (Lev 19:18). Today we might further object that love of neighbor is not a Christian innovation: other great religions, particularly the oriental ones, also have it as a fundamental principle. We ought neither to dispute these facts nor deprecate the ideal and practice of the Old Testament or other religious traditions in an attempt to prove the novelty of Christian charity.[29] Rather, we must listen to what Jesus says and try to understand it: "As I have loved you . . ."

Jesus' love for us is the incomparable standard for the love we must bear for others, even at the cost of one's own life if necessary, excepting no one for any reason. Jesus puts it in eminently clear terms: "But to you who hear I say, love your enemies, do good to those who hate you; bless those who curse you, pray for those who mistreat you . . . and lend expecting nothing back" (Luke 6:27-38).[30] To love "as" Jesus, who died for the salvation of all humanity, is therefore to love unconditionally, with no restrictions. But this is not all.

Jesus' love for all people is rooted in the love that binds him to the Father and reveals the Father's love for us. Universal Christian charity thus has an essentially vertical or, more precisely, mystical dimension. It is participation in what one might call the "morals of God"; it alone will be the law of the new world, the new Jerusalem. It accompanies faith: without love, nothing is valuable (1 Cor 13:1-13). To love "as" Jesus is to be "perfect, just as your heavenly Father is perfect" (Matt 5:48), to express, like Jesus, in our own way, God's holiness.

"This is how all will know that you are my disciples, if you have love for one another." This is the "sign" of the Christian in the world, the irrefutable, immediately verifiable, proof of Christian identity. For this love appears in a way of life, not only a series of actions, however admirable or even heroic they may be.[31] To walk faithfully in this way is constantly to be a certain way, blossoming from day to day in the peace and joy that nothing can harm; it is to bear fruit for time and eternity.[32] Happy the disciples of Christ whose charitable life, "as" Jesus', gladdens the heart of God and humanity!

You fought day and night for the whole fraternity so that in love and harmony the number of his elect might be saved. To all you were open; you
bore no grudge. All strife and division were abhorrent to you. You wept
for your neighbor's sins and thought of his failings as your own. You never
regretted doing what was good; rather, you were "open to every good enterprise" (Titus 3:1). Your excellent and admirable conduct was your rai-
ment, and it was in the fear of the Lord that you did everything. The Lord's
commandments and precepts were written boldly in your hearts.[33]

"A little while . . . now . . . soon": these words must always be retained if we are to have a proper understanding and experience of the
mystery of Christ, the faith, the Church, and the liturgy.

Jesus dwelt "a little while" on this earth. Resurrected, "now" he is
near God who has glorified him by raising him from the dead. He will
come again "soon," radiant with "the glory as of the Father's only Son,
full of grace and truth" (John 1:14).

Through faith, we possess "now" what we hope for, we know unseen
realities that shall "soon" be unveiled (Heb 11:1). This tension between
"already" and "not yet" is the dynamic of Christian life. It is completely
oriented toward the encounter with the one who has come, is coming
now, and will come.

The time between the two manifestations of the Lord is that of the
Church and its mission, the witness of "religious truth" (Titus 1:1), whose
expression and criterion is the love that unites the disciples. It is the
"sign" that Christians must present to all people of their newness of life,
of the resurrected who "now" acts in them through his Spirit.

Finally, in the liturgy, most perfectly in the Eucharist, the mystery in
which we "now" share is recapitulated. The assembly is the image, the
"sacrament," of the gathering in "the city of God," "the new Jerusalem
prepared" in heaven. The Lord himself becomes present to his own under
the "signs" of bread and wine. He feeds them with his flesh and blood.
The communion that binds them to the risen Lord is the sacrament of
charity and the Church's unity. When the celebration is over, each believer, renewed by participation in the liturgy, is sent to bring the good
news of salvation and to witness to it in the life the Lord has given.

God our Father,
we are sustained by your sacraments;
we are renewed by this pledge of love at
your altar.
May we live by the promises of your love
which we receive,

and become a leaven in the world
to bring salvation to mankind.[34]

YEAR A / SIXTH SUNDAY OF EASTER

The Spirit—Presence
of the Lord

Evangelization, Baptism, Gift of the Holy Spirit

Sometimes, events that are undoubtedly painful or tragic for groups, societies, even nations, can have happy results. Thus it was at the beginning of the Church. The persecution that followed Stephen's martyrdom forced the Greek-speaking disciples to flee Jerusalem.[1] One of them was Philip, a member of the Seven, the group that the apostles had instituted to serve the Greek-speaking community.[2] He went to a village in Samaria: there, his preaching of Christ, accompanied by many signs, found great success[3]: "There was great joy in that city"[4] (Acts 8:5-8, 14-17).

The news came to Jerusalem, where the apostles who had avoided the persecutions had stayed. We are particularly interested in their response.[5] They decided to send Peter and John themselves, who were regarded as "pillars" of the Church (Gal 2:9).[6] This was not to check up on what Philip, on whom they had "laid hands" at the institution of the Seven (Acts 6:6), had done, but rather to give the Holy Spirit to these new converts, who had as yet only received baptism.[7] Jesus had said to the apostles: "You will be baptized with the holy Spirit"; "You will receive power when the holy Spirit comes upon you, and you will be my witnesses in Jerusalem, throughout Judea and Samaria, and to the ends of the earth" (Acts 1:5, 8). When he appeared "on the evening of the first day of the week," the resurrected "breathed on them and said: 'Receive the holy Spirit' " (John 20:22). Then came the day of Pentecost, when they were "all filled with the holy Spirit" (Acts 2:4).

On that occasion, Peter proclaimed to the multitudes: "Repent and be baptized, every one of you, in the name of Jesus Christ for the forgiveness of your sins; and you will receive the gift of the holy Spirit" (Acts 2:38). He added: "For the promise is made to you and to your children and to all those far off, whomever the Lord our God will call" (Acts 2:39).

The Samaritans evangelized by Philip were the first of these. Since then, believers "from every nation, race, people, and tongue" (Rev 7:9), have received baptism and, with the prayer of the apostles (or their successors) and the laying on of hands, the "seal of the holy Spirit."[8]

Let all the earth cry out to God with joy.

Shout joyfully to God, all you on earth,
    sing praise to the glory of his name;
    proclaim his glorious praise.
    Say to God, "How tremendous are your deeds!"

Let all on earth worship and sing praise to you,
    sing praise to your name!

Come and see the works of God,
    his tremendous deeds among men.
He has changed the sea into dry land;
    through the river they passed on foot;
    therefore let us rejoice in him.
He rules by his might forever . . .

Hear now, all you who fear God, while I declare
    what he has done for me . . .
Blessed be God who refused me not
    my prayer or his kindness!
(Ps 66:1-3a, 4-5, 6-7a, 16, 20)

Witness to Your Hope with Gentleness and Reverence

Christians today often find themselves in a situation similar to that of the first recipients of the First Letter of Peter: being scattered in the midst of a population that does not share their faith and hope.[9] Such is the case, for example, in countries where most of the population is baptized, even though only a small number of them truly belong to a Church community.[10] Therefore, the short apostolic catechism we read today is still important for us (1 Pet 3:15-18):"Sanctify Christ as Lord in your hearts."

Peter, taking a line from Isaiah (8:13),[11] speaks of the Lord as the biblical tradition spoke of God. To recognize, in the full conviction of faith— "in one's heart"—that Christ alone is holy, is to regard him as the only source of confidence, besides whom "there is no salvation" (Acts 4:12). To fear nothing and no one is to give him glory, to recognize him as the only holy one. Likewise, to fear anyone is to doubt, in one's heart, the holiness of the Lord, to despoil him of something that belongs to him alone.[12] Thus, we who believe in the Lord's holiness are always ready to give an account before all who ask of the hope that is ours.

Even ordinary, daily life presents occasions for this. Faith and the gospel—the recognition of Christ as the only holy one—involves behaviors, choices, postures, and renunciations that often separate Christians from their milieu. Sometimes a great deal of courage is needed to hold firm, to keep from being drawn into conflicting currents, succumbing to solicitations, to the commands of a more or less pagan world. Fidelity to Christ, the gospel, and fundamental Christian values occasionally requires costly, even heroic, sacrifices, and more often than one might think. Each of us knows that we must often forego human respect to act in conformity with the faith and to give an account of it.

In any case, it is with "gentleness and reverence," without aggressiveness or pride, that Christians must witness to their belonging to Christ, explaining their behavior, affirming their need to act as they do, refusing to submit to demands that are incompatible with their faith. History provides us with many examples of martyrs who remained respectful to their persecutors.[13]

> When the proconsul insisted: "Swear by Caesar's fortune," Polycarp responded: "If you think I am going to swear by Caesar's fortune, as you say, and pretend not to know what I am, listen, for I tell you frankly: I am a Christian. If you want to learn the Christian teaching from me, appoint a day on which you will hear me." The proconsul replied: "Persuade the people." Polycarp said: "I will gladly discuss with you; for we have been taught to give to the authorities and rulers established by God their proper respect, if it does no harm to us. But the people I do not regard as worthy to hear my defense."[14]

Such assured bearing indicates "a clean conscience," that is, an untroubled conscience and, at the same time, a conduct that will present no grounds for reproach. Hopefully, one will only suffer for having done good. To be faithful amid persecutions is to give homage to God and to his holiness by following Christ's footsteps (1 Pet 2:20, 21). "But rejoice to the extent that you share in the sufferings of Christ," writes Peter. "When his glory is revealed you may also rejoice exultantly. If you are insulted for the name of Christ, blessed are you, for the Spirit of glory and of God rests upon you" (1 Pet 4:13-14).

"For Christ also suffered for sins once, the righteous for the sake of the unrighteous, that he might lead you to God. Put to death in the flesh, he was brought to life in the Spirit." This conclusion to our reading, which may be a fragment of catechesis or a baptismal hymn, shows that the apostle's exhortations are situated in the perspective of life in Christ. Authentic Christian morality flows from paschal faith. It has no other basis than the mysterious spiritual solidarity between Christ, dead and resurrected, and those who, by their baptism, have been joined to his passover.

United to the Father, Through the Son, in the Spirit

The last conversation between Jesus and his disciples, such as John reports it, does not follow the strictly logical structure of a planned discourse. It is composed of units of varying length, variously joined to each other. We read one of these today, outlined by two parallel declarations that Jesus made to his disciples: "If you love me, you will keep my commandments . . . Whoever has my commandments and observes them is the one who loves me" (John 14:15-21).

Fidelity to the Lord's commands flows from and expresses the love one has for him. As Jesus himself says, it is the decisive criterion—perhaps even the only reliable one—that designates those who truly love him. To inscribe it deeply in the disciples' memory and heart, Jesus repeats it six times, like a refrain.[15] But what "commands" is he talking about?

During the course of his preaching, Jesus often did say: "Do this," "Act thus," "Do not do this," and "Do not behave in this manner." But a compilation of all such sayings cannot provide a list of prescriptions that are sufficient for one to know one's obligations. Such a reading of the Gospels would be not only be reductive: it would indicate a misunderstanding of both spirit and letter. Rather, the Gospels proclaim that Jesus himself is his disciples' rule of life, "the way and the truth and the life" (John 14:6). In his company, we may be sure of discovering our true good. He knows this: he can and wants to lead us to it because he loves us: he has given his life for us (John 15:13). What other bond can we have with him than that of love, the strongest and most intimate bond on earth and in heaven? And how then could we fail to keep his commands? They are the footsteps his passage has left on the earth, given so that his friends may come with him to the Father who waits at the end of the road.

Not that the Lord leaves us alone in the night of our exodus. He has asked the Father to give us "another Advocate to be with [us] always, the Spirit of truth . . ." Invisible to human eyes, but perceptible with the eyes of faith, the Advocate allows the disciples to believe without having seen (John 20:29), to recognize "on that day"[16] that the Lord is in his Father, that we are in him and he in us. The Spirit manifests itself by what it does in each of us, in the Church, and in the world. It is by being attentive to this that we perceive the Spirit's active presence.

> You will ask me how I could know his presence. Because he is living and active: scarcely had he entered me than he awakened my slumbering soul. My heart was as hard as a rock and stricken; he shook it, softened it, and wounded it. He it is who uproots, builds up, plants, waters the dry earth,

lightens the dark places, opens locked rooms, and heats what was cold; even better, he straightens the crooked paths and levels the rough places, so much and so well that my soul blesses the Lord and all my being sings praises to his holy name. You well understand that the Bridegroom Word, who has entered me more than once, has never given me a sign of his presence by voice, image or any other appeals to the senses. No movement on his part warns me of his coming, no sensation has ever hinted to me that he was entering my interior retreats. As I have already said, I understood that he was there due to certain movements of my own heart: the fleeing of the vices and the repression of my carnal appetites has made known to me the strength of his virtue. The uncovering and accusation of my hidden feelings has led me to admire to depth of his wisdom; even the slightest amendment of my way of life has given me the experience of his sweet bounty; seeing the renewal and reformation of my mind, that is, the interior man in me, I have perceived something of his beauty; finally, contemplating the wonder of his greatness in all this has left me speechless.[17]

God—as the Bible teaches from the very beginning—reveals himself through his activity in the history of the world and in people, directing them toward the fulfillment of his plan. The mystery of salvation unfolds as it takes flesh. The prophets tirelessly proclaimed this, exhorting the people to allow themselves to be drawn by God into the dynamic of salvation history, to be ready to welcome the one who would come to fulfill all things.

Jesus' coming has fulfilled the longing of all hopes. In him, the Son of God made man, Lord of a new humanity firmly reconciled with its creator, salvation history has reached its zenith. Human history is then that of salvation acquired "once for all." Now we wait for the return of the Son of Man who will appear in his glory and will gather around God the huge crowd of those redeemed by his blood.

This does not mean that the earth is lacking the Lord's presence. His word is preached to all nations. Those who acknowledge him in their heart as the only holy one pass with him from death to life when they are baptized in his name, and they receive the Spirit in the sacrament that confirms—seals—their baptism. Faithful to the commandments the Lord has left them, they can and must, by the testimony of a life of charity, reveal God's love for all people to the whole world.

In the Eucharist, where past, present, and future come together, the mystery of salvation is present, revealing and communicating itself through the mediation of liturgical signs, whose meaning is perceived by faith. The proclamation of God's word focuses its convergent rays on what happens here and now, when the mystery is actualized. The Father sanctifies the bread and wine, sending "his Spirit upon these gifts to make them holy, so that they may become for us the body and blood of our Lord, Jesus Christ,"[18] whose invisible presence receives visible attestation in the sacrament we celebrate and receive.

The Love of the Lord Fills the Universe

For God, There Is No Difference Among People

All the major events of the Church's beginnings reported in the Acts of the Apostles are of great interest to us. We need to understand these beginnings to know from whence we have come. They tell of the wondrous and rapid spread of the gospel, the missionary zeal of the early Christian communities, the conversions and deeds that directed the Church's life. Also, they show the apostles being led to make decisions that would have weighty consequences for the future. Such was Peter's baptism of Cornelius and his household. Today, we read a résumé of Luke's epilogue to this story (Acts 10:25-26, 34-35, 44-48).[1]

Peter was making a pastoral visit to some of the communities: thus he came to Lydda[2] and Joppa.[3] There, on the terrace of a house where he had gone to pray at noontime, he had a strange vision. A kind of huge canvas containing all sorts of animal food forbidden to Jews descended from heaven three times, while a voice invited him to take and eat. While he was wondering about this, messengers from Cornelius arrived. Their master had also had a vision: he had been told to seek a certain Simon, called Peter, who was the guest of another Simon, a leathertanner, in Joppa by the seashore. Peter offered the messengers hospitality and, the next day, left with them and some of the faithful from Joppa to go to Caesarea, some thirty miles away, arriving the following day. Cornelius was waiting for them (Acts 10:1-24).

Cornelius' falling to his knees and prostrating himself at Peter's feet could only have displeased Peter. Yet his surprise must have been even greater when he saw the large audience—relations and close friends—that the centurion had gathered in his house (Acts 10:24). On the road, the messengers must have told Peter that Cornelius was a God-fearing man. Though a foreigner,[4] he had converted to Judaism, although he had not been circumcised.[5] The account he gave Peter of his vision was another indication of his piety: it took place at three in the afternoon, while he was praying in his house (Acts 10:30). Even if there had been no pagans among them, Peter was surrounded by people with whom, as a good Jew, he could have nothing to do; yet he entered their house! He was able to ignore the interdiction because God had shown him "that [he] should not call any person profane or unclean." In effect, he was saying, "here I am, and I should like to know why you summoned me." And the response: "Now therefore we are all here in the presence of God to listen to all that you have been commanded by the Lord" (Acts 10:28-29, 33).

This response pleased Peter: "In truth, I see that God shows no partiality. Rather, in every nation whoever fears him and acts uprightly is acceptable to him."[6] He then proclaimed Jesus Christ to them: the beginning of his ministry in Galilee after John's baptism; his anointing with the Holy Spirit, the good he did everywhere he went; his condemnation and death on the cross; his resurrection on the third day and his appearances to "the witnesses chosen by God in advance"; his command to them "to preach to the people and testify that he is the one appointed by God as judge of the living and the dead. To him all the prophets bear witness, that everyone who believes in him will receive forgiveness of sins through his name" (Acts 10:37-43).

Then an extraordinary thing happened. Peter had not finished these words "when the holy Spirit fell upon all who were listening to the word. The circumcised believers who had accompanied Peter were astounded that the gift of the holy Spirit should have been poured out on the Gentiles also." As at the first Pentecost in Jerusalem (Acts 2:7), these Gentiles of Caesarea were "speaking in tongues" and, impelled by the Spirit in their hearts, singing songs of praise to God.

The irruption of the Spirit cut short Peter's speech. How would he have ended it? Would he have said, as he did on Pentecost: "Repent and be baptized, every one of you, in the name of Jesus Christ for the forgiveness of your sins; and you will receive the gift of the holy Spirit" (Acts 2:38)?

We need not ask the question: he was preempted by God's irresistible initiative. "Can anyone withhold the water for baptizing these people, who have received the holy Spirit even as we have?" And Peter "ordered them to be baptized in the name of Jesus Christ."

One can imagine that the experience had a profound impact on him. When the conversion of the Gentiles led to "much debate" "in the Church of Jerusalem, "Peter got up and said to them, 'My brothers, you are well aware that from early days God made his choice among you that through my mouth the Gentiles would hear the word of the gospel and believe. And God, who knows the heart, bore witness by granting them the holy Spirit just as he did us. He made no distinction between us and them, for by faith he purified their hearts. Why, then, are you now putting God to the test by placing on the shoulders of the disciples the yoke that neither our ancestors nor we have been able to bear? On the contrary, we believe that we are saved through the grace of the Lord Jesus, in the same way as they' '' (Acts 15:7-11).

This intervention, based on what had happened at Caesarea and approved by James, was decisive: the Church's doors were opened to all, without restriction. Such was the considerable impact of Cornelius' baptism, in which the Spirit had forced Peter's hand.

> The LORD has made his salvation known; in
>   the sight of the nations he has
>   revealed his justice.
>
> Sing to the LORD a new song,
>   for he has done wondrous deeds;
> His right hand has won victory for him,
>   his holy arm.
> The LORD has made his salvation known:
>   in the sight of the nations he has
>   revealed his justice.
>   He has remembered his kindness and his faithfulness
>   toward the house of Israel.
> All the ends of the earth have seen
>   the salvation by our God.
> Sing joyfully to the LORD, all you lands;
>   break into song; sing praise.
> (Ps 98:1, 2-3ab, 3cd-4)

The Love that Comes from God Is Rooted in Faith

Charity is and must be the distinctive mark of the Christian—that by which one is judged. When they live in charity, Christians inspire the respect, indeed the sympathy, of those who do not share their faith. When they live otherwise, they are spurned and given no credibility. Men and women who say they believe in God and even in Christ reject the Church because of the lack of charity among the Christians they know. Even the baptized break with the ecclesial community for the very same reason. Some turn toward groups or sects that seem to have the community life they have not found in the Church. All this must make us more attentive to the true nature of the love about which the First Letter of John, especially, speaks (1 John 4:7-10).

"Beloved, let us love one another, because love is of God; everyone who loves is begotten of God and knows God . . . for God is love." Christian charity is not a vague, benevolent feeling, so general and undefined that it ends up not being able to touch anyone. Rather, it expresses itself concretely, like all personalized and efficacious love: "Children, let us love not in word or speech but in deed and truth," even to giving our life for each other or, on a more ordinary level, sharing our goods with those in need (1 John 3:16-18). This charity is indispensable to the definition of faith, which would otherwise be a lie (1 John 3:17). Whatever one says, whatever religious postures one takes, "whoever is without love does not know God, for God is love." Although experienced on the human level, charity must be supernatural: it is rooted in God. But John adds: "Everyone who loves is begotten of God." They will be recognized as such, publicly and solemnly, by the Lord of glory on the day of judgment: he will give them the inheritance of the kingdom prepared for them since the creation of the world (Matt 25:31-40). For the time being, no one has the imperative of judgment. On the contrary, the behavior of many who do not speak of Christ must stimulate the charity of those who proclaim themselves Christians, instilling in them a healthy shame and a deep admiration. Knowing that "love is of God," that "God is love," Christians adore his hidden and forgotten presence in the hearts of so many men and women who do not really know him.[7] But, at the same time, they guard themselves from making love a god, sacrificing everything to it, a god that excuses and justifies everything.[8] Could one truly call this love? Augustine saw and expressed the ambivalence of and the sentiments attached to the word "love." Speaking about the amorous life he had led in his youth, he wrote; "I still did not love, yet I loved to love . . . I looked for what I might love, in my love of love."[9] He was speaking of another love and in a wholly other perspective when he said: "Love and do what you will." Here, in an often cited text, "love" is the fraternal charity of which John speaks.[10] A principle of discernment, it allows one to determine at any moment what obedience to the Lord's command entails. Far from favoring any sort of laxity—"love permits all" Augustine's formula, affirming the primacy of charity, makes it the principle of Christian perfection.[11] "Love, and you can do nothing but good."[12]

In fact, God alone really knows what love is. He taught it to us by send-

ing his Son "among us" (John 1:14): Jesus is the love of God made man
(1 John 4:16). In him, God has loved us with a human heart. The sending of his only Son into the world, "an offering for our sins," shows very
concretely that God has loved us first, for ourselves, without the least
hope of return, for we were sinners. God's love is just the opposite of
that which we mean when we say, with Augustine: "I love to love."

This experience of God's love teaches us that love is a marvelous grace
that is given to us before we expect it. The charity that comes from God
surpasses all other loves. It forms a communion whose basis is God's
love, which guarantees its cohesion, its unfailing nature.

> The source of man's love for God can only be found in the fact that God
> loved him first. He has given us himself as the object of our love, and he
> has also given us its source. What this source is you may learn more clearly
> from the apostle Paul who tells us: "The love of God has been poured into
> our hearts." This love is not something we generate ourselves; it comes
> to us "through the Holy Spirit who has been given to us."
>
> Since we have such an assurance, then, let us love God with the love
> he has given us. As John tells us more fully: "God is love, and whoever
> dwells in love dwells in God, and God in him." It is not enough to say:
> "Love is from God." Which of us would dare to pronounce the words of
> Scripture: "God is love"? He alone could say it who knew what it was to
> have God dwelling within him.[13]

"Live On in Me"

Bound to Christ like branches to a vine, the disciples bear much fruit and
give glory to the Father.[14] After having said as much in images, Jesus,
"when the hour had come for him to pass from this world to the Father,"
spoke more clearly about in what the fertility of his disciples consists,
what the fruit is that they must bear (John 15:9-17).

As throughout this whole discourse, Jesus' thought moves in a spiral,
returning to certain central ideas, from which others spring forth like blossoms on a tree. It is reminiscent of pictures we see in some films of buds
rapidly becoming full-blown flowers. The development of Jesus' thought
has its surprises. We imagine that he has finished with a subject when
suddenly he returns to it, not only repeating in different forms what he
had said before, but pronouncing new revelations. The whole forms a
large and wondrous bouquet. But admiring its exuberance is not enough.
One must go over these texts carefully, meditating on them, dwelling
on each saying and letting it resonate in oneself, discovering its manifold relationships with other sayings. The more one studies, the more

one finds endless riches, nuances, and new depths: wonder follows wonder.

At each turn, Jesus speaks of love. This is first of all the Father's love. It is at the beginning of the whole process—the "economy"—of salvation, and each of its stages. The Father has loved his Son who, in obedience, was made man in order to save the world.[15] Obedient even to death, death on a cross, Jesus was highly exalted and made Lord, to the glory of the Father (Phil 2:6-11), in whose love he dwells. Because he loves the Father and shares in his love for the world (John 3:16), he gave his life for us. He has chosen us for his friends, even before we have made the slightest movement toward him. He has revealed to us everything he learned from the Father, which can be said very simply: God loves us, or, as John says, "God is love" (1 John 4:8).

Now, Jesus waits for only one thing from us: our loving response manifested not in beautiful professions but in fidelity to his commandments, which can be summed up in one: "Love one another as I have loved you."

> All the sacred words of the gospel are filled with the Lord's commandments. Why, then, does the Lord say that love is his commandment? "This is my commandment: love one another." Because every commandment flows from love alone; all his precepts are really one, and their sole foundation is that of charity. A tree's branches all come from the same root: so are all the virtues born of charity alone. The branch of a good work cannot stay green, if it is separated from the root of charity.
>
> Therefore, the Lord's commandments are at the same time many and one: many in the diversity of their works, one in the root of love.
>
> How can we keep this love? The Lord himself tells us: in most of the precepts of his gospel, he orders his friends to love one another in him, and to love their enemies because of him. Whoever loves his friend in God and his enemy because of God possesses true charity.[16]

On the eve of the day when he was going to give his friends the greatest proof of his love by dying for them, Jesus rose from the table, removed his cloak and tied a towel around his waist. Then, with water he had poured into a basin, he began to wash his disciples' feet and dry them with the towel (John 13:2-5). After he had put his cloak back on and took his seat at the table again, he explained the meaning of his actions. "You call me 'teacher' and 'master,' and rightly so, for indeed I am. If I, therefore, the master and teacher, have washed your feet, you ought to wash one another's feet. I have given you a model to follow . . ." (John 13:14-15). To be servants to one another: such is the charity that is an imitation of Christ and the basis by which one will be judged great in the kingdom.[17]

In response to a personal vocation, great numbers of men and women devote their lives in this world to the service of their fellows. Others do so for a certain number of years, or undertake it in response to a situation that personally affects them, e.g., the sickness, disability, or advanced age of someone close. Still others enter religious institutions, whether ancient or modern, with a charitable vocation. But the duty of active charity obliges every Christian, not just a few. There is no one way of life that is its definitive expression: the question that each Christian must answer is how, though one be withdrawn from the world, one can and must, with the means at one's disposal, exercise the Christian's fundamental duty, how one can be concretely faithful to the Lord's command. Benedict devoted a whole chapter of his Rule to what he called "the instruments of good works," which the monks must perform, and for which they will be held accountable on the day of judgment. Among these "instruments" he cites: assisting the poor, clothing the naked, visiting the sick, burying the dead, helping those undergoing tribulation, consoling the suffering.[18] Christian charity is not to be confused with a vague, general feeling of compassion. What is important about it is that it deals with the solidarity that unites to Christ and in Christ all people whom he has loved so far as to die for them.

Finally, Jesus added that if we bear fruit, everything we ask the Father in his name will be granted to us. He will receive our prayer with that of his Son, our Lord, because, like him, we do his will in loving one another.

Salvation history is a history of love, the unfolding in time of the plan of God who is love. He "so loved the world that he gave his only Son" (John 3:16) to save us. Jesus showed this love of God that dwelt in his heart by doing good throughout his earthly life, by dying for all people.

All are called to enter into this mystery, since God, whose love always anticipates us, shows no partiality (Acts 10:36). By his Spirit, which often goes beyond our expectations and prejudices, he never ceases to make new converts. In all ages, we see men and women astonish us with the suddenness and depth of their faith. In countries that were but recently objects of missionary preaching, we now see firmly established Churches whose zeal, community life, and devotion to service witness to a marvelous spreading of the Spirit.

Love of God and others is at the root of the zeal of the apostolate, as it burned in Jesus' heart, who was eager to see the earth engulfed in the fire of the Spirit (Luke 12:49). ''The love that was in Christ impelled him, gripped him, made him agonize over our salvation. This is the love that comes to us in brotherly love. This is the living and eternal source of the Church in its missionary zeal. Saint Paul was doubtlessly thinking of Christ when he wrote his great hymn to love: 'Love is patient; love is kind . . . It bears all things, believes all things, hopes all things, endures all things.' (1 Cor 13:4). Christ's love compelled him. How much must we then ask God and Christ for a little of this brotherly love, though it be as small as a mustard seed!''[19]

To love others because one loves God is, for the Christian, the greatest commandment, that which always and everywhere must direct one's life: a debt that one can never pay (Rom 13:8).

As the Eucharist is the ''source and summit of the Christian life,''[20] so is it the ''sacrament of love, sign of unity, bond of charity.''[21]

> What matter language, race,
> what matter voice or face;
> the just person living in love,
> the Lord will make his friend.
>
> The Lord makes us his friends,
> He fills us with joy!
>
> We cannot love God:
> He has loved us!
>
> We cannot choose Christ:
> He has chosen us!
>
> We cannot grasp the Spirit:
> He has seized us![22]

The Church of the Risen Lord and the Life of the Spirit

The Spirit and the Church Decide Together

The Holy Spirit had forced Peter's hand in the baptism of the Roman centurion Cornelius, garrisoned in Caesarea.[1] On his return to Jerusalem, the apostle had to justify his conduct in front of the assembly of the faithful. Divine intervention had so clearly been present that they could not help but approve of this baptism.[2] But the dissensions that arose from this matter clearly indicate that the admitting of the uncircumcised into the community of disciples posed a serious problem. Cornelius was at least a "God-fearing man," one who therefore observed the prescriptions of the Law.[3] The debate arose again with greater intensity when Paul and Barnabas, on their missionary travels, spoke directly to the Gentiles, many of whom converted.[4] The conflict broke out at Antioch of Pisidia.[5] This Sunday's reading briefly recalls the situation which led the community at Jerusalem to make a decision which would profoundly affect the future of the Church (Acts 15:1-2, 22-29).

"Some who had come down [to Antioch] from Judea were instructing the brothers: 'Unless you are circumcised according to the Mosaic practice, you cannot be saved.' " One should not judge these Christians too quickly, or be indignant at their "interference." Originally Pharisees, like Paul (Acts 23:6; Phil 3:5), or Judeans of James' company,[6] their conversion to Christianity was not doubtful. Their deep and heartfelt attachment to the Law and the traditions of their fathers had led them to the gospel. Convinced that everyone must follow the same road, they tried to persuade the converts at Antioch to imitate them. Their zeal created a good deal of trouble in the community. Serious controversy arose. "It was decided that Paul, Barnabas, and some of the others should go up to Jerusalem to the apostles and presbyters about this question."[7]

At Jerusalem, the debate became very spirited. After a while, Peter rose up and recalled how, through him, the Gentiles had heard the gospel message and come to faith. "And God, who knows the heart, bore witness by granting them the holy Spirit, just as he did us. He made no distinction between us and them, for by faith he purified their hearts. Why, then, are you now putting God to the test by placing on the shoulders of the disciples a yoke that neither our ancestors nor we have been able to bear? On the contrary, we believe that we are saved through the grace of our Lord Jesus, in the same way as they" (Acts 15:8-11).[8]

This resolute speech silenced the dispute. "They listened while Paul and Barnabas described the signs and wonders God had worked among the Gentiles through them." Then James spoke. They must "stop troubling the Gentiles who turn to God . . . but tell them by letter to avoid pollution from idols, unlawful marriage, the meat of strangled animals, and blood" (Acts 15:12-20). With the approval of the whole Church, the apostles and presbyters thus directed a letter to the Gentile converts in Antioch, Syria, and Cilicia. They appointed Paul and Barnabas to deliver it, accompanied by two delegates from the Jerusalem Church, Judas and Silas.

Animals sacrificed in the temples were cut up, and the meat that was not used for cultic purposes was sold in the market. The Jews knew that idols had no real existence. But to eat the flesh of sacrifices had an unbearable odor of idolatry, and this proscription was retained for converts to Judaism as well. By abstaining from such food, the Gentile converts would avoid offending the consciences of the Jewish Christians.[9] Likewise with the forbidding of strangled meat. This was, and still is, ancestral Jewish practice.[10] As for the "unlawful marriages," they were those forbidden by the Law between close relatives, a term that was understood in the large sense (Lev 18). They could only scandalize Christians with a background of Jewish religious culture.

Thus the stipulations placed on the Gentile converts were not the result of a condescending tolerance regarding certain demands. The decision of the Council of Jerusalem was manifestly not a compromise that, in order to placate those who were still attached to ancient (and outdated) religious practices, demanded some concessions from the non-Jews.

Charity alone inspired the Jerusalem council. No concession was made to those who, "without any mandate from us have upset you with their teachings and disturbed your peace of mind" among the faithful at Antioch. On the other hand, the way the letter was expressed did reprove, without censuring, those who were responsible for this regrettable and painful conflict. To demand that the Gentile converts not offend the religious sensibilities of their fellows by observing some regulations, altogether minor and perfectly understandable (such as abstaining from "unlawful marriages") was an implicit acknowledgment that the Jerusalem Church trusted the Gentile converts and believed them to be very reasonable. The council's decree also did not miss the chance to praise Barnabas and Paul, "who have dedicated their lives to the name of our Lord Jesus Christ." This was a clear recognition of the undoubted authenticity of their missionary work. Thus, there was not the least concession on principles: "There is no salvation through anyone [but Jesus Christ], nor is there any other name under heaven given to the human race by which we are to be saved" (Acts 4:12). The name of "Christians," which the disciples first received at Antioch, and which they bore ever after, proclaims this (Acts 11:26). May the day come when all will bear that name alone, without divisions and quarrels based on different sensibilities and traditions—a time, ideally, that could bring about unity. May the day come when everyone will recognize that unity is enriched by diversity wrapped in truth, mutual respect, and charity: "If I differ from you, I do not lessen, but increase you."[11] Charity will sometimes demand not compromises but a willingness to restrict one's freedom when its use, even if legitimate, might scandalize the weak.

> Now food does not bring us closer to God. We suffer no loss through failing to eat, and we gain no favor by eating. Take care, however, lest in exercising your right you become an occasion of sin to the weak. . . . Therefore, if food causes my brother to sin, I will never eat meat again, so that I may not be an occasion of sin to him (1 Cor 8:8-9, 13).

The conflicts in the early Church about traditional observances eventually died down. But others arose between those who held to traditional practices and those who in the spirit of the Council of Jerusalem did not wish to impose other obligations on the disciples than those that were strictly necessary. It was not enough to lay down the law once. Some years after the firm and clear decision of the apostles and presbyters in Jerusalem—as Acts and Paul's letters testify[12]—the controversy reawoke, and patient explanation, even justification, was needed for a line of conduct long since established by the assembly of "the whole Church" in Jerusalem, presided over by Peter.

In any case, one thing ought to be remembered: the decision of the Council of Jerusalem came about collegially at the end of a debate where there was much serious discussion (Acts 15:7). The spirited confrontation of diverse thoughts did not prevent the apostles and presbyters from writing: "It is the decision of the holy Spirit and of us . . ." Every coun-

cil, where the debates have often been just as lively and lengthy, has repeated this formula, or its equivalent.[13] The Spirit given to the Church
does not dictate the conduct it must follow: it assists the Church's efforts
to work out its problems in fidelity to its vocation, its universal mission.
The Spirit awakens the Church's courage and daring by making it attentive to the signs of the times. In those days, the Spirit led the early Christian community beyond its particularities to welcome the newly converted
Gentiles. Now, it calls us to be open to new cultures, to invent new modes
of living the gospel, ever responsive to changing history.[14] The example
of the Jerusalem Church, of Peter, of the apostles and presbyters, says
to us: "Take heart!"

> *O God, let all the nations praise you!*
>
> May God have pity on us and bless us;
>   may he let his face shine upon us.
> So may your way be known upon earth;
>   among all nations, your salvation.
>
> May the nations be glad and exult
>   because you rule the peoples in equity;
>   the nations on the earth you guide.
>   May the peoples praise you, O God;
>   may all the peoples praise you!
> May God bless us,
>   and may all the ends of the earth fear him!
> (Ps 67:2-3, 5, 6, 8)

Beyond Time: The Holy City

Only a peculiar divine grace can permit a glimpse of something of the
divine mysteries. The seer, in order to give an account of this experience,
and what he saw in his ecstasy, must necessarily resort to images. Really,
any other form of language would tend all too much to reduce the contemplated reality, even so far as to empty it of its content. Images, on
the other hand, are open-ended and must remain so. They must not be
taken strictly literally, i.e., shorn of all vague or mysterious elements. Instead, we must keep them as they are before our eyes, for the seer passed
them on so that we in our turn and according to the grace given to us
may contemplate the mystery. So it is with the vision of "the holy city"
that John saw descend from heaven, from God (Rev 21:10-14, 22-23).[15]

The apostle begins by saying, in his own way, that his vision occurred
thanks to God's initiative, which took him by surprise: "[An angel] took

me in spirit to a great, high mountain."[16] This was, then, a mystical experience: i.e., "in spirit." Paul speaks of his visions in the same way. "I know someone in Christ who, fourteen years ago (whether in the body or out of the body I do not know, God knows), was caught up to the third heaven. And I know that this person (whether in the body or out of the body I do not know, God knows), was caught up into Paradise and heard ineffable things, which no one may utter" (2 Cor 12:2-4).

The angel shows John "the holy city Jerusalem coming down out of heaven from God. It gleamed with the splendor of God." The first thing that strikes the seer is the "massive, high wall" that encircles the city, conferring on its inhabitants absolute peace and security. The twelve gates—"three gates facing east, three north, three south, and three west"—are guarded by twelve angels. Over the gates are the names of the twelve tribes of Israel. These "obligatory" entrances are a reminder that "salvation is from the Jews" (John 4:22). But "the wall of the city had twelve courses of stones as its foundation, on which were inscribed the twelve names of the twelve apostles of the Lamb." Thus it is a city that one enters through gates bearing the names of the twelve tribes of Israel, but whose ramparts are grounded on the Lord's twelve apostles. The Old and New Testaments together assure the city its cohesion, its unity. We remember what Paul wrote: "You are fellow citizens with the holy ones and members of the household of God, built upon the foundation of the apostles and prophets, with Christ Jesus himself as the capstone" (Eph 2:20).

John sees no temple in the city, "for its temple is the Lord God almighty and the Lamb. The city had no need of sun or moon to shine on it, for the glory of God gave it light, and its lamp was the Lamb." What a remarkable surpassing of all hopes! God allows the seer to contemplate the concrete realization, so to speak, of the most mysterious promises of Christ.

A prophet like Ezekiel dreamed at length of a temple worthy of God's presence in the midst of his people (Ezek 40–44). The destruction of the Temple of Jerusalem by the Roman armies under Titus in A.D. 70 was regarded as the sign of the end of the world. "I saw no temple in the city."

Jesus had foretold the destruction of the Temple of stones that the disciples were admiring, and added that he would replace it with the temple of his body, "raised up" in three days (John 2:19). He had told the Samaritan woman: "Believe me, woman, the hour is coming when you will worship the Father neither on this mountain nor in Jerusalem" (John 4:21).

"I saw no temple in the city, for its temple is the Lord God Almighty and the Lamb."

We still live in the time of signs, rites, and sacraments; it could not be otherwise. At the end, because God will be "all in all" (1 Cor 15:28), "we shall see face to face" (1 Cor 13:12). The time of mediations, of faith and hope will be over. Only love will remain (1 Cor 13:13). But this does not mean a devaluation of the system of signs and liturgy that orders our lives now: quite the contrary. The liturgy, like faith, gives into our possession the realities to come, the object of our hope.

"The city had no need of sun or moon," which mark out the succession of day and night. Evermore, there will only be the day illuminated by the resplendent glory of God and the light of Christ, the lamb who was slain and raised. "The true light, which enlightens everyone, was coming into the world. . . . And the Word became flesh and made his dwelling among us, and we saw his glory, the glory as of the Father's only Son, full of grace and truth" (John 1:9, 14). That which we proclaim we will clearly see in the holy city coming down from heaven, from God, where faith will become contemplation.

> God has prepared
> a dwelling-place for men,
> he has laid the stones
> and lit the fire.
> Today,
> he multiplies the bread
> and binds our hands together:
> our hearts are but one!
>
> *God with us, God in us!*
> *We are the body of Christ!*
>
> Behold the promised land
> where the human assembly
> knows the love of God.
>
> Behold the feasting ground
> where the human family
> gives a face to God.
>
> Behold the house of peace
> whose inhabitants
> receive the gift of God.
>
> Behold the open Temple
> where the adoring people
> become witnesses of God.[17]

The Time of Presence in Absence

Jesus knew that his departure would be a tremendous trial for his disciples. Thus, when the hour had come for him to pass from this world to the Father, he spoke to them at length about the situation in which they would from then on find themselves. The first "farewell discourse," the third part of which we read today,[18] reveals that this time would contain many new works of God (John 14:23-29).[19]

Jesus' time on earth was very brief; only a small number of people knew him then. How could this short visit of God's messenger be seen as the realization of the promises of God's abiding presence, symbolized by the magnificent temple built by Solomon (1 Kgs 8:10-13), promised by the prophet along with the rebuilding of Jerusalem after the Exile (Isa 60)? Didn't the Lord's departure crush all hope of seeing the advent of the long-awaited liberator, as the two disciples of Emmaus sorrowfully exclaimed on the evening of Easter (Luke 24:21)? "Are you the one who is to come, or should we look for another?" (Matt 11:3). John the Baptist's question must have haunted the disciples from the moment Jesus said to them: "My children, I will be with you only a little while longer" (John 13:33). And what is left for us? Regret for not having known the Lord as a companion, but only in the obscurity and solitude of faith, waiting for his return?

"Whoever loves me will keep my word, and my Father will love him, and we will come to him and make our dwelling with him." How astounding this news is, even surpassing the hopes that Jesus' departure seemed to undermine! No one could ever have imagined such intimacy with the Father and his Son: both of them dwelling in each of us! Jesus spent only a little time among us, but in that time he taught us the Father's word and passed on to us the assurance of his love, as well as the knowledge of how to respond to it. Loving the Lord and keeping his word are the same thing: is he not the Word of God? To receive the word is to receive the Father and the Son, since it testifies to their presence.

> At the age that I have now reached, the most valuable proof to me, the strongest witness in favor of Christian truth is the visible presence of grace in certain people . . .
> Often, in the evening, I become conscious of the contradictions of my life while remembering the names and faces of people whom I have seen during the day. I wonder about the divisions between people. What is social inequality in comparison with inequality in the spiritual world?
> Sometimes, the "successful" man, full of material concerns, projects, wholly wrapped up in his profane work—too profane, alas!—listens to the

young man or social worker seated across from him, who thinks he is perhaps indifferent or distant. No, on the contrary, he is attentive; less, to be
sure, to the words themselves than to their hidden source, which he can
sense underlying the whole discourse: an inner fire that lights up every
word.[20]

Jesus did not say everything: his human estate and the limits of time
would not have permitted it. Not to mention that the evangelists would
have been hard-pressed to report everything that he did say and do (John
21:25). But, on his return to the Father, the Lord sent the Holy Spirit to
be the disciples' advocate (John 14:16-17) and inner guide: "He will teach
you everything and remind you of all that [I] told you." The Spirit is the
Church's memory; even so, we must understand in what sense this is
so. It was not given only to those to whom Jesus spoke at the Last Supper, at the hour when he was to pass from this world to his Father. Its
action in them was not only a reminding of forgotten sayings. The Gospels
twice speak explicitly about the disciples remembering, well after an event,
some saying of Jesus or Scripture. At the Lord's entry into Jerusalem "six
days before the Passover," "his disciples did not understand" the meaning of the event, "but when Jesus had been glorified they remembered"
what Scripture said: "Fear no more, O daughter Zion; see, your king
comes, seated upon an ass's colt." And they understood that this prophecy of Zechariah (9:9) was speaking of the Lord (John 12:14-15). Again,
after his three-fold denial, "Peter remembered the word that Jesus had
spoken: 'Before the cock crows you will deny me three times.'" The
recollection of this saying made him conscious of his fault and led to his
repentance: "He went out and began to weep bitterly" (Matt 26:75). But
there are countless instances in the Gospels and the apostolic writings
where the Spirit brought to mind a scriptural text or one of Jesus' sayings. In their light, the meaning of Jesus' deeds, the events of his life,
his other sayings, what happens in the Church and what it determines
to do appears in full light. Thus, the Holy Spirit is even today "the memory of the Church," not that it always repeats what was said and learned
before, but because it teaches us to act in conformity with Scripture and
the Lord's teaching in our own time. The Spirit is the heart and soul of
the Church's living tradition. It pushes it forward, giving it the courage
and audacity needed to confront new situations, to seek and find bold
solutions, drawing on its memory of the living Word.

Jesus then said to his disciples: "Peace I leave with you; my peace I
give to you." From one end of the world to the other, the word "peace"

expresses the first and foremost human longing. Alas, this peace finds countless obstacles in its path! ''Not as the world gives do I give it to you.'' It comes from on high. It is the peace that reconciles all people with God; a peace that the leaps and bounds of history, trials, persecution, and death cannot touch. This is the supreme good that recapitulates all the gifts of the messianic era.[21] ''Peace'' is the first word the risen Lord spoke to his disciples (John 20:19, 21, 26). Assured of this peace, fruit of the Lord's passover and gift of the Spirit, the disciples have nothing to fear; rather, they should rejoice. Christ has freely and knowingly, in sadness and agony, confronted wrongful persecution and death. But he emerged victorious. This must never be forgotten, especially when everything seems lost.[22] ''I am going away and I will come back to you.''

> This is the great promise of the gospel, that the Lord of all things, who had appeared outwardly to his disciples, would come to dwell in their hearts. Such was, as we ought to remember, the language commonly used by the prophets. And it was also used by our Savior when he came upon the earth: ''I will love him,'' he said, speaking of the man who loves and obeys him, ''and reveal myself to him. . . . We will come to him and make our dwelling with him.''
>
> Although the Lord was incarnate to the point of being able to be seen and touched, this was still not enough. He was exterior and separated. But after his ascension, he descended again through and in his Spirit, and then the promise was finally fulfilled. He came into the souls of those who believe and, by taking possession of them, he who was unique united them as one.
>
> By becoming incarnate, Christ provided an exterior and seeming unity, the sort that existed under the Law. He gathered his apostles into a visible society. But when he came again in the person of his Spirit, he made them one in a real sense, and not only in name.
>
> Thus, Christ came, not to make them one, but to die for them. The Spirit has come to make us one in the One who died and was resurrected, that is, to form his Church.[23]

Ever since the beginning, when sin appeared to have ruined the work of creation and brought God's design to an abrupt end, salvation history has known, in each of its stages, crises that seemed to threaten everything. But each time, there was a new beginning: life rose up from death, the dry bones that filled the barren plain came to life, and a whole people rose up to go, at the Lord's command, into the desert, which had blossomed (Ezek 37:1-14).

When God sent his Son into the world, those who recognized him as the expected Savior, promised by Scripture, were ecstatic with hope. Their liberator had finally come (Luke 24:21). He would lead his people out of the interminable and taxing cycle of the dark years, which followed a time of grace lost through a relapse into sin. He had proclaimed: "Repent, for the kingdom of heaven is at hand" (Matt 4:17). God's decisive intervention was therefore imminent[24]: what could the hostility of some people matter when Jesus' sovereignty appeared greater after every encounter, "a prophet mighty in deed and word before God and all the people" (Luke 24:19)? So the disciples were mortified when, on an evening full of foreboding, he announced his departure. True, he added that an advocate would be sent to them, that God would come to dwell among them and that Jesus himself would be definitively present in their midst. The meaning of these mysterious words passed on by the evangelist did not take long to appear to the apostles. Thereafter, it never ceased being unfolded under the wondering eye of successive Christian generations.

From Jerusalem, the good news spread farther and farther. Under the impulse of the Spirit, the Church, sometimes following lively debates, opened more and more to all cultures and, today, to all languages, even in the liturgy. Very recently, it was thought that the Spirit had said that only the language used for centuries by the Church of Rome should be used for the liturgy everywhere in the West. At Vatican II, the pope and the college of bishops "decreed in the Holy Spirit" not to lay obligations on Christians that do not come from the Spirit, though they may be the customary practice.[25] And under the Spirit's impulse, the Church is working definitively toward the inculturation of the gospel. Truly, the one whom the Father has sent in the name of the Lord is, as in the early days, at work in the world and in the Church. The glory of God and the light whose source is the lamb do not yet shine as resplendently as they will. But the Spirit proclaims: "Be joyful and thankful. Take heart!"

> Now I am going away.
> I am going to the Father.
> He will send you the Creator Spirit.
> To you I will return.
> The Spirit of wisdom rouses your hearts:
> Rise up! People of Easter!
> Rise up! Take courage!
>
> *Rise up! People of Easter!*
> *Rise up! Take courage!*
>
> In vain does the sun shine
> if the Spirit does not illuminate the town!

In vain do the masons labor
if the Spirit does not build the house!

In vain are words chanted
if the Spirit does not dwell in the
memory![26]

The Ascension of the Lord

"We believe in Jesus Christ . . . he ascended into heaven, and is seated at the right hand of the Father. He will come again in glory to judge the living and the dead."[1] This article of the Creed is closely connected to the one that proclaims "on the third day he rose again" the only Son of God, "born of the Virgin Mary," crucified under Pontius Pilate. Thus it refers to the mystery of Christ, and not merely to an episode in his life. This is why the ascension is presented from four different, but complementary views in the Acts of the Apostles and the Gospels.

Acts speaks of it with remarkable sobriety in a grand and hieratic setting. Hence the ascension is the end of Luke's Gospel. The fact that it is recounted here shows very concretely that this is the continuation of the Gospel. After this, Luke will concern himself with the apostolic preaching and the Church's history following Jesus' departure. This account of the ascension is read every year on the feast day (Acts 1:1-11).

The second reading is a theological and spiritual reflection on the mystery (Eph 1:17-23—Year A; Eph 4:1-16—Year B; Heb 9:24-28; 10:19-23—Year C).

Each year has its own Gospel. Matthew, Mark, and Luke all speak in their own way of the departure of the risen one from the company of his disciples, whom he will nevertheless never abandon. Christ, who has received from his Father all power in heaven and on earth, remains with his own, even to the end of the world (Matt 28:16-20—Year A). He is with his messengers, working with them and confirming the Word by the signs that accompany it (Mark 16:15-20—Year B). After having promised his disciples "power from on high" to accomplish their mission he left them, blessing them as he went (Luke 24:46-53—Year C).

This is the mystery of faith in its unity and its diversity: the mystery of the risen Christ and of God's Church born of the Spirit.

> Church of the living God
> go up onto the mountain:
> Lift your voice, joyful messenger,
> and cry to the world:

Alleluia. alleluia!
As he left,
The Lord will return!

He has come, light into darkness:
he has left us the commandment of love.
High priest of the good things to come,
he has traversed the heavens,
he has entered the holy of holies.

He has taken our sins upon himself,
he has known death, and behold he is alive.

He has taken his place near the Father,
he reigns for ages and ages.

His eyes are burning flames:
the cloak that enfolds him is steeped in blood.
His name? The Word of God,
his beloved, the true and faithful
witness.[2]

You Will Be My Witnesses to the End of the World

Luke presents the Acts of the Apostles as the sequel to his Gospel, both of them being dedicated to "Theophilus."[3] In the first of these books the evangelist dealt with "all that Jesus did and taught[4] until the day he was taken up, after giving instructions through the holy Spirit to the apostles whom he had chosen." The central figure in Acts is the resurrected Jesus. It is he whom the apostles are able to proclaim with confidence, because they have received multiple proofs of his resurrection. But here Luke also introduces the Holy Spirit, whose crucial role is emphasized throughout Acts.[5] With this introduction, the author says that now begins the account of what the apostles did: their acts, as the title of the book says (Acts 1:1-11).

From the Journey to Jerusalem to the Sending Forth

At the beginning of Luke's Gospel came the announcement to Zechariah the priest of the birth of a son: this occurred at the Temple in Jerusalem. A large portion of Jesus' ministry is situated in the framework of a long journey to Jerusalem (Luke 9:51–19:27)[6] where the Lord finally entered (Luke 19:28-48) and finished his preaching (Luke 20), before celebrating his last Passover and suffering his passion there. It was at Jerusalem that Jesus was buried and that he appeared to the apostles after his resurrection (Luke 24:36-49). The holy city is thus in Luke's Gospel the terminus of Jesus' road, the place toward which he set his step, "resolutely determined" (Luke 9:51) to accomplish his passover, the last stage of which was the sending of the Spirit to his disciples. This is why he orders the apostles not to leave Jerusalem but to wait there for what the Father had promised and Jesus had proclaimed to them: the baptism of the Holy Spirit.[7]

Jesus adds, however, that Jerusalem will soon become a point of departure. There it is that the apostles will first proclaim the Lord by testifying to his resurrection. But they will leave the city to bear the good news "throughout Judea and Samaria, and to the ends of the earth." It is the story of this expansion of the Gospel that Acts recounts.

Jerusalem is, in a double sense, the holy city for Christians. Jesus went there to accomplish his passover, from whence comes our salvation; and it was from there that the apostles went out to proclaim the good news to all peoples, including us.

> Of Zion they shall say:
> "One and all were born in her" (Ps 87:5).

> If I forget you, Jerusalem,
> may my right hand be forgotten! (Ps 136:5)

As He Was Taken from Us, the Lord Will Return

When Mary Magdalene discovered the empty tomb where Jesus had been laid "on the first day of the week," she ran "to Simon Peter and to the other disciple whom Jesus loved, and told them, 'They have taken the Lord from the tomb, and we don't know where they put him' " (John 20:1-2). This news threw the disciples into disarray. They needed time and several appearances of the resurrected Lord in order to come to believe that he really was alive. He patiently prepared them for a new form of his presence through his appearances and instructions. Despite this, they ask him: "Lord, are you at this time going to restore the kingdom to Israel?" How could they ask such a question? Had they learned nothing? We must not be more severe on them than Jesus was. Rather, we should listen to his response, which is also addressed to us: "It is not for you to know the times and seasons that the Father has established by his own authority." What purpose could such knowledge serve? It is enough to know that the power of the Holy Spirit is assured to those whom the Lord has chosen for witnesses. They still have only limited possibilities, bearing "treasure in earthen vessels" (2 Cor 4:7). But they are capable of everything with the one who is their strength (Phil 4:13).

"When he had said this, as they were looking on, he was lifted up, and a cloud took him from their sight." Nothing here strikes one's imagination, not even one of those terms that elsewhere, both in Acts and the other writings of the New Testament, evoke Jesus' glorious exaltation.[8] "He arose toward heaven, beyond his apostles' sight, beyond this world, like a traveler who leaves for a distant country, 'when he had finished speaking.' "[9] The only exception is that the cloud that hides Jesus from the apostles' sight indirectly evokes the coming of the sovereign judge at the end of time.[10]

The time of Jesus' visible presence has come to an end. A new era of salvation history—the last—begins without fanfare.

One Must Not Stand There, Looking at the Sky

At Jesus' transfiguration, Peter, James, and John, thrilled by the vision, wanted it never to end. "Master, it is good that we are here; let us make three tents, one for you, one for Moses, and one for Elijah" (Luke 9:33).[11] But a voice spoke to them out of the cloud. And Peter realized that he did not know what he was saying. The vision had been granted to the three disciples to persuade them to listen to the Lord (Luke 9:33, 35)[12] and to prepare them for the revelation of his paschal exodus.[13]

At the ascension, none of the apostles said a word, but they could not tear their gaze from the heavens, where Jesus had disappeared. What were they thinking? Luke does not tell us. As at the resurrection (Luke 24:4), two men appear. Their white garments designate them as angels.[14] "Men of Galilee, why are you standing there looking at the sky? This Jesus who has been taken up from you into heaven will return in the same way as you have seen him going into heaven."

"Men of Galilee": this appellation reminds the apostles that they are still of this earth and must not think themselves to have reached heaven already. It was in Galilee that the angels at the resurrection appointed the rendezvous with the disciples (Luke 24:7). The angels of the ascension send the apostles back to their native Galilee, where Jesus had begun his ministry (Luke 4:14). They address them as they did the women at the empty tomb: "Why?" The disciples should not then have searched for "the living one among the dead" (Luke 24:5). No more must they now look for him in the heavens, passively contemplating the cloud that had hidden him from their sight. "He will return in the same way as you have seen him going into heaven." Witnesses of both the ascension and the resurrection, the solemn assurance of this return is reiterated to them at the Lord's departure.[15] To know this is enough. In the meantime, and with a view to that day, the disciples must strive to proclaim the gospel to the "ends of the earth." The Lord's ascension marks the uninterrupted passage between the time of Jesus and that of the Church's mission.

Two other important teachings flow from what the "two men dressed in white garments" said to the apostles. Contemplation, which the Church has always held in high regard because it is the highest form of union with God in prayer, has nothing in common with the various forms of idleness or religious passivity, with their mystical pretensions. True contemplatives do not retire to their mountain to escape the battles on the plain. Their vocation does not place them outside—or above—the Church that labors to proclaim the gospel. Their prayer is a battle, often sorrowful, even despairing, because they are distraught, in their heart and flesh, at the thought that Love is not loved. The same is true for those who lead lives completely turned toward the Lord's manifestation on the last day. This expectancy, which keeps them awake day and night in prayers of intercession and praise, plunges them, no matter what one might think, into the center of the Church's life and the confrontation between the Light and the world's darkness.[16]

The second teaching concerns the liturgy.

> The liturgy is the summit toward which the activity of the Church is directed; it is also the fount from which all her power flows. For the goal of apostolic endeavor is that all who are made sons of God by faith and baptism should come together to praise God in the midst of his Church, to take part in the sacrifice and to eat the Lord's Supper.
>
> The liturgy, in its turn, moves the faithful filled with "the paschal sacraments" to be "one in holiness"; it prays that "they hold fast in their lives to what they have grasped by their faith." The renewal in the Eucharist of the covenant between the Lord and man draws the faithful and sets them aflame with Christ's insistent love. It is from the liturgy, poured forth upon us as from a fountain, that the sanctification of men in Christ and the glorification of God to which all other activities of the Church are directed, as toward their end, are achieved with maximum effectiveness.[17]

The celebration lasts only a short while and ends with the sending forth of the assembly: "Go in peace to love and serve the Lord"; "Do not stand there looking up at heaven"; "Go back to Galilee where your mission awaits you."[18] The liturgy, properly understood and experienced, renews and inspires the missionary spirit of those who participate in it.

To celebrate the ascension, contemplating and singing the glory of the Lord, is to pray that the gospel may be proclaimed to the whole world. Time is pressing, for "this Jesus who has been taken up from you into heaven will return in the same way as you have seen him going into heaven."

> *God mounts his throne amid shouts of joy;*
> *the LORD, amid trumpet blasts.*
>
> All you peoples, clap your hands,
>   shout to God with cries of gladness,
> For the LORD, the Most High, the awesome,
>   is the great king over all the earth.

God mounts his throne amid shouts of joy;
   the LORD, amid trumpet blasts.
Sing praise to God, sing praise;
   sing praise to our king, sing praise.

For king of all the earth is God;
   sing hymns of praise.
God reigns over the nations,
   God sits upon his holy throne.
(Ps 47:2-3, 6-7, 8-9)

Christ Raised to Heaven, Present in the Church

Christ: Head of His Body, the Church

Paul is a model of the contemplative and the missionary. His letters are strewn with great lyrical and spiritual hymns, with prayers of fervent mysticism. He never loses sight of the higher, concrete realities. So, as he looks on each particular community, he is raised, almost spontaneously, to the contemplation of the Church extended throughout the world, in which he sees Christ's mystery in its fullness. Such is the case in the passage from the beginning of the Letter to the Ephesians that we read today (Eph 1:17-23).[1]

Paul prays that his correspondents may receive from "the God of our Lord Jesus Christ, the Father of glory . . . a spirit of wisdom and revelation resulting in knowledge of him." The "knowledge" of God—which is extremely important in Paul's thought[2]—is not a human knowledge: it comes from the Holy Spirit who reveals the mystery of God—especially his love—announced by Christ. It is closely bound up with charity. It involves "a total devotion of the person to the one God and a complete acceptance of his will that governs a man's whole conduct and gives it its religious value."[3] "No one knows the Son except the Father, and no one knows the Father except the Son and anyone to whom the Son wishes to reveal him" (Matt 11:27). Actually, it is because God knows us—as his love testifies—that we are allowed to know him in our turn. "Just as the Father knows me and I know the Father" (John 10:15). Is it not analogous to the way a child quickly learns to know its parents, because they show it their love, while it does not recognize strangers?

This knowledge of God fills our hearts with his light. It enables us to understand that his call puts our life in a radically different perspective. It was shut up; henceforth it will be open to unlimited hope: "the riches of glory in his inheritance" promised to all the faithful, on whose behalf God's "surpassing greatness of . . . power" is poured out. But it is not up to us to command this interior light, which sometimes is so dazzling that one might wonder whether it is not a figment of the imagination, which takes its desires for reality. We remember what Festus, the Roman procurator, said when he was examining Paul, being amazed at his biblical erudition: "You are mad, Paul; much learning is driving you mad" (Acts 26:24).

Our certitudes are based on faith in Christ. In him, God has demonstrated his power, "raising [Christ] from the dead and seating him at his right hand in the heavens." This is the same power that God deploys in us, enabling us to achieve a similar glory. Our hope is not based on speculation, but on what God has really done for Christ. The resurrection raised him "far above every principality, authority, power, and dominion, and every name that is named not only in this age but also in the one to come. And he put all things beneath his feet." Nothing can any longer prevent our hope, even if an ill-wind makes it waver sometimes. It is like the flame of the Easter candle. "The flame is a weak and vacillating and always rises upward. A breath of air disturbs the flame, but it rights itself. An upward impulse restores its magic . . . The flame is a permanent verticality. Every poet who dreams of flame knows that the flame is living."[4] But Christians are not dreaming. When they look at the burning Easter candle, they see it as the symbol of the living Christ who, risen to heaven, draws them irresistibly toward the heights where the inheritance of the resurrected awaits them.

The Church, Paul says, is really the body of Christ. Without it, there would not be "the fullness of the one who fills all things in every way." The revelation of the mystery here reaches an unexpected peak. In the Letter to the Colossians (1:19), the apostle wrote: "For in him the fullness was pleased to dwell." Now, it is the Church that contributes to the fulfillment of Christ who, would otherwise be like a head without a body. Such a claim might seem rather exaggerated, even entirely inappropriate, in so far as it might mean that the glory of Christ could be truncated. Actually, Paul is here affirming, in a very strong and provocative way, a truth that is customarily expressed in milder terms. Christ has been enthroned at the right hand of God as conqueror of all the powers of evil, as the Savior of the world. By his blood, he has gained for God "a people of his own" (1 Pet 2:9), "eager to do what is good" (Titus 2:14), the Church, jewel of his glory. We may confidently say that without the Church, Jesus would not be the Christ: it fills up what might be lacking in his glory, in his fullness.[5]

"Make disciples of all nations"

Matthew's Gospel does not speak explicitly of Jesus' departure. However, it does end with an account of what is clearly Jesus' last appearance. The way the Lord speaks to the apostles signifies that the time of his visible presence among them has come to an end (Matt 28:16-20).

First of all, the scene recapitulates, in a few words, the resurrection appearances. Jesus had said that the apostles would see him again (Matt 28:10). Nevertheless, he is the one who takes the initiative of appearing: they will see him and recognize him.[6] "When they saw him, they worshiped . . ." As Matthew shows throughout his Gospel, this is the proper attitude for those who recognize Jesus as the Lord to whom respect is owed.[7] Yet despite this gesture of faith, "they doubted." This also fits in with the accounts of the resurrection appearances[8]: for the disciples, too, faith had to overcome doubt.

Matthew places this final appearance "in Galilee" on "the mountain." These details have more theological than topographical[9] value. Galilee was where Jesus began his ministry (Matt 4:13). Moreover, it was on the edge of the pagan world: it was called "Galilee of the Gentiles,"[10] The Lord's departure from the place of his first manifestation shows the continuity between the universal mission of the apostles and the Church on the one hand and Jesus' ministry on the other. The "mountain," too, is a "theological site" in Matthew's Gospel. It was on the "mountain" that Jesus proclaimed the "charter" of the kingdom (Matt 5:1–8:1), and on the shore of the Sea of Galilee, he taught the crowds (Matt 15:29). Thus, the location of Jesus' departure and his final instructions to the eleven disciples have definite meanings for Matthew: this should be kept in mind as we continue.

"All power in heaven and on earth has been given to me." This absolute and universal sovereignty recalls that which, in the vision of the prophet Daniel, is attributed to the mysterious Son of Man (Dan 7:13-14), a term Jesus often used to refer to himself.[11] It was on the "mountain" that he was transfigured (Matt 17:1-9), allowing Peter, James, and John to glimpse the glory that he would be given at the conclusion of his passover. The "mountain" of the ascension, finally, reveals that the Lord's cosmic dominion has been given him by God, that he did not seize it himself, as the devil had tempted him to do on the mountain in the desert (Matt 4:8-10). All this is recognized by the disciples as they abase themselves.[12]

In the name of this sovereignty, the resurrected Jesus solemnly invests

the Eleven with the mission for which he had chosen them: "Go, therefore, and make disciples of all nations, baptizing them in the name of
the Father, and of the son, and of the holy Spirit, teaching them to observe all that I have commanded you." Each of the three points of this
command must be dealt with separately.

They must leave the "mountain," crossing the borders of Galilee, going to "all nations," i.e., to the Gentiles living outside Israel.

Baptism is the sign of adherence to the gospel and of belonging to the
Lord. It is not like John's baptism, a simple purification rite that signifies
conversion (Matt 3:11-12). It is the "sacrament of faith." This means that
in order to receive baptism, one must believe in God—Father, Son, and
Holy Spirit—as Jesus has revealed him[13]: this confession of faith is the
heart of the Christian creed.

Merely saying "Lord, Lord" (Matt 7:21), a profession of faith, however, is not enough to make one a disciple. One must "keep the commandments," practice justice, mercy, and love of neighbor. Matthew
often speaks of these demands. The disciple translates faith into action,
into life. "Whoever does the will of my heavenly Father is my brother,
and sister, and mother" (Matt 12:50). It is to bear oneself as Jesus, who
gave us the commandments from the Father.[14]

Finally, the apostles must "teach" the disciples to keep the commandments. Their mission therefore consists not only in repeating Jesus' words,
which they do remember, maintaining intact and transmitting what is
known as the deposit of faith. They have a responsibility to teach all
people, following Jesus' example. Like "every scribe who has been instructed in the kingdom of heaven," they have to draw new and old
things from the "treasure" that they have received (Matt 13:52).[15] This
is what is done by the authors of the apostolic letters in the New Testament. They develop the Lord's teaching, drawing lessons from it that
may be applied to the needs of time, place, and community, in fidelity
to the Lord's word and the living tradition. This responsibility even im-
poses on them the duty to speak like Paul does regarding celibacy: "I
have not received any commandment from the Lord, but I give my opinion" (1 Cor 7:25). Such an "opinion" on the part of those whose mission it is to teach must not be taken lightly. The Church has always
exercised this teaching ministry—the magisterium—on the part of all the
disciples, to guide them on the paths of the Lord's commands. The responsibility properly belongs to the pope and the bishops, who must exercise it while becoming themselves more and more disciples of Christ.[16]

For all members of the Church are disciples, who spend their whole lives trying to understand what Jesus taught.

After having established the apostles' mission, the resurrected Jesus declares to them: "And behold, I am with you always, until the end of the age." This, the last saying of the Lord reported in Matthew's Gospel, is a solemn promise that fulfills all earlier promises.[17] It is spoken not only to the first disciples, but to all those who, in the course of the ages, will form the people of God, gathered by Christ. To all those who will believe in him, the Lord will be present to assist, console, rescue, and strengthen them. Could the head separate itself from the body?

> When our Lord Jesus Christ ascended to heaven on the fortieth day, he laid a charge on his body that remained on the earth: he saw that many people would honor him because he had ascended to heaven, and he knew that this honor is useless if his members on earth are trampled underfoot . . .
>
> See how far his body stretches, see how he does not want to be trampled underfoot: "You are to be my witnesses in Jerusalem, throughout Judea and Samaria, and even to the ends of the earth." See where I am, who have ascended: I ascend because I am the head. My body still remains on the earth. Where is it? Everywhere. Be careful not to strike it, to do it violence, trampling it underfoot.
>
> These are the last words of Christ, who ascended to heaven.[18]

The Lord's ascension is a mystery that directly concerns the Church, "the fullness of him" whom God has established "above all things."

The Church is the place of manifestation of the invisible, though active, presence of the risen Lord, his sovereignty and power "always, until the end of the age."

Through baptism, one becomes a disciple of Christ in the Church, and one remains a disciple, thanks to the teaching of those whose duty it is to teach, as well as to the faithful observance of "all that [the Lord has] commanded you."

In and through the Church, the Father's work is continued: the assembling of all people under a single head, his Son, in the Spirit.

> Christ has ascended near to God, triumphant,
> To prepare the house, near to God.
> He remains with us in the land of the living,
> He remains with us, near to God.
> He will open to us, near to God, his kingdom,
> Welcoming sinners near to God.
>
> In heaven we will be near to God forever:
> No cold, no hunger near to God.

And we will sing, full of joy, full of love,
And we will sing near God.
And we will love, near to God, the universe
Completed by our hands, near to God!

In heaven we will have, near to God, happiness
In glory and peace, near to God.
For we will enter into the joy of the Lord,
For we will enter near to God.
And we will find, near to God, our Lady
And our brothers the saints, near to God.[19]

Christ Raised to Heaven, and the Church—His Body

Raised High Above the Heavens to Fill the Universe

The Letter to the Ephesians does not speak of the ascension as we typically understand it. But the passage from this "letter from prison"[1] that we read today shines a brilliant light on the mystery. The apostle reminds us of the riches of the Christian vocation, the gifts freely given to us, and the way the Church, the body of Christ "ascended far above all the heavens, that he might fill all things," is built. Moreover, at the center of his exposition, Paul quotes a verse of Psalm 68, traditionally used in the Latin liturgy for the ascension[2] (Eph 4:1-16).

The Christian calling, initiated by God, must be translated into a way of living marked with "all humility and gentleness, with patience . . ." and mutual support inspired by love; it encourages us to make every effort "to preserve the unity of the spirit through the bond of peace." These exhortations, coming from an apostle imprisoned "for the Lord" have lost none of their challenge for us today, in a troubled world and in a Church which is itself disturbed by conflicts and divisions which severely threaten its credibility. Must not the Church, rather, present to the world a model community wherein—since each member has received God's grace "given to each of us according to the measure of Christ's gift"— diversity is acknowledged as a blessing, and exists in harmony, mutual respect, and joy? A utopian fantasy? No; rather, a demand of faith. There is "one Lord, one faith, one baptism; one God and Father of all, who is over all and through all and in all." Once again, Paul reminds us that Christian morality is theological: to determine what one's behavior must be, it is necessary to return to faith, to turn toward God and Christ.

He "ascended far above the heavens, that he might fill all things." And we ask, "What does 'he ascended' mean except that he also descended into the lower regions of the earth?" This exaltation of Christ "far above the heavens" is the mystery celebrated today by the liturgy. The Apostles' Creed says that it followed "Christ's descent into hell," which here refers to the place where the just waited for the Lord to come and join them to his resurrection. In the Letter to the Philippians (2:6-9), Paul writes: Christ "humbled himself, becoming obedient to death, even death on a cross. Because of this, God greatly exalted him." Neither this text nor that from the Letter to the Ephesians is referring to that particular stage in Christ's passover that we call the ascension. Paul incorporates the Lord's exaltation into his one, great trajectory: "Though he was in the form of God, [he] did not regard equality with God something to be grasped" (Phil 2:6). He was made man, he took on "the form of a slave" (Phil 2:7). He died for the salvation of all people. That is why God lifted him above all and gave him "the name that is above every name." Henceforth, "Jesus Christ is Lord, to the glory of God the Father" (Phil 2:9-11). It is essential that when we celebrate one stage of Christ's mystery, we keep in mind the unity of the whole, even though the passover—death, resurrection, return to the Father, sending of the Spirit—is its summit.[3]

From this summit come gifts for "all": the charisms needed by the Church, especially those of governing and teaching. Thanks to them, "in roles of service the faithful build up the body of Christ," becoming "one in faith," "truth in love," "joined firmly together." Diversity and complementarity in functions is indispensable for every living organism, particularly the human body.[4] Even more is it so in the Church, the Body of Christ, of whom he is the head.[5] Thus "we become one in faith and the knowledge of God's Son, and form that perfect being who is Christ come to full stature."

> Word of God
> Come to take flesh
> in the virgin's womb,
> you veil your splendor
> in order to live as one of us.
> Today,
> more radiant than the sun,
> you disappear from our sight
> and return to the Father
> while the universe sings your praise:
>
> *You are the Lord,*
> *Glory to you, Son of Man!*
> *King of creation.*
>
> Rise up, Lord,
> show forth your power,
> and we will sing a hymn to your valor.

O Lord, our God,
how great is your name
throughout the earth.

Lord, our God,
you are so great,
clothed in majesty and glory.[6]

Proclaim the Gospel to All Nations

Mark's Gospel ends abruptly with the discovery of the empty tomb by Mary Magdalene, Mary, the mother of James, and Salome.[7] The canonical finale, whose last six verses we read today, seems to come from another hand. Nevertheless, it is regarded as an inspired text, like all other pages of Scripture.[8] It appears very early on—in the second century— and thus belongs to the Church's uncontested tradition (Mark 16:15-20).

The ascension is mentioned very succinctly, in one verse, like an article of the Creed. By way of contrast, the author dwells on the final mission the Lord imposed on the disciples, before leaving them, and the alacrity with which they performed it.

The "good news"—the gospel—a term that Mark is the only one to use without further qualification,[9] refers not to a doctrine but to the very person of Jesus.[10] He it is whom the disciples must announce to "the whole world," proclaiming him "to every creature." And because he himself is the object of this proclamation, "Whoever believes and is baptized will be saved; whoever does not believe will be condemned."[11] If it were a matter of doctrine—however sublime—this manner of speaking would be completely unacceptable.[12]

The apostles went forth unhesitatingly "and preached everywhere." Their promptness cuts through all those hesitations, discussions, and even conflicts that according to the Acts of the Apostles preceded the decision that an openness to the Gentiles conformed with the Lord's command (Acts 1:8).[13] The finale of Mark's Gospel goes beyond such evasive details, recalling that in fact the apostles did go out to bring the good news to "the whole world." Mark himself presents this as typical of Jesus' ministry. He always shows the Lord going forward, marching at the head of his disciples to lead them ever further, beyond their horizons, to Tyre and Sidon, on the other side of the Sea of Galilee, i.e., to the Gentiles.[14]

When he was still with them, Jesus had already sent his disciples forth to preach, giving them the power to drive out demons and heal the sick.[15] When he left them, he reconfirmed this power with all his authority as

Lord. The missionaries of the gospel were thus able to work signs that confirmed the Word. At Pentecost, the believers spoke in ecstatic utterances, which would reoccur on other occasions.[16] Ananias cured Paul of his blindness through the laying on of hands (Acts 9:17-18). At Malta, where the boat that was taking Paul to Rome as a prisoner was shipwrecked, he cured the father of Publius, the chief figure of the island, by prayer and the laying on of hands (Acts 28:8). Afterward, they brought him many sick, whom he healed in the same way (Acts 28:9). Also at this place, when he picked up a piece of wood, a viper bit his hand. The inhabitants, familiar with the snake's poison, said: "This man must really be a murderer; though he escaped the sea, Justice has not let him remain alive." But while they were waiting for him to swell up or fall down dead, Paul "shook the snake off into the fire and suffered no harm" (Acts 28:1-6). At Philippi, he drove "an oracular spirit" out of a woman, which made a number of enemies for Silas and him because the woman's masters had made a considerable profit out of her power (Acts 16:16-24). Such were some of the signs performed by the apostles that are recounted in Acts.[17]

The history of the Church tells us that the confirmation of the Word by signs did not end with the apostles. Even today the Lord gives his disciples such power, sometimes spectacularly, more often in a plain manner. The discernment of spirits by Jean-Baptiste Vianney of Ars (1786–1859) gave the word of this very simple priest an extraordinary authority. The life of Don John Bosco (1815–1888) is strewn with duly attested deeds of miraculous order. But one could just as well cite some of our contemporaries whose decisions and actions, especially in the realm of charity, are accompanied by signs showing that God is with them. Truly, "the Lord blossomed when he rose from he tomb. He brought forth fruit when he ascended to heaven."[18]

The candle solemnly blessed at the beginning of the Easter Vigil burns throughout the liturgies of the Easter season. It evokes the manifestations of the risen Christ who, beginning on Easter itself, came into the midst of his disciples, especially "on the first day of the week," to show them that he, whom they had seen crucified, really was alive. After Pentecost, the Easter candle is not lit during ordinary celebrations. Not because Christ is absent, but because he is present in another way.

"Seated at the right hand of God," he is with all those who in obedience to their mission proclaim the good news throughout the whole world.

From him, the Church, the body of which he is the head, receives those gifts, allowing us all to reach for "the full stature of Christ" (Eph 4:13).

In him, "the firstborn of all creation" (Col 1:15) and "the firstborn from the dead" (Col 1:18), we can hold fast in faith.

In him, if we live "the truth in love," we will grow to the full stature of Christ" (Eph 4:15).

> We sing to you, resurrected,
> your sun rises on humanity,
> you have emerged victorious from the shadow of the tomb,
> the living sun of the new age.
>
> The whole universe is brought to light
> and finally able to call you "love."
> A new song for the lost children:
> the name of God is given to us.
>
> You have thrown wide for your people
> the gate of the ancient garden,
> where God invites all men to joy
> under the spreading tree of your cross.
>
> You who sleep, awaken,
> the night sends out the signal of the bridegroom.
> He comes to seek out believers,
> "Amen" of the glory of the living God.[19]

Christ, Our Hope, Raised to Heaven

High Priest in the Sanctuary of Heaven

The ascension is not an isolated episode. No scriptural text that presents the Lord being raised to heaven after his resurrection speaks of it thus. It is part of the mystery, it is a fact concerning the person and mission of the Son of God who came to dwell a little while among us, taking on human nature, and who, at a time established by the Father, returned to him. As the mystery of God and his Christ, this fact concerns all people, pointing them to their salvation, collectively and individually. It cannot be envisioned except in this double dimension. Scripture does not speak of God and Christ "in themselves" abstractly, but of God and Christ known in faith, such as they are for us: this is the mystery in its concrete reality.[1] To speak of the Lord's ascension, one must necessarily resort to images: "he ascended . . . he was raised to heaven." But one quickly goes beyond such images in order to meditate on and to contemplate Christ in glory, the benefits his exaltation "at God's right hand" brings to the world. We can see this, for example, in the Letter to the Hebrews.

In chapter 9, verses 24-28,[2] the author, in speaking of the meaning of the enthronement of the risen Christ near the Father, evokes the rite performed once a year in the Temple for the feast of atonement.[3] On that day, after having offered a sacrifice for his own sins and another for the sins of the people, the high priest entered the innermost sanctuary, and purified it with the blood of the goat sacrificed in the outer Temple.[4] These rites made it possible for sacrifices to be offered in the Temple, which was in this way washed clean of all defilement. In Jewish communities, Yom Kippur is still the great annual feast where the people are purified.[5]

Seen in the context of this ritual, the mystery of the ascension becomes much clearer, even resplendent. "Christ did not enter into a sanctuary made by hands, . . . but heaven itself." He appears "before God on our behalf. Not that he might offer himself repeatedly, as the high priest enters each year into the sanctuary with blood that is not his own." Christ has destroyed sin once and for all by his own sacrifice: one can only die once. But after death, each must appear for judgment. Christ too "will appear a second time, not to take away sin but to bring salvation to those who eagerly await him."

In his wake, we can, even now, "through the blood of Jesus . . . have confidence of entrance into the sanctuary." He has opened for us a "new and living way . . . through the veil, that is, his flesh" (Heb 10:19-23). Christ's passover fulfills what he had said: "I will destroy this temple made with hands and within three days I will build another not made with hands" (Mark 14:58); "But from this time on the Son of Man will be seated at the right hand of the power of God" (Luke 22:69). This is our high priest, who by his death and resurrection has torn away the curtain that separated us from the true sanctuary, which is God's dwelling in heaven.

Washed clean by the "pure water" of baptism, we may walk with greater confidence toward God. The Lord has left us, with the sacrament of his Body and Blood, the guarantee of eternal life.

> On this day has ascended to heaven
> the new and spiritual bread,
> and all the mysteries have been revealed
> in your Body, raised like an offering.
> Blest be this bread, O Lord!
>
> As light falling from heaven,
> he was born of Mary, like a divine seed,
> fell from the cross like a ripe fruit,
> and was raised to heaven as one raises the
> first-fruits.
> Blest be your will![6]

Witnesses of Christ Taken Up to Heaven

As it brings Jesus' earthly mission to an end, the ascension ushers in a new age, toward which the Lord himself had directed the disciples: the age of the Church and its mission. The last appearance of the risen Christ, which ends Luke's Gospel, leads the way to this future, and Acts will show its wonderful blossoming (Luke 24:46-53).

The Lord's passover—the Messiah must "suffer and rise from the dead on the third day"—is the finale of God's plan, the fulfillment of "what was written in Scripture."[7] It must be our constant touchstone. Scripture witnesses to Christ and his passover; at the same time, the Lord's passover sheds its light on Scripture, especially on Jesus' teachings and sayings. In the same way, "repentance, for the forgiveness of sins, would be preached in his name to all nations, beginning from Jerusalem," the realization of God's plan progressively revealed by Scripture, is the final stage of the Lord's passover.

"You are witnesses of these things." It would be impossible to express more simply and clearly what Jesus henceforth expects from his disciples. "Witnesses": people who attest confidently to what they have seen and know. Witnesses so credible that each of us can say: "To accept and understand that everything that happened to the Lord was willed by God is not enough. Look at the apostles: it took them a long time; Jesus himself had to explain to them the mystery of his death and resurrection. Without constant reference to his teaching and to Scripture, faith runs the risk of succumbing to doubt. If we can be witnesses, it is due to the testimony, in us, of the power from on high promised by the Father and sent by the Lord."

With this promise, Jesus left his disciples, while blessing them in a manner reminiscent of what is recounted in the eulogy to the high priest Simon (Sir 50:20). The apostles then returned to Jerusalem, filled with "great joy." Perhaps they had in their hearts the prophecy of Zechariah that proclaims another meeting at the end of time: "That day his feet shall rest upon the Mount of Olives, which is opposite Jerusalem to the east. . . . Then the Lord, my God, shall come, and all his holy ones with him" (Zech 14:4-5).

At the end of his Gospel, Luke has painted the ascension as a picture of stark holiness and majesty, like an icon.[8] The scene ends like a liturgy: "Go in peace." The Mass of the world is about to begin, with the proclamation of the gospel to all nations and the gathering of the faithful around the resurrected one who nourishes them with his Body and Blood, giving them a share in his paschal mystery while they wait for him to come again and take them with him.

> Today our Lord Jesus Christ ascended into heaven; let our hearts ascend with him. Listen to the words of the Apostle: "If then you were raised with Christ, seek what is above, where Christ is seated at the right hand of God. Think of what is above, not of what is in earth." For just as he remained with us even after his ascension, so we too are already in heaven with him, even though what is promised us has not yet been fulfilled in our bodies.
>
> Christ is now exalted above the heavens, but he still suffers on earth all the pain that we, the members of his body, have to bear. He showed this when he cried out from above: "Saul, Saul, why do you persecute me?" and when he said: "I was hungry and you gave me food."

Why do we here on earth not strive to find rest with him in heaven even now, by way of the faith, hope, and love that unites us to him? While in heaven he is also with us; and we, though on earth, are with him. He is here with us by his divinity, his power, and his love. We cannot be in heaven, as he is on earth, by divinity, but in him, we can be there by love.[9]

In the meantime, the apostles went to Jerusalem to give thanks in the Temple. The announcement of John the Baptist's birth was made at the Temple (Luke 1:5-23).[10] Jesus spent the last days of his life there (Luke 21:37-38). And it was at the Temple where Peter and John performed their first sign (Acts 3:1-10), where the apostles began to proclaim Jesus Christ (Acts 3:11-26), where they were arrested (Acts 4:1), and where, ignoring all dangers, and after having been freed from prison, they returned to preach boldly (Acts 4:23; 5:25).

At Easter, beloved brethren, it was the Lord's resurrection that was the cause of our joy; our present rejoicing is because of his ascension into heaven. With all due solemnity we are commemorating that day on which our poor human nature was carried up in Christ above all the hosts of heaven, above all the ranks of angels, beyond the highest heavenly powers to the very throne of God the Father. It is upon this ordered structure of divine acts that we have been firmly established, so that the grace of God may show itself still more marvelous when, in spite of the withdrawal from men's sight of everything that is rightly felt to command their reverence, faith does not fail, hope is not shaken, charity does not grow cold.

For such is the power of great minds, such the light of truly believing souls, that they put unhesitating faith in what is not seen with the bodily eye; they fix their desires on what is beyond sight. Such fidelity could never be born in our hearts, nor could anyone be justified by faith if our salvation lay only in what was visible.

And so our Redeemer's visible presence has passed into the sacraments. Our faith is nobler and stronger because sight has been replaced by a doctrine whose authority is accepted by believing hearts, enlightened from on high.[11]

The ascension is a mystery of hope. Christ, by entering the sanctuary of heaven, has opened up a way for us to follow him at his return. Christian life is sustained by this hope, the object of the Church's prayer—"Come, Lord Jesus!" (Rev 22:20)—expressed in the Eucharist that is celebrated every day "until he comes in glory."[12] But does this desire possess us as strongly as it should? "Christians, charged after Israel with always keeping alive the flame of desire, what has happened to our hope, twenty centuries after the ascension?"[13]

This very hope lies at the root of the apostolic mission and witness, with which the Lord charged his disciples when he left them. They go to the rendezvous fixed for them beyond the veil of the sanctuary, all the while proclaiming to every nation conversion and the forgiveness of sins.

> O Son of God resurrected,
> Why do we seek your face
> In the skies?
> You come to us on every shore
> Of humanity.
>
> Heaven is where you descend,
> You give living water to your people,
> Living Love,
> And you draw us like a stream
> Into your current.
>
> The joy promised to our thirst,
> How shall we seize it in both hands
> Before the evening?
> In partaking of your Supper
> And of your cross.
>
> You will return to transfigure
> The world eager to be reborn
> In your light.
> You are the glory of your Father,
> God revealed.[14]

Thanksgiving Prayer of Christ and the Church

A Small Community United by Prayer

In the Acts of the Apostles, Luke paints a picture of the early Christian community three times.[1] But before this, he notes that immediately after they had seen Jesus "going into heaven," the apostles gathered around themselves a small group of the Lord's disciples. In a way, this was the prototype Church (Acts 1:12-14).

The gathering took place in Jerusalem, not far from Mount Olivet, from which Jesus had ascended to heaven.[2] The apostles stayed in an "upper room" somewhere in the city. Such a vague term does not allow us to determine their exact location.[3] But it suggests that there already was a place in Jerusalem where the disciples could rally, though we do not know how long it had been available.[4] This means that the apostles and disciples could not have been in total disarray after the Lord's death.[5]

More important is the fact, certainly emphasized here, that this first "official" gathering took place around the apostles. Luke thus proceeds to name them[6]: they are the Church's nucleus, though not its whole. Other disciples were there as well. Luke also notes the presence of "some women," though he neither names nor numbers them. Coming from Luke, one would almost expect him to mention names. In his Gospel, he pointed out that there were women accompanying Jesus and the Twelve: they had been "cured of evil spirits and infirmities, Mary called Magdalene, from whom seven demons had gone out, Joanna, the wife of Herod's steward Chuza, Susanna, and many others who provided for them out of their resources" (Luke 8:2-3).[7] In Acts he will note the readiness of women—some of them "prominent" (Acts 17:4)—to receive the good news, their role in the spreading of the faith (Acts 16:3-4), and their zeal for works of charity, with Tabitha of Joppa as a model (Acts 9:36-43).

Among those who were in Jerusalem after the ascension, Luke names only "Mary the mother of Jesus." The one who bore the Savior in her womb is with the apostles when the Spirit descends to bring the Church to birth. This is not surprising: in the body of Christ, whom she bore, Mary continues to occupy a privileged place in the unfolding of her son's work.[8]

Jesus' "brothers," i.e., his relatives, are mentioned last, after the women. Why are they mentioned at all? Aside from Mary, it does not seem—as John testifies and Mark confirms (Mark 3:21)—that Jesus' relatives were very eager to follow him: "For his brothers did not believe in him" (John 7:5). But they wanted Jesus to dazzle Jerusalem with his miracles (John 7:3-4). They dreamed of seeing their kinsman gloriously exalted in this world. Jesus told them that they were deceived about his mission. He let them go up to Jerusalem for the feast of Booths. He went too, but later, "not openly but [as it were] in secret" (John 76-10). Thereafter, except for James, who played an important role in the Jerusalem community,[9] the brothers of Jesus who believed in him blended into the group of the disciples.

The atmosphere of this assembly is like that of a retreat. We hear nothing of the conversations that must have occurred. Not a word is said about what had happened, their feelings, doubts, or regrets after the Lord's departure. This is the silence where the future grows.

> All that is true
> can be noiseless
>
> Fruits without noise ripen
> And shed their leaves in silence
>
> The snow covers them without a word
> Frost grips the lake in stealth
> Death comes like sleep
>
> Silent act of begetting
> The sun's light does not scream
> No one hears the snow
> when it begins to melt
>
> The grass rises from the earth
> without saying a word
> There is no fanfare
> when the flowers open
>
> All that is true
> can be noiseless
>
> At least to our ears:
> It is not human to see
> what the owl sees.[10]

Instead, Luke says that they "devoted themselves with one accord to prayer." Unity of hearts, fraternal communion, and devotion to prayers are characteristics of the early Christian community, as Luke makes clear in his "pictures." After Pentecost, he will add "devotion to the apostles' instruction."[11] Finally, he says that the disciples, who, "breaking bread in their homes," "met together in the temple area" for prayer (Acts 2:46).[12]

It is in this same atmosphere of meditation, fraternal charity, and prayer, that the Church prepares to celebrate today, at Pentecost, a new pouring forth of the Spirit on the Lord's disciples.

> *I believe that I shall see the bounty of the* LORD
>   *in the land of the living.*

The LORD is my light and my salvation;
  whom should I fear?
The LORD is my life's refuge;
  of whom should I be afraid?

One thing I ask of the LORD;
  this I seek:
To dwell in the house of the LORD
  all the days of my life,
That I may gaze upon the loveliness of the LORD
  and contemplate his temple.

Hear, O LORD, the sound of my call;
  have pity on me, and answer me.
Of you my heart speaks; you my glance seeks.
(Ps 27:1, 4, 7-8a)

There Is No Shame in Suffering for Being a Christian

The cross of Christ is familiar to us. Without forgetting that it was an instrument of torture on which the Lord died, we regard it, quite rightly, as the instrument of his glory.[13] We never meditate on his sufferings without raising our eyes to heaven, where he is seated at the right hand of God. Even so, it is difficult to say just how this mystery of suffering-death-glorification guides our lives, by virtue of our Christianity. Yet this is the case, as Peter proclaimed in the fragment of his First Letter that we read today (1 Pet 4:13-16).

The apostle is speaking to those of the faithful who are enduring suffering and scorn "for the name of Christ."[14] This is to be expected, writes Peter. You must rejoice, you must count yourselves fortunate because "the Spirit of glory and of God rests upon you." Thus will you fully honor your title of "Christian." We know that people have always thought of those who endure suffering, torture, and death for a great and noble cause as glorious martyrs. Christian martyrs give glory to God. Their sharing in Christ's suffering enables them to share in his passover. "The centurion who witnessed what had happened glorified God and said, 'This man was innocent beyond doubt'" (Luke 23:47). Happy those martyrs whose sufferings endured "for the name of Christ" inspire such praise!

> We have found great joy, brother Cyprian, great consolation, great comfort, especially in these worthy praises that you have bestowed I will not say on the death, but rather on the glorious immortality of the martyrs. . . . What greater glory, what greater happiness could befall a man through the benefit of divine grace than to confess the Lord without fear, amid his tormentors, than to be fearless in the midst of the various and refined tortures of the power of the age, with a torn, bruised, mangled body, than to confess Christ the Son of God, with a fleeting, but still free spirit? . . . What is more beautiful than to become, in confessing the name of Christ, a partner in his passion, to judge, through divine grace, his own judge, to be spotless while confessing the name of Christ, not to bow before human and sacrilegious laws that are contrary to the Law, publicly swearing to the truth, submitting to the death that all the world fears, being assured by death itself of immortality, and overcoming all torments through these torments themselves, giving one's body to torture and to being rent by the instruments of torture? . . . Pray then, most beloved Cyprian, that the Lord, by his grace, may equip us and glorify us more and more each day, sustaining and affirming our strength and, like a great general with the soldiers whom he has only tested in the camp, lead us out of prison into the plain of battle. May he give us these heavenly arms, these invincible weapons, the breastplate of justice that nothing can break, the shield of faith that nothing can pierce, and the sword of the spirit that nothing can shatter.[15]

We readily join in the praise of martyrs, recognizing that by their sufferings and death, they give glory to God. But we must go further: it is impossible to be a Christian without seeing oneself ordinarily confronted with suffering in one form or another, and without accepting this perspective. The Lord himself said very clearly: "If they have called the master of the house Beelzebul, how much more those of his household!" (Matt 10:25); "Whoever wishes to come after me must deny himself, take up his cross, and follow me" (Mark 8:34); "If they persecuted me, they will also persecute you" (John 15:20). But he also declared: "Blessed are you when they insult you and persecute you and utter every kind of evil against you [falsely] because of me. Rejoice and be glad, for your reward will be great in heaven" (Matt 5:11-12).

To be sure, suffering is an evil. We do not seek it for its own sake. But one cannot say "yes" to Christ for a whole life without having to say "no" to many things, many advantages, satisfactions, and goods that are, certainly, ephemeral and often deceptive, but the refusal of which, "for the name of Christ," nevertheless involves denials that are painful, even crucifying, not to say heroic. Christian life exists under the sign of Christ's paschal mystery of death and resurrection (1 John 3:13-14). Paul echoes Peter: "I wish to know [Christ] and the power of his resurrection and [the] sharing of his sufferings by being conformed to his death, if somehow I may attain the resurrection from the dead" (Phil 3:10-11).[16]

There is no dolorous, stoic, or scornful view of suffering in this unanimous teaching of Scripture and tradition. Rather, there is a grappling in faith with the meaning and value of Christ's passover, and a willingness to share in it, as the Lord has promised.

The Glory of the Father and the Son

The chapter in John's Gospel that immediately precedes the story of the passion recounts Jesus' long prayer "when the hour had come for him to pass from this world to the Father." Addressed to the Father, this prayer, in its composition, resembles what one might call a Eucharistic prayer. Jesus pronounced it, "raising his eyes"[17] and blessing God for the fulfillment of salvation through the passover of his Son and for its bestowal on the disciples who received the gift of the Spirit.[18] This prayer has the Trinitarian structure of all liturgical and Eucharistic prayers: to the Father, through the Son, in the Spirit. The passage moves uninterruptedly from thanksgiving to intercession in the same format, leading always to the Father, through the Son, in the Spirit. With no parallels in the other Gospels, this text is extremely important: by placing before our eyes the mystery of salvation in its totality and by presenting it in its internal dynamic,[19] it is the perfect model for all Christian prayer and liturgy. Today we read the first part of it (John 17:1b-11a).[20]

"Father, the hour has come." Despite the fact that it is said at this particular time, this is not really a prayer "before" the passion but a prayer that is situated in the present moment of the mystery accomplished once for all at a historical hour, though that moment transcends time. Therefore we can say, in the Eucharistic Prayer: "Today you revealed in Christ your eternal plan of salvation" (Epiphany), "Christ became our paschal sacrifice" (Easter), "Christ ascended to heaven" (Ascension).

This is the "hour" of the Son's glorification that gives glory to the Father and reflects back on believers. Christ has received "authority over all'' from his Father. He exercises this universal lordship by giving eternal life to all those whom the Father has given him and to whom he has revealed himself: "For God so loved the world that he gave his only Son, so that everyone who believes in him might not perish but might have eternal life" (John 3:16); "I did not come to condemn the world but to save the world" (John 12:47).

The work performed by the Lord—his "signs"—allows one to recognize him as the messenger of God[21] and, at the same time, to glorify the Father toward whom the disciples' eyes are turned.[22] "No one has ever seen God. The only Son, God, who is at the Father's side, has revealed him" (John 1:18). Jesus can, in thanksgiving, recognize that he has brought the Father's work, which was given to him, to its end, and present it to him in homage: "It is finished" (John 19:30). Now, Jesus has only to return to the Father to receive from his hand the glory that he had in his presence before the world began.[23]

From the offering of his life and the recollection—anamnesis[24]—of what he has done, Jesus moves to intercession as we have learned to do in the Eucharistic Prayer. He prays for his disciples who are in the world while he will henceforth be with God. They too contribute to his glory and the Father's. They know that his is their calling: "By this is my Father glorified, that you bear much fruit and become my disciples" (John 15:8). They also know that the Spirit is given to them to prepare them for it: "[The Spirit] will guide you to all truth . . . He will glorify me, because he will take from what is mine and declare it to you" (John 16:13, 14). Everything that belongs to Christ belongs to the Father, just as everything that belongs to the Father belongs to Christ. Through him, with him, in him and in the Spirit, we belong to God.

> Christ, who promised to make his disciples one in God with him, who promised that we would be in God and God in us, has realized this in a mysterious way: he has accomplished this great work, this stupendous privilege for us. It seems that it was in rising toward the Father that he did this, that his corporeal ascension is his spiritual descent, that his assumption of our nature to God is the descent of God to us, that he has truly, albeit in a hidden sense, borne us to God, or that he has led God to us, depending on which point of view one adopts.[25]

Jesus passed from this world to his Father in prayer, a prayer that gave thanks to God for the work which reached its summit at the "hour." So too the Church prays, following the example of the disciples gathered together in the upper room, while waiting for the gift of the Spirit. It blesses God who chose the Church to make known to the whole world "the only true God" and the one whom he sent, Jesus Christ. It gives thanks for Christ's heavenly glory and the gift of faith that makes him known to those who faithfully keep his word.

If we suffer with him and for him, with him and in him we will experience joy and gladness when his glory is revealed. "The Spirit of glory, the Spirit of God" is upon us: may the day come when we will appear fully as what we already are!

> The earth rejoices,
> it bears its first fruit of glory:
> Jesus has risen to the Father!
> In joy, the earth brings forth the promise!
> Calm in its humility,
> it draws the light from on high.
>
> *Come, Spirit of God!*
> *Come engulf the universe in your glory!*
>
> You are the life of all life,
> the youth that renews everything.
>
> You are the heart of the world,
> beating in the rhythm of love.
>
> You are the joy and hope
> that bear us to the Father.[26]

The Lord Dwells with His Own

A Twelfth Witness to the Resurrection

Just before his account of Pentecost, Luke tells of the selection, suggested by Peter, of a replacement for Judas, to be "counted with the eleven apostles."[1] Nothing about the origins of the Christian community can be a matter of indifference for us. There are always teachings that point to later developments in the Church. The apostles chosen by the Lord had authority over the Church at this time. Yet God himself was clearly present, his Spirit guiding the first steps of the Church established by his Son (Acts 1:15-17, 20a, 20c-26).[2]

No specific date for the gathering is given, only the phrase "during those days." Not many years ago, this was said at the beginning of the proclamation of the Gospel in the Mass: "In those days." One thing is certain: a group had formed even before Pentecost.[3] Already it was large: "about one hundred and twenty persons." Most importantly, Peter appears here as the leader of the community, the first of the apostles.[4] He is the one who suggests to the community that a replacement for Judas should be found, and establishes criteria for the candidates. But why "is it necessary" to appoint someone to Judas' place? The argument that Peter draws from Scripture—"For it is written in the Book of Psalms: 'May another take his office' "—hardly seems convincing to us. Rather, we feel that a seemingly haphazard selection of scriptural texts is a forced way of saying something. But this is not the only time that the New Testament refers to Psalm 69, particularly with respect to the events of the passion.[5] If this psalm is read as a prophecy of what would happen to Jesus, it is perfectly natural to apply to Judas a verse that seems to fit him so well. He did not profit by his treachery: he cast away the money he had received, and it was used to buy a piece of barren land (Ps 69:26). As for Psalm 109, it is the prayer of a persecuted just man:

> O God, whom I praise, be not silent,
>   for they have opened wicked and treacherous mouths against me.
> They have spoken to me with lying tongues,
>   and with words of hatred they have
>   encompassed me

and attacked me without cause.
In return for my love they slandered me,
   but I prayed.
They repaid me evil for good
   and hatred for my love . . .

And I am become a mockery to them;
   when they see me, they shake their heads.
(Ps 109:1-5, 25)

How can we read this passage without thinking of Christ and his passion when a friend betrayed him? Doesn't the verse, "May another take his office" (Ps 109:8b) suggest a replacement for Judas? This is what Peter thinks. Jesus chose a group of twelve; the fact that one proved traitor must not disrupt this group: appointing a replacement is authorized by Scripture. Thus the group will not feel that one of its members has been cut off.[6]

Peter suggests choosing a man from among those who accompanied Jesus the whole time he lived on earth, "from the baptism of John until the day on which he was taken up from us," i.e., during the time of his public ministry. This man will be, along with the Eleven, "a witness to [Jesus'] resurrection," which cannot be separated from what Jesus did and taught ever since his first appearance on the banks of the Jordan. The testimony of the Twelve is and remains a foundation of the Church's faith.[7] Nothing can replace it. Hence, not every member of the Twelve will be replaced when he dies, e.g., James, the brother of John, the first to perish by the sword (Acts 12:2). Those who will later be called "successors of the apostles"—the bishops—together assure the continuity of the Twelve's authority in the Church's mission and pastoral government.[8] Thus their number has no limit. However, the Twelve are still the privileged and official witnesses to the resurrection.[9]

Two men are presented who fit Peter's criteria: "Joseph called Barsabbas, who was also known as Justus, and Matthias." The assembly prays that God, who knows the human heart, may show which one he chooses. They cast lots, and Matthias is chosen.

Jesus told the apostles: "It was not you who chose me, but I who chose you" (John 15:16). The appointment of Matthias shows that one does not arrogate the ministry to oneself: one is called to it by God and the Church. To offer oneself as a candidate under the impulse of grace is a good and proper thing: "Whoever aspires to the office of bishop desires a noble task" (1 Tim 3:1). However, this desire must be tested: one must submit oneself to the Church's discernment, through which God's will is made

manifest. Joseph Barsabbas must have been a man with remarkable qualities, since he was called "the just" (Justus).[10] Yet Matthias became the
twelfth apostle; after that, he is mentioned no more in Acts.[11]

Before leaving us, Jesus laid the foundations of his Church: the apostles
who accompanied him throughout his ministry and who became witnesses of his resurrection. Through them, the gospel has been preached
to all nations and faithfully passed on to us. Their ministry is perpetu-
ated in the college of bishops, with the pope as its head. "This college,
in so far as it is composed of many members, is the expression of the
multifariousness and universality of the people of God; and of the unity
of the flock of Christ, in so far as it is assembled under one head."[12] The
Lord's promise never ceases to be realized: he watches over his own (Luke
12:32).

> The LORD has established his throne in heaven.
>
> Bless the LORD, O my soul;
>   and all my being, bless his holy name.
> Bless the LORD, O my soul,
>   and forget not all his benefits.
>
> For as the heavens are high above the earth,
>   so surpassing is his kindness toward
>   those who fear him
> As far as the east is from the west,
>   so far has he put our transgressions from us.
>
> The LORD has established his throne in heaven,
>   and his kingdom rules over all.
> Bless the LORD, all you his angels,
>   you mighty in strength, who do his bidding.
>   (Ps 103:1-2, 11-12, 19-20ab)

"God Is Love"

Today we continue to read John's exposition on the love that is in God.[13]
Actually, what John offers is a kind of eminence, a meditation on this
mystery. It is in God and through him that the contemplative sees very
simply what he will discover in being constantly drawn on in the light
of this bright fire. Thus one returns to the center where new wonders
appear. This mystical witness should not therefore be regarded as a treatise that follows the forms of discursive logic.[14] Nor is this to be regretted,
for John opens up infinite horizons for our own penetration of the mystery (1 John 4:11-16).

God so loved us that he sent us his only Son (John 3:16). In the face
of such a revelation, the human spirit falters: how can we possibly re-

spond to this infinite love; how can we even know if we love God? For "no one has ever seen God." "Whoever remains in love remains in God and God in him. In this is love brought to perfection among us." This is because God is not content to point to what he reveals: he communicates it. "He has given us of his Spirit" of love so that we in our turn might love those whom he loves without measure, so that we might be like him.

> If God would stop giving, he would cease to be God. The spring that flows no more is no longer a spring. And I who am a spring of likeness to my Father, I lose my being in so far as wishing to seize it I oppose its flow.
>
> Existence is not a brute fact. All existence is vigor, tension, expansion, movement towards the other, and response to its call. If Being is love, to exist is to love. But the point of this verb has been dulled: one must find words that express more precisely what one means. To love is to forget, to sacrifice, to lose oneself, to give up everything.
>
> Whether it is a poor flower or a grand bouquet is God's concern alone. But, however little I give, may that little be everything.[15]

This God whom we cannot see is seen in the face of the other. At the same time, he reveals himself more and more to our heart.[16] Love for others is a public confession of faith in God and his Son, the Savior of the world: it witnesses that God's love is among us (John 15:17). Not in words alone but in acts must one say to the world: "God is love."

> God so loved the world that he gave it his only Son. Ask no more who has united earth and heaven, the cross, and greatness in Jesus Christ: "God so loved the world." Is it incredible that God loves, and that bounty is given? Let this not encourage strong souls to a love of glory, or more vulgar souls to love of wealth, or anyone anything that bears the name of love! No cost, no peril, no travail, no pain; and see the wonders of which man is capable. So if man, who is only weak, attempts the impossible, will not God, to satisfy his love, do the extraordinary? Let us then say with good cause in all the mysteries: "God so loved the world." This is the master's doctrine, and the beloved disciples understood it well . . . This is the whole of Christian faith; this is the source and summary of every creed . . . God has loved: this says everything.[17]

In Faith, Truth, Unity, and Joy

When the "hour had come for him to pass from this world to the Father," Jesus, in a profoundly moving prayer, entrusted his disciples to the one whom he was about to rejoin. This confident intercession reveals that the Lord, who is now seated at the right hand of the Father in heaven, watches over his own today even better than he could while he was visibly present in their midst. For this prayer, said before the passion, belongs to the resurrected Lord raised in God's presence as his Son (John 17:11b-19).[18]

The Gospels tell us this: the whole time he was with them, Jesus watched over his disciples. They clearly recognized this: even when the Lord sent them out "without a money bag or a sack or sandals," they lacked nothing (Luke 22:35). With infinite patience, he kept them faithful to the Father's name, he taught them the Word, striving, in ever new ways and without being discouraged, to open their minds to it. Despite what he demanded of them, not one of them was lost, except Judas, through his own fault. Jesus, nevertheless, did not lack vigilance on his behalf and did not test his weakness. This reminder of the defection of one of the Twelve—"Even my friend who had my trust and partook of my bread, has raised his heel against me" (Ps 41:10)—is a solemn and tragic appeal to our fidelity and, paradoxically, an assurance. Nothing can corrupt the one who remains attached to the Father and his Son, whoever trusts in them.

> Jesus has revealed the Father's name to the disciples, to those men who were given him. He has told them that he was sent by the Father, and they believed him. He has told them that his Word is living truth. He has bestowed on them the glory the Father has granted him. He has given them his love. All this is true, and yet they are still who they are. One must imagine then that these treasures exist in them like seeds lying in the earth, without their knowledge. Despite their cowardice and lack of understanding, all this is within the disciples thanks to the miracle of all-powerful grace. When, after the Lord's departure, the Spirit will come, its fire will warm the seed and cause it to sprout. Then, human will and knowledge will grow alongside the divine reality the Lord has made to rest in them. Indeed, until that time it was in them while they were absent. Now, it will be in them and they in it. Now, they believe and bear witness, without knowing how they have received this supreme grace of being carried over the dark abyss.[19]

Jesus first asks his Father that his disciples may remain faithful to the Word. It will give them cause for joy in the midst of their trials. Even if the "world" persecutes them, they will see in this hate an acknowledgment of their Christian authenticity.[20] After being beaten for their preaching, the apostles "left the presence of the Sanhedrin, rejoicing that they had been found worthy to suffer dishonor for the sake of the name" (Acts 5:41).

Jesus does not ask his Father to take the disciples from the world, but to guard them from the evil one; indeed, they are "sent into the world." To try to evade this would be a temptation, a lack of faith and confidence in God as well as a desertion. When Christians pray, they say: "Our Father who art in heaven, hallowed be thy name. Thy kingdom come . . . deliver us from evil."

> What will separate us from the love of Christ?
> Distress, anguish, persecution, hunger,
> want, peril, the sword?
>
> *Save us, Lord,*
> *Gather us in your love!*
>
> What will separate us from the love of Christ?
> Yes, I am confident that neither death, nor life, nor angels,
> nor the present, nor the future, nor powers will do so.
>
> *Save us, Lord,*
> *Gather us in your love!*
>
> What will separate us from the love of Christ?
> Neither the powers of height nor depth,
> nor any other creature,
> nothing can separate us from the love of God,
> manifested in Jesus Christ, our Savior.[21]

Finally, Jesus asks his Father that the disciples may be "consecrated in truth" and that they may be "one." In a hostile world, the Christian life that is faithful to God and to his Christ, the witness given by prayer and the proclamation of the good news are worship of God.[22] They are offerings acceptable to him, as was Christ's. Without this, worship rather offends God than pleases him.

Throughout his life, Jesus prayed: when he participated in the synagogal liturgies or Temple celebrations, when he spent whole nights in solitude. But the veil was lifted on the eve of his passion: when the "hour had come for him to pass from this world to the Father," he prayed aloud in his disciples' presence. The prayer he addressed to his Father reveals him as the Lord, such as he is before God and for us.

Sent by the Father for our salvation, he eternally intercedes for his own so that they may pursue the mission conferred on them, in fidelity to the Word in truth, unity, and joy. As he loved his own in the world to the end (John 13:1), Jesus, seated at the right hand of the Father, loves them for eternity. Through his prayer as beloved Son, he continues to watch over his disciples, that none of them may be lost. He, the only one who has ever seen God, sees him also in those to whom he has made the Father known.

All the more reason that we, who have never seen God's face, should recognize him in those around us. Each of us is a reflection of the invisible face of God for others. In loving one another, it is God whom we love! The love of God revealed in Jesus Christ and poured out in our hearts by the Holy Spirit is the source and object of the preaching of the Church founded on the apostles, witnesses of all that Jesus did and of his resurrection. This is also the love that gathers us together to remember Christ's passover in the celebration of the Eucharist, sharing the same bread, drinking the same cup while saying to each other: ''God so loved the world!'' And we pray: ''Father . . . grant that we, who are nourished by his body and blood, may be filled with his Holy Spirit, and become one body, one spirit in Christ. May he make us an everlasting gift to you.''[23]

> On that night,
> Jesus prayed for his disciples,
> he who was their joy in this world,
> who wanted them to be faithful.
>
> Now joy and fidelity
> can open our hearts
> opening to the infinite:
> Christ is living in the presence of God.
>
> Father, send your Spirit,
> sanctify your people!
>
> The Son came into the world for you:
> you will be his witnesses
> in the world.
>
> The Son is consecrated to the Father for you:
> you will serve the Father
> in truth.
>
> Over you the Son has watched in the night:
> you will keep his word
> till the dawn.[24]

Behold Christ, Standing at the Right Hand of God

Christian Martyrdom and Christ's Passover

The very carefully written story of Stephen's martyrdom takes up a good deal of space in the Acts of the Apostles.[1] The death of the first martyr, shedding his blood to witness to Christ,[2] was an extremely important event in the early Church; thus it deserved to be set down at length and in detail. But the way Luke does so betrays his intent, i.e., to offer his readers the perfect model of a disciple. Particularly significant is the end of the story (Acts 7:55-60).[3]

At Stephen's trial, the judges are struck by the look on his face, which is like that of an angel (Acts 6:15). At the end of his speech, "filled with the holy Spirit," he looks "to heaven" and sees "the glory of God," and Jesus—the Son of Man—"standing at the right hand of God." We are reminded of Daniel's vision: "As the visions during the night continued, I saw One like a son of man coming, on the clouds of heaven; he reached the Ancient One and was presented before him" (Dan 7:13). Likewise with a verse from one of the messianic psalms: "The Lord said to my Lord, 'Sit at my right hand' " (Ps 110:1). But whereas the psalm says that the Messiah was "seated" and Daniel saw the Son of Man coming toward God, Stephen sees Jesus "standing" at the right hand of God. When one realizes how precise Luke's vocabulary is, it is obvious that such a change means something.[4] The fact that Jesus "stands" in God's presence indicates his relationship with the believer. He is "standing" like a lawyer for the accused before his judges. Jesus had promised: "Remember, you are not to prepare your defense beforehand, for I myself shall give you a wisdom in speaking that all of your adversaries will be powerless to resist or refute" (Luke 21:14-15).[5] Now, Stephen proves the truth of that promise. His accusers "could not withstand the wisdom and the spirit with which he spoke" (Acts 6:10). The judges themselves are unable to answer him. They can only cover their ears and shout at him.

One might imagine that the Son of Man is "standing," ready to come "in a cloud with power and great glory" (Luke 21:27). Luke, like the other evangelists,[6] proclaims this judgment. But he indicates that something is to happen first, namely the announcement of the gospel to the nations (Acts 1:7-8, 11); and this will also be a time of persecutions: "Before all this happens, however, they will seize and persecute you, they will hand you over to the synagogues and to prisons, and they will have you led before kings and governors because of my name. It will lead to your giving testimony" (Luke 21:12-13).

The early Christians were profoundly affected by the Lord's words and their experience of the cost involved in being his witnesses. The martyrs were esteemed as "true disciples" of Christ, following him, by grace, in laying down their lives. "Then I will be a true disciple of Jesus Christ, when the world sees my body no longer," writes Ignatius of Antioch in a letter composed on his way to martyrdom in Rome.[7] And again: "Now I begin to be a disciple."[8] To be "a true disciple": this longing is a constant theme in his letters.[9] Origen relates "baptism of blood" to "baptism of water." Likewise, the sacrifice of the martyrs is connected to the Eucharist: "I am the wheat of God, ground by the teeth of wild beasts to become a pure bread of Christ."[10] Polycarp, martyred in 155, pronounced this beautiful thanksgiving as he celebrated his last Eucharist.

> Father of your beloved and blessed Son, Jesus Christ, through whom we have come to know you, God of angels and powers, of all creatures and all the just who live in your presence, I bless you, because you have judged me to be worthy of this hour, and because you have allowed me to share in the number of the martyrs, in the cup of Christ, for resurrection to eternal life of body and soul, in the incorruptibility of the Holy Spirit.
>
> May I be received among them in your presence today as a rich and acceptable sacrifice, as you prepared and foreshadowed it, and as you fulfilled it, true God in whom there is no deceit.
>
> For this, and for all things, I praise you, I bless you, I glorify you through the eternal high priest, Jesus Christ, your beloved Son, through whom, to you, in the Holy Spirit, be glory now and in the ages to come. Amen.[11]

The veneration the Church has given the martyrs has been the cause of their liturgical cult, ever since the end of the second century. Commemoration is made of the day of their death, known as *Dies natalis* or *Natale*, that is, the "anniversary day of their birth" in heaven. The first non-martyrs to be so venerated were, in the East, Athanasius, bishop of Alexandria from 328 to 373, and, in the West, Martin, bishop of Tours from 372 to 397.

The identification of Stephen's martyrdom with Christ's passover is emphasized by this story. Like Jesus, he is accused by bribed witnesses, and for the same pretended cause: speaking against the Law and the Temple.[12] The indignation of the Sanhedrin appears in their shouts after Stephen's speech, as it did in their tearing their garments during Jesus' trial.[13] Stephen is dragged "out of the city" to be stoned, as Jesus was to be crucified.[14] Both pray that God might forgive their executioners.[15] At the end, Stephen hands over his spirit to the Lord Jesus in a loud cry, as Christ had handed over his spirit to his Father.[16] On the cross Jesus bowed his head: Stephen falls to his knees in an act of adoration.[17]

Among the witnesses, Luke mentions "a young man named Saul." The executioners' cloaks are laid at his feet. This scene must have had a profound impact on the man who, some time later, on the road to Damascus, would hear the Lord say to him: "I am Jesus, whom you are persecuting" (Acts 9:5). These words must have brought Stephen's martyrdom, of which he had approved, before his eyes (Acts 26:10). Might not this memory be behind Paul's doctrine of the mystical body, of which Christ is the head and we are the members?

The story of Stephen's martyrdom is not merely the re-telling of an edifying episode in the Church's early years. It is a proclamation of the gospel lived out to the point of supreme sacrifice by a witness of Christ. It invites us to look toward heaven as Stephen did, and to proclaim the glory of the Lord "standing at the right hand of God."

> The LORD is king, the most high over all the earth.
>
> The LORD is king; let the earth rejoice;
>   let the many isles be glad.
> Justice and judgment are the foundation of his throne.
>
> The heavens proclaim his justice,
>   and all peoples see his glory. . .
>   all gods are prostrate before him.
>
> Because you, O LORD, are the Most High over all the earth,
>   exalted far above all gods.
> (Ps 97:1, 2b, 6, 7c, 9)

"Yes, I am coming soon! . . . Come, Lord Jesus!"

The Bible ends with the solemn promise of the Lord's return, standing at the right hand of God, to which the Church responds with a cry of faith and hope, expressing its fervent desire to come through the gates of heaven. This revelation is both a final and urgent appeal to believers not to let down their guard, not to be lukewarm, not to withdraw. Now more than ever is the time to witness to the Lord Jesus. Clearly, then, the message at the end of the Book of Revelation has lost none of its importance for us (Rev 22:12-14, 16-17, 20).

"Remember, I am coming soon!" This declaration heard by the seer of Patmos recapitulates the message not only of Revelation, but of the whole of Scripture.[18] From one end of the Bible to the other, one finds the theme of God's coming, of the kingdom of God, of the Savior: "He has come. He comes. He will come." Calling to mind the past, the present joy, and the hope for a still more marvelous future is, at each turn of salvation history, the central theme of the prophets' preaching, the meditation of the sages, the annals of biblical historians, and the prayers of the psalms that foresee the day when all hopes and promises will be fully realized. This watchful waiting sustains courage in trials, inspires conversion, renews fervor. When it falters, it seems that God has passed beyond our sight, as if he were hiding himself or leaving us. In fact, he is always present, but we cannot see him because of our short-sightedness, or because our eyes are fixed on the things of this earth.

After John, whose vehement preaching was an attempt to awaken the ancient hope—"Prepare the way of the Lord" (Luke 3:4); "One mightier than I is coming after me" (Mark 1:7); "The kingdom of heaven is at hand!" (Matt 3:2)—Jesus appeared proclaiming: "This is the time of fulfillment" (Mark 1:15).[19] There is no Savior to wait for beside him. He is "the Alpha and the Omega, the first and the last, the beginning and the end."[20] With him, the last stage of salvation has begun to play itself out on this earth. It will end with his return, which will mark the end of time and the beginning of endless ages. On that day he will come with a "recompense [that he] will give to each according to his deeds."

Such certitude in this promise is a vibrant call to stir up one's missionary energy. The Lord has conferred a task on each one of us. When he returns, he will demand an accounting of our management (Matt 25:14-30).[21] Certainly, there is nothing unjust or arbitrary about this demand: Jesus, having returned to the Father, gives all those who believe in him the ability to do "the works" he does, and "greater ones than these" (John 14:12). Our faithfulness may lead to martyrdom: "Blessed are they who wash their robes so as to have the right to the tree of life and enter the city through its gates!"[22]

He who speaks this way is "the root and offspring of David, the bright morning star." This is a very fine summary of the entire mystery of Jesus, the Word made flesh (John 1:14) who is "the true light, which enlightens everyone, coming into the world" (John 1:9) and shines in the heavens: "The city had no need of sun or moon to shine on it, for the glory of God gave it light, and its lamp was the Lamb" (Rev 21:23). John hears a voice saying, like God, "I am."[23] For, "the Word was God. . . . and we saw his glory, the glory as of the Father's only Son, full of grace and truth" (John 1:1, 14).

He comes without delay, the holy city come down from heaven to redeemed humanity, "prepared as a bride adorned for her husband" (Rev 21:2). The same bride of the Song of Songs, that wonderful and passionate book endlessly read, meditated on, and expounded upon by the mystics, who find in it an expression of the intense desire of God, whose Spirit embraces the soul.

> "My lover belongs to me and I to him" (Cant 2:16). What do these words "me" and "him" mean?
>
> Understand that it is the heart speaking here, not the mind: nor is it addressed to our mind. To what, then? To nothing! Instead, tasting a wonderful emotion and being deeply moved by the delectable words of the Bridegroom, when he is silent, she can neither keep silent herself nor express all her feeling. If she speaks, it is less to say something than not to be silent. Her words come from the fullness of her heart, but cannot express its richness. Feelings have their own tone, which will always betray them.
>
> These words come not be choice, but by an impulsive movement. This is so with any passionate love, especially love for God; the feelings cannot be restrained, but break forth with little concern for the logical succession of phrases and ideas. The only thing desired is that these words lose none of their force. Thus it happens that one is content not to speak, nor even to cry, but to sigh. So the Bride, seized by an extraordinary and holy passion, only breathes to give more air to the flame that consumes her. It matters little what she says or how she says it. Everything that rises to her lips, forced upward by her love, she lets out, not concerning herself with clear articulation. For she is so full of feeling that she can no longer keep it within.[24]

The Book of Revelation began in a hieratic, though warm, manner, much like a liturgy (Rev 1:4-8), "on the Lord's day" (Rev 1:10). It likewise ends with a final, solemn admonition. Nothing may be added to or taken away from the holy Scriptures: "not the smallest letter or the smallest part of a letter will pass from the law" (Matt 5:18; Luke 16:17). One who does so will lose "his share in the tree of life and the holy city."[25] "The one who gives this testimony says, 'Yes, I am coming soon!' " This is the last word of revelation contained in Scripture. We receive it in faith, life, and the liturgy in order to hasten the coming of the day when the mystery of the union between God, humanity, and the whole world will be consummated in love: "Amen! Come, Lord Jesus! *Marana tha!*"[26]

> We give you thanks, holy Father,
> For your holy name
> That you have made to dwell in our hearts,
> And for the knowledge, faith, and immortality
> That you have revealed to us through your servant, Jesus.
>
> *Glory to you forever!*
>
> All powerful master,
> You created the universe because of your
> name
> And give everyone food and drink in
> abundance so that they offer you thanks.
> But to us, you have given the grace of
> spiritual food and drink and eternal life
> through Jesus, your servant;
> Above all, we give you thanks because you
> are mighty.
>
> *Glory to you forever!*
>
> Remember, Lord, your Church, deliver it
> from every evil and make it perfect in your
> love.
> And gather this holy Church from the four
> winds, bringing it into your kingdom that
> you have prepared
> To you belong power and glory forever!
> Let grace come and the world pass away!
> Hosanna to the God of David!
> If anyone is holy, let him come!
> If he is not, let him repent!
> *Marana tha!*
> Amen![27]

"That they may be one in us; that the world may believe"

This Sunday, we read the last part of the great prayer of thanksgiving and intercession that Jesus addressed to his Father when the time had come for him to leave the world (John 17:20-26).[28]

Now that he is to return to the Father, Jesus places in his Father's hands the work he has accomplished, for which he was sent into the world. This is a memorial of what he has done, an offering in thanksgiving and prayer so that his mission might come to maturation. The same is true today with our Eucharistic Prayer, which follows the same pattern.

> In memory of his death and resurrection,
> we offer you, Father, this life-giving
> bread,
> this saving cup.
> We thank you for counting us worthy
> to stand in your presence and serve you.
> May all of us who share in the body and
> blood of Christ
> be brought together in unity by the Holy Spirit.[29]

Christ gives the Father thanks for having made his name known to those who welcomed his messenger. Matthew (11:25-26) and Luke (10:21-22) report a similar prayer of Jesus' during his ministry. "I give praise to you, Father, Lord of heaven and earth, for although you have hidden these things from the wise and the learned you have revealed them to the child-like. Yes, Father, such has been your gracious will. All things have been handed over to me by my Father. No one knows the Son except the Father, and no one knows the Father except the Son and anyone to whom the Son wishes to reveal him."

The Lord's thanksgiving is not merely his own; even more must we make it our own. The faith that has been given to us allows us to recognize Jesus as the one sent by God. Children of God through baptism, we may properly address him as the Lord taught us, saying: "Our Father who art in heaven." The Spirit that has been poured forth into our hearts, while leading us to an ever deeper knowledge of God, draws us toward the day when "we shall see him as he is" (1 John 3:2). Then, with the whole of creation, we will say nothing else than that thanksgiving which is perfectly in accord with that of the glorified Son. We were promised a share in his glory, being "one" as the Father and the Son are "one": "I living in them, you living in me," Jesus said.

This union will be fully realized when all the saved will be assembled around Christ in heaven. But it must also work here and now, made perfect, so that the world might believe that Jesus has been sent by the Father and that the Father loves all people as he loves his own Son. Every blow to this unity is thus a blow to God and his Christ, to their credibility. In order to really understand this, one must remember that all of Christ's work and the fulfillment of the Father's will is at stake here. "For in him all the fullness was pleased to dwell, and through him to reconcile all things for him, making peace by the blood of his cross [through him], whether those on earth or those in heaven" (Col 1:19-20). The Lord Jesus died to reconcile the whole world with God (Rom 5:10), and to gather all people in peace to "create in himself one new person" (Eph 2:15). The mission of the Church and of all Christians is to preach this reconciliation and work for it (2 Cor 5:18-19). All those who bear the name of Christian profess this faith. They may not perpetuate the divisions that history has created between them. Their duty is to pray and work in every way for unity, while asking God for forgiveness for their sins and those of their fathers. A better cognizance of this fundamental demand is a blessing of our age.

> Nevertheless, The Lord of Ages wisely and patiently follows out the plan of his grace on our behalf, sinners that we are. In recent times he has begun to bestow his graces more generously upon divided Christians who are remorseful over their divisions and longing for unity.
> Everywhere large numbers have felt the impulse of this grace, and among our separated brethren there increases also, from day to day, a movement fostered by the grace of the Holy Spirit, for the restoration of unity among all Christians.[30]

We celebrate the liturgy this Sunday with eyes turned toward Christ in glory, standing at the right hand of God. He watches over his own while waiting for the time when he will bring them into the city, through whose gates he was the first to pass. That day will not be slow in coming. The Church at prayer cries out its hope and desire to see the rising of "the bright morning star . . . Come, Lord Jesus!"

Nevertheless, this contemplative vision does not free us from the mission conferred by the Lord on his disciples. Our concern is the same as that which Christ expressed in his prayer to the Father: the unity of the human race through and in the unity of the Church. This is why Jesus poured out his blood. This is why he left us the sacrament of the Eucharist: so that by his passover we all might be gathered into one body with him as head. The unity that comes from and leads to God—Father, Son and Spirit—is beyond any conceivable human power. But it was for this that Christ offered himself up, prayed to the Father, and sent his Spirit. Such is the prayer of all of us who, personally and in community, work for the coming of the reign of God.

> In the night that was all around him,
> Jesus, in the shelter of the garden,
> prayed for his disciples.

In the glory that surrounds him,
near to the Father forever,
he prays for his brethren.

Father, may they truly be
one in love!

So that my disciples may witness
that you are in me, and I in you.

So that my brethren may one day contemplate
that glory you have given me.

So that my Church may shine with the love
with which you have glorified it.

So that the world may recognize in me
the Messiah whom you have sent.[31]

Pentecost

As its name indicates, Pentecost is the feast that takes place fifty days after Easter.[1] It is the crowning finale of the celebration of the Lord's resurrection, which lasts throughout Eastertime[2] and ends with the pouring out of the Spirit over the apostles and in the Church. Hence the importance of Pentecost in the liturgical year, where the richness of the liturgy tries to do justice to the many components of the mystery as it is celebrated.

> When the work that the Father gave the Son to do on earth (cf. John 17:4) was accomplished, the Holy Spirit was sent on the day of Pentecost in order that he might continually sanctify the Church, and that, consequently, those who believe might have access through Christ in one Spirit to the Father (cf. Eph 2:18). He is the Spirit of life, the fountain of water springing up to eternal life (cf. John 4:47; 7:38-39). To men, dead in sin, the Father gives life through him, until the day when, in Christ, he raises to life their mortal bodies (cf. Rom 8:10-11). The Spirit dwells in the Church and in the hearts of the faithful, as in a temple (cf. 1 Cor 3:16; 6:19). In them he prays and bears witness to their adoptive sonship (cf. Gal 4:6; Rom 8:15-16, and 26). Guiding the Church in the way of all truth (cf. John 16:13) and unifying her in communion and in the works of ministry, he bestows upon her varied hierarchic and charismatic gifts, and in this way directs her; and he adorns her with his fruits (cf. Eph 4:11-12; 1 Cor 12:4; Gal 5:22). By the power of the gospel he permits the Church to keep the freshness of youth. Constantly he renews her and leads her to perfect union with her Spouse. For the Spirit and the Bride both say to Jesus, the Lord: "Come!" (cf. Rev. 22:17).
>
> Hence the universal Church is seen to be "a people brought into unity from the unity of the Father, the Son and the Holy Spirit."[3]

The inauguration of the new covenant, the promulgation of the new Law announced by the prophets, the gathering of the community in latter days prefigured by the assembly—*ecclesia*—in the desert, beginning of the coming harvest, Pentecost is the final manifestation of God—the theophany—that has given birth to the Church.

The liturgy commemorates the Pentecost that occurred in Jerusalem fifty days after Easter, yet transcends time. In fact, the liturgical celebration constantly makes this event present; from year to year it allows those who celebrate Pentecost to share in the graces of the mystery.[4]

The liturgical celebration of Pentecost encompasses two Masses: one on Saturday evening, the other on Sunday. At the Vigil Mass on Saturday evening, there are three readings from Scripture.[5] The second and third are always the same: Romans 8:22-27; John 7:37-39. For the first reading, on the other hand, one may choose between four Old Testament texts: Genesis 11:1-9; Exodus 19:3-8a, 16-20b; Ezekiel 37:1-14; Joel 3:1-5a. Probably very few of us ever participate in the Pentecost Vigil Mass;[6] but the texts are there, offered for our meditation in preparation for the feast day.

For Mass on Pentecost Sunday there are, as usual during Eastertime, three readings from the New Testament (Acts 2:1-11; 1 Cor 12:3b-7, 12-13; John 20:19-23).[7] The first reading is the account of the first Pentecost.

Thus it is a richly spread table that the liturgy for Pentecost offers, where everyone can feed on the living bread of the Word, entering into the mystery and taking its best fruits.

Drawing Life from the Wellspring of the Spirit

Spirit who hovers over the waters,
Calm our disturbances,
The troubled waves, the clamor of words,
The whirlwinds of vanity,
And in the silence raise up
The Word that recreates us.

Spirit of fire, always hidden
In your origin, by your flame,
Come and consume the chaff in us;
To the foundations of our lives,
Come thrust like a sword
The Word that sanctifies.

Spirit who breathes in a whisper
To our spirit the name of the Father,
Come gather all our desires,
Make them rise like an army
That answers to the light,
The Word of the new day.

Spirit of God, sap of love
Of the huge tree whereon you graft us,
May all those around us
Appear to us as a gift
In the great body
Where the Word of Communion
is the culminated.[1]

Word and Spirit are intimately linked. The Spirit is the source of the Word, making it known, inspiring one's heart to respond to it in prayer and action. The Word reveals the Spirit at work in the world from the beginning. Spirit and Word direct and animate the Church, guiding believers in their search for God and his will. By receiving the Word so that it may penetrate and grow in the heart, one creates a silent space in which the Spirit speaks. This is what we are invited to do in the Pentecost Vigil Mass.

When God Descends to Prevent Evil

The story of Babel concludes the dramatic history of the beginning of the world, such as it is found in the Book of Genesis. Even though it is nearly three thousand years old, this text is still extremely important for us today. It reaches to the deepest places of human and religious existence by its symbolism, which spans the ages, and to which every culture can relate. Read on the Pentecost Vigil, this passage deserves to claim our attention, even if we can see only some of its implications (Gen 11:1-9).[2]

The story is typically called "The Tower of Babel." Actually, it deals with the building of a "city and a tower with its top in the sky," a city with, in the strict sense of the word, a "skyscraper." And it is "the city" that people would eventually give up building. When "men were migrating in the east," they came to a plain in Mesopotamia and settled there, and decided to build on a large scale, making bricks and mortar for this purpose. They began this enormous enterprise to reach to heaven and to make a name for themselves. But God brought their Promethean project to an end. He came down to these people and confused their common language that had allowed them to undertake such an ambitious project, thus scattering them throughout the earth. They wanted to make a name for themselves, and ended up only with that of the uncompleted city: Babel, which means "to stammer," "to stutter," "to confound," or "confusion." But what significance does this have for the salvation history recorded in the Bible?

When they reflected on the beginning of history, the sages of Israel concerned themselves not so much with what happened, but how and why something happened. Drawing on the experience of several centuries, they asked about life and creation, evil and suffering, death, sexuality, the natural catastrophes that still belonged to the collective memory. Their central question was: "What is man, with his dignity as king of creation, but also his faults, especially this propensity to revolt against God?"

The oral and written traditions were gathered together to respond to this basic question. They drew on the culture of the ancient Middle East, though not without the old myths undergoing profound changes, even in their spirit, through the faith of the redactors. Thus was explained the initial revolt of man and woman against God, whose dire consequences were readily apparent to all (Gen 1:1–11:9). Babel, then, was the account of a general rebellion, before God made his covenant with Abraham, the father of believers.[3]

When one reflects on the human situation and its stance with respect to God, one looks around and wonders about the significance of certain types of behavior. The author of the Babel story must have perceived the megalomania of Babylonian secular and religious buildings, especially in those temples formed like pyramids, with a sanctuary and a terrace at the top from which to observe the stars: they were called ziggurats.[4] "What folly!" thinks the wise man; "Who do these people think they are?" He sees this sort of enterprise as a defiance flung at God, the only master of time and space, and a magnified repeating of the first sin, when Adam listened to the tempter's words: "You certainly will not die! No, God knows well that the moment you eat of it you will be like gods who know what is good and what is bad" (Gen 3:4-5). Pretending to be autonomous, wanting to arrogate to oneself the right to choose the means and scope of one's growth—is not this in what human sin consists, forgetful of one's creaturely condition?[5]

Whatever the origin of sin, the causes of the dispersion of peoples over the earth and the diversity of languages—questions with which the text is really concerned—over everything, even in an enigmatic episode like Babel, is suspended God's intervention.[6] Why does God intervene? Is he afraid that if this human enterprise succeeds, it will endanger his sovereignty? Does he think that he alone can make a name for himself? Does he want to remind us that he alone can open the door to heaven? Is the dispersal from Babel and the confusion of language, like the expulsion from paradise (Gen 3:23-24), a result of human pretention, wanting "to be like gods" (Gen 3:5)?[7] In short, does God descend to punish? Holding to the text, without projecting the result of later interpretations on it, one must say that God's intervention appears to be preventive. He halts a human enterprise that is in danger of leading to worse excesses.[8] Thus, this ancient text is a call to reflection, today more than ever when the progress of science and technology is constantly rolling back the frontiers of the impossible. What are the real reasons why people endlessly and frantically push toward complete mastery over time, space, nature, the universe? Are there boundaries that must not be passed if their efforts and actions are to remain human? What judgment does (or will) God make regarding these ambitions and their realizations? Babel does not give a ready-made response. But, should one be tempted to forget, this scriptural story reminds us that people cannot attempt and pursue everything for which they have the capacity, without asking certain questions. If they do not . . .[9]

A Christian reading of the Bible, i.e., one made in light of the fulfillment of God's plan, discovers a precise meaning in the Babel episode. Babel is perceived to be the symbol of the misery of humanity wanting to escape its creaturely condition and establish its autonomy without reckoning with God's plan. The rupture of the communion between man and woman, between Adam and Eve and nature (Gen 3:16-19), is aggravated by the rupture at Babel of the unity among people who, unable to understand and communicate with each other, are scattered over the face of the earth, and soon will be enemies.[10]

God is not unmoved at the risk of excess that threatens the people. In some way, he prevents it by bringing their foolish enterprise to an end. Hope then becomes possible. There is a counterpoint between the story of Babel and the calling of Abraham (Gen 12:1-3). Once again God intervenes, but this time to begin a new dialogue: "All the communities of the earth shall find blessing in you" (Gen 12:3). The initiative in word and action belongs to God. At Babel, people wanted to settle permanently: God asks Abraham to take up a nomadic life. At Babel, people wanted to achieve their own renown: God promises Abraham a name glorious over all the earth. At Babel, the human enterprise is interrupted; with Abraham, the promise of a blessing of all the nations on the earth is given the solemn guarantee of God's word. At Babel, humanity is dispersed; the gathering of the great people come from Abraham will stretch as far as the eye can see.

The event of Pentecost responds to the tragedy of Babel. The Spirit of God, descending on the disciples, will gather the far-flung peoples: There is "one Lord, one faith, one baptism; one God and Father of all" (Eph 4:4-6). The gift of tongues gives to each the possibility of understanding the unique word of God in their own tongue.[11] For this gift is not intended to make everyone multilingual. "The meaning is doubtlessly that the disciple of Christ has the ability to reconcile in himself the diversity among people and discover the very word that will reach each person, like a path that penetrates to one's most secret soul. The plurality of languages continues. It is only surpassed in meaning; it is vanquished in the hope of faith."[12] But to be able to speak to others the word that will reach them, one must begin by listening humbly to the word that comes from God and, confessing the name of the Lord Jesus Christ, putting one's attainment of heaven in his hands.

> I have been like those
> Who built the tower
> In the huge plain of Calneh,
> In the land of Babylon,

So that from the waters of the flood,
Should they come again, they would be safe;
Or so that they might reach heaven,
As they thought in their pride.

A strong wind blew,
The terrible clamor of the Spirit
Destroyed the mountains of pride
And this monstrous tower.

And the one language,
Was split into seventy,
So that they might not gather for evil,
But go out to do good.

I too have raised
The rampart of the tower of sin;
In my pride I have built with stones
The insolent edifice.

Its clever architect
Is the infernal Lucifer,
And the laborers of the evil Prince
Are the bands of the demon legion.

They too will be thrown down and destroyed
With the machines they have built;
And I, I will escape their snares
As the Hebrews did before.[13]

When God Descends to Make a Covenant

In each of God's interventions in salvation history, he clearly seems to be working according to a set plan, from which nothing can make him deviate. At the same time, it appears that each stage is a preparation for another, where God's initiative will again be made manifest. So the narration and celebration of a divine manifestation begin with the evocation of what God has already done, and are open to what is still to come. Memorial of the past, reception of a present gift, hope for a future guaranteed in the present, such is the triple dimension of every account of God's wonders and every liturgy that celebrates them. Here we have one such, in a text that must be read and understood in its liturgical context (Exod 19:3-8a, 16-20b).[14]

"You have seen for yourselves how I treated the Egyptians": this is the anamnesis of God's intervention three months earlier, when "at midnight" he descended to force Pharaoh to let the people go (Exod 12:29), and then to enable them to pass through the Red Sea (Exod 13:17-21). This recollection of God's loving and powerful care—"I bore you up on eagle wings and brought you here to myself''[15]—is the pledge of what he will soon do: ''You shall be my special possession . . . You shall be to me a kingdom of priests, a holy nation.''

''Special possession'' chosen among ''all other people, though all the earth is mine,'' says God. This choice implies a responsibility for all other people, as indicated by the title ''kingdom of priests,'' i.e., representative to God for all people, and for God in the world,[16] the ''holy nation'' consecrated to God's service.[17] Because of the privileged status that God, source of all holiness, has bestowed on it, Israel must display his holiness to the world. The grace it has received must be shared with all others; those who know God already must proclaim him. The Church acknowledges this responsibility in appropriating for itself the titles given to Israel.

> Father, all-powerful and ever-living God,
> we do well always and everywhere to give
> you thanks
> through Jesus Christ our Lord.
>
> Through his cross and resurrection
> he freed us from sin and death
> and called us to the glory that has made us
> a chosen race, a royal priesthood,
> a holy nation, a people set apart.
>
> Everywhere we proclaim your mighty works
> for you have called us out of darkness
> into your own wonderful light.[18]

Thus, on the third day, comes the manifestation of God, with all the classical accouterments: thunder, lightning, clouds.[19] These express both God's proximity and his inaccessibility. He comes, and one knows he is present in power and mystery,[20] though one cannot see him.[21] The scene is like a liturgy, as is the ceremonious meeting between Moses and God. The trumpet blast, like the sound of the shofar—the liturgical horn— gathers the assembly. Moses, the mediator, ascends the mountain like a priest going up to the altar. He is brought into God's presence, revealed and concealed in signs. The author of the Letter to the Hebrews recalls this theophany at Sinai, comparing it to the manifestation of the Lord, of which Christians have a foretaste.

> You have not approached that which could be touched and a blazing fire and gloomy darkness and storm and a trumpet blast and a voice speaking words such that those who heard begged that no message be further addressed to them . . .

No, you have approached Mount Zion and the city of the living God, the heavenly Jerusalem, and countless angels in festal gathering, and the assembly of the firstborn enrolled in heaven, and God the judge of all, and the spirits of the just made perfect, and Jesus, the mediator of a new covenant (Heb 12:18-19, 22-24).

The purifying blood of Christ opens a way to the mountain of God, to which the daily liturgy draws the caravan of believers.

> *Citizens of heaven,*
> *Dwellers in the house of the Lord,*
> *We march toward the Father,*
> *In the Son, through the Spirit.*

> We draw near to the mountain of Zion,
> The city of the living God,
> The heavenly Jerusalem.

> We draw near to the multitudes of angels,
> A solemn feast,
> The assembly of the first-born
> Whose names are written in the heavens.

> We draw near a God who judges the universe,
> The spirits of the just made perfect,
> Jesus, mediator of a new covenant.[22]

The covenant does not tear down the rigid boundary between God and his people: this is an essential recognition of the distance between God and his creature, wholly necessary if God is to speak to his people. In the community of the new covenant, this distance is maintained, but the Word is made flesh: it gives itself, sacrifices itself and opens a way into the mystery of God. Nevertheless, the Church, too, must listen to God's word in fear and trembling, appreciating at its true value the grace by which it is able to draw near to God in his Son Jesus Christ and respond to him in the fire of the Spirit.

> Open the doors of
> the wedding hall, my God;
> yes, do not close on me the door
> of your light, O my Christ!

> Do you think, son of men,
> that you can force me with your words?
> What are you saying so senselessly:
> that I hide my face?
> How do you suspect me so easily
> of closing doors and gates?

How do you suppose
that I am ever separated from you?
What have you said:
that I inflame you, burn you and crush you?

———

Consider my blessings,
look on my economy,
learn what my gifts are!
I have shown myself to the world
and have shown my Father,
I have poured forth abundantly
my Holy Spirit,
in truth, on all flesh;
I have revealed my name
to all men;
and that I am creator,
that I am the author of the world, through
my works,
I have shown and am showing now
everything that must be done. Amen.[23]

When God, Through the Spirit, Will Bring Life from Chaos

The famous "Vision of the Dry Bones" in the Book of Ezekiel occupies an important place in the history of biblical revelation. It should be understood in the context of today's liturgy (Ezek 37:1-14).

"Our bones are dried up, our hope is lost, and we are cut off." This is the cry of a people reduced to nothing, devastated, incapable of making the least effort to rise up, devoid of all vitality, which knows only how to bewail the past and curse its fate.

By the streams of Babylon
  we sat and wept
  when we remembered Zion.
On the aspens of that land
  we hung up our harps.

O daughter of Babylon, you destroyer,
  happy the man who shall repay you
  the evil you have done us!
Happy the man who shall seize and smash
  your little ones against the rock!
(Ps 137:1-2, 8-9)

Happy the people who in such situations see a prophet rise up to encourage them, exhorting them to raise their heads, and who listen to him. It is an unpleasant task for whomever God calls to such a mission, especially when he knows that the people's downfall has been due to their own fault, their perversion (Ezek 16; 20:1-31). Yet an Ezekiel can see that this situation will not last forever. Isn't God's honor itself threatened? If he does not come and raise up his people, the pagans will jeer and say: "Where is their God?"[24] He is certainly powerful enough to rebuild what human sin has destroyed.[25] He himself often reminds us of this: "Then you shall know that I am the Lord."[26] This is the message he charges Ezekiel with passing on to those who think that they are hopelessly forsaken: "Prophesy and say to them: Thus says the Lord God: O my people, I will open your graves and have you rise from them, and bring you back to the land of Israel. Then you shall know that I am the Lord, when I open your graves and have you rise from them, O my people! I will put my spirit in you that you may live, and I will settle you upon your land; thus you shall know that I am the Lord. I have promised, and I will do it, says the Lord."

To accomplish this resurrection, God needs the cooperation of his prophet. He has brought him to a valley of chaos and death beyond time and space. Ezekiel has given an account of the indescribable scope of the disaster: especially the completely dried-up bones. "Son of man, can these bones come to life?" What can be said to such a question, in the face of such a haunting sight? "Lord God, you alone know that." Then the prophet is commanded to pronounce a prophecy over the bones, on God's behalf. And the incredible happens: a loud noise, a violent shaking, and the bones join together, covering themselves with sinews, flesh, and skin. "But there was no spirit in them." Then comes a new prophecy, on God's order: "From the four winds come, O spirit, and breathe into these slain that they may come to life." They come to life, rising up as an entire people—"a vast army."

This transformation occurs because of a solemn invocation—"epiclesis"[27]—of the Spirit who, out of dried and scattered bones, makes a living people. Thus the Spirit is the one who gives or restores life, who creates or recreates.[28]

> Come, Holy Ghost, Creator, come
> From thy bright heavenly throne,
> Come, take possession of our souls
> And make them all thy own.[29]

"So shall my word be that goes forth from my mouth; it shall not return to me void, but shall do my will, achieving the end for which I sent it," says God (Isa 55:11). So it was at the creation (Gen 1:2; 2:7) and the Exodus. It will be so always: "I have promised, and I will do it." In a way, the great vision of the dry bones is a striking summary of salvation history yesterday, today, tomorrow. The living God, the God of the living (Luke 20:38), gives and restores life not only to our mortal bodies, but to the immense crowd that none can number, "from every nation, race, people, and tongue" (Rev 7:9). For, through his Spirit, he makes "all things new" (Rev 21:5).[30]

> The one who makes me descend from on high
> and rise up from the low places;
> he it is also who gathers what is in the middle
> and throws it to me.
>
> He has scattered my enemies and my adversaries,
> and has given me power over bonds,
> that I might untie them:
> by my hands he has slain
> the seven-headed dragon;
> and made me trample his roots,
> so that I may destroy his seed.
> You were at my side,
> and you rescued me.
> Your Name surrounds me on all sides,
> your right hand has dispersed the poison of
> the wicked,
> your hand has leveled the road for the faithful,
> for those who have faith in you.
> You have chosen them from among the tombs
> and separated them from the dead;
> you have taken lifeless bones,
> and wrapped them with flesh;
> they were motionless,
> and you have given them vital energy.
>
> Incorruptible was your way and your face,
> and your creation was corruption,
> so that the world might be brought to nothing, then renewed
> and that your rock might support the universe.
> On it you have built your kingdom,
> and it has become the abode of the saints.
> Alleluia![31]

When God Pours Out the Spirit Over All Creatures

There are at least two ways to speak about a prophetic text. The first is to see it in the context of the book it comes from and the whole of the prophet's preaching: his personality, the circumstances in which his ministry occurred, the situations and problems that confronted him and led him to speak. Having done this, one will usually end up considering a still larger context: the whole of prophetic preaching understood in its largest sense, the chain of ideas, conceptions, and themes of which this particular text is one link.[32] Such a reading is fruitful: one cannot even complain about how uneconomical it is, at least in the sense that one cannot read a biblical text without considering the rest of the Bible. Even so, one can approach a scriptural passage from another angle without isolating it completely from a biblical context, by reading and meditating on it in another environment, particularly that of the liturgy. When dealing with the Old Testament, this is the most direct route[33] to its Christian reading, with which the liturgy is concerned.[34] Such is the case with the passage from the Book of Joel that announces a marvelous pouring out of the Spirit (Joel 3:1-5a).

"The Lord said to his people: 'I will pour out my spirit upon all mankind. Your sons and daughters shall prophesy, your old men shall dream dreams, your young men shall see visions; even upon the servants and the handmaids, in those days, I will pour out my spirit.'" Usually, the Spirit is given for a particular mission, such as that of a prophet or a leader of the people. It is promised most fully to the Messiah.[35] Its effusion often occurs during either an ecstasy or vision, or produces them. The one proclaimed by Joel is general, i.e., all will benefit from it: men and women, young and old, even servants. It is not therefore reserved to a particular group or caste, priestly or otherwise. "Would that all the people of the Lord were prophets!" (Num 11:29). Moses' wish will be fulfilled beyond all hope. "In those days," the Spirit itself will instruct each in "dreams" and "visions."[36] Piercing to the depths of their hearts, their spiritual sense, the Spirit will enable them to know the Law, to find their delight in it, and to cling to it as to the most precious of gifts. This knowledge of the Law is associated with the knowledge of God. "I will place my law within them, and write it upon their hearts; I will be their God, and they shall be my people. No longer will they have need to teach their friends and kinsmen how to know the Lord. All, from least to greatest, shall know me, says the Lord" (Jer 31:33-34). "I will put my spirit within you and make you live by my statutes, careful to observe my decrees" (Ezek 36:27). And Jesus says to his disciples: "But when he comes, the Spirit of truth, he will guide you to all truth. He will not speak on his own, but he will speak what he hears, and will declare to you the things that are coming" (John 16:13).

The effusion of the Spirit prepares for "the day of the Lord, the great and terrible day," the day of final judgment. But "everyone shall be rescued who calls on the name of the Lord." Therefore one must hasten to teach it to the whole world.

> LORD, *send out your Spirit,*
> *and renew the face of the earth.*
>
> Bless the LORD, O my soul!
> 　O LORD, my God, you are great indeed!
> You are clothed with majesty and glory,
> 　robed in light as with a cloak.
>
> How manifold are your works, O LORD!
> 　In wisdom you have wrought them all
> 　the earth is full of your creatures;
>
> *Bless the LORD, O my soul!*
>
> They all look to you
> 　to give them food in due time.
> When you give it to them, they gather it;
> 　when you open your hand, they are filled with good things.
>
> 　. . . if you take away their breath, they perish
> 　and return to their dust.
> When you send forth your spirit, they are created,
> 　and you renew the face of the earth.
> (Ps 104:1-2a, 24, 35c, 27-28, 29bc-30)

The Holy Spirit, Our Help

Paul is particularly sensitive to the tragic situation of people who are prisoners to a sin from which they cannot free themselves. He has personally experienced this tension. Working fervently to defend the Law, he learned on the road to Damascus that he had been wrong. During his ministry and his missionary travels, he was constantly confronted with the resistance of a human nature opposed to grace. To be sure, he was also a joyful witness to God's action when it encountered, as it did in his case, sincere souls of good faith. But he also knows that a first generous impulse, however great it may be, is not enough. A fierce battle must still be fought: one must always reckon with the burden of what Paul calls the "flesh," that is, whatever holds one back from the things above.[37] In the passage from his Letter to the Romans that we read today, the apostle evokes this situation very strikingly, without softening his description of the pain, but at the same time showing that far from being desperate, it is the forbearer of a glorious future (Rom 8:22-27).

In fact, in this passage, the words "groan," "labor pains," "weakness," alternate almost line by line with "wait," and "hope." If the present appears in somber colors, it also contains points of light that announce here and now what is to come. But the Spirit is the main concern of the passage.

"All creation is groaning." The truth of this statement must not lead Christians to pessimism and discouragement. They should rather see in it the pangs of childbirth. For, "we also groan within ourselves." But we have already received the Holy Spirit.[38] We know that it is, for us, the guarantee of the promised adoption and of "the redemption of our bodies." "The Spirit itself bears witness with our spirit that we are children of God, and if children, then heirs, heirs of God and joint heirs with Christ" (Rom 8:16-17). To know this does not make us insensitive to suffering or prevent us from alleviating it as much as possible: it comes from the sin and disorder that have been brought into creation. But— and of this we can be certain—suffering is not the last word; it is not the harsh, necessary result of a pointless life. Our cries of suffering are confident appeals to the one whom we call: "*Abba*, Father!" (Rom 8:15). True, we do not yet see what is promised us.[39] But "we wait with endurance," and our hope shall not be deceived.

"In the same way, the Spirit too comes to the aid of our weakness; for we do not know how to pray as we ought, but the Spirit itself intercedes with inexpressible groanings. And the one who searches hearts knows what is the intention of the Spirit, because it intercedes for the holy ones according to God's will." By instilling and strengthening in us the keen desire for what will soon be brought to light, the Holy Spirit helps us withstand the pains of childbirth not only courageously, but joyfully. It thus guides Christians on their march toward the day when their adoption will be made manifest, and teaches them to pray as they ought: "Our Father . . . Thy kingdom come!" God cannot help but satisfy the ardent longing of his children, whose desire is in accord with his will for them and for the world.

The firm bond between the condition of creation and that of humanity is a conviction often expressed in the Bible, especially in the account of the first sin: "Because . . . [you] ate from the tree of which I had forbidden you to eat, 'Cursed be the ground because of you! . . . Thorns and thistles shall it bring forth to you' " (Gen 3:17-18). We also know of this solidarity from experience. Today we are more modest about such claims in so far as we are aware of the immensity of the universe and the relative insignificant size of the planet we inhabit. Nevertheless, as we are more and more aware, we have, for better or worse, a solidarity with this planet of ours, both on the material and spiritual levels; so much greater is our responsibility.

> If Paul and the Bible only conceive of the redemption of the universe as a function of human redemption, it follows that our striving by our own work to bring about the redemption of the universe would be mere deception if it were not ordered to human redemption. Likewise, all so-called ascetic effort to submit the body to the soul that does not aim at the redemption of this soul by opening it to charity will never be accomplished. The Gnostics might think matter evil in itself; for Paul, as for the Bible, evil belongs only to man, or, more precisely, in the egoism of a man who, instead of ordering himself to God and others, attempts to order others and even God to himself.
>
> It necessarily follows that every conquest of the universe that does not promote the establishment of the reign of charity among men, the "establishment of a universal brotherhood," according to a favorite expression of the Constitution *Gaudium et spes*, far from preparing the redemption of the universe, cannot help but concur in its ruin. On the other hand, each time that by his labor man attempts, even without seeming to do so, to bring the universe to the service of love, one can say that he is preparing mysteriously but really for its redemption, for, according to *Gaudium et spes*, where it invokes Romans 8:19-21, "charity and its works will remain."[40]

The Spirit, Living Water Flowing from the Heart of Christ

A brief reading from the Gospel according to John closes the series of readings for the Pentecost Vigil Mass. "Jesus stood up and exclaimed, 'Let anyone who thirsts come to me and drink. Whoever believes in me as scripture says: "Rivers of living water will flow from within him." ' " The evangelist says, without elaboration, that in saying this, Jesus said this "in reference to the Spirit that those who came to believe in him were to receive." The word of the Lord, proclaimed forcefully and solemnly—Jesus "stood up" and "exclaimed"—would be very enigmatic if the evangelist had not noted that it took place "on the last and greatest day of the feast." Doubtlessly, the key to the interpretation of this saying lies in this note. Let us then look at this particular liturgical context (John 7:37-39).[41]

Of the three great Jewish feasts—Passover (*Pesach*), Pentecost (*Shabbat*) and that of Booths (*Sukkoth*)—the last was and is the occasion of greatest popular merrymaking. It has been said: "Whoever cannot perceive the joy of this feast does not know what joy is."[42] This character comes from the feast's origin as a celebration of the end of the harvest, around the beginning of the Jewish year in September-October.[43] During this time, the people lived in huts of branches in fields or orchards. The custom of building tents (*sukkoth*) during the seven days of the feast still exists today.[44]This practice was later combined with the memorial of the Exodus, whose "marvels" were recalled in certain rites. Each day, the priests went to draw water from the fountain of Siloam—the name has to do with one who has been "sent" (John 9:7)—and brought it back solemnly, in a golden pitcher, to pour at the corner of the altar. This was the living water that Moses called up in the desert (Exod 17:6), as well as that which the prophet Ezekiel saw flow, in a vision, beneath the threshold of the Temple. Becoming a torrent, it fed the whole country and, descending into the Jordan Valley, purified the waters of the Dead Sea (Ezek 47:1-12). In an oracle, the Lord spoke thus to the prophet: "I will sprinkle clean water upon you to cleanse you from all your impurities, and from all your idols I will cleanse you. I will give you a new heart and place a new spirit within you, taking from your bodies your stony hearts and giving you natural hearts. I will put my spirit within you and make you live by my statutes, careful to observe my decrees. You shall live in the land I gave your fathers; you shall be my people, and I will be your God" (Ezek 36:25-28).[45] Full of so many memories and themes, the feast of Booths also points to the fulfillment of all promises, the full realization of what is proclaimed by the great deeds performed by God in the past: the new Exodus of joy and glory, the definitive purification of the people, the coming of the Messiah, the effusion of God's Spirit, and its manifestation on the last day. Such a feast could only be celebrated in great joy, a popular rejoicing that culminated on the eighth (last) day of the celebration. It was on just this "greatest day" that Jesus, "stood up" and proclaimed the saying reported by John.

"Let anyone who thirsts come to me and drink." In Jesus, the believer will find the quenching of all desires, all the hopes remembered and extolled in the feast of Booths. In him is fulfilled the passage of Scripture that says: "Rivers of living water will flow from within him"[46] This text is not found anywhere else, as such, in the Bible. But the Psalms, as well as Exodus and Numbers, look back to the episode of the rock that Moses struck, bringing forth water to quench the people's thirst.[47] In addition, the Jewish commentators traditionally make much of Ezekiel's vision (Ezek 47:1-12). The prophet Zechariah (13:1) alludes to this spring, saying that it will wash away the defilements of the inhabitants of Jerusalem. Psalm 46 probably does so as well: "There is a stream whose runlets gladden the city of God, the holy dwelling of the Most High" (Ps 46:5-6).

It may also be understood as the water of the Red Sea that saved the people, allowing them to pass through with dry feet while it engulfed their enemies (Exod 14:21-29). It is also the water by which one is filled with the Holy Spirit. Finally, Paul sees the passage of the Red Sea as a baptism, and he says of the rock of Horeb, "the rock was the Christ" (1 Cor 10:4).

Jesus himself declared to the Samaritan woman: "But whoever drinks the water I shall give will never thirst; the water I shall give will become in him a spring of water welling up to eternal life" (John 4:14).[48] From the lance wound in his side John says that "blood and water flowed out" (John 19:34), with which he associates the Spirit (1 John 5:6-7). One can then understand how the evangelist can write: "He said this in reference to the Spirit that those who came to believe in him were to receive." This saying, which at first is quite enigmatic, evokes so many biblical reminiscences that one can, in meditating on it, forever joyfully "draw water from the fountain of salvation."[49]

> The Spirit was in the prophets, allowing them to prophesy. Now it dwells through Christ in those who believe, and coming first to dwell in Christ, when he was made man. Since Christ is God, the Spirit is substantially rooted in him from eternity, and belongs properly to him. This is why God anointed him for us, and Scripture says that he receives the Spirit as man. It is not for himself that he acquired a share in God's gifts, but for human nature, as I have already taught you.
>
> When the holy evangelist tells us: "There was, of course, no Spirit yet, because Jesus had not yet been glorified" (John 7:39), we may understand that he means the full and perfect dwelling of the Holy Spirit in men.[50]

Jesus, the Christ, has been glorified by the Father. Announced "in times past . . . in partial and various ways" (Heb 1:1), the pouring out of the Spirit has occurred; each of us has received it at our baptism and confirmation. It is renewed throughout our life when we pray in the Church, and especially when we beg the Father that it may "make us an everlasting gift to him, and enable us to share in the inheritance of his saints, with Mary, the virgin Mother of God, with the apostles, the martyrs, and all the saints."[51]

> I saw living water
> flow from the heart of Christ, alleluia!
> All those washed by this water
> will be saved and sing, alleluia!
>
> *Alleluia, alleluia, alleluia!*

I saw the spring
become a huge river, alleluia!
The assembled sons of God
sung their joy at being saved, alleluia!

I saw the Temple
now opened to all, alleluia!
Christ returns in victory,
showing the wound in his side, alleluia!

I saw the Word
give us the peace of God, alleluia!
All those who believe in his name
will be saved and sing, alleluia!

Alleluia, alleluia, alleluia![52]

Sunday Mass—Pentecost

The Lord Jesus' resurrection marks the decisive turn in salvation history from the past to the present, which will last till Christ's return. Before "the first day" of this long week in which the world now lives, the Spirit was only in Jesus: his baptism at John's hands in the Jordan showed this to the people.[1] Given to all those who believe in him (John 7:39), the Spirit, transmitted through the risen Lord who was glorified by the Father,[2] enables them to live as children of God. It gives the apostles the strength and courage necessary to become witnesses of the Lord in the world, and to preach "the forgiveness of sins . . . to all nations, beginning from Jerusalem" (Luke 24:47).[3] Why then was it necessary to wait fifty days after Easter for the outpouring of the Spirit?

Granted, the communication of the Spirit to the first disciples and the Church cannot be separated from the paschal event. John knows this. He reports that, "on the evening of that first day of the week," when the Lord appeared to the disciples, "he breathed on them and said to them: 'Receive the holy Spirit. Whose sins you forgive are forgiven them, and whose sins you retain are retained'" (John 20:19-23).[4] But, on that day, the disciples were in a house where "all the doors were locked." At Pentecost, the Spirit made them open the doors, speaking without fear to the people who gathered as "a noise like a strong driving wind" filled the whole house (Acts 2:1-11).[5] This was a public event.

On this "fiftieth day" was celebrated the feast of Weeks—*Sabu'ôt*—,a commemoration of all the covenants, from Noah to Sinai.[6] One can therefore see the outpouring of the Holy Spirit on this day as the solemn promulgation of the new covenant and the birth of the Church. Shrouded in the secrecy of its paschal baptism, where the Spirit brought it to maturity, the Church blossoms on Pentecost, and it is quite clear that the fruits of the Lord's passover surpass the promise of the buds.

Once again, God reveals his mystery through what he does. After having spoken for so long through the prophets (Heb 1:1), God reveals himself as Father by sending his only Son to save the world. The gift of the Spirit inaugurates the last age by communicating to humanity the secret

force that animates his life and the Son's. "The love of God has be
poured out into our hearts through the holy Spirit that has been give
to us."[7] "For the Spirit of the LORD fills the world, is all-embracing, and
knows what man says,"[8] and through it, God shows that he wants to
communicate his love to all.

Baptism into the death and resurrection of Christ opens one to the action of the Spirit, "and where the Spirit of the Lord is, there is freedom"
(2 Cor 3:17). Nothing and no one can prevent it from blowing where and
as it will: "You can hear the sound it makes, but you do not know where
it comes from or where it goes" (John 3:8). Born at Pentecost through
the breath of the Spirit, the Church cannot escape its impulse. The Church
is constantly prompted to proclaim the gospel to the whole world. If it
should fall asleep, the Spirit reawakens it, sometimes rather brusquely;
under the Spirit's impulse, the Church, though thought to be "out of
breath," renews its youth from age to age.

> Love that hovered over the waters
> And rocked them with the first wind,
> Our souls sleep.
> Seize them with a new rhythm
> That flows from Christ their source
> To overflow among men.
>
> You are the voice that groans
> Amid the sorrows of our world.
> The name of the Father;
> But you are also
> The voice that brings his response:
> the love of God covers the earth.
>
> You are the genesis of all ages,
> You are the wind that cries birth
> To the hidden soul;
> You engender us from within,
> You make the silence reverberate
> In the depth of every being.
>
> Love descending today,
> Come stir up the secret waters
> Of our baptism,
> Which from the death of Jesus Christ
> Makes us rise up in his life.
> All is love in Love itself.[9]

The Spirit Makes One People of All Nations

Each year on Pentecost Sunday we read the only account of the first manifestation of the Holy Spirit, reported in the Acts of the Apostles. The scene is so well known to us that we are easily tempted to listen to it rather distractedly. But if we pay close attention, it is clear that Luke is describing a scene that does not easily lend itself to the imagination. The best icons and most successful pictures of Pentecost must be understood in the light of this text (Acts 2:1-11).

At Jerusalem

The Gospel According to Luke presents Jesus' ministry in the framework of a long journey that begins in Nazareth and ends in Jerusalem. In the synagogue of Nazareth, "where he had grown up," Jesus began his preaching and ministry in Galilee.[1] Then comes the long journey to Jerusalem,[2] into which Jesus made his solemn entry and where, in the Temple, he ended his ministry.[3] After his passion,[4] it is at Jerusalem that the risen one appeared to the apostles and gave them his last instructions.[5] There he left them and was lifted up to heaven[6] after having ordered them to remain in the city till they were "clothed with power from on high,"[7] to be his witnesses "in Jerusalem, throughout Judea and Samaria, and to the ends of the earth."[8] Finally, it is at Jerusalem that the Spirit is given to the apostles and the first disciples. It is from the city where Jesus' ministry ended that the universal mission will go out, as the Acts of the Apostles testifies. This carefully constructed montage underscores the continuity between the apostles' and the Lord's mission, the causal link between his passover, the blossoming of the Church and, after Pentecost, the proclamation of the good news to all the nations.[9]

The Day of Pentecost

A new theophany occurring "fifty days after Easter," during the feast of Weeks, which commemorated the many previous divine manifestations, could only be a significant event of salvation[10] (especially covenant) history.

In the desert of Sinai after their departure from Egypt, after having declared themselves ready to follow God's prescriptions, the people led by Moses prepared for God's manifestation (Exod 19:1-15). In the "upper room" of the house in Jerusalem (Acts 1:12-14), a group of disciples was gathered: the apostles, with Peter their leader; some women, including Mary, the mother of Jesus, and some of his relatives. They all waited in prayer for the Holy Spirit that the Lord had promised them.[11]

At Sinai, the mountain, burning like a furnace, trembled; there was thunder and lightning: a terrifying spectacle (Exod 19:16-19).[12] At Jerusalem, "suddenly there came from the sky a noise like a strong driving wind, and it filled the entire house in which they were. Then there appeared to them tongues as of fire, which parted and came to rest on each one of them." But the manifestation aroused no fear in them.

The Gift of Tongues

"And they were all filled with the holy Spirit and began to speak in different tongues, as the Spirit enabled them to proclaim." The Old Testament notes that there were people who, seized by the Spirit, would suddenly find themselves in ecstatic and prophetic trances.[13] Similar experiences occurred in the primitive Church.[14] Though it is impossible to say exactly in what this gift consisted, it seems that it was both a charism of prophecy and a kind of spiritual delirium during which one praised God in a language that was incomprehensible, even to the speaker. The Christians at Corinth knew this charism and valued it highly. Paul, who had experienced it himself (1 Cor 14:18) and recognized its value—"I should like all of you to speak in tongues"—nevertheless shows some reserve about it: "but even more to prophesy" (1 Cor 14:5). Actually, if there is no one to interpret the speech and thus give an account of its prophetic content, whether revelatory or didactic, it is of no use to the community (1 Cor 14:6). "On the other hand, one who prophesies does speak to human beings, for their building up, encouragement, and solace" (1 Cor 14:3). "But in the church I would rather speak five words with my mind, so as to instruct others also, than ten thousand words in a tongue" (1 Cor 14:19). And he adds a final argument: "So if the whole church meets in one place and everyone speaks in tongues, and then uninstructed people or unbelievers should come in, will they not say that you are out of your minds?" (1 Cor 14:23).[15] But this was not the case at Pentecost, even if some people at first thought that the apostles were drunk (Acts 2:13). Peter's speech showed that something quite different was happening (Acts 2:14-41).

From Babel to Pentecost

The noise "like a strong driving wind" gathered a large crowd around the house. "They were confused, because each one heard them speaking in his own language." Paul says, "But if there is no interpreter, the person should keep silent in the church and speak to himself and to God" (1 Cor 14:28). Here, the apostles were not speaking at random. They spoke words that were perfectly intelligible to everyone in the crowd, though they heard them all in their native tongue.[16] Just how could this happen? Clearly, it is a matter of little importance to us.[17] On the other hand, it is clear that Pentecost was the opposite of Babel. Following the confusion of language, people were dispersed "all over the earth" (Gen 11:1-9).[18] At Pentecost, God gathered the people, though they came from different cultures, differences that were not obliterated. But thereafter, there would be only one, universal Church, consisting of the communion of local Churches. All of them were enabled to hear and understand the Word and celebrate the Name in their own tongue, without establishing one universal language.[19]

> Today the Church, united by the Holy Spirit, speaks in the language of every people. Therefore if somebody should say to one of us, "You have received the Holy Spirit, why do you not speak in tongues?" his reply should be, "I do indeed speak in the tongues of all men, because I belong to the body of Christ, that is, the Church, and it speaks all languages. What else did the presence of the Holy Spirit indicate at Pentecost, except that God's Church was to speak in the language of every people?"[20]

From Every Nation Under Heaven

The crowd that gathered was formed of "devout Jews from every nation under heaven," who had come to Jerusalem for the feast. Their list symbolizes the whole of humanity.[21] Abraham had received from God the promise that he would be the father of many peoples (Gen 17:4-6). The covenant at Sinai had been a beginning of the realization of this promise. The people had received an assurance that God would make of them "a kingdom of priests, a holy nation" to keep the name of the Lord among all the nations of the earth (Exod 19:6). The infant Jesus had been greeted by the old man Simeon as "a light for revelation to the Gentiles, and glory for your people Israel" (Luke 2:32). John the Baptist, announcing the one

to come, said: "And all flesh shall see the salvation of God" (Luke 3:6).
When Paul and Barnabas turned to the Gentiles, they were conscious of
obeying the Lord's command and cited once again the oracle from Isaiah
(49:6): "I have made you a light to the Gentiles, that you may be an instrument of salvation to the ends of the earth" (Acts 13:47). The Acts
of the Apostles recounts how, especially through Paul, the gospel was
preached to all the nations. The story of Pentecost shows that the Church
was born to be "universal." "The Spirit brought all the scattered peoples
to unity, and offered the Father their first-fruits."[23]

The Christian Pentecost inaugurated the age of the Church "proceeding from the love of the eternal Father, founded by Christ in time and
gathered into one by the Holy Spirit"[24] which dwells in it, like an internal principle of life and growth.

By the preaching of missionaries of the gospel whose words it inspires
and whose zeal it sustains, the Spirit excites faith and converts hearts.
In the sanctified waters of baptism, the sacrament of the death and resurrection of Christ, it brings those believers marked with oil to life as children of God and the Church. By the Spirit's power, the bread and wine,
fruits of the earth and the vine, offering of human labor, become the Body
and Blood of Christ, sacrament of the new and eternal covenant,[25] leaven
of the Church's unity, perfect worship of the Father to whom belongs
all honor and glory.[26]

Through the other sacraments instituted by the Lord, efficacious signs
of the Father's love, the Spirit sanctifies the people of God: sins are forgiven; the union of man and woman becomes a sign of the union of Christ
and the Church (Eph 5:32); ministries and works are bestowed on the
ecclesial community, structuring the body of Christ; the sick, anointed
with holy oil in the name of the Lord receive forgiveness for their sins
(Jas 5:14-15), the grace to live through their trials in communion with the
passion of Christ and, being at peace, to hand over their souls to God.

The same Holy Spirit does not limit itself to sanctifying the people of
God by sacraments and ministries, leading them and giving them the
crown of virtues; it also distributes among all the faithful, "to each person as he wishes" (1 Cor 12:11), the special graces that make one able
to assume the various offices and charges that can renew and develop
the Church, in accord with what Paul says: "To each individual the
manifestation of the Spirit is given for some benefit" (1 Cor 12:7).

Finally, the event of Pentecost is a mystery of universal importance.
The miracle of tongues unhesitatingly entrusts the proclamation of the

ospel to fragile human language, which is always changing. No longer is there a sacred language, determined once and for all or received from the past as the only one capable of authentically transmitting the good news, of such a lofty state that one must use it to speak of God and to address him in prayer: not even that used by Jesus himself to teach and pray to his Father; still less that which was used in the writing of the Gospels. The Spirit has been given to the Church so that it may assume every human language and all of the cultures expressed therein. In each one the good seed of the Word must be sown with both hands, because, in each, the fruits of the Spirit may be borne a hundredfold. In its calling, the Church is confronted with the challenge of constantly translating the gospel into the native speech of "every nation under heaven." It has been given "inscrutable riches" of Christ so as to announce it to the pagan peoples (Eph 3:8) and bring the riches of the nations to Christ, so that he may offer them to his Father.

> *Lord, send forth your spirit,*
> *and renew the face of the earth.*
>
> Bless the LORD, O my soul!
> O LORD, my God, you are great indeed!
>
> How manifold are your works, O LORD!
> . . . the earth is full of your creatures.
>
> . . . if you take away their breath, they perish and return to their dust.
> When you send forth your spirit, they are created,
> and you renew the face of the earth.
> May the glory of the Lord endure forever;
> may the LORD be glad in his works!
> Pleasing to him be my theme;
> I will be glad in the LORD.
> (Ps 104:1ab, 24ac, 29bc-30, 31, 34)

Gift of the Risen Christ and the Spirit for the Common Good

The Gifts of the Spirit for the Common Good

"Breath of God": like the wind, which no one knows where it comes or goes, the Holy Spirit has no face.[1] It manifests its presence by what it does, by its "gifts." But how can one determine that a particular interior impulse (inspiration) or gift really comes from the Holy Spirit? How can one distinguish the true from the false, the authentic from the illusory? These are common questions, and not only regarding extraordinary phenomena. In certain times and places, the multiplicity of unusual actions or abilities can become a real problem.[2] But what Paul says in the passage from the First Letter to the Corinthians that we read today may always be used as a touchstone (1 Cor 12:3b-7, 12-13).[3]

In order to determine if certain actions, desires, movements, and undertakings are or are not inspired by the Spirit, one must examine them individually, judging them by their fruits. This might take some time A hasty judgment is more easily refuted; on the other hand, what is authentic will not suffer from being submitted to the test of time.[4] Here Paul gives a certain and generally applicable criterion: "And no one can say, 'Jesus is Lord,' except by the holy Spirit." This means that the action of the Spirit, whatever its manifestations, always holds to this fundamental confession of faith. This criterion is much more concrete than it might appear at first sight. It is by referring to the creed—otherwise known as "the rule of faith"—and the truth of the gospel that the presence of the Spirit can be verified.

"There are different gifts," and it would be impossible to draw up a definitive list of them. We cannot pretend to force the wind of the Spirit into predetermined channels, limiting it to certain paths, establishing what it must do to the exclusion of anything else, since "you can hear the sound it makes, but you do not know where it comes from or where it goes" (John 3:8). Paul is quite right to say: "The fruit of the spirit is love, joy, peace, patience, kindness, generosity, faithfulness, gentleness, self-control'' (Gal 5:22-23);[5] "For light produces every kind of goodness and righteousness and truth'' (Eph 5:9).[6] These are not simply the "gifts of grace'' that come from the Holy Spirit but the signs of its action. They are our basis for judgment, beginning with the most visible, the easiest to verify.[7] But Paul insists primarily on this point: the various gifts of the Spirit are given for the common good. We seem here to pierce to the foundation of Paul's thought, which is expressed in the "hymn to love,'' the love that underlies everything and for which every charism is given (1 Cor 13:1-7). The gifts of prophecy and speaking in tongues can only last a short while. Love alone will never fade (1 Cor 13:8-10); it is for this that we must seek (1 Cor 14:1). Consequently, there is no reason to be saddened if the more "extraordinary'' charisms do not appear as frequently as one might like. It would be a mistake to try to "reactivate'' them: a vain enterprise and not a little suspect. Holiness does not come from such phenomena, but from the love that the Spirit pours out in our hearts,[8] and the prayer and works that it inspires for the common good.

The best illustration of this activity of the Holy Spirit lies in the ecclesial community. There are different ministries and works, distributed by the Spirit among the faithful. These are necessary, so that the Church may exist in an harmonious structure, for it is always the same Spirit, the same God and Father who acts in the Church. If love presides, there need be no conflict between charisms, no jealousy, no disastrous pride, or rivalry between believers who have received different gifts. Instead, their mutual needs will then be made clear, and the common good will be assured. "As a body is one though it has many parts, and all the parts of the body, though many, are one body. . . .''

One expects Paul to conclude: "So it is with the Church, which is a living body.'' But in fact, he writes: "So also [it is with] Christ.''

> Instead of saying "Church,'' he says "Christ''; in so doing, he speaks from a height that confuses his listener. This is what he means: "So it is with Christ who, properly understood, is the Church.'' Just as the head and the body form one man, Christ and the Church form a whole. This is why he replaces "Church'' with "Christ,'' meaning the whole body. As our bodies are one, he says, even though they contain many parts, so in the Church are we all one. Though the Church may contain many members, they all form but one body.[9]

Note, then, that the diversity of ministries and works is fundamentally different than that which we find in other social or political organizations. Like the unity that it assures, this diversity is supernatural: it comes from

God, from Christ. The body of the Church does not result from the coming together of the faithful: rather, it is the Spirit of Christ that unites them in the Church. The body thus formed is of a mystical, sacramental order. Hence one may rightly say that if the Church makes the sacraments, it is no less true that the sacraments make the Church.[10] Therefore, "there is neither Jew nor Greek, there is neither slave nor free person, there is not male and female; for you are all one in Christ Jesus" (Gal 3:28), because all are baptized in the same Spirit, the only source of life and the diversity of their graces.

> The metaphor is very suitable in the present context. It is as if one said of the plants in Paradise: "All have been watered from the same well." Likewise it is said here: We have all been washed with the same Spirit, we have all received the same grace.[11]

The Risen Jesus, the Spirit, and the Mission

John's Gospel was the last one to be written. It was meant for Christians who already knew the traditions recounted by Matthew, Mark, and Luke, and who were familiar with the assembly on "the first day of the week," which commemorated Christ's passover and celebrated the Lord's Supper. Indeed, many passages in the Fourth Gospel seem to belong to a liturgical setting; one often has the impression that it contains material which John first preached in a liturgy. In any case, the meaning of the Gospel often becomes much clearer when it is proclaimed in the midst of the assembly. This is doubtlessly the reason for the obviously hieratic character of certain scenes, as well as the seemingly haphazard way the evangelist gathers together the stages of the mystery that Matthew, Mark, and Luke present in more sequential order. We should keep this in mind while reading the Gospel passage chosen for Pentecost Sunday (John 20:19-23).[13]

It was "the evening of that first day of the week," the day of the Lord's resurrection, "when the doors were locked, where the disciples were, for fear of the Jews, [when] Jesus came and stood in their midst." The Lord's death had thrown them into confusion, even so far as to make them forget what Jesus had told them in order to prevent this very reaction (John 14:1-27). Mary Magdalene's discovery of the empty tomb, verified by Peter and John, was not enough to comfort them. Then, suddenly, "Jesus came and stood in their midst and said to them, 'Peace be with you,'" In the mouth of the Lord, this is not a simple salutation. It is the messianic salutation par excellence. Coming from Jesus at this moment,

˅ is also a revelation; and one subsequently finds it at the beginning of the apostolic letters[13] and in the Book of Revelation (1:4), not to mention in the liturgy itself.

"When he had said this, he showed them his hands and his side." John, the mystic, is known for his insistent realism when he speaks of the Lord's humanity: "And the Word became flesh" (John 1:14); "What we have seen with our eyes, what we looked upon and touched with our hands concerns the Word of life" (1 John 1:1); "Whoever eats my flesh and drinks my blood has eternal life" (John 6:54).[14] There is the same insistence here. He whom the disciples see on the evening of Easter is the crucified, who is now living again. His "flesh" bears the unmistakable signs of the nail and lance wounds. "Blood and water flowed out [of his side]" (John 19:34). This pouring out of water and blood, elsewhere connected with the pouring out of the Spirit (1 John 5:8),[15] has been traditionally understood as the source of life and the sacraments: water of baptism, blood of the Eucharist, birth of the Church, the new Eve, from the open side of the new Adam.[16] But in order to "see" this and receive the riches of the Lord's passover, one must "believe."[17] The joy that overwhelms the disciples when they recognize the Lord by the signs of his passion is an act of faith that, with the peace the Lord bestows on them, allows them to overcome the scandal of the cross. It may take a while, as the apostles know all too well.[18] John asks us if we believe that the Son of God made flesh, who died on the cross with his side wounded by a lance-blow is alive in our midst? "An eyewitness has testified, and his testimony is true; he knows that he is speaking the truth, so that you also may [come to] believe" (John 19:35), and so that "you may have life in his name" (John 20:31).

The witnesses are the messengers of the Father's Messenger, who came not "to condemn the world, but that the world might be saved through him" (John 3:17). "Now this is eternal life, that they should know you, the only true God, and the one whom you sent, Jesus Christ" (John 17:3).[19] The disciples' task is thus clearly laid out: they are to reveal to the world the Father and "the one whom [he] sent." In fulfilling this mission, they will pursue Christ's work: to save the world,[20] to give eternal life to those who believe in him (John 3:36). This was why the Father "has given everything over to him" (John 3:35), especially the Spirit that he gave without measure (John 3:34).

Glorified by the Father, he can now communicate the Spirit to those who believe in him (John 7:39).[21] Jesus "breathed on them and said: 'Receive the holy Spirit.' '' The breath of God made man a living being (G 2:7). It restored life to an immense number of dry bones (Ezek 37:1-14). Now, the one through whom ''all came to be'' (John 1:3) breathes on his disciples the Spirit that makes them new creatures. It creates a new world where everyone who receives the Lord's word, proclaimed by his messengers, can see his sins forgiven, for this Word is ''spirit and life'' (John 6:63).

Joseph was told by the angel to give Mary's child the name ''Jesus,'' for he would save ''his people from their sins'' (Matt 1:21). Zechariah, ''filled with the holy Spirit'' (Luke 1:67), saw the dawn of salvation through the forgiveness of sins in his son's birth (Luke 1:77). And when Jesus came to be baptized, John the Baptist pointed to him and said: ''Behold, the Lamb of God, who takes away the sin of the world'' (John 1:29).

During his ministry, Jesus was not content, like John, to preach conversion and the forgiveness of sins: he claimed this power for himself[23] and exercised it with the same right as God. '' 'But that you may know that the Son of Man has authority to forgive sins on earth'—he said to the paralytic, 'I say to you, rise, pick up your mat and go home' '' (Mark 2:10-11; Luke 5:24). In giving his messengers the Spirit, the risen Lord confers his own power on them without restriction. Because Jesus has returned to the Father, the disciples will even be able to exercise it more than he could[24]: through their ministry, the word of forgiveness is offered to everyone. They will proclaim to the whole world: God ''has reconciled us to himself through Christ and [has] given us the ministry of reconciliation. . . . We implore you on behalf of Christ, be reconciled to God!'' (2 Cor 5:18-20).

The Church, the body of Christ formed and animated by the Spirit, is a community of pardoned sinners, who themselves forgive and announce to the world the good news of reconciliation with God. In the Church, the various gifts of grace lead to different ministries. But each person, with the gifts bestowed on him or her, must work for the common good: the spreading of the peace the Lord has brought to the world by his preaching, death, and resurrection. The risen Lord is here in our midst. He appears in the efficacious signs of his presence and action that can be seen in the liturgical celebration.

Thus God's word is proclaimed and, in acclaiming it, we say: ''Glory to you, O Lord!''

We commemorate ''the death he endured for our salvation, his glorious resurrection and ascension into heaven,''[25] giving thanks for the bread

wine, as he did at the Last Supper, saying: "Do this in memory of
e."

By the Holy Spirit, the bread and wine "become the Body and Blood
of our Lord Jesus Christ."[26]

Reconciled with our brothers and sisters, we exchange a sign of peace
and go forward, in joy, to receive the Body and Blood of Christ, proclaiming: "Behold the Lamb of God who takes away the sins of the world."
Through this sacrament from which flow, and toward which converge,
the sanctification of humanity, the glorification of God, evangelization,
and the other sacraments, we are "brought together in unity by the Holy
Spirit."[27]

> On the evening of the resurrection,
> On Sunday, the first day of the week,
> You appeared to the Eleven,
> Behind closed doors, at night;
>
> And the first breath
> that we had lost in Paradise,
> You gave to them again,
> And through them to our human nature.
>
> I who in my soul hold closed
> To your word the doors of my mind,
> And who dwell in darkness,
> In the land of shadow,
>
> Do not, under my darkened roof,
> Allow the Evil One to dwell forever;
> But open the bridal chamber of my heart,
> Making it glow with dazzling light.[28]

Witnesses of Christ with the Holy Spirit

Living Under the Guidance of God's Spirit

No matter what subject he is addressing, Paul always thinks of it in reference to God, to Christ, to salvation, to the Church, to faith: in other words, he always sees the theological dimension, even in questions that seem to be purely practical. His responses always flow from this all-encompassing vision of the mystery. At least, he always wonders what is at stake in a particular situation, seeing its significance in the light of revelation. Many of the situations the Apostle deals with confront us today, but the value of his teaching is not bound to the situation that provokes it. An example of this is the passage we read today from the Letter to the Galatians (Gal 5:16-25) [1]

The Lord Jesus Christ "gave himself for our sins that he might rescue us from the present evil age in accord with the will of our God and Father" (Gal 1:4). And it was for our "freedom" that Christ handed himself over (Gal 5:1) and gave us the Spirit under whose direction he has placed us. For "the Lord is the Spirit, and where the Spirit of the Lord is, there is freedom" (2 Cor 3:17). Therefore we must live as "guided by the spirit."

This life of liberty does not authorize us to do simply anything, and it never comes without a struggle. We must still deal with all the lusts of what Paul calls "the flesh." Note that the Apostle always thinks of the human being as a whole: body and soul. This is God's creation, and the Son of God, in becoming man, took "flesh" of a woman. In our bodies, we are, like all other living creatures, limited beings: we are born, we die, and every day we are faced with all the constraints of a body. Unlike all other creatures, we are aware of these limits, and we know that we will die. In this sense, nothing is different for the Christian, though we may not be disheartened like those "who have no hope" (1 Thess 4:13). But "the flesh," in Paul's terminology, has a different meaning.

281

denotes that which is within the human person that draws toward earthly things, toward sin. In this sense, "flesh" is opposed to "spirit," which draws us toward heavenly things.

"Now the works of the flesh are obvious." To attempt to draw up a list of such things would be a useless if not impossible task if it were not limited to certain examples indicative of different types of perversion to which the "flesh" leads. Paul enumerates some of them. He does not pretend that his list is complete,[2] but it is extensive enough to make us understand that we must take a serious look at our own conduct.

A list of fruits of the Spirit is no easier to draw up, but at least it is clear when one attempts to do so that everything one can enumerate is a variation of faith, hope, and love: thus "joy, peace, patience, kindness, generosity, faithfulness, gentleness, and self-control."[3] These are no less numerous than the fruits of the "flesh," but they are more homogeneous. The carnal person, swayed by all the tendencies of the "flesh," its desires, lusts, and impulses, tries at once to reach in all directions, as disorderly as a wild plant, or a tree that has never been pruned. The power of the Spirit, on the other hand, unifies the person, who then bears innumerable fruits, all of good quality, for eternal life (John 15:16). Those who obey the tendencies of the "flesh" "will not inherit the kingdom of God." Those on the other hand who let themselves be led by the Spirit flower in an absolute freedom that has nothing in common with licentiousness. It is not a law that surrounds them, confronting them with constantly painful demands with which they must always struggle. Their law is interior: it is love, the first gift of the Spirit, from which come all the others. Whoever lives under this law of spiritual freedom is filled with a profound joy and peace, which shed their light over everything, and which nothing can touch.

Letting oneself be led by the Spirit, however, opposed as it is to the tendencies of the "flesh," never comes without a struggle. One must renounce all assurance except that of the cross. Choosing this means that one must crucify one's flesh with its "passions and desires." This is folly, according to human wisdom; it flies in the face of all those solicitations that tell one to give in to the immediate satisfaction of all desires and impulses. But this folly is wisdom in the eyes of faith: it enables one to share in Christ's victory over sin, a victory in which we may have all the more confidence since it does not rely on our own strength, but on the power of the Spirit, given as a gift to those who ask for it and wish to receive it.

Come, true light. Come, eternal life. Come, hidden mystery. Come, named treasure. Come, ineffable reality. Come, incredible person. Com happiness without end. Come, sun that never sets. Come, unfailing long ing of all those who must be saved. Come, waking call to those who sleep. Come, resurrection of the dead. Come, O Powerful One, who work and transform everything by your will alone. Come, O invisible and completely intangible one. Come, you who are always immovable and who at each moment move me, and come to us, lying in hell, O you who are above the heavens. Come, O Name beloved and repeated everywhere, but whose being and nature is always forbidden for us to express. Come, eternal joy. Come, untarnished crown. Come, our God with the purple of the high king. Come, crystalline sash studded with jewels. Come, inaccessible sandal. Come, royal purple. Come, right and true sovereign. Come, you who have desired and still desire my miserable soul. Come, Alone to the alone, since you see that I am alone. Come, you who have divided me from the rest of the world. Come, who have become my desire, who have made me desire you, you the completely unreachable. Come, my breath and my life. Come, consolation of my poor soul. Come, my joy, my glory, my endless delight.[4]

The Spirit: Advocate, Witness, and Guide

When the apostles were arraigned for the second time before the Sanhedrin, Gamaliel, a Pharisee and doctor of the Law "respected by all the people" and a member of the high council, spoke to the assembly, after having the accused men removed. He reminded them of what had recently happened regarding two men, one Theudas who had claimed to be "someone important" and, during the census, Judas the Galilean. They had both won disciples: one "four hundred men," the other quite a following. Both of them died, and their partisans scattered. Thus Gamaliel advised not being too concerned with Jesus' disciples. "For if this endeavor or this activity is of human origin, it will destroy itself. But if it comes from God, you will not be able to destroy them; you may even find yourselves fighting against God."[5] The argument of durability is not a decisive criterion for judging whether some movement has a divine origin or not. However, without knowing it, Gamaliel was agreeing with what Jesus had said to his disciples when "the hour had come for him to pass from this world to the Father": he promised them Another, come from the Father to be with them: an advocate, a witness, a guide (John 15:26-27; 16:12-15).

The Holy Spirit is called "Paraclete," from the Greek *paraklētos*. In the legal language of the New Testament era, this term meant someone who

...es to the aid of an accused in a trial: "an advocate, a witness for the ..fense, an intercessor."[6] Several different translations are possible, and different editions of the Bible commonly choose one term and use it wherever the word appears in John's writings.[7] But "the difference in contexts suggests that the translation should be varied from place to place. In this particular passage, the legal context and the role attributed to the Spirit recommend the translation 'advocate.'"[8]

Jesus is referring to the coming of the Holy Spirit, who is charged with testifying on his behalf and assisting with counsel the disciples who would also testify to the Lord. This way of speaking suggests that the Holy Spirit will act in the context of a legal action. Indeed, it is in just such a framework that John presents the whole of Jesus' ministry. Confronted, accused by the "world,"[9] Jesus constantly appeals to the witness of his Father, the Scriptures, his works that attest to his authority, the authenticity of his mission, and the truth of his words.[10] During the great trial that ends in his condemnation to death, he is asked about his teaching and his disciples (John 18:19-24). He is presented as a criminal to Pilate, who can find no cause for complaint against him (John 18:38), but who, not daring to release him, hands him over to be crucified (John 19:12-16). Jesus faces this trial alone: at his arrest, he requests and is granted that his disciples not be bothered (John 18:8-9); Peter denies him (John 18:15-18, 25-27); around the cross, there are only four women—his mother, his mother's sister, Mary the wife of Clopas, Mary Magdalene—and John (John 19:25). He loses the trial, which leads to his being immediately executed. But Jesus knows that events will take another turn. As he had foretold, the Father raises him up "on the third day." Another trial begins that will end with a sentence without appeal against death and the Prince of this world (Rev 20:10-14), while the Lamb who was slain will be with "the one who sits on the throne," eternally glorified by the countless multitude of those "purchased for God" (Rev 5:1-14). Before that, though, comes the fight on both sides, in which the Advocate plays a part.

Because it "proceeds from the Father," who alone knows his Son (John 10:15)[11] and who is "the Spirit of truth," this Advocate gives a decisive and irrefutable witness to the Lord, not only in words, but, in conformity with its nature, by acting on Christ's behalf.[12] It does so by lending concrete assistance to the disciples, who in particular are charged with testifying in our midst. They will have to do so in the aftermath of Pentecost and throughout the history of the Church when, brought before judges, they are asked to give an account of their faith, or of the behaviors, choices, or denials that it demands.[13] Even today, some people will be witnesses of Christ at the cost of their lives: imprisoned, tortured physically or morally, and put to death.[14] Countless others will witness by conforming their lives to the gospel and the rule of the kingdom—the Beatitudes—or by fighting for justice, rights, and the respect for all people. The force of this witness, as great as it is when given individually, is all the stronger when it is given collectively, by the Church community. Finally, the announcement of the good news is also testimony to Christ (Matt 24:14). In all of these, it is the Spirit who witnesses "on behalf" of Christ, whose disciples bear his name. It gives them strength and courage, a strength and courage that often seem to surpass human possibility, enabling them to stand firm before their judges, steadfast in the faith despite threats, ill treatment, and death. It inspires and sustains their noble determination to live and fight, following to the end the demands and hints of the gospel. It inspires the speech of those who preach the good news, the zeal and the various undertakings of those men and women who are inflamed with the love of Christ and neighbor.

The Advocate is also a Guide "to all truth." Over the person and life of Jesus, over his words and deeds, it throws an ever dazzling light. It gives to the disciples and the Church an ever deeper wisdom. What it has heard, as alone it can, it will repeat throughout the centuries, hiding nothing.[15] Not like a scribe or doctor who would comment endlessly on a particular text, but like an inner master who makes the living Word grow in our hearts and in the Church, that it might bear new fruits in abundance in every season. Through the Holy Spirit, Jesus teaches in plain words everything that concerns the Father and the coming of the kingdom (John 16:25).[16] Authoritative interpreter of the Scriptures who reveals the mystery of God and of salvation, the Spirit guides Christians and the Church to a knowledge of the "signs of the times," enabling them in every age to penetrate to the meaning of history.

> Sweet is its presence, sweet our knowledge of it, light is its yoke. The rays of light and knowledge announce its brilliant coming. It comes with the feelings of a true guardian; for it comes to save, to heal, to teach, to counsel, to strengthen, to enlighten minds, first of all in the one who receives it, then, through him, others as well. And like the bodily eye, first in darkness, then suddenly gazing on the sun, is brightened and sees distinctly what it had not seen, thus the soul of whoever is honored with the visit of the Holy Spirit is enlightened and sees in a superhuman way what it did not know. . . . This person enjoys the presence of one who truly leads him to the light.[17]

When he left his disciples, Jesus did not leave them to themselves with the mission of continuing his work and remembering what he had done, and what he had taught. He sent them, "from the Father," the Spirit who would act in them and in his Church with the power and authority of an Advocate, a Witness, and a Guide. Thanks to the Spirit, the Word is still living in the world, being poured out and raising up new disciples everywhere, witnesses of Christ with the Holy Spirit "that God has given to those who obey him" (Acts 5:32), so that the kingdom may come.

It is the Holy Spirit by whom we are restored to paradise, ascend into the kingdom of heaven, and come to be adopted sons. The Spirit gives us the confidence to call God Father, to share in Christ's grace, to be called children of the light, to have a share in eternal glory, to be filled with every blessing, in this age and in the age to come, to see as in a mirror, as if they were already present, the gifts promised us and which, in faith, we look forward to enjoying. If the pledges are such, what will the fulfillment be like? And if the first-fruits are so great, what shall we say of the fullness?[18]

The Spirit of the Father in the Lord's Prayer

Under the Control of the Spirit, Not the Flesh

Life according to the "flesh" is life under the power of sin and the instability it creates in the world. Such a life cannot be pleasing to God: the only possible result is death, the punishment for sin. On the other hand, there is no condemnation for those who belong to Christ and live through his Spirit dwelling in them; Paul explains how and under what conditions in the Letter to the Romans (Rom 8:8-17).

The gift of the Spirit, inaugurated by Christ's passover, characterizes the nature of the last times. Poured out first on the apostles and, through them, on all disciples, the Spirit continues Christ's work. It sanctifies the waters of baptism where believers are born to new life, and it changes other sacred signs into sacraments that truly bestow grace. Source of many and varied charisms, it organizes the Church, making it, in its unity, the body of Christ (1 Cor 12:4-30). The Christian is thus more and more assimilated to Christ, "belonging" to him to an ever greater degree, in so far as the Christian lives through the indwelling of the Spirit. One is never fully a Christian in this life but is always progressing toward that fullness. In the end, "we will all attain to the unity of faith and knowledge of the Son of God, to mature manhood, to the extent of the full stature of Christ" (Eph 4:13).[1] "Taken possession of by Christ," we may never think ourselves "as straining forward to what lies ahead" (Phil 3:12-13). Our body "is dead because of sin," but the Spirit of him "who raised Christ from the dead will give life to your mortal bodies also, through his Spirit that dwells in you." Baptized into the death of Christ, we thus participate fully in his passover and resurrection, and he "will raise our mortal bodies and make them like his own in glory."[2]

Although we have become "just," we must still reckon with the temptation of sin. The Spirit allows us not only to conquer it but to destroy it. Again, this comes from following the same path as Christ, while acknowledging the vast difference between him and us. Conceived by the

Holy Spirit, he received it in full at his baptism in the waters of the Jordan. "At once the Spirit drove him out into the desert" (Mark 1:12), where he won his first victory over Satan, who then stayed away until the time of the decisive battle (Luke 4:13). Throughout his ministry, Jesus walked under the guidance of the Spirit, who enabled him to triumph over death. Immediately after being resurrected, the Son began to use the Spirit to transform into his image all those for whom he had died on the cross (2 Cor 3:18).[3]

Like Jesus, the disciple must allow himself to be led by the Spirit, to live with the Spirit that "dwells in him," to submit to its inspiration and action, not to "grieve" (Eph 4:30).

> Into the heart freed from illusions will be born divine and mysterious thoughts that will leap about like the fish, like dolphins leaping head-first into a calm sea. A light breeze stirs the sea, and the Holy Spirit agitates the depths of the heart. "God sent the spirit of his Son into our hearts, crying out, '*Abba*, Father!'"[4]

Indeed, "those who are led by the Spirit of God are children of God." They live no longer under the rule of fear, but rather that of love and confidence. "Through the Spirit," who attests in us to our divine sonship, we cry out to God and call him: "*Abba*, Father!" Now, we are heirs as well: "heirs of God and joint heirs with Christ." This inheritance promised us[5] is the kingdom,[6] glory,[7] eternal life[8]: "kingdom and glory" (1 Thess 2:12), "eternal life to those who seek glory" (Rom 2:7). The Spirit is the object of the promise (Gal 3:14), of which it is both the pledge (Eph 1:13) and the first-fruit (Rom 8:23).

> If we now, on receiving the pledges, cry "*Abba*, Father," what will we do when, resurrected, we will see him face to face? when all the members, wave upon wave, will shout a hymn of exultation, glorifying the one who will have raised them from the dead and given them eternal life? For, if already with simple pledges surrounding him, man cries "*Abba*, Father," what will he not do with the complete grace of the Spirit, once given him by God? It will make us like God and will accomplish the will of the Father, for it will make man into the image and likeness of God.[9]

In order that this may be true, one must "suffer with [Christ] so that we may also be glorified with him." "We were indeed buried with him through baptism into death, so that, just as Christ was raised from the dead by the glory of the Father, we too might live in newness of life" (Rom 6:3-4). The liturgy of Pentecost thus returns us to that of Easter Sunday.

If then you were raised with Christ, seek what is above, where Christ is seated at the right hand of God. Think of what is above, not of what is on earth (Col 3:1- 2).

It is the Spirit who makes us capable of pursuing this path and participating in the life of Christ, in his humility, his obedience to the Father, his trust, his patience, his charity. But it also enables us to participate in his kingdom, in the benefits of his resurrection, in the full enjoyment of the gifts of the Spirit. It belongs to us to be the son of God who, through the Spirit, will reach, in eternal glory, his full stature.

> Come, Holy Spirit, come!
> And from your celestial home
> Shed a ray of light divine!
>
> Come, Father of the poor!
> Come, source of all our store!
> Come, within our bosoms shine!
>
> You, of comforters the best;
> You, the soul's most welcome guest;
> Sweet refreshment here below;
>
> In our labor, rest most sweet;
> Grateful coolness in the heat;
> Solace in the midst of woe.
>
> O most blessed Light divine,
> Shine within these hearts of yours,
> And our inmost being fill!
>
> Where you are not, man has naught,
> Nothing good in deed or thought,
> Nothing free from taint of ill.
>
> Heal our wounds, our strength renew;
> On our dryness pour your dew;
> Wash the stains of guilt away:
>
> Bend the stubborn heart and will;
> Melt the frozen, warm the chill;
> Guide the steps that go astray.
>
> On the faithful, who adore
> And confess you, evermore
> In your sev'nfold gift descend;
>
> Give them virtue's sure reward;
> Give them your salvation, Lord;
> give them joys that never end. Amen.
> Alleluia.[10]

We Will Come to His House to Dwell

The liturgy on Pentecost Sunday contains two Gospel readings that were read only a few weeks ago.[11] But they are not simply reprises of texts we have already heard. Pentecost presents a new and very definite context in which they are to be understood, as the liturgy understands in plucking out this extract from the first of Jesus' discourses after the Last Supper, from John's Gospel (John 14:15- 16, 23b-26).[12]

It is noteworthy that the revelation concerning the sending of the Spirit begins by Jesus saying: "If you love me, you will keep my commandments . . . and [my Father] will give you . . ." The New Testament, on the whole, more often urges us to believe in Jesus than to love him.[13] John, though he insists on the love of God and of Christ, for God and for Christ, does not at all misunderstand the importance of obedience to the commandments: "Those who keep [God's] commandments remain in him, and he in them" (1 John 3:24); "The way we may be sure that we know him is to keep his commandments. Whoever says, 'I know him,' but does not keep his commandments is a liar, and the truth is not in him" (1 John 2:3- 4).[14] The Old Testament already demanded that love for God find concrete expression in the keeping of the commandments: "Hear, O Israel! The Lord is our God, the Lord alone! Therefore, you shall love the Lord, your God, with all your heart, and with all your soul, and with all your strength. Take to heart these words which I enjoin on you today" (Deut 6:4-6). In the new covenant "in his blood," of which Jesus speaks in the "farewell discourses," the Law is more than a personification of God: obedience to the commandments is first and foremost obedience to God and to his Christ out of love; to love God and Christ is to obey the commandments. Jesus himself experienced and understood his love of the Father in obedience to his commandments. He told his disciples: "If you keep my commandments, you will remain in my love, just as I have kept my Father's commandments and remain in his love" (John 15:10).

On his part, the Lord wants his disciples to love him not only in words, but in truth and in action: "And I will ask the Father, and he will give you another Advocate to be with you always." The identity of this other "Advocate," and especially the manner in which he will be with us always, are not as easy to determine as it might seem at first glance. Jesus distinguishes between himself and this other: we have always understood this to be the Holy Spirit. But John writes: "We have an Advocate with the Father, Jesus Christ, the righteous one" (1 John 2:1). It is inconceivable that after his return to the Father Jesus ceased to be interested in his own, like someone who would leave them in the hands of a capable guardian. In order to understand the mystery of this new presence, the result of Jesus' prayer, and what exactly this most precious of gifts[15] sent by the Father is, one must carefully follow the intricate line of John's thought.

"We will come to him and make our dwelling with him." The Advocate is not therefore a kind of proxy sent to replace the absent Lord: on the contrary, it assures his presence as well as the Father's. They will "come to" the one who remains faithful to Jesus' word, and they will dwell "with" him. Not with the others—those who do not love the Lord and do not keep his word—for "it is love that divides the saints from the world."[16] This presence of the Father and the Son through the Holy Spirit fulfills, beyond all hope, the aspiration of religious people who build places for their god to dwell. The hour is come when, to adore the Father "in Spirit and truth," one must go neither to the sacred mountain nor to Jerusalem (John 4:21-24): "Do you not know that you are the Temple of God, and that the Spirit of God dwells in you? . . . for the temple of God, which you are, is holy" (1 Cor 3:16-17).

"The word you hear is not mine; it comes from the Father who sent me." Jesus speaks like the prophets—"The word of the Lord"—but with an authority that no one has ever had or will ever have. "This much have I told you while I was still with you": he focuses on the time when his presence will no longer be visible; namely, our time.[17]

The Father will send "the Advocate, the holy Spirit" not only at Jesus' prayer, but "in his name." The Father does nothing without his Son, and the Son always does what the Father wishes. "In the beginning was the Word, and the Word was with God, and the Word was God. He was in the beginning with God. All things came to be through him, and without him nothing came to be . . . And the Word became flesh" (John 1:1-3, 14).

> From among many of our Lord's sayings, these have been chosen to guide our understanding, for they reveal to us the intention of the giver, the nature of the gift, and the condition for its reception. Since our weak minds cannot comprehend the Father or the Son, we have been given the Holy Spirit as our intermediary and advocate, to shed light on that difficult doctrine of our faith, the incarnation of God.[18]

"The Advocate, the holy Spirit that the Father will send in my name—he will teach you everything and remind you of all that [I] told you."

What then do we do, brothers, when we teach you? If the anointing of the Spirit teaches you all things, do we work in vain? Why bother? We need only to leave you to its anointing, and this anointing will teach you . . .

You see the great mystery, brothers: the sound of our words strikes your ears, the Master is already inside. Do not think that one can learn anything from a man. We can direct your attention with the noise of our voice; but if there is nothing inside you to teach you, that noise is useless . . .

The teachings of the outer master are like helps or signs. But the one who teaches hearts has its seat in heaven. . . . It speaks inside of you, when no one is present; even if someone is at your side, he is not in your heart. And if there is no one in your heart, may Christ be in your heart, may his anointing be in your heart, so that your heart may not thirst in a desert, without springs to water it. It is the inner Master who teaches, Christ who teaches, his inspiration that teaches. Where his inspiration and anointing are not present, the noise of words outside is useless.[19]

The "inner Master" leads to the greater and greater penetration of the mystery of Jesus and of the Father whom the Son reveals.

This teaches us, at least for the future, to have faith in what we do not see. The world seems to follow its well-trodden path. There is nothing heavenly on the face of society; in the day's news, there is nothing of heaven; on the faces of the masses or the great or wealthy or mighty, there is nothing of heaven; in the speech of the eloquent, in the actions of the powerful, in the counsels of wise men, in pomp and splendor, there is nothing of heaven. And yet, the Spirit of God is present. . . . Let us always keep this divine truth in our minds: the more hidden God's hand, the more powerful it is; the more it is silent, the more it is formidable. We are in the powerful service of the Spirit; whoever speaks like him, risks more than he can guess; whoever pains him, loses more blessing and glory than he could possibly imagine.[20]

Everyday Pentecost

Without failing to do justice to the historical sequence of events, the liturgy readily views the mystery of salvation in its totality. At the end of the fifty days of Easter, it shows that Easter is fulfilled only when the wind blows at Pentecost, the wind of which a breath was felt in the first light of dawn "on the first day of the week."

> The Spirit descended on the Son of God become the Son of Man: through him, it came to dwell in the human race, to rest upon men, to reside in the work modeled by God; it realized the Father's will in them and renewed them by enabling them to pass from their decay to the regeneration of Christ.[1]

Following the Gospels,[2] particularly Luke (4:1, 14-15), Peter, in the Acts of the Apostles, recalls that Jesus' public ministry began at the Jordan with his baptism in water and the Spirit.[3] John insists on the lance thrust that opened Jesus' side when he "handed over the spirit" on the cross (John 19:34, 30). In speaking thus, the evangelist perhaps wants to suggest that it was in dying that Jesus gave the Spirit to the world. In any case, he accords a great deal of importance to the mystery of the water and blood that flow from the wound of the crucified. And John explicitly associates the gift of the Spirit with the Lord's passover (John 7:37-39).

The mystery of Pentecost is thus that of the Church, the Body of Christ. It appears on "the fiftieth day," when the Spirit was poured out on the first Christian community, giving it the strength and confidence to testify publicly to the resurrection.

This memorable day, however, was not by itself the real beginning. The readings for Mass on the Vigil of Pentecost attest to this, recalling a series of prefigurations and prophecies. The confusion of languages at Babel brought an end to the attempt to build a city and future not dependent on God. But the hope still remained of a day without end when people of every nation, race, and tongue would be gathered into the city that would descend from heaven.

The covenant at Sinai, concluded amidst fire and thunder, would provide the framework of the Christian Pentecost, when "suddenly there came from the sky a noise like a strong driving wind," and there appeared "tongues as of fire, which parted and came to rest on each one of . . ." those who were in the house.

The vision of the dry bones revived by the Spirit points to the immense gathering of people who will form the Body of Christ, different though they may be in ministry and charism.

The prophet Joel reveals how, in the last days, the Lord will pour out his spirit on every creature who will invoke the name of the saving God.

John's Gospel recalls the words of the one whom we must invoke in order to be saved: "Let him come to me, let him drink who believes in me."

As for Paul, he never ceases to exhort us to be open to the gift of the Spirit, to let ourselves be led by the one who draws us toward the possession of the promised inheritance, the pledges of which we have already received.

The celebration of Pentecost does not simply commemorate a past event, however great it might be. It celebrates a mystery which happened once and for all time, but which also unfolds throughout time. It proclaims the permanence of Pentecost.

The Spirit continues to build the Body of Christ, of which we become members by baptism and the Eucharist (1 Cor 12). It revives those who, crucifying their "flesh" with its egoistic tendencies, allow themselves to be taught and led by its impulses (Gal 5:16-25). It makes them sons of God and inspires in them the prayer: "*Abba*, Father!" (Rom 8:8-17). It joins with the gradual dawning of the new heavens and the new earth, the whole creation that cries out in pain while awaiting its deliverance. "For in hope we were saved" (Rom 8:18-23).

Pentecost—"fifty days after Easter"—Pentecost of every day: the Spirit is given in abundance to those who pray the Father to send it to them in the Lord's name.

> Open your hearts to the breath of God,
> His life is grafted to the souls that he touches;
> May a new people
> Rise from the waters
> Over which hovers the Spirit of your baptism!
> —Let us open our hearts to the breath of God
> For he breathes in our mouths
> More than we do ourselves!
>
> Offer your bodies to the tongues of Fire:
> May it inflame the heart of the earth!

Your foreheads are marked
With sacred signs:
The words of Jesus and of Victory!
—Let us offer our bodies to the tongues of Fire
So that they may announce the mystery
Of our glory.

Give your being to the seed of the Spirit
Come to be joined to all suffering:
The Body of the Lord
Is formed with the sorrows
Of the Man crushed by injustice.
—Let us give our being to the seed of the Spirit
So that he may give us his strength
In his service.

Turn your eyes to the inner guest,
Desiring nothing more than this presence;
Live with the Spirit
So as to be the one
Who gives his Name to your Father.
—Let us turn our eyes to the inner guest,
For he dwells in our silence
And our prayers![4]

From Bethlehem to Emmaus

The story of the pilgrims on the road to Emmaus (Luke 24:13-35)[1] is, among the twenty-three Gospel passages read on the Sundays of Eastertime, one of those that touches us most and most directly concerns us. This wonderful story is a sort of parable, filled with highly evocative details. It used to be read to the newly baptized on Easter night. But everyone, in hearing it proclaimed and meditating on it, can see the reflection of all of Christian life, and not just its beginning. The slow growth of Easter faith in hearts slow to understand the Scriptures that announce Christ and his passover, the light which suddenly shines forth on the occasion of an unexpected encounter or a decisive conversation, the joy of the discovery that one immediately wants to share with others: in one way or another, we have all had this experience. But the story of the pilgrims to Emmaus also evokes the Eucharist where Christ is recognized in the sign of the breaking of the bread; the necessity, for Christians, of telling each other ''The Lord has truly been raised'' and, for the Church, of proclaiming it to the whole world. Emmaus cannot be located on a map with any certainty. This is no cause for regret: the humble inn can be found on our own paths; we may stop there on any evening when our heart is sad, returning when we wish, so as to give thanks for our encounter with the Lord.

The same is true of the poor stable of Bethlehem where one evening Mary and Joseph took refuge because there was no room at the inn, ''when the time came for her to have her child, and she gave birth to her firstborn son.'' There, at Bethlehem, ''the house of bread,''[2] Mary laid her newborn son in a manger (Luke 2:6-7).[3] In the light of the prophecies, we recognize that this child, poor among the poor, is Emmanuel, ''God with us'' (Isa 8:8, 10),[4] the only Son of God was sent ''in the likeness of sinful flesh [to condemn] sin in the flesh'' (Rom 8:3). What quietly begins there reaches its height with the passover of the Lord, his death and resurrection.

Between the obscure stable at Bethlehem, where the Son of God appeared in our flesh, and the humble inn of Emmaus, where the resurrected was recognized in the breaking of the bread, there are many connections. To stop and think about them for a while, at the end of the Easter season, will shed greater light on the mystery celebrated in joyful exultation during the fifty days as "one feast day, or perhaps better, as one 'great Sunday.' "[5]

From Christmas to Easter—One Mystery

The Church's tradition has always sensed a hidden connection between Christmas and Easter. The Greek and Latin Fathers expressed it in unparalleled terms, yet very concisely. The thanksgiving of Christmas anticipates that of Easter.

> Let no one argue that such thanksgivings are only suitable for the paschal mystery. Consider rather that Easter is the last act of the divine economy. And what ending is not preceded by a beginning? Which is the earlier moment? Of course, that which inaugurates the economy of the passion. Thus the miracle of Easter has a share in our praise of Christmas.[6]

Christmas announces Easter in much the same way that a seed contains the promise of the fruit. The feast of the theophany, the Epiphany of the Lord, celebrates the beginning of the mysteries of Christ that display extraordinary continuity. Together they lead to the fulfillment of humanity, to its new birth in Christ, the new Adam of a humanity freed from sin (1 Cor 15:45-49). "The creation of man was a wonderful work, his redemption"; and by the incarnation of his Son, his death and his resurrection, "still more wonderful."[7] In order to share in this salvation, the disciple of Christ must, with and in him, travel the same road: from Christmas to Easter.

> Be lifted on the cross with Christ, die with him, be buried with him, O joyful heart, so as to rise with him, to be glorified with him, to reign with him, to see God in all his majesty, this God adored and magnified in the Trinity, whom we desire so much to know, as clearly as prisoners of the flesh can.[8]

St. Bernard of Clairvaux, the last of the Western Fathers, expresses in his distinctive mixture of poetry and mysticism, of strength and tenderness, what he sees while contemplating the manger.

> It is as if God the Father sent upon the earth a purse full of his mercy. This purse was burst open during the Lord's passion to pour forth its hidden

contents—the price of our redemption. It was only a small purse, but it was very full.[9]

From Christmas Night to Easter Night

In its calm sobriety, the Western liturgy is not typically carried away by great mystical enthusiasms, quick connections between ancient figures and present-day realities. But it has kept an antiphon of strange and mysterious beauty, from the Book of Wisdom.

> For when peaceful stillness compassed everything
>   and the night in its swift course was half spent,
> Your all-powerful word from heaven's royal throne
>   bounded, a fierce warrior, into the doomed land . . .
> (Wis 18:14-15)[10]

Within the liturgical context of the nativity, this antiphon suggests the silent coming, in the middle of the night, of the eternal Word sent by the Father, coming to dwell among humanity to save it. However, this text is drawn from an evocation of the all-powerful intervention of the Word of God during the night of the Exodus: "a fierce warrior . . . bearing the sharp sword of your inexorable decree. And as he alighted, he filled every place with death; he still reached to heaven, while he stood upon the earth" (Wis 18:15-16). It is in shocking contrast with an atmosphere of sweetness, peace, divine benevolence toward humanity. Is this a clear and obvious misunderstanding by the Church, a free appropriation of a symbol that can be interpreted in many ways? Certainly not. Rather, it is a remarkable insight. This connection to a meditation on the Exodus reveals a profound awareness of the unity of God's plan that unfolds in an astonishingly coherent manner from Christmas night to Easter night, from Bethlehem to Emmaus.

A Time of Journeying in Faith

The Gospels of Bethlehem and Emmaus show men and women whose faith progresses in the rhythm of their journey from one place to another, from astonishment to joy over what they discover and finally understand. They are all simple, humble people. Accustomed to a harsh and deceptive reality, they say nothing until verifying for themselves what has been proclaimed to them. "Let us go, then, to Bethlehem to see this thing that has taken place, which the Lord has made known to us," the shepherds say to each other (Luke 2:15). And the two disciples on the road to Emmaus tell the stranger that "some women from our group . . . have astounded us: they were at the tomb early in the morning and did not find his body; they came back and reported that they had indeed seen a vision of angels who announced that he was alive. Then some of those with us went to the tomb and found things just as the women had described, but him they did not see.'' Without hesitation, they testify to what they have seen (Luke 2:17; 24:22-24, 35). They allow themselves to be judged by the reality of the astonishing things they have witnessed. We do not know what became of them: but their faith has left its mark on history.

Both at Christmas and Easter, all these people who wait, who hope—without always knowing for what, sometimes against all hope—suddenly begin to stir, to walk, even to run. Alerted by the angels, the shepherds of Bethlehem abandon their flocks in the middle of the night and hasten to the Shepherd of Israel (Luke 2:16). The magi, because of a rising star, set out on a long journey to offer homage to the newborn King (Matt 2:2).

At Easter, Simon and John, the women, and Mary Magdalene come and go, running from the house to the tomb, then returning to the house (John 20:1-10). Cleopas and his companion walk from Jerusalem to Emmaus. On the way, they meet the stranger. When they have recognized the Lord, they return ''immediately'' to Jerusalem.

The journeyers of Bethlehem and Emmaus do not follow the same road of faith, nor do they have the same experiences. But all of them go through trials, traveling for a while in the dark, leaving their homes; and this exodus marks a sharp break between the past and the future. At the end of the road, they bow down to adore the one they have recognized in the light and shadow of faith: the Christ-Savior, the prophesied Son of David, the Son of God.[11] ''My Lord and my God!'' (John 20:28). Then they leave by another road, as the magi had done (Matt 2:12), or by unknown roads on which the Lord sends them to proclaim the good news, as the disciples had done (Matt 28:17-20).

Both at Bethlehem and at Emmaus, the road of faith is marked with signs. ''And this will be a sign for you: you will find an infant wrapped in swaddling clothes and lying in a manger.'' (Luke 2:12). ''He was made known to them in the breaking of the bread,'' at the moment he disappeared (Luke 24:35), whereas on the road, when he marched at their side, ''their eyes were prevented from recognizing him'' (Luke 24:16). Certainly, there is a great difference between the body of a child, no different from any new-born, and the body of the dead and risen Lord. With the latter, too, it was possible to say, ''Yes, it is he.'' Did he not show the marks of the nails and the lance wound to Thomas (John 20:27)? Yet, the relationship one has with the risen Lord is different. He appeared, suddenly, behind the locked doors of the house where his disciples were hiding (John 20:19). He disappeared, and they could not hold onto him, as they could not at Emmaus (Luke 24:31).

True, when he was in his earthly form, Jesus, who let himself be approached and touched, whom the crowd pressed on from all sides, was no less impossible to hold onto. As a child, he escaped the death that Herod had ordained for him (Matt 2:13-15). The people of Nazareth could not lay hold of him when they sought to throw him off the cliff outside their town (Luke 4:29-30). He escaped the crowd after the multiplication of the loaves (Matt 5:22-24). He was present yet impossible to seize: such was always the case with Jesus; he is more present than ever today and still impossible to seize, because now he is clothed with the glorious flesh of the resurrected.[12] In faith, we recognize his presence in the sign of bread and wine, in the Spirit's action in us—in the Church and in the world— the Spirit whom the Father sends us at Jesus' request and in his name (John 14:16, 26).

From Bethlehem to Emmaus, from Emmaus to the Lord's last manifestation, we journey in faith, going "from glory to glory" (2 Cor 3:18), on a road filled with signs.

A Time of Silence in the Presence of the Word

Bethlehem and Emmaus may also be described as times of silence in the presence of the proclaimed Word. After having taken center stage for a moment, the shepherds and magi of Bethlehem, the two disciples of Emmaus, break their silence only in order to speak their testimony. They say nothing of themselves, they efface themselves before the message that has been given them: then they disappear, and are never spoken of again.

Human speech—as Babel exemplifies—is unable to gather and unite people. Only the Word of God can make one people out of the diversity of races, languages, and cultures. But it acts with a certain discretion, even when it must be proclaimed. And even people who are given the ministry of preaching must be careful that the noise of their words does not drown out the Spirit, the inner master.[13]

Before spending three years traveling through towns and villages proclaiming the good news, the Word of God spent many years of silence in Nazareth. Jesus' words are short and concise. When he taught the disciples to pray, he warned them to avoid rambling on and on (Matt 6:7). He taught them to act, eschewing hollow words. "Let your 'Yes' mean 'Yes,' and your 'No' mean 'No.' Anything more is from the evil one'' (Matt 5:37). The disciples and all servants of the Word must first listen to it and let it penetrate them in silence.

At Bethlehem there is the silence of wonder and adoration, of the offering of presents, of Mary who "kept all these things, reflecting on them in her heart" (Luke 2:19). Only the angels in heaven sing: "Glory to God in the highest and on earth peace to those on whom his favor rests" (Luke 2:13-14). The shepherds will glorify and praise God, but after leaving the place where they found the child (Luke 2:20).

Easter is also wrapped in silence. The words of the risen Lord could not be more succinct: "Peace be with you." And the disciples can only keep saying: "The Lord has truly been raised!" Then they shut themselves up in the silence of the house, united in their devotion to prayer (Acts 1:14). It will take the dazzling coming of the Spirit to make them speak again. Then, all who hear them understand them in their own tongue (Acts 2:11). From that moment on, nothing and no one can prevent them from saying what they have seen and heard (Acts 4:20). "Woe to me if I do not preach [the gospel]," Paul writes.

At Emmaus, the breaking of the bread suffices. Words would only destroy the power of the moment. It is as if time has stopped in this inn, giving way to the Other, to the common and yet unique action by which the eyes of the two disciples are opened (Luke 24:31). On the road, they could not stop speaking, trying to ease their sorrow. Now they are speechless. They return to Jerusalem. But their story is of less importance than the still-echoing words: "The Lord has truly been raised and has appeared to Simon!" (Luke 24:34).

It is also in silence that the word proclaimed in the liturgy must be molded and grow. If the celebration does not allow for some moments—however brief they might be—in which to interiorize the Word and to pray, it will run out of breath. The liturgy does not confuse communion and communication, speech and babbling. "I give thanks to God that I speak in tongues more than any of you, but in the church I would rather speak five words with my mind, so as to instruct others also, than ten thousand words in a tongue" (1 Cor 14:18-19).

A Time of Births and Beginnings
In Bethlehem of Judea, the Son of God was born of the Virgin Mary. In this little child, God placed himself in our hands. He taught us that he was not far from us. We cannot lift ourselves to heaven, but he can come

to earth. Every living thing looks to him for nourishment (Ps 145:13-14): yet among them, he begged for food and lodging for his Son. God risked him in this cruel and faithless world that sought to control and manipulate him and finally put him to death as a criminal. The shadow of the cross hangs over the cradle of the nativity. But this child is the King of the world, "the Alpha and the Omega, the first and the last, the beginning and the end" (Rev 22:13). His birth marks the beginning of the last age, at the end of which all creation, which experiences the pangs of childbirth, will be "set free from slavery to corruption and share in the glorious freedom of the children of God" (Rom 8:20-23). The shepherds of Bethlehem must have been astonished that the angels came to tell them of the birth of a child, accustomed as they were to be forgotten, if not despised, left out of the great events of history. We ourselves know that they were, for this very reason, the first to be concerned. A new world was born, where "the poor of God"[14] would take the place of honor— "How blessed are they!"[15]—and where each person would be judged on what he had done or failed to do on their behalf (Matt 25:31-46). "In times past, God spoke in partial and various ways to our ancestors through the prophets; in these last days," which begins at Christmas, "he spoke to us through a son, whom he made heir of all things and through whom he created the universe" (Heb 1:1-2). When the magi came to Bethlehem, the first crack appeared in the wall that divided the nations. All this we have learned from a child who could not yet speak.

At Easter a new mode of God's presence in the world begins. After being shed in drops of blood on the cross, God's love is poured out into the world through the Spirit. The risen one comes to believers where they are, in their homes behind locked doors, and on their paths. They do not always recognize him immediately; he often seems more absent than present, and one even wonders whether his apparent presence is merely an illusion. But he left signs that do not deceive the faithful: the water of baptism and the laying on of hands that bestow the anointing of the Spirit, and especially the bread broken and the cup of the new and eternal covenant in his blood. One need not go to Bethlehem or Jerusalem to meet him and offer him gifts of gold, incense, and myrrh. Instead, he himself comes, wherever Christians are gathered in his memory; he is the offering the Church presents to the Father.

His passover explains for us the Scriptures "beginning with Moses and all the prophets" (Luke 24:27). The Spirit leads us toward all truth (John 16:13), it teaches us everything, and reminds us of everything the Lord has told us (John 14:26). Fed by this Word, by the Body and Blood of Christ, after having given thanks, the assembly goes forth in the peace of Christ. It knows that the good news does not belong to it, for it must not stay in one place, looking toward heaven. Jesus, before leaving this earth, ordered the apostles to go into the entire world. This, then, is the "ordinary" time of the Church, the time of mission inspired by the Spirit who makes all things new.

> No longer let us avoid
> The Spirit who regenerates us:
> The Lord is risen!
>   New blood flows through
> The whole Body.
> The time of darkness
> Has changed into light:
> The man was dead, and he is alive.
>
> No more let us resist
> The one who draws us on:
> The Lord is risen!
>   In his flesh suddenly rises
> Eternity.
> He gives weight
> To days, to weeks,
> Leading them to joy.
>
> Let us be no longer without hearth or home
> When Jesus accompanies us:
> The Lord is risen!
>   See the bread on the table
> Of the baptized.
> Present of God
> Offered together,
> Christ today opens our eyes.
>
> We will go forth bearing aloft
> Our faith in the victory:
> The Lord is risen!
>   The universe sings the glory
> Of the redeemed.
> Fire and water
> Take away the past,
> God calls us with the Lamb.[16]

NOTES

The Easter Triduum—Pages 1-5

1. The conversion of the Gentiles would accelerate this distinction. The so-called "Council of Jerusalem" decreed that Gentile converts should not be forced to follow the prescriptions of Jewish law, particularly circumcision, the indispensable sign of membership in the Jewish community (Acts 15:5-35). From that day on, the separation was practically final.

2. Paul, it is true, continued to go to the synagogue on the sabbath every time he was in a city where there was a Jewish community. But this was primarily in order to meet the Jews and announce to them the good news of the gospel (Acts 13:5, 14; 14:1; 16:13; 17:2, 10, 17; 18:4, 19; 19:8; 28:17, 23). He acted this way out of principle: "It was necessary that the word of God be spoken to you first, but since you reject it and condemn yourselves as unworthy of eternal life, we now turn to the Gentiles" (Acts 13:46). This happened at the synagogue of Antioch of Pisidia.

3. Even today, the Jewish custom reckons days not from midnight to midnight, but from sunset to sunset. Most importantly, the sabbath has always begun on Friday evening. Vestiges of this practice remain in the Christian calendar. Sundays and feast days begin with a prayer known as "First Vespers," celebrated the evening before. The institution of Sunday Mass on Saturday evening follows from this tradition.

4. Matt 28:1; Mark 16:2; Luke 24:1; John 20:1.

5. Luke 24:13; John 20:19, 26.

6. Testified to by Ignatius of Antioch (d. 110), *Lettre aux Magnésiens* IX, 1, in *Sources chrétiennes* 10 (Paris: Cerf, 1951) 103; and the *Doctrine des douze Apôtres* or *Didachè* (1st c.), 14, 1, in *Sources chrétiennes* 248 (Paris: Cerf, 1978) 193. See A.G. Martimort, *The Church at Prayer: The Liturgy and Time*, vol. IV (Collegeville, Minn.: The Liturgical Press, 1985) 11-15.

7. Vatican II, Constitution on the Sacred Liturgy, no. 106.

8. See *Days of the Lord: Advent, Christmas, Epiphany*, vol. 1, pp. 7-9.

9. The Jewish year begins in the spring. Nisan, the first month, falls within March-April.

10. Pope Victor turned this argument into a question of unity, if not of faith itself. Irenaeus, bishop of Lyon (ca. 135-202), wrote to the pope to dissuade him from pronouncing excommunication against those Churches that celebrated Easter on 14 Nisan, arguing that the divergence of traditions on the subject of a liturgical date does not threaten the unity of faith. Such a conflict seems unintelligible to us today, lacking as we do sufficiently clear notions of the doctrinal positions that supported the Eastern tradition. In any case, such a controversy points to the great importance that was placed on Easter very early on in the Church. The whole matter is laid out by Eusebius of Caesarea (ca. 265-338), *Histoire ecclésiastique*, XXIII-XXV, in *Sources chrétiennes* 41 (Paris: Cerf, 1955) 66-72, the letter of Irenaeus to Pope Victor, 70-71.

Another problem arose, however: how was 14 Nisan (lunar calendar) to be determined in the solar calendar? The Council of Nicaea (325) determined it thus: Easter would be celebrated on the Sunday following the first full moon after the spring equinox. This is why Easter will fall between March 22 and April 25.

Finally came the reform of the Julian calendar by Pope Gregory XIII (1572–85): in 1582, October 5 became October 15. The Eastern Churches have never accepted this reform: hence, in most years, they do not celebrate Easter on the same date as the Western Church.

In a declaration on the revision of the calendar, Vatican II accepted the principle of fixing Easter on a particular Sunday in the Gregorian calendar "with the assent of those on whom the issue will have an effect, especially those brethren separated from communion with the apostolic See." Nor did it oppose the institution of a perpetual calendar in civil society, provided that it would preserve the seven-day week with Sunday (Text in *Concile oecuménique Vatican II. Constitutions, décrets, déclarations, messages* (Paris: Centurion, 1967) 204–05.

11. Matt 16:21; Mark 8:31; Luke 9:22.

12. *Lettre 23*, in J.-P. Migne, *Patrologie latine*, 16, col. 1030. Cited in A. Nocent, *Célébrer Jésus Christ. L'année liturgique*, vol. 4; *Les trois jours saints. Le Temps pascal* (Paris: J.-P. Delarge, 1976) 45.

13. *Sermon 258*, 3, in *Sources chrétiennes* 116 (Paris: Cerf, 1966) 351.

14. There is a good summary of this evolution in A.G. Martimort, o.c. (see n. 6 above), p. 305.

15. It did not, however, suppress certain individual formularies, e.g., the Dominican or Lyonnaise rites of the Mass. Likewise, Pope Paul V, on October 1, 1612, promulgated a decree that approved a monastic breviary for the Benedictine monks.

16. We ought not to forget that in 1911, Pius X (1903–14) began a reform of the Roman breviary—*Ordo psallendi*—and that he published a new *Graduale Romanum* in 1907 and a new Antiphonal in 1912. However, as important as these reforms may have been, they did not have any noticeable impact on the format of the "three holy days." See A.G. Martimort, *The Church at Prayer: Principles of the Liturgy*, vol. I (Collegeville, Minn.: The Liturgical Press, 1986) 63–76.

17. This title is found in I. Schuster, *Liber sacramentorum*, 2nd French edition (Brussels: Vromant, t. 3, 1938) 19. The author justifies it by noting that ancient practice "expanded the signification of the Christian Passover so that the liturgical cycle comprised the whole mystery of human redemption, from the Last Supper to the dawn of the resurrection."

18. *General Norms for the Liturgical Year*, no. 19, approved by Paul VI on February 14, 1969, and made effective on January 1, 1970.

19. The missal approved by Paul VI on April 3, 1969, comprises the Easter Vigil and the Mass of the day under the title: "Easter Sunday: The Lord's Resurrection." Thus there are clearly three days involved: from Holy Thursday evening till the Liturgy of the Passion on Good Friday; from Friday evening till the Easter vigil; and Sunday.

20. The *Constitution apostolique promulgant l'Office divin restauré par décret du 2e concile oecuménique du Vatican* was signed by Paul VI on November 1, 1970. The Office itself was published in Latin on April 11, 1973. The French translation of *La Liturgie des Heures* was approved on August 2, 1979, and published the same year (Cerf-Desclée-Desclée De Brouwer-Mame).

21. The Liturgy of the Hours contains an Office of Vespers for those who do not participate in the evening Eucharist. It does the same on Good Friday.

22. It should be recognized that when they were sung, they were more like concert pieces. A contemplative and prayerful hearing of them is possible now, thanks to the general availability of quality recordings.

23. Is it necessary to point out that the complete works of Bossuet (1627–1704), Bourdaloue (1632–1704), Massillon (1663–1742), to mention only the classics, contain many sermons on the Passion?

24. In certain churches, particularly in France, the altars of repose for Holy Thursday were often scarcely Eucharistic: rather, they evoked Christ's burial, or Calvary. People would make a sort of pilgrimage from one to another. In some places, one even spoke of the "visit to the holy places." Liturgists denounced this idea, but often without much success. In-

deed, were not crucifixes available for the veneration of the faithful? And also collection baskets to receive their offerings for the "holy places in Jerusalem"?

Chrism Mass—Pages 6–13

1. It was not always this way. In fourth-century Jerusalem, one celebrated two Masses: one in mid-afternoon at the *Martyrium* (the name of the major church) would bring Lent to a close; the other, near the cross, was celebrated to commemorate the institution of the Eucharist.

At Rome, from the 4th—6th c., Holy Thursday was set aside for the reconciliation of the penitents: there was no celebration of the Last Supper. In the 7th c., there were two Masses in churches served by priests: in the morning, to close out Lent, and in the evening, in memory of the Last Supper. But during a noon Mass, the pope consecrated the chrism and blessed the oils. In the liturgical book known as the "Gelasian Sacramentary" (sixth-seventh centuries), there are three Masses: for the reconciliation of penitents, for the holy chrism, for the Last Supper.

At the end of the 8th c., the Roman liturgy took precedence over local customs: there was no more than one Mass, as in the papal liturgy, with the consecration of the chrism and the blessing of the oils in the cathedrals.

See A.G. Martimort, *The Church at Prayer: The Liturgy and Time*, vol. IV (Collegeville, Minn.: The Liturgical Press, 1986) 53–54.

2. There is no Vespers or Compline because of the Eucharistic celebration in the evening.

3. A ritual Mass is one that performs the celebration of a sacrament (baptism, confirmation, ordination, anointing of the sick, marriage), the blessing of an abbot or abbess, the consecration of a virgin, a religious profession, the consecration of chrism and the blessing of the oils.

4. Some bishops celebrate the Chrism Mass in another church in the diocese. This decentralization allows all Christians in the area the chance to participate when it takes place close to them. It can also assemble all the priests of a given area.

In dioceses that are unusually spread out, or for other local reasons—e.g., two distinct linguistic communities—the bishop may celebrate two Chrism Masses, on different days.

5. The Missal is eminently realistic: it says that "it is desirable that, if possible, all the priests take part in it," but also that "the priests who concelebrate with the bishop should come from different parts of the diocese."

6. A detail worth noting: at the Chrism Mass the *Gloria* is sung.

7. The use of the oil of catechumens is not obligatory for baptism: the priest can, instead, lay his hand on the one who is being baptized. For the sacrament of the sick, he can use oil that he blesses himself.

8. Those who read and use *Days of the Lord*—like most people—are not likely ever to participate in the Chrism Mass. Instead of following its outline, then, it seems preferable to confine ourselves here to the subjects of reflection, meditation, and prayer that it presents.

9. We speak of the "consecration" of chrism and the "blessing" of the oils. This last occurs at the end of the Eucharistic Prayer, before the doxology "Through him, with him, in him . . . ." The consecration of the holy chrism comes after Communion. It includes a developed consecratory prayer in which the priests who are concelebrating participate by stretching their right hands toward the chrism, while the bishop invokes God (epiclesis). For the oil of anointing of the sick and the oil of the catechumens, the bishop alone says the prayer of blessing.

10. The texts of the New Testament are too numerous to cite. The coming of the Spirit on Jesus at his baptism in particular points to his being the Lord's anointed (Matt 3:13-17;

Mark 1:9-11; Luke 3:21-22; see John 1:29-34). See "Esprit de Dieu" in *Vocabulaire de théologie biblique* (Paris: Cerf, 1970) col. 395–97.

11. Opening prayer. See *Vocabulaire de théologie biblique*, col. 397–401.

12. Verse six of this chapter forms the entrance antiphon for the Chrism Mass.

13. The Missal contains two prayers that may be used. This is the second. The first says: "when [those who are to be baptized] are anointed with this holy oil, make them temples of your glory, radiant with the goodness of life that has its source in you. Through this sign of chrism grant them royal, priestly, and prophetic honor, and clothe them with incorruption."

14. Vatican II, Dogmatic Constitution on the Church (*Lumen Gentium*), no. 10. The council paid a great deal of attention to the doctrine of the priesthood of Christ, of all the people of God, and of those who are ordained priests: ibid., nos. 10, 11, 15, 21, 26, 28, 31, 34, 41, 66; Constitution on the Sacred Liturgy, nos. 14, 83; but it referred to it in other documents as well: the Decree on the Ministry and Life of Priests (*Presbyterorum ordinis*), the Decree on the Pastoral Office of Bishops in the Church (*Christus Dominus*), and the Decree on the Apostolate of Lay People (*Apostolicam actuositatem*).

15. This is what is said, with certain nuances, in the two formulas offered by the Missal.

16. Preface of the Chrism Mass.

17. Constitution on the Sacred Liturgy, no. 2.

18. Other celebrations are equally significant: the consecration of a bishop in his cathedral, and the ordination of priests, the Eucharist at a gathering or a diocesan synod, etc., and, of course, that celebrated by the pope surrounded with bishops, especially during a pastoral trip. But these are special celebrations that do not greatly illuminate the general dimensions of the Church and its nature.

19. A strict definition expresses in unambiguous terms, as clearly and briefly as possible, everything contained in the reality, and distinguishes it from all other things. The definition of a material thing is easy. The difficulty begins when one speaks of a non-material "thing" (a reality) that proves to be impossible to encompass in a strict definition. How could we give a definition of love, hate, etc.? And what of spiritual realities *a fortiori* regarding God himself? This is also the case with the Church. The catechism used to say that the Church is "the society of the faithful governed by the pope and the bishops under the authority of the pope." This is true, as applied to a certain, very restricted aspect, and with a very specific understanding of "society." But it is not a "definition" that expresses everything about the Church in its greatest and most primal reality.

20. Dogmatic Constitution on the Church, no. 6. The major texts are nos. 1-8 and 13-25.

21. In today's "catechisms," like the recent *Belief and Belonging* (Collegeville, Minn.: The Liturgical Press, 1990), published in French by the bishops of Belgium (Tournai, Desclée, 1987) it is fruitless to try to find a "definition" in the pages devoted to belief in the Church. See pp. 50-65 in the English edition.

22. There are dioceses—and Churches—without territorial limits, e.g., the vicarate of the armies, the national or supra-national exarchates of the Eastern Churches.

23. As, for example, pastoral zones or sectors, deaneries, superiors, archpriests.
To speak of the local Church as a parish is somewhat inexact.

24. Since the creation of the national episcopal conferences, one can speak of the Church *of* such and such a country or of the Church that is *in* such and such a country. But not in the same sense. It would be more appropriate to speak of them as "Churches."

25. Thus speaks the bishop at the Chrism Mass, when after the renewal of sacerdotal promises by the priests, he addresses the assembly, asking the people to "pray also for me."
"To hold Christ's place" means that the Lord is not present visibly, that the bishop is his representative.

26. This is what the mention of the pope, the bishop—the whole episcopate—means in

the Eucharistic Prayer. It is not merely an intercession on their behalf. One does not name one's own priest or the vicars general of the bishop, even though they may have received episcopal ordination. Besides, we know that the omission of the name of the bishop—or, more often, the name of the pope—has often been the expression of a rupture in communion.

27. Until the middle of the 5th c.—it was still possible then—custom and discipline reserved preaching to the bishops alone. It was pointed out to Pope Celestine I (422-32) that in Gaul some priests were stirring up dissensions by indiscreetly disputing questions concerning grace, and by preaching things contrary to the truth. The pope sent a letter to the Gallican bishops, sternly chiding them. He said: "The bishops are responsible for this disorder, since they have allowed simple priests to preach above their heads" (Letter "*Apostolici verba,*" in J.-P. Migne, *Patrologie latine,* vol. 50, col. 528).

28. Vatican II, Decree on the Ministry and Life of Priests, no. 5.

29. Vatican II, Constitution on the Sacred Liturgy, no. 61.

30. See above, n. 3.

31. Vatican II, Constitution on the Sacred Liturgy, no. 5.

32. "The Church on earth is by its very nature missionary, since, according to the plan of the Father, it has its origin in the mission of the Son and the Holy Spirit" (Vatican II, Decree on the Church's Missionary Activity, no. 2).

33. Vatican II, Decree on the Apostolate of Lay People, no. 2.

34. Ibid.

35. Ibid., no. 3.

36. Ibid.

37. Chrism Mass, prayer after communion.

38. Ibid., opening prayer.

39. The same is the case for many priests, even if some of them remember having participated in one during their days in the seminary.

40. See also Rom 12:1; 1 Cor 3:16; Eph 2:20-22; Heb 13:15.

Holy Thursday—Pages 14–22

1. "Where it seems pastorally appropriate," says the Missal, one moves from the homily to the washing of feet. One also consecrates as much bread as is needed for communion today and tomorrow. Finally, the reserved Eucharist is solemnly born to an altar of repose at which the people are invited to keep vigil during the evening. But this does not affect the normal flow of the Mass.

2. Eucharistic Prayer II.

3. Eucharistic Prayer I (Roman Canon).

4. Eucharistic Prayer III.

5. Matt 26:26-29; Mark 14:22-25; Luke 22:14-20; 1 Cor 11:23-25.

6. "God our Father, we are gathered here to share in the supper which your only Son left to his Church to reveal his love. He gave it to us when he was about to die and commanded us to celebrate it as the new and eternal sacrifice" (Opening Prayer).

7. Eucharistic Prayer III, Holy Thursday.

8. Cut off from its origin in the tradition and rite of the Jewish Passover, the Eucharist becomes we know not what. It could be seen, for example, as a simple meal among friends, which eventually came to be celebrated in a more or less religious ambiance. And proceeding from such a basis, one "invents" often aberrant ways of acting that have nothing to do with tradition. "When you meet in one place, then, it is not to eat the Lord's supper," Paul wrote (1 Cor 11:20).

9. Matt 26:17-19; Mark 14:12-16; Luke 22:7-13.

10. See "Pâque" in Dictionnaire encyclopédique de la Bible (Paris: Brepols, 1987) 957–60.

11. The rite of unleavened bread is laid out in Exodus 12:15-20. This code was edited during the Babylonian Exile: therefore, its rite of Passover is of a later date than others with which it might be connected: Exod 24; Lev 23; Num 9; 28; Deut 16; Josh 5; 2 Kgs 23; 2 Chron 30; 35; Ezra 6; Ezek 45. But at Jesus' time, the Bible was taken as a whole, with a traditional interpretation that often went beyond the literal meaning of the text. The ritual retained by the liturgy of Holy Thursday, though later, was nonetheless incorporated into very ancient customs, particularly nomadic customs that were obliterated by certain forms of centralization (Deut 16).

12. Melito, bishop of Sardis (d. ca. 190), Homélie sur la Pâque, in Sources chrétiennes 123 (Paris: Cerf, 1966) 95–101. This text is read on Holy Thursday in the Office of Readings of the Liturgy of the Hours.

13. The Latin Church keeps the custom of using unleavened bread for the Eucharist, whereas the Eastern Churches use leavened bread.

14. Lev 1:5, 11; 9:12; 4:6-7, 16; 17:11.

15. 1 Pet 1:18-20; Heb 9:1-28; 10:19, 29; 12:24; 13:12, 20.

16. A life is voluntarily given to God either as a sign of adoration or because one is found to be unworthy of the gift of life. Where human sacrifices are prescribed, an animal is substituted.

17. Matt 26:17-35; Mark 14:12-25; Luke 22:7-38; John 13:1-17:26.

18. The clearest difference lies in John's omission of the "institution account," where he instead reports the washing of the feet (John 13:1-10), and Jesus' lengthy discourse (John 13:31-17:26), which is not found in the Synoptics, except for an echo in Luke (Luke 22:24-34).

19. The gospel was preached for many years before it was written down: the earliest, Mark's, may be dated ca. 65–70, thus after Paul had written several of his letters (the First Letter to the Thessalonians was undoubtedly written during the winter of 50–51).

20. The date of Jesus' last Passover supper can be a source of discussion between the testimony of the Synoptics and John.

21. Mark 15:28; Luke 22:37; 1 Pet 2:24; John 1:29 allude to this "Fourth Song of the Suffering Servant."

22. Actually, this marks the beginning of a major part of John's Gospel (13–20), known as "The Book of Glory" (or "The Manifestation of Jesus' Glory"), when his "hour" had come, a term by which the evangelist denotes Jesus' glorification by his death, resurrection, and return to the Father (See John 2:4; 7:6; 12:23, 27).

23. One thinks immediately of chapter 6. But Jesus' first sign, at Cana in Galilee (John 2:1-12), also has a Eucharistic flavor. See X. Léon-Dufour, Le partage du pain eucharistique selon le Nouveau Testament, Parole de Dieu (Paris: Seuil, 1982) 311–17.

24. This is the only time John 13:1-15 is used in the Sunday, Feast Day, or Weekday Lectionary. The only other place it is found is in the Mass for the unity of Christians, with Matt 18:19-22 ("For where two or three are gathered together in my name . . ."), Luke 9:49-55 (". . . whoever is not against you is for you") and five other passages from John.

25. The Bible reports certain actions and gestures that announce what God is going to do. A piece of Saul's mantle is torn off: Samuel tells him that in the same manner, the kingdom will be torn from him (1 Sam 15:27-28). Jeremiah watches a potter throw away flawed vessels from his wheel: this symbolizes the way God acts toward his people (Jer 18:1-12). See also 1 Kgs 11:30; 22:11-12; Jer 13:1-11; 18:1-12; 19:10-11; 27–28; 32; Ezek 4:1-3, 9-17; 12:1-20; 24:3-14; 37:15-28.

26. It was common to wash one's feet upon entering one's house (Judg 19:21; Luke 7:44; 1 Tim 5:10), but not during the meal. Those who owned slaves had them do the washing. But women also did the same for their husbands, daughters for their fathers, and disciples for their masters. We must not, therefore, exaggerate the humbling character of this ges-

ture. But it did express deference to whomever received the washing. Thus Peter quite understandably found it improper for Jesus to wash the disciples' feet.

27. Following some of the Fathers, it is possible to see the washing of feet as a symbol of the purification of sins by the sacrament of penance: P. Grelot, "L'interprétation pénitentielle du lavement des pieds," in *L'homme devant Dieu. Mélanges H. de Lubac* I (Paris: Aubier, 1963) 75–91.

28. Gen 31:14; Deut 10:9; 12:12; 14:27-29; 18:1-2; Num 18:20.

29. See E. Cothenet, *Exégèse et liturgie*, Lectio divina 133 (Paris: Cerf, 1988) 49–53, which deals with the "care with which the evangelist moves from the laying aside to the taking up again of the cloak."

30. Ibid., p. 53.

31. Vatican II, Constitution on the Sacred Liturgy, no. 47.

32. Commission Francophone Cistercienne, *La nuit le jour,* (Paris: Desclée-Cerf, 1973) 84 (Fiche de chant H LH 139).

Good Friday—Pages 23–36

1. Pope Leo the Great (440–460), *Homélie sur la Passion*, 8, 6-7, in *Sources chrétiennes* 74 (Paris: Cerf, 1961) 60–61, and in *The Liturgy of the Hours*, Office of Readings for Good Friday.

2. The earliest witnesses to the liturgy of Good Friday in Rome date from the middle of the 7th c.

On the history of the liturgy of Good Friday from its origins in Jerusalem, see A.G. Martimort, *The Church at Prayer: The Liturgy and Time*, vol. IV (Collegeville, Minn.: The Liturgical Press, 1986) 54–55.

3. Before the council, the priest wore black liturgical garments, but today they are red, as for a martyr's feast.

4. Antiphons of the Morning Office for Good Friday.

5. Verse following the short reading for the mid-morning office.

6. For Sundays in Ordinary Time, only the first reading is chosen on the basis of the Gospel, the second coming from a "semi-continuous" reading of an apostolic writing. During Christmas-Epiphany, Lent and Eastertime, the Liturgy of the Word has a somewhat different structure, as explained in *Days of the Lord*, vols. 1, 2, 3.

7. The other three are also found in Isa: 42:1-9; 49:1-7; 50:4-11.

8. It was the "Fourth Song of the Servant" that the official to the court of the Candace, i.e., the queen of Ethiopia, was reading when he met Philip and asked him: " 'I beg you, about whom is the prophet saying this? About himself or someone else? Then Philip opened his mouth and, beginning with this scripture passage, he proclaimed Jesus to him' " (Acts 8:26-40).

9. See Lev 5:14-15; 14:1-32.

10. See John 19:37.

11. Psalm 22—"My God, my God, why have you forsaken me?"—presents the same shift in tone at the end: "I will proclaim your name to my brethren; in the midst of the assembly I will praise you: 'You who fear the Lord, praise him' . . . To him my soul shall live; my descendants shall serve him. Let the coming generation be told of the Lord that they may proclaim to a people yet to be born the justice he has shown" (vv. 23-24, 31-32).

12. The Letter to the Hebrews can be dated ca. 66-67. At any rate, it was written before the destruction of the Temple in A.D. 70, for it supposes that the Temple cult was still in existence: see for example, Heb 9:9.

13. Matt (27:46) and Mark (15:34) put this verse in Jesus' mouth at the moment of his death.

14. See Matt 27:50; Mark 15:37; John 19:30.

15. L. Malègue, *Augustin ou le Maître est là*, t. 2 (Paris: Spes, 1933) 245–46.

16. John Chrysostom (ca. 350–407), "Homélie pour le Vendredi saint," in *Homéliaire patristique*, Lex orandi 8 (Paris: Cerf, 1949) 65.

17. Pius XII's liturgical reform reintroduced the Communion of the Faithful on Good Friday (it had been reserved for the celebrant alone since the 13th c.). The later reform of Vatican II replaced Hos 6:1-6 and Exod 12:1-11 with the two texts we read today.

18. Refrain of the Gospel acclamation.

19. John 2:4; 4:21, 23; 5:26; 7:30; 8:20; 12:23, 27; 13:1; 16:25, 32; 17:1. See above, "Holy Thursday," n. 24, p. 310.

20. The beginning of John's Gospel is commonly called the "Prologue." It is a kind of hymn on the mystery, which the subsequent text will unfold.

21. John 3:14; 8:28; 13:1-3.

22. John 1:14; 11:40; 12:41.

23. John 3:11, 32-33; 8:13-14, 46; 14:6; 18:37.

24. John 10:11-18; 12:24.

25. The historians Philo and Flavius Josephus did not have much good to say about his person or his administration. He plundered the Temple treasury to finance an aqueduct and he responded to opposition with violence. They remark that he behaved with unusual cruelty toward the Samaritans. Dismissed from his office, he was recalled to Rome to give an account of his actions.

26. Nersès Snorhali (1102–73), *Jésus, Fils unique du Père*, in *Sources chrétiennes* 203 (Paris: Cerf, 1973) 186.

27. The importance of witnessing in the Church is not only that testimony has more weight if it is given collectively. It is a theological necessity, because the Church is the Body of Christ. Besides, it is not uncommon for the convincing testimony of individual Christians, rightly or wrongly, to be opposed to that of the universal or neighboring Church, which is regarded as completely inadmissable, devoid of credibility.

28. D. Rimaud, *Les arbres dans la mer* (Paris: Desclée, 1975) 122–23 (Fiche de chant H 119).

29. Eucharistic Prayer I, for reconciliation.

30. The apostolic constitution *Missale romanum*, which promulgated the Missal reformed according to the norms of Vatican II, was signed by Pope Paul VI on April 3, 1969. The Latin edition (*Typica*) of the new Missal was published on Holy Thursday, March 26, 1970.

31. The first witness to a Good Friday liturgy, at the end of the 4th c. in Jerusalem, notes that the celebration of the Lord's death contained certain prayers after the reading of the passion. The prayers of the faithful are found in the celebration of the Passion at Rome in the 7th c. See A.G. Martimort, o.c., 54–55.

32. *General Instruction of the Roman Missal*, no. 45.

33. These "personal" intentions are appropriate after the general intercessions in the Mass and especially in the Office: *The Liturgy of the Hours* locates them explicitly in the morning and evening offices.

34. *General Instruction of the Roman Missal*, no. 47.

35. The Missal says that "the priest may choose from the prayers in the Missal those which are more appropriate to local circumstances, provided the series follows the rule for the general intercessions," as set forth in the *General Instruction of the Roman Missal*, no. 46: the needs of the Church, public authorities and the salvation of the world, those oppressed by any need, and the local community. Under these guidelines, it is difficult to see which intentions among those proposed by the Missal could be omitted. Could the prayers for the Jews and those who do not believe in Jesus Christ or in God, for instance, be less appropriate for a community assembled on Good Friday, after the reading of the Passion? Would it not seem more proper to desire to add one or another special intention, as the local Ordinary, the Missal says, "may permit or decree in case of serious public need"?

36. This liturgy is described in a very striking way by Egeria (4th c.), *Journal de voyage* (P. Maraval), in *Sources chrétiennes* 296 (Paris: Cerf, 1982) 290–91; or Etheria, *Mon pèlerinage en Terre sainte* (H. Petre), Foi vivante 180 (Paris: Cerf, 1977) 85–88. (There is disagreement about the name of the author of this *Journal*: today she is called Egeria, rather than Etheria.) On the movement of the veneration of the cross into the presbyterial churches of Rome, then into the papal liturgy and the Gallican liturgy, see A.G. Martimort, o.c. (n. 2), 54–55.

37. The Missal suggests this antiphon:

We worship you, Lord,
we venerate your cross,
we praise your resurrection.
Through the cross you brought joy to the world.

though it adds: "or other suitable songs."

38. Commission Francophone Cistercienne, *Sur la trace de Dieu* (Paris: Desclée, 1979) 72–73 (Fiche de chant H 164).

39. *Homélie ancienne pour le Samedi saint*, in *Liturgie des Heures, 2. Carême-Temps pascal*, pp. 373–74.

The Easter Celebrations—Pages 37–38

1. *Calendarium romanum*, Cité du Vatican, 1969, no. 20.
2. D. Rimaud, *Les arbres dans la mer* (Paris: Desclée, 1975) 137 (Fiche de chant I 166).
3. P. de la Tour de Pin, *Une lutte pour la vie* (Paris: Gallimard, 1970) 310 (Fiche I 78).

Easter Vigil—Pages 39–66

4. On the origin and evolution of the Easter Vigil, see A.G. Martimort, *The Church at Prayer. The Liturgy and Time*, vol. IV (Collegeville, Minn.: The Liturgical Press, 1986) 35–38.
5. As early as the 4th c., this acclamation accompanied the lighting of lamps for the community meal.
6. Pope Urban VIII (1623–44) removed these holy days from the list of "obligatory feasts."
7. On all this—origin, development, decay, and renewal of the Easter Vigil—see A.G. Martimort, o.c., vol. IV, 35–41.
8. The Congregation for Divine Worship was begun on Holy Thursday, March 26, 1970. Hence one often speaks of the "Missal of 1970."
9. Pius V's Missal contained twelve readings from the Old Testament: Gen 1:1–2:2; Gen 5:32–8, 20; Gen 22:1-19; Exod 14:24–15:1; Isa 54:17–55:11; Bar 3:9-38; Ezek 37:1-14; Isa 4:1-6; Exod 12:1-11; Jonah 3:1-10; Deut 31:22-30; Dan 3:1-24; then, after the blessing of the water, Col 3:1-4 and Matt 28:1-7.

Pius XII's *Ordo* contained only four readings from the Old Testament: Gen 1:1–2:2; Exod 14:24–15:1; Isa 4:2-6; Deut 31:22-30.

Paul VI's Missal contains seven: Gen 1:1–2:2; Gen 22:1-18; Exod 14:15–15:1; Isa 54:5-14; Isa 55:1-11; Bar 3:9-15, 32–4:4; Ezek 36:16-17a, 18-28. But it also says that they may be limited to three, or even to two. However, in any case, Exod 14:15–15:1 must be read.

10. Augustine (354–430), *Traité sur la nuit sainte*, in *Saint Augustin. L'année liturgique*, selected sermons, translation and annotations by V. Saxer, Les Pères dans la foi (Paris: Desclée de Brouwer, 1980) 82–83.

11. It would be a mistake to attribute the fall-off in the practice of faith to the change to a living language in the liturgy: however, this has clashed with some people's sense of dignity; occasionally, this conflict has forced people who were satisfied in their faith to

recognize their own doubts. It is intolerable to hear texts proclaimed in a living language and to be at variance with their message. Such we find in the man who said to his priest: "They can do whatever they want in the funeral ceremony. But they shouldn't speak of resurrection around a dead man." One simply cannot hide inside one's own meditation or religious reverie when the liturgy constantly calls for "full, active, and conscious participation." One must concentrate on the entire liturgy in light of one's faith—not pious religiosity—for it is easy to be distracted by merely beautiful and isolated moments of piety.

12. Said by the priest while lighting the Easter candle.

13. Proclamation of the Passover (*Exultet*).

14. Early on, the deacon had to compose a new hymn to the Easter candle every year, while the priest, in the Eucharist, had to give thanks "as he is able," as Justin says (ca. 100–165), (*Apologies*, I, 67, 5, Textes et documents, trans. L. Pautigny [Paris: Picard, 1904] 143). But very soon certain quality texts were circulated and their use was mandated. Thus we find it today in the Missal, which offers two other shorter forms.

In the Middle Ages, the text of the *Exultet* was often illustrated in such a way that the assembly could see the illustrations as the deacon, at the ambo, unrolled the scroll on which the text was written, much as we might do today with a slide projector. On a simpler note, we still have the custom of the priest cutting a cross on the Easter candle while he says: "Christ yesterday and today, the beginning and the end, Alpha and Omega; all time belongs to him and all the ages; to him be glory and power through every age for ever." Likewise the priest may stick five grains of incense into the candle: "By his holy and glorious wounds, may Christ our Lord guard us and keep us." This is a way of defining the Easter candle and reminding those who will see it during the fifty days of Easter that the glorified Christ, marked as he is by the stigmata of his passion, dwells in our midst as light without end.

15. See above, n. 9.

16. Prayer after the seventh reading.

17. "According to the Palestinian Targum (2nd c. B.C.), the Jews commemorated, during the night of the Passover, the memory of the 'Four Nights,' which were those of the creation of the world, Abraham's sacrifice, the Exodus and the coming of the Messiah" (P. Jounel, in A.G. Martimort, o.c., vol. IV, 42).

Targum—literally "translation, interpretation"—refers to a version of the Old Testament used in the synagogues. The Targum included in its text elements of explanation and paraphrase that had originally and for a long time been transmitted orally. See *Dictionnarie encyclopédique de la Bible* (Paris: Brepols, 1987) 1311–13.

18. R. le Déaut, *La Nuit pascale. Essai sur la signification de la Pâque juive à partir du Targum d'Exode 12,42*, Analecta biblica 22 (Rome: Pontifical Biblical Institute, 1975) 64–65. Two modifications have been introduced into the citation: as in the liturgical translations, Yahweh has been replaced by God or Lord; instead of "the *Memra* of Yahweh," one writes "the Word of God."

19. Suggestion for the general introduction to the Liturgy of the Word in the Missal.

20. Ibid.

21. J. Servel (Fiche de chant L 82).

22. It is not, in fact, the first to have been written. See the introductions in various Bibles, or the articles "Pentateuque" and "Genèse" in *Dictionnaire encyclopédique de la Bible* (Paris: Brepols, 1987) 1002–03; 523–25.

23. As opposed to the "prophets of the future" who appeal to what will happen.

24. The ordered and rhythmic character of the composition, with the recurring refrain at the end of each day; the rigorous symmetry of the two parallel series of three days: first the separation, then the arrangement of the created elements; the taste for numbers; the hieratic character of the whole that gives an impression of cold beauty and grandeur. The

framework of the week, and the importance given to God's resting on the seventh day, suggest a liturgical work, perhaps intended to be read at the feast of the new year, consecrated to the creator God.

25. The verb "to create" (*bara*) appeared first in the Bible to designate the new creation of the last days, the decisive intervention of God that will be accomplished by his all-powerful word: Isa 41:20; 45:8; 48:6-8; 65:18; Jer 31:22, 35; Ezek 11:19; 36:26-35; Ps 51:12.

26. 1 Cor 11:7; 2 Cor 4:14; Col 1:15. Some of the Fathers thought that Christ was the image of God according to which the human person was created: humanity is the image of his Image which is Christ, or, literally, the icon of his Icon.

27. Rom 8:16-17, 29; 2 Cor 3:18; Col 3:10.

28. Peter Chrysologus (ca. 380–450), *Sermon 148*, in J.-P. Migne, *Patrologie latine*, 52, col. 596.

29. The second story of creation (Gen 2:4b–4:26), which belongs to another tradition, highlights the fragility of the human being who comes from the earth, an ephemeral breath, a passing shadow.

30. The Bible—Exod 20:3-6—formally forbids all images of God made by human hands.

31. D. Rimaud, *Les arbres dans la mer* (Paris: Desclée, 1975) 156 (Fiche de chante P 156).

32. The priest's prayer after the first reading.

33. Columban (ca. 540–615), *Instruction 11,2*, in *Lectures chrétiennes pour notre temps* (Abbaye d'Orval, 1971) Fiche W 27.

34. The Missal offers a choice between these two psalms.

35. It is a technique of torture to submit the victim to a fake execution.

36. This presents the serious problem of how much authority one person has over another when it comes to the point of ordering someone to do the most horrible things.

37. Thus: Matt 3:17; Mark 12:6; Luke 1:55-73; John 3:16; Acts 3:25; Gal 3:16; Heb 6:13-14; 11:12, 17; James 2:21.

38. Among others: at Rome, in the catacombs of Callistus (twice), of Priscilla, the fresco of Saint-Vital at Ravenna, as well as numerous pieces of gold ornaments, sarcophagi, miniatures, etc.

39. This story is read at two other times in the liturgical year: the Second Sunday of Lent, Year B, in a shorter form (Gen 22:1-2, 9a, 10-13, 15-18) that accents Abraham's obedience (see *Days of the Lord*, vol. 2, opening pages of the chapter on the Second Sunday, Year B) and Thursday of the Thirteenth Week in Ordinary Time, in its entirety, as part of the "semicontinuous" reading of the Book of Genesis.

40. In the contemporary literature, the return from Exile is compared to victory over primeval chaos (Isa 35; 40:1-8; 43:16-20), the triumph of light over darkness at the beginning (Isa 49.9, 50.1-10, 60.1-2), the driving back of the waters that also recalls the flowing back of the Red Sea during the Exodus (Isa 51:9-10; Hab 3:8-15; Ps 104:5-9; 106:9).

41. D. Rimaud, o.c. (n. 31), 156.

42. Origen (ca. 185–253), *Homélies sur la Genèse*, VIII, 6, in *Sources chrétiennes* 7 (Paris: Cerf, 1943) 167–68.

43. It would be worthwhile to reread Exod 12:1–13:16, a collection of texts composed at different times that explain how to celebrate the memory—memorial—of the Exodus, and what meaning it has for the present.

44. See above, n. 40.

45. The following reconstruction has been proposed. In their flight, the Hebrews crossed an area of lakes and marshes. The Egyptians began to pursue them. An east wind, regarded as a sign of God, began to blow, creating a momentary passage on the shallows, allowing the people somehow or other to pass over. The Egyptian chariots, on the other hand, were swallowed up, creating such a heavy loss that pursuit was abandoned.

46. Such things exist in the history of every people. For example, the taking of the Bastille at the beginning of the French Revolution, on July 14, 1789. Was it, in itself, a tragic and

lamentable event? Yes, to be sure, if one keeps to the brute fact: a poorly defended state prison in which there was only one prisoner; a wild crowd who led the assault and put the governor and his guards to a cruel death. But it was also experienced as an important event and remains in the collective memory as the symbol of the victory of the people over tyranny. All the more so since there is nothing left of this bastion, except the remains of a counterscarp—but what does it make one think of?—in a Paris Metro station.

47. V. Hugo, *La légende des siècles*, La Pléiade (Paris: Gallimard, 1950) 5.

48. Exod 12:26-27: 13:8, 14.

49. John 2:13 (cleansing of the temple); 6:4 (multiplication of the loaves); 13:1 (the Last Supper and the Passion).

50. John 1:29, 36.

51. D. Rimaud, o.c. (n. 31), 156.

52. See the two prayers in the Missal, which may be said after this reading.

53. This is the name given to the second part (chs. 40–55) of Isaiah, because it begins with the words "Comfort, give comfort to my people," and because "consolation" is its main theme, whereas the first part (chs. 1–39) primarily contains threatening oracles.

54. There is an untranslatable play on words in Hebrew, between *abanim* ("stones") and, a little further on, *banim* ("children").

55. This conclusion is also read during Ordinary Time, Year A, but in three parts: 55:1-3; 55:6-9; 55:10-11 (on the Eighteenth, Twenty-fifth, and Fifteenth Sundays). See those Sundays in *Days of the Lord*, vol.4.

56. Dante, *La divine comédie*, trans. Lucienne Portier, *Paradis*, canto XXXIII, 139–45 (Paris: Cerf, 1987) 526.

57. Ezek 15:8; 16; 20:4; 22:2; etc.

58. The psalms do not hesitate to ask God to intervene "for his name's sake." Thus Psalm 109:21; 143:11.

59. See also Rev 19:1.

60. Ezekiel, the priest become a prophet, does not have his predecessors' prejudices against the cult. He will be the one who inspires its restoration after the Exile, the concern for which is expressed in chapters 40–48 of his Book. See in particular Ezek 47 on the living water that will flow from the new temple.

61. Heb 9:15; 12:24.

62. Rom 6:4; 2 Cor 5:17; Eph 4:24; Col 3:10.

63. When there is a baptism, one sings either Ps 51 or Isa 12, which also appears after the fifth reading. Ps 42 is used for celebrations in which there is no baptism.

64. A portion of this text (Rom 6:3-4, 8-11) is read on the Thirteenth Sunday of Ordinary Time, Year A. See *Days of the Lord* vol. 4.

65. As it is generally practiced today in the Western Church, baptism appears to be more of a washing ritual.

66. Theodore of Mopsuestia (ca. 350–428), *Commentaire sur saint Jean*, Book II, in *Lectures chrétiennes pour notre temps* (Abbaye d'Orval, 1972) Fiche F 5.

67. Pss 112 to 117 (according to the Vulgate numbering scheme; 113 to 118 according to the Hebrew), known as the "Hallel" psalms because they begin with "Alleluia," were sung at the end of the paschal meal; Jesus and the apostles would have done so at the end of the Last Supper (Matt 26:30; Mark 14:26).

68. In the evening Mass, one reads in Luke (24:13-35) the story of the pilgrims to Emmaus, because it relates how these two disciples encountered the risen one on the evening of the resurrection.

69. The first examples of this reflection are found in the apostolic preaching reported in the Acts of the Apostles and in the other writings and catechesis of the New Testament, from which large portions are read throughout Eastertime. Later Christian tradition con-

tinued to reflect on the paschal mystery, while expressing in different ways the fundamental core of the Christian creed, without which our faith would be in vain (1 Cor 15:2).

70. This is the finale of the Gospel of the Passion According to Matthew, as read on Passion (Palm) Sunday, Year A.

71. This calm, sober dignity contrasts with the exuberances of apocryphal writings—such as the Gospel of Peter—which because of their grandiose details, fall into the absurd. See: F. Amiot, *La Bible apocryphe. Evangiles apocryphes* (Paris: Fayard, 1952) 141-44. One simple example: The soldiers "saw three men come out of the tomb. Two young men supported the third, and a cross followed them. The heads of the first two reached to heaven, but the head of the one they led reached above the heavens" (p. 142).

72. See Matt 16:21; 17:23; 20:19.

73. Acts 2:36; 3:15; 5:30; 10:40; 1 Cor 1:23; 2:2; 15:4; Gal 3:1; 1 Thess 1:10.

74. This greeting is reminiscent of those of the messianic proclamations: Zeph 3:14; Joel 2:21; Zech 9:9; Luke 1:28 (annunciation to Mary).

75. Sometimes, apologetic has started from the empty tomb. But this is not, in the strict sense, a "proof." Matthew himself notes the story that explains the empty tomb by saying that Jesus' body was stolen (Matt 28:11-15).

76. Matt 28:16-17; Mark 16:14-20; Luke 24:36; John 20:19-23; 21:1; Acts 1:3.

77. Romanus the Melodist (6th c.), *Hymnes*, 40, 12, in *Sources chrétiennes* 128 (Paris: Cerf, 1967) 401.

78. The appearances of Jesus that follow this story (Mark 16:9-20) belong to the canonical text of the Gospel, but it is the opinion of exegetes that it was added much later, at an unknown date. See the notes on this in the *Jerusalem Bible*.

79. The sabbath did and still does begin on Friday evening at sunset, and ends on Saturday at the same time.

80. He is perhaps referred to in Acts and four of Paul's letters: Acts 12:12, 25; 15:37, 39; Col 4:10; 2 Tim 4:11; Phil 24; 1 Pet 5:13.

81. M. Quésnel, *Comment lire un évangile*: Saint Marc (Paris: Seuil, 1984) 291-92.

82. Mark's Gospel is characterized by its missionary, universalist spirit, and by its dynamism. Jesus constantly makes his disciples "go on" (Mark 1:38); he is always going somewhere.

83. Jerusalem is particularly important in Luke's work. Everything begins there (Luke 1:5-22. There is the announcement of the birth of John the Baptist); and a large portion of the Gospel deals with Jesus going to Jerusalem (Luke 9:51-19:27) where he exercises his final ministry (Luke 19:28-22:38). And it is in Jerusalem that the mission begins with the coming of the Spirit (Acts 2), and where the first Christian community is gathered (Acts 2:1-47).

84. At the beginning of Acts, where he takes up the thread of events, Luke speaks of the forty days in which Jesus gave the apostles proofs of his resurrection and his last teachings on the kingdom of God (Acts 1:1-5).

85. Luke 1:11-20, 26-38; 2:9-15; 22:43. See also: 4:10; 9:26; 12:8-9; 15:10; 16:22; 20:36.

86. Luke 7:36-50; 8:2-3; 10:38-42; 23:27-31; Acts 1:14; 8:3, 12; 9:2; 16:13; 21:5; 22:4.

87. E. Charpentier, "Christ est ressuscité," in *Cahiers Evangile* 3 (1973) 51.

88. Josh 3:10; Judg 8:19; 1 Sam 17:26, 36.

89. Commission Francophone Cistercienne, *La nuit, le jour* (Paris: DescléeCerf, 1973) 92-93.

90. Conclusion of the blessing of the baptismal water.

91. Blessing of the water.

92. Prayer at the conclusion of the Liturgy of Baptism, after the renewal of the baptismal profession of faith.

93. Preface of the Easter Vigil.

94. Commission Francophone Cistercienne, *Prières aux quatre temps. Des poèmes et des chants,*

Vivante liturgie 101 (Paris: Publications de Saint-André-Centurion, 1986) 61–62 (Fiche de chant I 253).

Easter Sunday—Pages 67–76

1. P. de la Tour du Pin, *Une lutte pour la vie*, N.R.F. (Paris: Gallimard, 1970) 306–07 (Fiche de chant I 77).
2. Antiphon for Morning Office (Lauds).
3. Entrance antiphon.
4. Paschal hymn, in Commission Francophone Cistercienne, *Guetteur de l'aube* (Paris: Desclée, 1976) 61 (Fiche de chant I 249).
5. Opening prayer.
6. During this season, we read no fewer than 60 extracts from it; 20 during Sunday Eucharists, 40 during the week. On the Acts of the Apostles, see text, pp. 78–79.
7. The text of the Apostles' Creed as it has come down to us is attested to in Greek and Latin in writings of the 4th c., but one can find its content, with the very same order and form, in the "rule of faith" cited by Tertullian, priest of Carthage (ca. 160–220). Rufinus (345–410), in his *Commentaire sur le Symbole des Apôtres*, gives the popular account of the Creed: the apostles themselves, before leaving each other, formed this creed, so as to have a common reference point for their teaching. Later (6th c.) this "tradition" was embellished: each of the articles came from one of the apostles. This "tradition" at least witnesses to the great antiquity of the Apostles' Creed.
8. At two other times the liturgy draws from this speech of Peter's and the account of what followed. On the Sixth Sunday of Easter, Year B, we read verses 25–26 and 34–35 while focusing on what is reported in verses 44–48: the descent of the Spirit on those who had heard the Word. On the feast of the Lord's Baptism, Year A, we read only verses 34-38, because they evoke everything "beginning in Galilee with the baptism John preached." (See *Days of the Lord*, vol. 1, 297–98). This is a good example of how the liturgy uses a text for its own purposes, while not twisting its meaning.
9. The Letter to the Colossians was written ca. 60–61. At that time, the dangers to the community came from the preaching of the "Judaizers" and the seductive threat of Hellenistic cults, or at least of some of their elements.
10. H. de Lubac, *Paradoxes* (Paris: Editions du Livre francais, 1946) 79–80.
11. John Chrysostom (ca. 372-September 14, 407), *Septième homélie sur la Lettre aux Colossiens*, 4, in *Oeuvres complètes*, t. 10, trans. J. Bareille (Paris: Vives, 1873) 50.
12. In the context of 1 Cor, the apostle's intervention was provoked by a case of grave misconduct about which the community had done nothing. "This is intolerable," writes Paul. The scandal must be denounced immediately so that the feast of Christ's passover may be celebrated in sincerity and truth (1 Cor 5:1-6a). But what he says has universal importance. Therefore the liturgy does not do violence to Paul's thought by proclaiming what he says in general from the particular circumstances that he is addressing.
13. Matt 13:33; Luke 13:21. In Matthew, this saying of Jesus comes after the short parable on the mustard seed (Matt 13:31-32). The three parables of the kingdom—the weeds, the mustard seed, the yeast (Matt 13:24-43—are read on the Sixteenth Sunday of Ordinary Time, Year A. See *Days of the Lord*, vol. 4.
14. Matt 16:6, 11; Mark 8:15; Luke 12:1.
15. Not so long ago, the discipline of the Lenten fast was so strict that in some places the mistress of the house would carefully clean all the pots and pans on the evening of Mardi Gras to remove every trace of fat; and containers of fat, carefully closed, were placed

in a cupboard some distance from the stove, so that during Lent the cook would not use it in a moment of forgetfulness.

16. Rom 6:6; Eph 4:22; Col 3:9.

17. Pope Leo the Great (440-61), "Sermon XII sur la Passion," 7, in *Sources chrétiennes* 74 (Paris: Cerf, 1976) 161-63.

18. Read during Mass on Easter Vigil, Years A, B, and C, respectively.

19. John's Gospel begins by presenting the inaugural week of Jesus' ministry, before the first Passover (John 1:19-2:12). It ends with the account of another week that begins on the day of the Lord's resurrection (John 20:1-29).

Chapter 21 is a kind of epilogue added by either the evangelist himself or by one of his disciples (see the notes in the *Jerusalem Bible*). Even so, it belongs to the canonical text of the Fourth Gospel.

20. John names only Mary Magdalene, but has her say: "we don't know" where the body was laid. This "we" implies that she was not alone.

21. The Bible acknowledges different senses of the verb "to see": Deut 33:20; Isa 6:5; John 1:18; 2:11; 11:15; 1 John 1:1-3; etc.

22. The Greek verb used here (*oida*) means "to know" or "to have seen."

23. This is particularly the case with the "signs of the times," about which we often speak today. They allow us to understand many things about Scripture and its demands, which, on their part, make us attentive to the "signs of the times," enabling us to "see" their meaning.

One must also remember that "particular visions" and "revelations" are to be judged in the light of Scripture, i.e., their coherence with it; they may be regarded as signs only in so far as they contribute to a better understanding of Scripture. Thus the visions and apparitions in the New Testament: Paul's vision on the road to Damascus, and Ananias' (Acts 9:1-9); that of Cornelius in Caesarea and Peter in Joppa (Acts 10:1-33; 11:1-18).

24. The evangelist says nothing about Peter's reaction, whether it took him a while to believe. But he emphasizes that John "believed" from what he had "seen."

25. There are numerous examples; e.g., Francis of Assisi (1182-1226) and Catherine of Siena (1347-80), charged by God with missions of reform, the one with respect to the Church, the other with respect to the papacy. Bernadette Soubirous (1844-79) conveyed to the priests the demand of what she had "seen" that a church be built and a pilgrimage be instituted to the grotto of Massabielle. All the saints have shown complete obedience and deference to those with authority in the Church, even when they were faced—and this was almost always the case—with incomprehension and reticence. This humble obedience is in fact the first and simplest criterion of authenticity. Narrow-minded rebellion or stubbornness has undermined the best intentions of reformers, and often led them to schism.

26. H. Urs von Balthasar, *Adrienne von Speyr et sa mission théologique* (Paris: Apostolat des editions, 1976) 225-26.

27. Commission Francophone Cistercienne, *Sur la trace de Dieu* (Paris: Desclée, 1979) 78 (Fiche de chant I 271).

28. This Gospel (Luke 24:13-35) is read during the evening Mass on Easter Sunday. It may also be found on the Third Sunday of Easter, Year A.

29. P. de la Tour du Pin, o.c. (n. 1), 296 (Fiche de chant I 144).

30. See Luke 2:51.

The Fifty Days of Easter—Pages 77–83

1. See *Days of the Lord*, vol. 1, 21-30.

2. Ibid., vol. 2, ch. 1, "Forty Holy Days."

3. Ibid., 20-21.

4. *General Norms for the Liturgical Year* approved by Pope Paul VI on February 14, 1969, nos. 22–24.

5. There is no other instance in the liturgical year where every day of a week has the title of "solemnity."

6. The only exception is the the Vigil Mass for Pentecost, where the first reading is taken from the Old Testament (Gen 11:1-9; or Exod 19:3-8a, 16-20b; or Ezek 37:1-14; or Joel 3:1-5).

7. Also for every day of the week. We read 60 extracts from Acts: 20 on Sundays, 40 during the week.

8. The First Letter of Peter is also read in the Office of the Octave of Easter, from Monday to Saturday.

9. The First Letter of John is also read in the Office for the Sixth Sunday of Easter to Thursday of the Seventh Week.

10. The Book of Revelation is read in the Office from Monday of the Second Week of Easter to Saturday of the Fifth Week.

11. There is no real methodical and complete commentary for this Book. But the notes of the *Bible de Jérusalem*, by J. Dupont, allow one to read it under the guidance of a specialist who provides essential explanations.

12. See: J. Dupont, "La question du plan des Actes des Apôtres à la lumière d'un texte de Lucien de Samosate," in *Novum Testamentum* XXI (1979), 220–31. The author's position has developed from the division he proposed in 1953, in the *Bible de Jérusalem*.

13. Acts 2:17; 7:49; 8:27; 9:15.

14. See E. Cothenet, "Les épîtres de Pierre" in *Cahiers Evangile* 47 (1984), with selected bibliography.

15. The Acts of the Apostles refers to this Silvanus (or Silas): 15:22, 40; 18:5; see 2 Cor 1:19; 1 Thess 1:1; 2 Thess 1:1.

16. It contains five chapters divided into 105 verses. During the Sundays of Easter, we read 42 of them.

17. The Letter has five chapters divided into 105 verses. We read 30 of them during the Sundays of Easter.

18. Nonbiblical apocalyptic writing flourished between 150 B.C. and A.D. 70: *Book of Enoch, Book of Jubilees, Testament of the Twelve Patriarchs, Psalms of Solomon, Assumption of Moses, Apocalypse of Baruch, Apocalypse of Esdras, Book of the Secrets of Enoch*.

19. Commentaries on the Book of Revelation are innumerable.

20. In the Old Testament, the apocalyptic genre is represented by the Book of Daniel, especially chapters 7–12.

21. Some passages in the prophetic books of the Old Testament point toward apocalyptic, properly so-called: Isa 24–27; 34–35; Ezek 1; 38–48; Joel 3–4; Zech; Jer 25:11-14. John's Revelation is inspired by them, and by the Book of Daniel: there are 57 allusions to it!

22. In some sects, there are those who claim to find precise meanings in numbers, proper names, and other details, from which to make predictions with an assurance that is undeterred by repeated refutations backed up by facts.

23. L. Bloy.

24. Rev 1:9; 2:2, 3, 19; 3:10; 13:10; 14:12.

25. In Masses during the week in Ordinary Time, we read 38 extracts from the Fourth Gospel.

26. We also read John 20:19-31 (Second Sunday, all three years) and John 10:1-10, 11-18, 27-30 (Fourth Sunday, Years A, B, and C, respectively). "The last discourse" is not quite an appropriate title. Rather, we have here a series of conversations between Jesus and his disciples. Moreover, the Fourth Gospel, in opposition to the Synoptics, does not report an institution of the Eucharist here. Nevertheless, these conversations are found in the context of the Last Supper taken by Jesus with his own (John 13:1-2, 31).

27. See Exod 12:25-27; 13:8, 14-15.

28. See the farewell speeches of Jacob (Gen 47:29-49:33), Moses (Deut 31-33), Joshua (Josh 23-24), Samuel (1 Sam 12), Tobit (Tob 14), Macc (1 Macc 2:49-70), Paul (Acts 20:17-35).

29. A. Lion, *Lire saint Jean*, Lire la Bible 32 (Paris: Cerf, 1972) suggests that one may see in John's Gospel almost three equal divisions, the keys to which are given by one word each: "life" (John 1-6), "death" (John 7-12), "love" (John 13-20).

It is true that the "Book of the Hour" (John 13-20) begins by affirming that Jesus' journey toward the cross is inspired by the great love he has for his own in the world (John 13:1). But Jesus speaks of more than this.

30. Above, p. 77.

Second Sunday of Easter—Pages 84-90

1. John reports Mary Magdalene's discovery of the empty tomb and the Lord's later appearance to her, as well as Peter and the "other disciple" running to the tomb to verify the fact (John 20:1-18). But it is only "on the evening of that first day" and "a week later" that the disciples see the risen one together.

2. Chapter 21, the "appendix" or "epilogue," according to modern editions of the New Testament, was added later, either by the evangelist himself or more likely by one of his disciples. This fact does not deny the canonicity of these 25 verses, nor does it diminish their importance for us.

The "canonicity" of a text, or of a book of the Bible, i.e., its belonging to the "canon" (the received *corpus*) of Scripture, is not tied to its "authenticity," i.e., its attribution to a particular author, but its acceptance by the Church as inspired Scripture. There are anonymous books in the Bible that are attributed to such and such an author: e.g., the Book of Proverbs, supposedly written by Solomon. One can dispute the authenticity of a particular Letter, e.g., the Second Letter of Peter. Today, it is nowhere suggested—not even in the title in official liturgical books—that the Letter to the Hebrews was written by Paul, as was thought for centuries. Rather, "canonicity" and "inspiration" go hand in hand: all these books are "canonical" and they alone are "inspired." This is what faith attributes to them. This is why the establishment of the "canon"—the list—of Scripture is given to the Church by tradition (Vatican II, Dogmatic Constitution on Divine Revelation, 8). The Council of Trent, in its fourth session (1546), "judged it proper" to promulgate such a list. The authenticity of a book or part of a book is the object of external criticism (what tradition says about it) and internal (an examination of the book itself). The question of authenticity affects many other works: writings, documents, works of art.

3. I. de la Potterie, "Genèse de la foi pascale d'après Jn 20," in *New Testament Studies* 30 (1984), pp. 26-49, which we will follow here very closely.

4. This passage is read on Tuesday in the Octave of Easter.

5. It is customary to present Thomas this way, and to see him, if not actually as a model, at least as a man who is like us and thus reassures us, because he demanded solid proofs before he would believe.

6. Matt 28:17 (at the moment of Jesus' appearance in Galilee); Mark 16:11-14; Luke 24:11, 13-35.

7. See the final chapter in this book: "From Bethlehem to Emmaus."

8. P. Claudel, *Corona benignitatis anni Dei*, in *Oeuvre poètique*, Pléiade (Paris: Gallimard, 1967) 424-25.7.

9. See above n. 2.

10. John notes the reactions of the people who had seen the blind man begging day after day, after he was healed. Some said it was he. But others said, "No, he just looks like him."

He himself said: "I am [the one]." Then others asked him, "How were your eyes opened?" They even asked his parents: "Is this your son, who you say was born blind?" (John 9:1-41).

11. Commission Francophone Cistercienne, *Tropaires des dimanches*, Le Livre d'Heures d'En-Calcat (Dourgne, 1980) 34.

12. Eucharistic Prayer for this Sunday.

13. Ibid., acclamation III.

*Year A: The Church—Paschal Community—*Pages 91-96

1. The other two (Acts 4:32-35 and 5:12-16) are read on the Second Sunday of Easter, Years B and C.

Luke loves these beautiful transitions that allude to what he has said and prepare for what will follow. These "summaries" play such a role. At the same time, they are of more general interest: they present an overview of the events and speeches reported.

One should not be surprised to find anomalies, repetitions, and a certain lack of obvious order in these summaries. These are not due to negligence on the part of the author or a lack of mastery of the many sources used, but a literary method. Luke generalizes to the point of ignoring the nuances of what follows; but in so doing he gives his readers a guiding thread to his work.

2. The verb "to persevere" is characteristic of Paul's vocabulary: Rom 12:12; Col 4:2; Eph 4:18. It means "to hold fast" to something. It is frequently associated with prayer (Luke 18:1).

3. Ph. Menoud, *La vie de l'Eglise naissante*, Foi vivante, 14 (Paris: CerfDelachaux et Niestlé, 1989) 60.

4. "Communion" in Greek is *"koinonia."* It is rarely found in the New Testament. It is used only once—here—in the Acts of the Apostles. Its precise meaning is a matter of question.

5. Even in monastic and religious communities whose members make a personal vow to communal life, actual behavior must constantly be examined to measure its closeness to this ideal. Benedict, for instance, insists on this point. Not all have the same needs, and this must affect what is given to each (*Rule*, chs. 34, 36, 37). Even so, one must "radically extirpate . . . the vice of ownership" (ibid., ch. 33), which is that one regards what one has (or has received) as properly reserved for purely individual benefit. It is no more and no less than the ideal presented in Acts toward which Benedict aims.

6. Like the Jewish Passover supper, the Eucharist was at this time a domestic celebration.

Nothing here allows us to determine how frequent it was at the time of which Luke is speaking. One certainly "broke bread" when the community gathered on "on the first day of the week" (Acts 20:7) and also when an unusual circumstance, e.g., an apostle's passing through, would collect the local Church. Among many witnesses on the Christian custom of assembly (see A.G. Martimort, *The Church at Prayer: The Liturgy and Time* , vol. IV [Collegeville, Minn.: The Liturgical Press, 1986] 13-15). Writing to the emperor Trajan in A.D. 110, Pliny the Younger, governor of Bithynia, said, "Their whole fault or error is confined to gathering on a fixed day, before dawn, to sing to Christ, as to a God."

7. A.-G. Martimort, "L'assemblée liturgique," in *La Maison-Dieu* 20 (1949), p. 164, remarks that in praying for the absent, the assembly above all takes into consideration the fact that certain categories of people find it impossible to partake in the assembly: "absent due to circumstances." Thus the sick, travelers, and prisoners are almost always mentioned in ancient liturgies. In our day, it is no less the case that some people, because of their life situations, responsibilities, or commitments, are prevented from coming to the assembly. Because of this, they must have a particular place in the assembly's prayer.

8. This is what Paul writes to the Corinthians (1 Cor 11:20-21).

9. Luke usually speaks of "prayer" in the singular (Acts 1:14; 2:42). Thus he is referring to Christian prayer, of which the "Our Father" is a model.

10. See Acts 3:1; 16:16.

11. ". . . and it was in Antioch that the disciples were first called Christians" (Acts 11:26). The foundation of the Church in this city took place following the scattering of the disciples due to the violent reaction that rose up against Stephen (Acts 11:19).

12. Psalmic prayer belongs to the Old Testament. Reading Scripture is part of the synagogal liturgy (though Christians add the Gospels and the apostolic writings to it). Hymns, on the other hand—most notably hymns to Christ—are characteristic rather of the Christian liturgy. See in A.G. Martimort, n. 6, above.

13. What does it mean to say: "I am a nonpracticing Christian"; "I believe in God, but I do not pray"? To be sure, such statements cannot in themselves guarantee an absence of faith: who could judge this with any certainty? But what is the faith so expressed? Does it really revolve around God the Father and the one he has sent, Jesus Christ, his Son? Even if it does inspire one's actions, especially the way one treats one's neighbor—"I am just as honest and caring as any practicing Christian; more so than most of them!"—is it not corrupted by religious individualism and ready to fall apart, since it cannot see how it is nourished by the source of all faith? Or, in other words, at what point must we talk about theological faith?

14. The *Benedictus* (Luke 1:68-79), the *Magnificat* (Luke 1:47-55), the *Nunc dimittis* (Luke 2:29-32), in the Offices of Morning, Evening, and Compline.

15. Acts 4:33; 5:13. In the Gospel too, Luke emphasizes the contrast between the unfavorable attitude of the leaders with respect to Jesus and the welcome accorded him by the crowd: Luke 19:47; 20:19, 26; 21:37-22:2.

16. On this letter, see above, pp. 79, 80 [First Letter of Peter] 111-12.

17. The "Eighteen Benedictions"—*Shemoneh Esreh*—are one of the most solemn formulas. "Blessed be you, Lord, our God and God of our fathers, God of Abraham, God of Isaac and God of Jacob, great, powerful and holy God. Most high and merciful God, who orders all things, who recalls the pious actions of the Fathers and will send a redeemer to the sons of their sons, for your name, in love: blessed be you, Lord, Abraham's shield" (trans. L. Bouyer, *Eucharistie. Théologie et spiritualité de la prière eucharistique* (Tournai, 1966) 75–76.

18. J. Loew, *Ce Jésus qu'on appelle Christ* (Paris: Fayard, 1970) 47.

19. *Odes de Salomon* (collection of 42 anonymous hymns of the first half of 1st c.), 15, in A. Hamman, *Naissance des lettres chrétiennes*, Ichtus I (Paris: Éditions de Paris, 1957) 38 (slightly revised translation).

Year B: Community, Faith, and Hope—Pages 97–102

1. See above, n. 1, "The Church—Paschal Community, p. 322.

2. We are becoming more and more aware today that the disparity between rich and poor, whether individuals or countries, is an intolerable scandal. We are gradually recognizing that this is an urgent problem that must be remedied. But—and this is where the vicious character of wealth is revealed most clearly—economic structures and mechanisms themselves lead to the rich getting richer and the poor getting poorer.

3. J. Dupont, "L'union entre les chrétiens dans les Actes des Apôtres," in *Nouvelle revue théologique* 91 (1969), p. 909; *Nouvelles études sur les Actes des Apôtres*, Lectio divina 118 (Paris: Cerf, 1984) 310.

4. Deuteronomy instituted a number of measures to promote this: every three years the tithes should go not to the sanctuary but to those who have no share in the inheritance; every seven years, there should be a relaxation of debts and freeing of Hebrew slaves (Deut 15:1-23). Elsewhere, Leviticus instituted the jubilee: every fiftieth year, property was to be returned to the original owner, and strict prescriptions were laid down that the property not be dissipated as the jubilee drew near (Lev 25).

5. Evagrius Ponticus (ca. 345-99), *Traité pratique ou Le moine*, 97, in *Sources chrétiennes* 171 (Paris: Cerf, 1971) 705.

6. *La Doctrine des douze Apôtres*, (*Didachè*), 4, 8, in *Sources chrétiennes* 248 (Paris: Cerf, 1978) 161. This is a catechetical, liturgical, and disciplinary manual (1st c.).

This text and the three following are cited in J.-B. Franzoni, *La terre appartient à Dieu*, translation reviewed by the author, published by P. de Béthune and R. Gantoy (Paris: Centurion, 1973) 61-67.

Unless indicated otherwise, the translations of these patristic texts are those found in this work.

7. Basil (329-79), *Homélie 6 contre la richesse* (*Lc 12,16*), 7, trans. A. Hamman, *Riches et pauvres dans l'Eglise ancienne*, in Lettres chrétiennes 6 (Paris: Centurion, 1972) 76.

8. Ambrose (339-97), *Homélie 8 sur le Ps 118*, 2, in J.-P. Migne, *Patrologia latina* 15, col. 1303-04.

9. John Chrysostom (ca. 350-407) *Homélie sur la Première Lettre à Timothée*, 4, in J.-P. Migne, *Patrologia graeca* 62, col. 562-63.

10. After this reading, as in Year A, the Lectionary contains Ps 118.

11. See above, p. 81. Beginning with the Third Sunday, one follows the order of the chapters (2, 3, 4).

12. The verb "to believe" occurs nine times in this letter, six alone in 5:1-13. Also in this text is the only use of the substantive "faith" in the theological sense, describing an interior attachment to God.

13. This is the Gospel for this Sunday.

14. Augustine (354-430), *Commentaire sur la Première épître de saint Jean*, treatise VII, 4, in *Sources chrétiennes* 75 (Paris: Cerf, 1961) 321.

15. To acknowledge this definition is not to devalue whatever love nonbelievers have for one another, especially that love they have for the poor and weak. All human love is a marvelous thing. It really comes from God, who created us in his image. In every love, the believer can recognize, with amazement, a reflection of the God-Love, all the more astonishing when those who love do not know God. Nevertheless, one cannot speak of them as "anonymous Christians," since to do so is not to respect them as they are, and often (quite rightly) provokes a strong reaction from them. On the other hand, hate is a monstrosity and a blasphemy. Lack of charity among Christians is always a scandal to both believers and nonbelievers.

16. Bernard (1090-1153), *Sermon pour la Cène du Seigneur*, 1, in J.-P. Migne, *Patrologie latine*, 183, col. 271.

17. The theme of victory over the world is developed at length in Revelation. Of the 30 instances of the use of the terms "to conquer," "conqueror" and "victory" in the New Testament, 21 of them occur in John's writings (16 in Rev).

18. This citation combines two texts: Ps 34:21 and Exod 12:46.

19. Zech 12:10.

20. Irenaeus (ca. 135-202), *Contre les hérésies*, III, 24, 1, in *Sources chrétiennes* 211 (Paris: Cerf, 1974) 475.

21. Vatican II, Pastoral Constitution on the Church in the Modern World (*Gaudium et Spes*), no. 69.

Year C: The Presence of the Risen Christ in the Community—
Pages 103-106

1. See above, "The Church, Paschal Community," n. 1.
This third "summary" marks a turning point in the Acts of the Apostles. If the healing of a lame man at the Temple and Peter's subsequent speech provoked a reaction from the leaders of the people, the Sanhedrin contented itself with forbidding Peter and John to preach in Jesus' name (Acts 3-4). But the apostles ignored this injunction: they performed many signs and wonders (third "summary"). This renewal of their activity led to their arrest (Acts 5:17-42), soon followed by the martyrdom of Stephen (Acts 6:8-7:60) and a violent persecution against the Church in Jerusalem that forced the disciples to leave (Acts 8:1-3). Thus began the mission outside the City, which is the focus of the rest of the book, where Luke particulary concerns himself—from chapter 13 on—with Paul's missionary activity.

2. Likewise: Matt 4:24-25; Mark 3:7-12; Matt 14:35-36; Mark 6:54-56.

3. See also Acts 3:6-7 (the healing of a crippled man who begged at the Beautiful Gate of the Temple); 9:33-35 (the healing of a paralytic in Lydda); 9:36-42 (the raising of a woman in Joppa).

4. Augustine (354-430), Traité 49 sur saint Jean, 2, in J.-P. Migne, Patrologie latine, 35, col. 1747.

5. On Rev see above, pp. 81-82.

6. The combination "word-witness" is found five times in Revelation: Rev 1:2, 9; 6:9; 20:4; 12:17. The word "testimony" is also typical of its vocabulary: Jesus is the Witness (Rev 1:5; 3:14); he gives his testimony either through himself or through "those who give witness to Jesus," i.e., the Christians (Rev 12:17; 19:10 and also 6:9; 11:7; 12:11).

7. The author attaches a good deal of importance to this book that the voice ordered him to write. He speaks of it 23 times: Rev 1:3; 22:7, 10, 16, 18-19; etc. This is an innovation in the prophetic tradition: previously, more importance was accorded to the prophet's speech than his book. Jeremiah is an exception (Jer 36).

8. Mark 9:9; Matt 17:9, 22; 20:18.

9. Isa 42:1-4; 49:1-6; 50:4-9; 52:13-53:12.

10. Luke 22:69; John 5:27; Acts 7:56.

11. Matt 17:1-9; Mark 9:2-9; Luke 9:28-36. The story of the transfiguration in the Gospels has a definite paschal feel about it. See Days of the Lord vol. 2. The garment also recalls Jesus' seamless tunic that was taken from him on the cross (John 19:23). See above, "Good Friday" Mysteries of Calvary, p. 30.

12. Matt 28:5, 10; Mark 16:6; Luke 24:38.

13. Nersès Snorhali (1102-1173), Jésus fils unique du Père, 958-60, in Sources chrétiennes 203 (Paris: Cerf, n.d.) 225.

14. L. Groslambert (Fiche de chant I 168).

Third Sunday of Easter

Year A: Raised According to Scripture, Recognized in the Breaking of the Bread—Pages 107-115

1. The Gospels themselves, whose historical value ought not to be doubted, are not presented as chronological records of Jesus' life: neither Luke, who writes a "whole sequence of events" (Luke 1:3), nor John, who accompanies Jesus from his baptism in the Jordan to his death on the cross, pretend to be such. They wrote their books to instruct

the faithful to whom they were writing. Because of this, they each chose certain things out of the multitude of recollections transmitted by tradition (see Luke 1:2) and oral preaching. After learning about the whole, each evangelist organized his selection of Jesus' words and actions according to a personal plan that corresponded to his purpose. Although the Gospels of Matthew, Mark, and Luke are called "Synoptic," side by side, they are not simply copies of each other: their common elements are not always found in the same order or context.

2. This is what Jesus said in his first preaching at Nazareth (Luke 4:21), after having read a prophecy from Isaiah (61:1-2).

3. Acts reports five speeches by Peter: Acts 2:1-41; 3:1-26; 4:1-22; 5:17-41; 11:1-18. The liturgy runs through them in order during Eastertime: on the Third and Fourth Sundays of Year A, it draws from the first; on the Third and Fourth Sundays of Year B, it contains portions of the second and the third; the Third and Fourth Sundays of Year C, finally, contain portions of the fourth and fifth. Each of these speeches occurred in a particular context, but the Lectionary, of course, does not address the context. The liturgy does not attempt to run through or recall those events that marked the history of the primitive Church in succession; it does not follow the unfolding of the apostles' or one of the apostles' activity: Peter in this case. It pronounces the preaching of the apostles—of Peter—which, outside any historical context, is of perennial importance, for it is on this that our faith rests.

4. *La Divine liturgie de saint Jean Chrysostome*, Editions des Bénédictins de Chevetogne, 4th ed. (Gembloux, 1957) 36–38.

5. This is the Gospel for this Sunday.

6. Gen 45:5-8; Isa 53:10-12; Wis 2:13, 18; etc.

7. The Acts of the Apostles (2:34-36) also appeals to Ps 110:1 which, with Ps 16, is referred to later on: Acts 13:33-37.

8. On 1 Pet, see above, pp. 79–80.

9. See "Crainte de Dieu," in *Vocabulaire de théologie biblique* (Paris: Cerf, 1970) col. 219-22; "Crainte," in *Dictionnaire encyclopédique de la bible* (Paris: Brepols, 1987) 310.

10. This way of speaking presents the Exodus as a "figure" or "parable": one can speak, in this sense, of the "typology" of the Exodus. See Ps 105.

11. John 1:29, 36; 19:36; Rev 5:6.

12. One of the Palestinian Targums says that this lamb "had been created at the dawn of the world," in other words, that God had known from the beginning that he would substitute a lamb for Isaac.

The Targums—literally "translations, interpretations"—were versions of the Old Testament in Aramaic—the spoken language—used in some synagogues so that everyone might understand the reading, which was done in Hebrew. These translations included elements of explanation and interpretation. They were originally made orally, being written down much later. See "Versions anciennes de la Bible" in *Dictionnaire encyclopédique de la Bible* (Paris: Brepols, 1987) 1311-13.

13. Melito of Sardis (d. ca. 190), *Sur la Pâque*, 4–5, in *Sources chrétiennes* 123 (Paris: Cerf, 1966); in *La Liturgie des Heures, 2. Carême-Temps pascal*, p. 420, with a slightly modified translation.

14. The evangelist edited this story with a good deal of care and finesse: we must therefore read it attentively. Also, it holds a great place—even in terms of length—in the last chapter of Luke's Gospel: 23 verses out of 53, while the appearance to the apostles accounts for 13 verses, and that to Peter only one.

15. This first part contains 15 verses; the second—the denouement—only seven. Several places today claim to be the Emmaus of the Gospel, which was apparently situated some 60 "stades" (the currently accepted reading)—around seven miles—or a "two-hour walk" from Jerusalem (as is said in certain versions). The village of Imwas has an appropriate name, but it is much too far away (160 stades, around 14 miles). Qubeiba is 75 stades; Moza, with

its neighbor Bet Zayit, is 40 stades. Finally, there is Abu Ghosh, 60 stades away. We cannot be sure that any of these was actually Emmaus. It is worth noting that at Imwas, one can see the ruins of a 12th c. church with traces of two earlier ones: one built ca. 225–250, which was destroyed and replaced in the 5th c. by a Byzantine basilica. At Abu Ghosh— from the name of a bandit chief of the 19th c. who held pilgrims for ransom—there is a beautiful basilica built during the crusades and magnificently restored—Notre-Dame de l'Arche d'Alliance—which is also built over the ruins of an earlier Byzantine church.

16. See Peter's speeches on Pentecost (Acts 2:32-36), after the healing of the lame man at the Temple (Acts 3:13-16), before the Sanhedrin (Acts 4:10-11; 5:30-32); also that of Paul at Antioch of Pisidia (Acts 13:27-31); and 1 Cor 15:3-6.

17. Acts 3:18; 13:27-33; 17:3; 26:22; 28:29.

18. See Origen (ca. 185–253), *Commentaire sur l'Evangile selon saint Matthieu* I, Book X, 5-6, in *Sources chrétiennes* 162 (Paris: Cerf, 1970) 157–61.

19. At this time, the Eucharist was still celebrated in the course of a meal: Acts 20:7, 11; 1 Cor 10:16.

20. The Acts of the Apostles was written ca. A.D. 80–90. This is the date commonly accepted by exegetes today: *Bible de Jérusalem*, 1567; "Actes des Apôtres," *Dictionnaire encyclopédique de la Bible* (Paris: Brepols, 1987) 12–13.

21. Augustine (354–430), *Sermon 235, 3*, in J.-P. Migne, *Patrologie latine* 38, col. 1118-19.

22. Commission Francophone Cistercienne, *La nuit, le jour* (Paris: Desclée, 1973) 53 (Fiche de chant P LH 123).

23. See above n. 14.

Year B: He Is Living in Our Midst—Pages 116–123

1. Verse 16 is omitted because it recalls the circumstance that led Peter to make this speech: the healing of the crippled beggar at the Beautiful Gate of the Temple. See n. 3, p. 326. The end—vv. 20-26—which is also omitted, is an expansion, in the form of a scriptural argument, on what God "spoke of long ago through his holy prophets." Such a recollection of the promises is still of interest today, but in the context of this speech, it points directly to those who were listening to the apostle at the time. Thus the entire passage would have a circumstantial character. By omitting these seven verses, the Lectionary very judiciously, without really curtailing the text or changing its meaning, has retained the essence of the announcement of the resurrection, which is important always and everywhere.

2. Isa 42:1-4; 49:1-6; 50:4-9; 52:13–53:12.

3. Vatican II, Declaration on the Relation of the Church to Non-Christian Religions (*Nostra aetate*), no. 4, is very expressive on this point: "Even though the Jewish authorities and those who followed their lead pressed for the death of Christ (cf. John 19:6), neither all Jews indiscriminately at that time, nor Jews today, can be charged with the crimes committed during his passion. It is true that the Church is the new people of God, yet the Jews should not be spoken of as rejected or accursed as if this followed from holy Scripture."

4. The apostolic discourses on the resurrection, always constructed along the same lines— recollection of circumstances, proclamation of the resurrection, appeal to the Scriptures— invariably end with an exhortation to conversion.

5. 1 John 2:1-5a (Third Sunday); 3:1-2 (Fourth Sunday); 3:18-24 (Fifth Sunday); 4:7-10 (Sixth Sunday); 4:11-16 (Seventh Sunday). To these five extracts, read in the order of the chapters in which they appear, one should add that selected for the Second Sunday: 5:1-6. On this letter, see above p. 80.

6. So, for example, the author of the Book of Proverbs: Prov 1:8; 2:1; 3:1; 4:1; 8:32. The *Rule of Saint Benedict* also begins with these words: "Listen, my son."

7. "My little ones" occurs frequently: 1 John 2:1, 12, 13, 28; 3:7, 18; 4:4; 5:21. This letter seems to be directed to a group of Churches.

8. 1 John 1:6-8; 2:6; 3:5-9; 5:18, 21.

9. "*Pecca fortiter, et crede fortius*" ("Sin boldly, and believe more boldly yet") said Luther. Some polemicists have made poor use of this formula, distorting its meaning and wrenching it from its context. It was meant to be provocative; it does not mean that one can sin without constraint the moment one has unshakable faith: this would be a mockery of God. Instead, it means that in so far as one sins, one must, in order to escape from sin and receive forgiveness, appeal all the more strongly to God who forgives.

10. Augustine (354–430), *Commentaire de la Première lettre de saint Jean*, I, 7, in *Sources chrétiennes* 75 (Paris: Cerf, 1961) 129-30.

11. "To know," in John's vocabulary, has the strong sense of "to be united with," "to be intimately attached to."

12. John returns to this point several times: 1 John 2:3-6, 10; 3:7-10; 5:2-3.

13. It seems that John has in mind certain doctrinal and moral deviations. He castigates those who teach such doctrines, calling them "antichrists" (1 John 2:18, 22; 4:3; 2 John 7); "liars" (1 John 2:22); "false prophets" (1 John 4:1); "deceitful men" (2 John 7).

14. "Gnosticism" refers to a doctrine in which intellectual knowledge ("gnosis") has primacy over everything else and is sufficient for salvation.

Every distortion in Christology generates errors in other areas and ends up supporting many false conceptions, especially with regard to the Church. This is seen as either a purely spiritual or purely human reality when one makes a distinction in Christ between the Son of God and the man Jesus.

15. See text, pp. 99–100, and n. 15, p. 324.

16. At the beginning of the Acts of the Apostles, Luke writes that "over the course of forty days" Jesus appeared to the apostles, to whom he gave proofs in many convincing ways of his resurrection and to whom he spoke about the "kingdom of God" (Acts 1:3). This does not contradict what he says in the Gospel. Luke, no more than the other evangelists, pretended to establish, after a strict investigation, a detailed chronology of Jesus' appearances: dates, places, number, etc. This would have had no relation to his purpose, and more importantly, would have been of scant interest for our faith. Rather, it is necessary to have assurances about the seriousness of the apostles' testimony. At the beginning of Acts, Luke recalls that, in fact, the apostles received numerous proofs of Jesus' resurrection. In the Gospel, the resurrection itself is given. See above, n. 1, p. 325.

17. Tradition has retained different appearances of the resurrected. In 1 Cor, Paul enumerates the appearances of which he has heard or which came to him at the time he dictates the letter. It is a long list, but certainly not complete. One notes in particular the appearances to Peter and the Twelve, which are testified to everywhere: ". . . he appeared to Kephas, then to the Twelve. After that, he appeared to more than five hundred brothers at once, most of whom are still living, though some have fallen asleep. After that, he appeared to James, then to all the apostles. Last of all, as to one born abnormally, he appeared to me." (1 Cor 15:5-8).

18. The Eleven are always mentioned, even when it is added that other disciples were also present.

19. The Synoptics testify to this. They each give a list of the Twelve: Matt 10:1-4; Mark 3:13-19; Luke 6:12-16.

20. What else could explain what life is, when we know its mechanisms and manifestations or the love that determines what one becomes, what one does when it is present? See G. Martelet, *Résurrection, Eucharistie et Genèse de l'homme* (Paris: Desclée, 1972).

21. W. Vischer, "Etudes sur l'Ancien Testament," in *Foi et vie* 4 (1939).

22. John 2:17-22; 12:14-16; 14:26; 15:26; 16:13-14.

23. Acts 3:22-25; 7:37.

24. Acts 1:20; 2:25-31, 34-36; 4:25-28; 13:33, 35-37.

25. Acts 2:38; 3:19; 4:10-12; 5:31; 10:43; 17:30; 20:21; 26:20.

26. Isa 42:1-6, 10; 45:14-16, 20-25; 49:1-9; 55:5; 60; Ps 96-100; Jonah.

27. Guerricus of Igny (ca. 1070–1157), *Premier sermon pour la Résurrection*, 5-6, Sermons II, in *Sources chrétiennes* 202 (Paris: Cerf, 1973) 225–27.

Year C: Church of the Resurrected and Witness of the Apostles— Pages 124–132

1. See above, pp. 124–126.

2. The first is read on the Fourth Sunday of Easter, Year B (Acts 4:8-12).

3. The Lectionary only contains what is really the speech. Acts 5:17-27a recalls in what circumstances Peter and the apostles were once again arraigned before the Sanhedrin. They had paid no attention to the interdiction that forbade them to preach the name of Jesus. Arrested, they were thrown into prison to await trial. Miraculously delivered, they immediately went back to preach at the Temple, the very place they had been arrested.

The Lectionary also omits vv. 33-40a, which tell of what one member of the Sanhedrin—Gamaliel—said, recommending that the apostles not be bothered: "For if this endeavor or this activity is of human origin, it will destroy itself. But if it comes from God, you will not be able to destroy them; you may even find yourselves fighting against God." The council followed his advice. They again forbade the apostles to preach, and after having them scourged, released them.

On this omission of the details of circumstance, see n. 1, p. 327.

4. This was the argument put forth to condemn Jesus: "We found this man misleading our people . . . He is inciting the people with his teaching" (Luke 23:2, 5). In all ages, and even today, the charge of subversion has been leveled against Christians and the Churches, resulting in their persecution or the forbidding of their activities.

5. Jesus did the same. He refused to respond to Pilate, who dealt thus with the accusations against him (Matt 27:14; Mark 15:5; Luke 23:9; John 19:9-12).

6. Eucharistic Prayer IV thus recalls the uninterrupted unfolding of salvation history: creation, covenant, prophets, sending of the Son "in the fullness of time," and for the fulfilling of the plan of God's love, the passion and resurrection of the Lord who gave the Spirit to the faithful and through whom the bread and wine become the Body and Blood of Christ.

7. Exod 14:13; Ps 105:8, 10, 21; Isa 49:7; 43:11; 45:15; Acts 7:25; Heb 2:10.

Luke's Christology is very biblical and is not without a polemic against the worship of the Greek gods and the emperors who usurped the title "Savior." Not like these does Jesus save. Rather, he is the "liberator" (*goel* in Hebrew) of the chosen people, as the Bible conceives of it.

8. The theme of salvation runs throughout Luke's work and characterizes the whole of Jesus' life, from his infancy and public life to his death on the cross: Luke 1:47; 2:30; 3:6; 23:39-43.

9. "I saw" occurs 56 times in Rev.

10. Twenty-eight times. See also John 1:36: "Behold, the Lamb of God."

11. See 1 Pet 1:19; 2:23.

12. Note that the author of the Fourth Gospel says that Jesus died at the same hour the paschal lamb was sacrificed (John 19:14). He insists on the fact that not one of Jesus' bones was broken: he thus cites Ps 34:21, but it was also prescribed that the bones of the paschal lamb should not be broken (Exod 12:46; Num 9:12).

13. There is no reason to try to identify these personages with those found in other visions, especially those of Daniel and Ezekiel. Some Bibles translate "living creatures" by "animals." In Ezek, they are certainly cherubim whose wings cover, like a canopy, the ark of the covenant and who take on the aspect of strange beings. In any case, they evoke the glory which surrounds the throne—or the chariot—of God. Likewise in Rev.

14. Acclamation of the assembly after the "Our Father."

15. See n. 2, p. 321.

16. It appears in every manuscript.

17. One remark by the author indicates that he has very carefully read what has gone before. He writes: "This was now the third time Jesus was revealed to his disciples after being raised from the dead." The two other appearances are reported by John; we read them every year on the Second Sunday of Easter.

We also note that the author has retained the evangelist's description of the characteristics and typical reactions of Peter and John. When the disciples ran to the tomb on Easter morning (John 20:3-9), John understood and immediately "he believed." On the shore of the sea of Tiberias, he is the first to understand and recognize the Lord. Finally, the anonymous editor connects his account to the finale of the evangelist's writing. John wrote: "Then the disciples returned home" (John 20:10), and they are shown in Galilee, their home, having returned to their previous profession of fishermen.

18. Many have attempted to discover the secret. Jerome (ca. 347–420) saw it as the number of species of fish, as was known in his day. Others have noted that the sum of the numbers from 1 to 17 $(1 + 2 + 3 + . . . + 16 + 17)$ is 153. Still others, that "if one respresents each number by a corresponding quantity of points, and lines them up underneath each other, one will form an equilateral triangle with each side seventeen points long" (See B. Schwank, "Le Christ et Pierre à la fin des Temps," in Assemblées du Seigneur, 2nd series, no. 24 [Paris: Publications de Saint-André—Cerf, 1969] 60). These attempts to show how the number 153 can be symbolic of a whole are more indicative of ingenuity than exegetical power. Jerome's interpretation would be the most satisfying if it were well founded. But that there were 153 known species of fish is of course, a supposition.

19. Also, tradition reports that Peter, Andrew, James, and John his brother left their nets—"they were fishermen"—in order to follow Jesus, who had said to them: "Come after me, and I will make you fishers of men" (Matt 4:18-22; Mark 1:16-20). Luke places this calling and Jesus' saying after a miraculous catch (Luke 5:1-11). And this all happened on the shore of the Sea of Tiberias.

20. No translation can capture the assonances and the sibilant quality, nor the pithiness of the Latin formula.

21. Gregory the Great (pope from 590 to 604), Homélies sur les évangiles 24, in J.-P. Migne, Patrologie latine, t. 76, col. 1187.

22. Matt 10:2-4; Mark 3:16-19; Luke 6:14-16. John's Gospel does not contain this list. But it does note that after Simon came to him, Jesus gave him the name Cephas, "(which is translated Peter)" (John 1:42).

23. In the story of the miraculous catch followed by the call of Simon, James, and John, we read in Luke's Gospel that the nets where broken by the weight of the fish (Luke 5:6).

24. John 18:15, 25-26.

25. Matt 26:75; Mark 14:72; Luke 22:62.

26. The discourse on the Good Shepherd is read on the Fourth Sunday of Easter: John 10:1-10, Year A; John 10:11-18, Year B; John 10:27-30, Year C.

27. Ignatius of Antioch (d. 110), Lettre aux Romains, I, 1, in Sources chrétiennes 10 (Paris, Cerf, 1951) 124, greets the Church of Rome as the one "which presides in charity."

28. A. Valensin (1873–1944), La joie dans la foi (Paris: Aubier, 1955) 124.

29. In order to express welcome into the Christian community, the priest, followed by

the parents and godparents, traces the sign of the cross on the infant who is to be baptized (*Rituel du baptême des petits enfants* (Mame-Tardy, 1984) 75, 116, 153, 178).

30. Eusebius of Caesarea (ca. 265–338) says that according to one tradition, "he was crucified head downward, on his own request," *Histoire ecclésiastique*, III, 1, 1, in *Sources chrétiennes* 31 (Paris: Cerf; 1952) 97.

31. This text is read on Saturday of the Seventh Week of Easter, with the last verses (23–25), in which the author does justice to the preceding conclusion with an inscription that takes it up and expands it (John 20:31). He writes: "So the word spread among the brothers that that disciple would not die. But Jesus had not told him that he would not die, just 'What if I want him to remain until I come? What concern is it of yours?' "

"It is this disciple who testifies to these things and has written them down, and we know that his testimony is true. There are also many other things that Jesus did, but if these were to be described individually, I do not think the whole world would contain the books that would be written."

32. Augustine (354–430) *Traité 124 sur saint Jean*, 5, 7, in *Corpus christianorum, series latina* 36 (Brepols, p. 685). French text in *La Liturgie des Heures*, 2, Temps pascal, Saturday of the Sixth week, p. 733.

Fourth Sunday of Easter

Year A: The Paschal Exodus in the Wake of Christ—Pages 133–139

1. See above, p. 107.

2. This announcement comes from what is called the "kerygma," from the Greek word *kèrugma*, which means "proclamation." The kerygma is thus distinguished from the catechesis and preaching that develop and explain its content, revealing its implications for all areas of Christian life, for the Church, and for the world. The study of the kerygma acknowledges that the gospel was preached before it was written. Hence it is expressed in somewhat stereotyped formulas. See the article "kérygme," in *Dictionnaire encyclopédique de la Bible* (Paris: Brepols, 1987) 717–720; *Dictionnaire de la foi chrétienne. 1. Les mots* (Paris: Cerf, 1968) col. 405. *Le vocabulaire de théologie biblique* (Paris: Cerf, 1970) has no article on "kerygma," but see what is said in the articles "Confession," "Nouveau Testament," "Enseigner," "Evangile," "Prêcher," which indicate the meaning of the term.

3. The fifty days of Easter are "as one feast day, or better as one 'great Sunday' " (*General Roman Calendar*, no. 22). See above, p. 77.

4. We can all think of many such manifestations of joy: "Hooray!"; "Bravo!"; etc. People who do not know what it is all about ask the reason for this kind of general rejoicing, and are sometimes surprised to find themselves drawn into the collective enthusiasm before finding out the cause.

5. In Acts, this text comes from Peter's first speech (Acts 2:14-41), of which the first part (Acts 2:14, 22-28) is read almost in its entirety on the Third Sunday of Year A.

6. Peter cites this text in the verse just before we pick up the reading.

The way Peter speaks gives no warrant to those doctrines that have been called "adoptianist." Though nuanced differently, they all had recourse to the notion of adoption to explain how Jesus was the Son of God. For some—in the 2nd and 3rd c.—Jesus was a man whom God, by adoption, made his Son. For others—in the 8th c.—(the Spanish "adoptianists"), it was the human nature of the unique person of Christ that had been adopted by God. All of these were condemned as heretics. Today, some ways of speaking about Jesus and Christ suggest an unconscious and insidious form of adoptianism. When one insists on the humanity of the God-man, one may seem more or less to forget his divine nature. In the end, he would be a kind of "superman" who became a "supersaint."

7. Three other psalms are cited in Peter's speeches: Ps 2:1-2 (Acts 4:25-26); Ps 16:8-11 (Acts 2:25-28); Ps 118:22 (Acts 4:11)

8. See n. 4, p. 327.

9. It is said that Ananias laid his hands on Saul and said to him: ". . . the Lord has sent me . . . that you may regain your sight and be filled with the holy Spirit" (Acts 9:17). At Ephesus, we find that Paul himself baptized twelve people, then laid his hands on them so that they might receive the Holy Spirit (Acts 19:5-6). Likewise, Peter and John went to Samaria to some disciples who had received "baptism in the name of the Lord Jesus" but not the gift of the Spirit; the apostles bestowed this on them by the laying on of hands (Acts 8:14-17). In the last two cases the distinction between the rites is clearly marked. In the case of Saul, it is more difficult to be sure. In any case, however, the point of these stories is not of a liturgical or ritual order. Indeed, it is always emphasized—as in Peter's speeches—that baptism and the gift of the Spirit go hand in hand.

10. The prophets had dimly foreseen and announced this universality of salvation: Isa 57:19; Joel 3:5.

11. Even so, Acts testifies that the apostles, especially Peter, did not understand this from the first. A vision was needed for Peter to go into a pagan house and there announce Jesus Christ; moreover, the Holy Spirit took the initiative to descend on Cornelius and those with him, so that Peter felt himself bound to baptize them (Acts 10:9-48). On his return to Jerusalem, Peter had to explain the whole affair "step by step" to satisfy the community, assuring them of the ground of his action and inspiring them to glorify God (Acts 11:1-18). Nevertheless, there were still misgivings about the Gentiles until the question was officially decided at the Council of Jerusalem (Acts 15:6-29).

12. Acts 2:41, 47; 4:4; 5:14; 6:1, 7; 9:31; 11:21, 24; 16:5; etc.

13. See n. 2, above.

14. From the point of view of their destination, the letters may be divided in the following manner: ten are addressed to a particular Church (Rom, 1 Cor, 2 Cor, Gal, Eph, Phil, Col, 1 Thess, 2 Thess, 2 John); six to a group of Churches or Christians (Heb, Jas, 1 Pet, 2 Pet, 1 John, Jude); five to individuals (1 Tim, 2 Tim, Titus, Phlm, 3 John).

15. See n. 3, p. 329.

The Lectionary has not retained what this letter says about the Christian's requisite submission to civil authorities, even harsh taskmasters (1 Pet 2:13-18). A little further on, it speaks of the submission of a wife to her husband, and the submission of Christians to one another (1 Pet 3:1-12). Such a speech does not go over well today. We must understand what the author wants to say, and make some necessary "translations." But even so, the letter does not equivocate: the verb "to submit" occurs six times in 105 verses, and only 36 times in the rest of the New Testament! For this Sunday of Easter, the Lectionary has retained only the paschal core of this catechesis, the basis of the specific demands enunciated by the author, which are applicable to many situations.

16. In our usual understanding, "to lie" means knowingly to affirm, by words or acts, the opposite of the truth, with the intention to deceive. The Bible knows this meaning of "deceit"; but it also recognizes another meaning. Deceit can mean to turn from the God of truth toward deceitful idols, to do evil, to make a covenant with it, to imitate Satan, "liar and the father of lies" (John 8:44). On the other hand, the saints, those who are pure and "follow the Lamb wherever he goes . . . on their lips no deceit has been found; they are unblemished" (Rev 14:4-5). This is the level at which the text here speaks of "deceit." See *Vocabulaire de théologie biblique* (Paris: Cerf, 1970) col. 737–40.

17. R. H. Benson, *L'amitié de Jésus Christ* (Paris: Perrin, 1923) XI-XII.

18. One might wonder about the literary genre of chapter 10 of John's Gospel. We usu-

ally speak of it as a parable. In the strict sense, this term denotes a story that, through the persons and situations it depicts, illustrates or is the point of departure for a teaching: "Likewise . . . in the same way," etc. Chapter 10 of the Fourth Gospel does not exactly fit this framework. Nor is it an allegory, a story in which each element symbolizes something else. (Note that these two types are not entirely separate: there are sometimes allegorical elements in a parable.) This is why we speak here of an enigma, a story whose meaning must be divined.

19. Two other extracts from this chapter are read on the Fourth Sunday of Easter of Years B (John 10:11-18) and C (John 10:27-30).

20. In the Fourth Gospel, chapter 10 follows the story of the healing of the man born blind and the reactions of the Pharisees (John 9). In their eyes, Jesus is not the Messiah, and cannot be: "We know that God spoke to Moses, but we do not know where this one is from" (John 9:29). Jesus responds to this not by giving proofs, but by a solemn and peremptory declaration: "Truly, I assure you . . . ."

21. With the Gospels of the Samaritan woman (John 4:4-42) and of Lazarus (John 11:1-45), that of the man blind since birth (John 9:1-41) was one of the three great texts in the final preparation of the catechumens for baptism. See *Days of the Lord: Lent*, vol. 2, Third, Fourth, and Fifth Sundays, Year A.

22. Even a city-dweller can appreciate the appropriateness of these features, if he or she has ever tried to approach a flock of sheep: inside the sheepfold, they stampede, running into each other, to get far away from the gate; outside, they try to run out of reach of the stranger.

23. Jesus thus implicitly says that he is the new Moses, responding to what the Pharisees said to the blind man: "We know that God spoke to Moses" (John 9:29).

24. Jesus can undoubtedly point to the crowd of little ones—"the lambs"—that surround him. Thus he can present to those who oppose him an argument *ad hominem*. Of course, in itself, the success of a preacher in attracting a following is not a sure basis for judging his legitimacy, his being sent by God, the value of his teaching. Success might lead one to wonder, but statistics are not in themselves part of the rule of discernment.

25. John 3:16; 4:14; 6:27-40; 10:28; 12:25.

26. J.-H. Newman (1801-90), *Douze sermons sur le Christ*, trans. P. Leyris (Paris: Eglof, 1943) 54.

Year B: Children of God Under the Staff of Christ—Pages 140-146

1. This is the "kerygma": see n. 2, p. 331.

2. It is of Paul that Festus is speaking, presenting the imprisoned apostle to King Agrippa and his sister Bernice: "Instead, [his accusers] had some issues with him about their own religion and about a certain Jesus who had died but who Paul claimed was alive" (Acts 25:19).

3. This speech of Peter's is the third recounted in the Acts of the Apostles.

4. The Acts of the Apostles has been called "The Gospel of the Holy Spirit" because of the experience of the Spirit among the apostles, then in the various Christian communities, in Jerusalem and beyond Judea, even in Rome, the capital of the empire.

5. It was actually the Sanhedrin who condemned Jesus and handed him over to Pilate to carry out the sentence.

6. On this, see the article in *Vocabulaire de théologie biblique* (Paris: Cerf, 1970) col. 827-32.

7. Acts 3:6; 4:10, 30. Christians are those who invoke the Lord's name (Acts 9:14, 21; 22:16; 1 Cor 12:2).

8. The *Hallel* was composed of the psalms of praise (hence the name), 112-17 according to the Greek Bible and the Vulgate, 113-18 according to the numbering of the Hebrew Bible. The first is the one usually followed in modern Bibles, and it is used in the Eastern Churches and the Roman liturgy.

9. "Then, after singing a hymn, they went out to the Mount of Olives" (Matt 26:30; Mark 14:26).

10. "Then beginning with Moses and all the prophets, he interpreted to them what referred to him in all the scriptures" (Luke 24:27).

11. See n. 7, p. 332.

12. No fewer than 123 times. Ps 136, with its refrain "For his mercy endures forever" is the best example.

13. See M. Morgen, "Les épîtres de Jean," in *Cahiers Evangile* 62 (1988); F. Smyth-Florentin, "Voyez quel grand amour le Père nous a donné," in *Assemblées du Seigneur*, 2nd series, 25 (Paris: Publications de Saint-André—Cerf, 1969) 32-38.

14. P. Teilhard de Chardin (1881–1955), cited in Cl. Cuénot, *Pierre Teilhard de Chardin. Les grandes étapes de son évolution* (Paris: Plon, 1958) 467.

15. The two syllables of the Latin word *Deus.*

16. Augustine (354–430), *Commentaire de la Première épître de saint Jean*, IV, 6, in *Sources chrétiennes* 75 (Paris: Cerf, 1961) 233.

17. See n. 18, pp. 332-333.

18. One day, on a mountain road, as some people were walking along, being guided by a shepherd. On the side of the road lay a dead sheep. The shepherd went over to it and came back, saying: "It is not mine." The others, city-dwellers, could not believe their ears: "The animal is not marked. All sheep look alike. How can you say that it is not one of your flock?" The shepherd was indignant: "All sheep look alike! I know my own." Jesus must have known real shepherds.

19. This is what God calls himself: Yahweh (Exod 3:14). Whatever its precise meaning, "I am" ("who I am," "who I will be") it denotes something of absolute value in revelation. God alone can say "I am." Modern Bibles often write it in capital letters: "I AM." See the article in *Vocabulaire de théologie biblique* (Paris: Cerf, 1970) col. 1387-90.

20. See also Ps 23:1; Jer 31:9.

21. Gregory the Great (pope from 590–604), *Homélie sur l'Evangile* 14, 4, in *La Liturgie des Heures, 2. Carême et Temps pascal*, pp. 580–581.

22. Ibid.

23. Commission Francophone Cistercienne, *Tropaire pour les dimanches*, Le Livre d'Heures d'En-Calcat (Dourgne: 1980) 36 (Fiche de chant I LH 175).

Year C: The Great Multitude Gathered by the True Shepherd—
Pages 147–152

1. On the day of Pentecost many people from different parts of the world were converted, following the first announcement of the resurrection. All were Jews or proselytes, that is, those joined to the chosen people by observance of the Law and circumcision (Acts 2:1-41). Yet this diversity, which the author emphasizes, has a connotation of universality. On their return home, these first converts shared their discovery with others and formed the core of small Christian communities in pagan countries.

The persecution that followed Stephen's martyrdom forced the disciples to scatter, with only the apostles remaining in Jerusalem. Thus Philip came to announce the gospel in Samaria, where many converted. Peter and John were sent to lay their hands on the newly baptized (Acts 8:5-19). Samaritans were not Gentiles, properly speaking, but they were regarded as such—or worse—by the orthodox Jewish community: they did not go to the Temple in Jerusalem and had their own sanctuary on Mount Gerazim.

Peter resolved to baptize the Gentiles because the Spirit had visibly descended on Cornelius and his family. This led to some trouble in the Jerusalem community: Peter had to justify his actions (Acts 10:9–11:18). After several conflicts the question was resolved, in principle, at the Council of Jerusalem, which recognized that the gospel could be announced to the Gentiles (Acts 15:7-29).

2. From this point on, Acts follows the evangelization that led Paul to Rome, the capital of the pagan world. At the beginning of this, his first missionary journey, the apostle abandoned his first name of Saul (or Saoul) for that of Paul (Paulus in Latin, Paulos in Greek). Acts calls him Saul 9 times, Paul 128 times.

3. Acts 13:14; 14:1; 16:13; 17:10, 17; 18:4, 19; 19:8.

4. On reaching Rome, he will ask prominent Jews to come to the place where he is held prisoner, and they will respond to his invitation (Acts 28:17, 23).

5. Paul's speech is recorded in vv. 16-42. The Lectionary omits them in order to come immediately to what happened after this first encounter (the invitation to Paul and Barnabas to return to speak on the following sabbath) and what happened at the second.

6. Luke 3:6 cites this text.

7. Luke never misses a chance to talk about the reception of the good news by some of them, sometimes many of them: Luke 1-2; 13:16; 19:9; Acts 2:41, 47; 4:4; 5:14; 6:1, 7; 18:8; 21:20; 28:24.

8. See n. 5, above.

9. He does so at greatest length in Rom (9:1–11:36).

10. The others: Rev 14:1-4; 15:1-4; 19:10. All four point to the ultimate vision of chapter 21 (the heavenly Jerusalem).

11. The Gospels testify to this (Mark 11:25; Luke 18:11). Ancient paintings, such as those of the catacombs, always picture people standing while praying. This stance is still the traditional one in the East. The Roman liturgy has restored some favor to it. Heb (10:11) says: "Every priest stands daily at his ministry."

12. We no longer speak, and quite rightly, of liturgical "ornaments," but rather "vestments." They enable one to see what position the various "actors" in the liturgy have, especially the one who presides: thus they have the value of visible signs, utterly indispensable in a structured assembly, an image of the Church, one body with different members (1 Cor 12:12-31). At the same time, the "liturgical vestments" show that those who wear them exercise a ministry—a service, a function—that goes beyond what they are themselves. Not that "liturgical vestments" are depersonalizing, like uniforms; they are not like garments an actor puts on to become another persona in the theater. Through the person who wears them, they point to Another. We sometimes forget that all liturgy is a collection of signs. In a very general way, to speak of the "presider of the liturgy," "concelebrating priests," "other ministers," "the assembly," "the choir" of monks and religious, means precisely this.

13. Matt 21:1-11; Mark 11:1-10; Luke 19:28-38; John 12:12-15.

14. Some exegetes see the palms as evoking the feast of Booths (*Succôth*) celebrated in Sept.–Oct., which certain Christian communities would have preserved for a while. On the other hand, Ch. Augrain, "La vision de la foule innombrable: Ap 7, 9.14-17," in *Assemblées du Seigneur*, 2nd series, no. 25 (Paris: Publication de Saint-André—Cerf, 1969) 43, argues that an allusion to the feast of Booths cannot be proven. Whatever the case may be, the triumphal character of the procession is evident enough.

15. Monastic liturgy calls the gathering of the community the "station." It takes place in one wing of the cloister near the church; one processes into the church when all are in their places.

16. See also Rev 5:10; 1 Pet 2:9.

17. See: Vatican II, Dogmatic Constitution on the Church (*Lumen Gentium*), nos. 10-11, 34.

18. Here the evocation of the feast of Booths is particularly suggestive. During this feast, the people live in tents (or booths). Then there will be only one, that of God, where all will be admitted. See n. 15, p. 335.

19. Vatican II, Constitution on the Sacred Liturgy, no. 6.

20. Ibid., no. 10.

21. Ibid., no. 8.

22. It is in the nature of things that every liturgy will begin and end in a defined manner. Paul, it is true, speaks of life as a "sacrifice holy and acceptable to God" (Rom 12:1) and of the proclamation of the gospel as "worship in the spirit" (Rom 1:9). But he does not say that these are liturgies in the precise sense we give this term. Actually, in many cases, Paul uses liturgical language, for example to speak of his missionary activity (Rom 15:16).

23. The liturgical year is animated by a similar dynamism that points to the day when God will be all in all. See: *Days of the Lord*, vol. 1, pp. 11-13.

24. One image alone will not express the mystery. This is why John uses different terms successively, or even at the same time: shepherd, sheepgate, lamb, and even lion (Rev 5:5-6).

25. Between the preceding sayings on the good shepherd and these here, John reports the discussions on Jesus provoked by the question: "How long are you going to keep us in suspense? If you are the Messiah, tell us plainly" (John 10:19-26). This section of the Fourth Gospel is strongly reminiscent of Jesus' trial before the Sanhedrin, especially as recorded by Luke (22:66).

26. John 6:39; 17:12; 18:9.

27. Sometimes editions of the Bible will write "ONE" in capital letters.

28. And also: John 8:16, 29; 14:9, 10; 17:11.

29. Gregory of Nazianzus (329-89), *Discours*, II, 117, in *Sources chrétiennes* 247 (Paris: Cerf 197) 239-41.

Fifth Sunday of Easter

Year A: The Risen Jesus—Way, Truth, Life—the Cornerstone—
Pages 153-161

1. Even at Jerusalem they belonged to different synagogues.

2. Targums: see n. 12, p. 326.

3. This episode contrasts with the pictures of the community painted earlier (Acts 2:42-47; 4:32-35; 5:12-16). There, the sharing of goods posed no problem; however, the community was homogeneous and smaller.

4. "Diaconate" (from the Greek *diakonia*) is a synonym for "service." Thus "deacon" (*diakonia*) etymologically means "servant," or "server" (at table).

5. One finds, in Acts and in the apostolic Letters, those in charge in the community called "overseers" (bishops), "elders" (presbyters), "servers" (deacons). But it is not easy to define the proper role of each, and still less to structure them into a hierarchical scheme.

6. Thus Philip, "one of the Seven," who received Paul into his home in Caesarea, is called "the evangelist" (Acts 21:8).

7. Philip evangelized Samaria (Acts 8:5); Stephen preached and performed signs and wonders (Acts 6:8).

8. This receives ample testimony in Stephen's famous speech (Acts 7:2-53).

9. Vatican II, whose Constitutions, Decrees, and Declarations were approved by the pope "in the Holy Spirit" has played a significant role.

10. John XXIII, Speech on the Opening of the Council (October 11, 1962).

11. "Dogma" is the ensemble of the truths of the faith contained in revelation (Scripture and Tradition) and propounded in the Church and through it, whether by the teaching of the ordinary and universal magisterium of the pope and the bishops, or by the "extraordinary" magisterium of the pope or an ecumenical council (e.g., Vatican II). Certain truths of the faith are sometimes solemnly defined by a council (papal infallibility, at Vatican I, in 1870) or a pope (assumption of the Virgin Mary, by Pius XII, November 1, 1950).

Therefore, there is a "development of dogma," i.e., of the coming to awareness and the progressive explanations of the truths of the faith contained in revelation. This "development" comes about by different causes: events in the Church, particularly challenges to the truths it teaches (from Nicaea in 325 to Trent in 1545-63, the first twenty ecumenical councils arose from confrontations with heresy), the need to respond to the concerns of the time (Vatican I in 1870, called to clarify the doctrine on the Church, which was not carried out, due to the war that interrupted its deliberations; and above all, Vatican II), the life of prayer (particularly the liturgy), the faith of the Christian people, theological and spiritual reflection in all its forms, preaching.

"Dogma" and the "development of dogma" do not change the objective content of the faith.

See Vatican II, Dogmatic Constitution on Divine Revelation (*Dei verbum*) and Dogmatic Constitution on the Church (*Lumen Gentium*), particularly chapter three (nos. 18-28)

12. Like everything that lasts in history, the development of dogma and its happy effects have not followed an ever-ascending line. They have known times of stagnation, crises and, sometimes, and in some places, even regressions. All rebirth, every leap forward has its explanation and cause in a return to the living sources of Scripture and the living tradition of the Church. We may simply point to the recent biblical, patristic, liturgical, pastoral, and spiritual renewals, that typically go hand in hand. Stagnation or paralysis in one of these areas leads to stagnation or paralysis in the others. Likewise, a renewal in one of them inspires a progression in the others.

13. This does not warrant calling the apostolic faith, catechesis, and preaching of the Gospels—especially of John, the "theologian" or the other New Testament writings, especially Paul's Letters—"primitive," in the pejorative sense of the term. Isn't it true that these Letters, though addressed to Gentile believers who were but recent converts, are often too difficult for Christians today, though they are rooted in the multisecular culture and tradition of the Church?

14 Matt 21:42; Mark 12:10-11; Luke 20:17.

15. Even before the writing of the New Testament, there were "collections" (*Testimonia*) of texts on the theme of the stone.

16. John 2:18-21; 1 Cor 3:16-17; 2 Cor 6:16-18; Eph 2:18-22; 2 Tim 2:19; Rev 3:12, 21-22.

17. Vatican II many times recalls the doctrine of the "common priesthood of the faithful": Dogmatic Constitution on the Church (*Lumen Gentium*), nos. 9, 10, 11, 26, 31, 34; Decree on the Apostolate of Lay People (*Apostolicam actuositatem*), nos., 2, 3; Decree on the Ministry and Life of Priests (*Presbyterorum ordinis*), no. 2; Decree on the Church's Missionary Activity (*Ad Gentes Divinitus*), no. 15.

18. At the Church's beginnings, there were few apostles. But the communities they founded had a missionary aspect, and this explains the extraordinary universal spreading of the gospel. This has been true at other times and places, too. Inversely, when Christian communities, however well supplied they are with priests, are concerned only with themselves, evangelization experiences a slowdown, and these local Churches become more and more tainted with paralysis: the Church's vitality and its missionary dynamism go hand in hand.

19. Bede the Venerable (ca. 672-735), *Commentaire sur la Première lettre de saint Pierre* 2, in *Lectures chrétiennes pour notre temps*, fiche R 5, Abbaye d'Orval, 1972; *La Liturgie des Heures*, vol. 2, Monday of the Third week of Easter, pp. 538-39.

20. One also may look at the meaning they had for the evangelists themselves. They wrote and edited their books in the light of the paschal faith of the Church and its experience: joys, difficulties, temptations of Christian life and of the communities; the search for an authentic evangelical spirituality, etc.

21. We read in succession: John 14:15-21 (Sixth Sunday, Year A); 14:23-29 (Sixth Sunday, Year C); 14:15-16, 23b-26 (Pentecost, Year C); 15:1-8 (Fifth Sunday, Year B); 15:9-17 (Sixth Sunday, Year B); 15:26-27; 16:12-15 (Pentecost, Year B); 17:1-11a, 11b-19, 20-26 (Seventh Sunday, Years A, B, C). Also, chapters 15–17 are read almost in their entirety in the Mass from Friday of the Third week to Thursday of the Seventh.

22. Exod 24:9-11; 33:18.

23. Augustine (354–430), *La cité de Dieu*, X, XXXIII, 2, in *Oeuvres de saint Augustin*, Bibliothèque augustinienne, 34 (Bruges: Desclée de Brouwer, 1959) 551–56.

24. Thus, for example, the word "society," when it is introduced into the definiton of the Church: "society of the faithful under the authority of the pope and the bishops." This definition is very clear; it uses the same idea of "society" that can be applied to any organized group. But it is precisely in this way that the definition is deficient, even if it adds that the Church was "founded" by Christ, and that the bishops were "instituted" by him.

25. Thus Vatican II, Dogmatic Constitution on the Church (*Lumen Gentium*), no. 6.

26. Ibid.

27. Vatican II, Decree on Ecumenism (*Unitatis redintegratio*), no. 6.

28. Vatican II, Constitution on the Sacred Liturgy (*Sacrosanctum concilium*), no. 1.

29. Vatican II, Dogmatic Constitution on the Church (*Lumen Gentium*), nos. 9, 4, 21.

Year B: *Live On in Me and Bear Fruit!*—Pages 162–169

1. Acts 2:42-47; 4:32-35; 5:12-16.

2. Acts 6:7; 12:24; 19:20.

3. There are three accounts of this conversion in Acts: 9:1-9; 22:4-11; 26:9-18. See also Gal 1:13-24.

4. See n. 17, p. 328 and n. 9, p. 352.

5. Acts 13:1–28:31.

6. Acts tells of Paul's three missionary journeys. From Antioch of Syria, he went—first journey—to Cyprus, Pamphylia, and Lycaonia, returning to Antioch (Acts 13:4–14:28). The conflict about circumcision led Paul and his companions to go to Jerusalem where the answer to the question was settled (Acts 15:1), after which the apostle returned to Antioch (Acts 15:1-35).

From Antioch, Paul left for a second journey that led him to Lycaonia, Galatia, Troas, Macedonia (Philippi, Thessalonica), Athens, and Corinth, returning to Antioch by passing through Ephesus (Acts 15:36–18:21).

Third journey: Galatia, Ephesus, Macedonia (staying in Corinth for the winter), Miletus, and returning to Jerusalem where Paul was imprisoned (Acts 18:22–22:30).

Finally, taken to Rome to be judged by the emperor, Paul reached the city by passing through Malta, Crete, Syracuse in Sicily, and Rhegium, at last landing at Puteoli (Acts 27:1–28:14).

Most editions of the Bible and the New Testament have one or more geographical maps on which these journeys are laid out.

7. Luke, in this passage, cites a series of events of which the apostle himself, in Gal 1:18-21, gave a detailed account. Between the first preaching at Damascus and the conflict that arose with the Jews of that city, he dwelt for two years in Arabia, where in solitude,

the convert deepened his growing faith in the light of Scripture. On his return to Damascus, he had to flee the city where he stayed for three years. Afterward, he went to Jerusalem to meet Peter, with whom he stayed for 15 days.

8. There is nothing inquisitorial about this. The point is not to preserve the community from dubious elements, but to force the candidate for admission to recognize the seriousness of its obligation by giving as clear an idea as possible of its demands. Such a concern is obvious in Benedict's "Procedure for admitting brothers" (*Rule*, ch. 58). One does not grant the postulant's first request for admission; one must show great reserve. If, nevertheless, he perseveres in his request, he is admitted first to the guest quarters, then to the novitiate. During a probationary period, one will see whether he is made for the monastic life. The *Rule* is read to him a first, second, and third time, and he is asked after each reading if he wants to continue or to leave, as he is free to do. Consequently, he can decide whether or not to make his profession with full knowledge. The catechumenate for baptism and the preparation for marriage fall into the same perspective: the respect owed both to the people involved and to the sacraments.

9. It is said in Acts that his name means "son of encouragement." Actually, *Barnabas* (in Greek) is the transcription of *Bar-nabu* or "son of Nabu" in Aramean.

10. Barnabas stayed with Paul till the Council of Jerusalem (Acts 15:2-30; Gal 2:1, 9). Then they had a falling out and went their separate ways (Acts 15:36-40).

11. The whole history of the Church witnesses to this: authentic mystics, far from avoiding these verifications, sought them out most submissively. And this all the more so when they benefited by the greatest graces.

12. He was one of them when Stephen was stoned (Acts 6:9; 7:58; 8:3; 9:1). He would often find them on his road: Acts 21:27; 24:19.

13. To pass from the one's road to a second, then a third, then back to the first, etc., is not a good way to get anywhere, and may end up turning one in circles. This is why, for example, when one passes from one religious institution to another—which may be perfectly legitimate and even profitable—one goes back to the beginning, i.e., the novitiate.

14. Augustine (354-430), *Commentaire de la Premiè épître de saint Jean*, VI, 3, in *Sources chrétiennes* 75 (Paris: Cerf, 1961) 283.

15. John 14:13-14; 15:7; 16:23-24.

16. Augustine, o.c. (note 14), ibid., 301.

17. This verb (*menein* in Greek) occurs 68 times in John's writings, 118 times in the whole New Testament; 11 times in John 15:1-17.

18. The Son dwells in the Father, and the Father in the Son (John 14:10-11; 15:10).

19. John the Baptist saw the Spirit descend from heaven onto Jesus and stay there, proving that he was the Son of God (John 1:32-34).

20. 1 John 3:18-24: second reading.

21. 1 John 4:16; John 6:56; 15:7, 9-10; 1 John 2:6, 27-28; 3:6.

22. Isa 27:2-5; Jer 2:21; 12:10; Ezek 15:1-8; 19:10-14; Hos 10:1; Ps 80:9-17; article "Vigne" in *Vocabulaire de théologie biblique* (Paris: Cerf, 1970) col. 1355-57.

23. The workers sent out at various hours of the day (Matt 20:1-15); the two sons, the one who said "yes" but did not go to work, the one who said "no" then repented (Matt 21:28-31); the murderous vineyard workers (Matt 21:33-41). Also, the Synoptics report Jesus' saying during the Last Supper: "I tell you, from now on I shall not drink this fruit of the vine until the day when I drink it with you new in the kingdom of my Father" (Matt 26:29; Mark 14:25; Luke 22:18).

24. It would be more appropriate to speak here of the "vine-stock"—on which the branches grow—whereas "vine" denotes the assortment of vine-stocks that make it up.

25. This is not really an allegory, in which every detail has a specific meaning. See n. 18, pp. 332-333.

26. Cyril of Alexandria (ca. 380–444), *Commentaire sur l'Evangile de Jean*, 10, 2, in *Liturgie des Heures*, vol. 2, Tuesday of the Fifth Week of Eastertime, p. 645.

27. John 2:11, 23; 6:2, 14; 7:31; 11:47; 20:30.

28. Matt 12:33; Luke 6:44.

29. Eucharistic liturgy, presentation of the cup.

30. Commission Francophone Cistercienne, *Tropaires des dimanches*, Le Livre d'Heures d'En-Calcat (Dourgne, 1980) 38.

31. This union of the disciples with the resurrected is the subject of John 15:1-8, 9-17 (Fifth and Sixth Sundays of Easter, Year B). John 15:18–16:11 deals with the relation of the disciples with the world (from Saturday of the Fifth Week to Tuesday of the Sixth). The rest of chapter 16 speaks of life "in the Spirit" after Christ's departure (Fifth and Sixth Sundays, Year C; Pentecost, Year B; and Trinity, Year C).

32. Commission Francophone Cistercienne, *Prières au fil des heures*, Vivante liturgie 99 (Paris: Publications de Saint-André—Centurion, 1982) 101.

Year C: "A Little While . . . Now . . . Soon"—Pages 170–177

1. See above, n. 6, p. 338.

2. One must look both at the letters to the community he founded and the one to Rome, where he would go.

3. There are two cities with the name of Antioch: one in Syria, Paul's starting and returning point; the other in Pisidia, in the Roman province of Galatia (in present-day Turkey).

Lystra, in Lycaonia, was Timothy's birthplace. Paul healed a man there who was lame from birth (Acts 14:8-10; 2 Tim 3:11). At Iconium (today Konya), the two missionaries were nearly stoned (Acts 14:4-5). Perga, in Pamphylia, is some eight miles from the port of Antalya (in Turkey).

4. Acts 3:5, 8, 23; 6:12; 23:14; 24:1; 25:15.

5. Acts 11:30; 15:2, 4, 22, 23; 16:4; 20:17; 21:18.

6. Acts 13:3. Luke (6:12-13) says that before choosing the Twelve, Jesus spent a night on the mountain, in prayer.

7. J. Dupont, "La première organisation des Eglises: Ac 14, 21-27," in *Assemblées du Seigneur*, 2nd series, no. 26 (Paris: Publications de Saint-André—Cerf, 1973) 64.

8. Acts 15:41; 16:5; 18:23. See: Matt 10:22; 24:13; Luke 21:12-19.

9. Thus he sent Timothy to the Thessalonians to strengthen them and encourage them in their faith, "so that no one be disturbed in these afflictions" (1 Thess 3:1-3).

10. Some of these letters were sent to several communities, in the manner of circular letters. The same concern inspired the letters that have come to us from James, Peter, John and Jude.

11. Such was the case particularly for the Corinthian Church with regard to serious disorder in the assembly (1 Cor 11) and grave misconduct for which those in authority had to shoulder the blame (1 Cor 5). But in almost every letter, we see the Apostle call on his authority to reprove his correspondents on various points, rectify their errors or deviational tendencies, decide their quarrels, etc.

12. Thus titles such as primate of Gaul or Aquitaine, or patriarch of Venice or Portugal.

13. The patriarchates, for example.

14. Thus the national episcopal conferences, even if they do not enjoy true jurisdiction over the whole of the country.

15. Among these innovative adaptations, one can look to the institution, in Zaire, or parishes run by laity, called "Bakambi" in the diocese if Kinshasa. In instituting them, Cardi-

nal Malula wrote: "In entrusting certain parishes to the laity, we are going beyond the limits of present legislation. We judge that this action is justified because of the particular circumstances of the archdiocese of Kinshasa: the lack of priests, and the urgent need for Africanization." See A. Turck, "Des ministères pour quelle Egilse?: Au Zaïre des paroisses officiellement confiées a des laïcs," in *Communautés et liturgies* 58 (1976) 32–37.

16. Mgr. Bakole wa Ilunga, archbishop of Kananga (Zaire), "A situation nouvelle, pastorale nouvelle," ibid. 57 (1975) 442.

17. In their present form, they date from the end of the 1st c.

18. Especially Hellenism and gnosticism. "Hellenism"—a rather vague and general term—refers to the current of Greek thought, elevated as it was, that tried to understand and express Being through philosophy. Christianity could not ignore it, since the gospel was preached in Greek to people imbued with Greek culture. John had to force Christians back to the essential: the knowledge, in faith, of the Son of God made man.

Gnosticism was characterized by a dualism that opposed nature and flesh, the sources of evil, with spirit, that alone, freed from the flesh, could allow one to come to knowledge and contemplation. Here, as well, John reacted by vigorously affirming the realism of the incarnation: "The Word became flesh" (John 1:14); Jesus has given us his flesh to eat, his blood to drink (John 6:51, 54).

19. "Apocalypse," another name for the book, means precisely "Revelation" (from the Greek verb *apokaluptein*, "to raise the veil," "to reveal").

We read another passage from it (Rev 21:10-14; 22-23) on the Sixth Sunday of Easter, Year C. Part of the book's finale (Rev 22:12-14, 16-17, 20) is read on the Seventh Sunday of Easter, Year C.

20. Ezek 40–42; Isa 65:17; 66:22.

21. See the article "Mer" in *Vocabulaire de théologie biblique* (Paris: Cerf, 1970) col. 740–42 and in *Dictionnaire encyclopédique de la Bible* (Paris: Brepols, 1987) 809.

22. "God saw how good it was" (Gen 1:13, 18, 21, 25). "God looked at everything he had made; and he found it very good" (Gen 1:31).

23. Job 25:7-14; Prov 8:23-31; Sir 42:15–43:33.

24. The canticle of Daniel 3:57-88 is found in *La Liturgie des Heures.*

25. P. Teilhard de Chardin, "La messe sur le monde," in *Hymne de l'univers* (Paris: Seuil, 1961) 30 and 31–32.

26. Exegetes claim that Jesus' first "farewell discourse," as it is found today in John's Gospel (13:31-14:31), is a composite text, edited and elaborated over time.

The interest of such studies cannot be denied, but they constitute no more than a preliminary to our hearing of the Word in the liturgy.

27. See John 2:21 (the "sign" of Cana); 11:4, 40 (the raising of Lazarus).

28. 7:33; 8:21; 12:35; 14:19; 16:16.

29. On the site known as Qumran, some seven miles south of present-day Jericho, there lived, in the 1st c. B.C., an important Jewish religious community—today we would call it monastic—whose communal life was based on the practice of humility, justice, and law, of "affectionate charity."

See the articles "Qumrân" and "Esséniens" in *Dictionnaire encyclopédique de la Bible* (Paris: Brepols, 1987) 1085–88 and 439.

30. Matt 5:39-47.

31. The Greek word used here—*entole*—means "commandment," "precept," but understood in a way that also means "mandate," "way," i.e., "way of life."

32. John 15:9-17; 17:23; 1 John 2:5; 4:10, 12, 17; Rom 13:8-12; 1 Cor 13; Gal 6:10.

33. Clement of Rome (pope ca. 90 to 100), *Lettre aux Corinthiens*, 2, 4–8, in *Sources chrétiennes* 167 (Paris: Cerf, 1971) 103.

34. Masses for various needs and occasions: for the Church, prayer after Communion.

Sixth Sunday of Easter

Year A: The Spirit—Presence of the Lord—Pages 178–183

1. Acts 8:1-4.
2. Acts 6:1-7: first reading for the previous Sunday, pp. 208–11.
3. Jesus had passed through Samaria, and for two days he announced the good news to the inhabitants of Shechem, many of whom believed in him (John 4:1-42). Certainly, the Samaritans would not have forgotten this encounter; they were well prepared to receive Philip's teaching.
4. Luke emphasizes that joy goes along with the reception of the Word: Acts 2:46; 5:41; 8:8, 39; 13:48, 52; 16:34.
5. The Lectionary, in order to come to this without delay, has omitted vv. 9-13, where one sees a certain Simon, "who used to practice magic," become a convert, receive baptism and become one of the most devoted followers of Philip's preaching.
6. Peter and John enjoyed undisputed authority among the apostles: John 20:3; Acts 3:1, 3; 4:13-19.

Jesus had sent out the seventy-two in pairs (Luke 10:1). It would seem, according to Acts, that this was customary in the primitive Church (Acts 11:30; 12:25; 13:46; 15:22, 39-40). It agreed with the prescription of the Law that there must be at least two witnesses (Deut 19:15).

7. In Western tradition, the bishops, "successors of the apostles," were, until recently, the "ordinary" ministers of confirmation, the sacrament that bestows the Holy Spirit. Even then, however, there were exceptions. A cardinal who was not a bishop and certain priests who were in charge of an area that did not constitute a diocese had the full right to perform the sacrament of confirmation within the limits of their jurisdiction. Still others, by a concession from the Holy See, had the same faculty (Code of Canon Law promulgated by Benedict XV, Pentecost 1917, p. 782).

The new Code promulgated by John Paul II on January 25, 1983, reaffirms these regulations, but it adds: "If necessary, the diocesan bishop may concede the faculty of administrating this sacrament to one or more specific priests," who may be assisted, in each instance, by other priests (no. 884). This is the common practice today, but it does not contradict the Latin tradition. Moreover, one should note the reasons for this extension of the practice. It allows for more regular and worthy celebrations of the sacrament, whereas previously, in many parishes, the bishop could only come to confirm every two or three years, or the confirmands had to come together from several parishes, sometimes numbering in the hundreds. In the Eastern Churches, priests have always been the ordinary ministers of confirmation, which may be given even to infants, after baptism.

8. In the 3rd c., the rite that constituted the second stage of baptism was called the "seal of the Holy Spirit" (Sphragis in Greek, sigillum in Latin). Our title for the second sacrament of Christian initiation—"confirmation"—says the same thing. The term is found in the second canon of the first Council of Orange, in 441.

9. The letter is addressed to Christians who live among the Gentiles "in Pontus, Galatia, Cappadocia, Asia, and Bithynia" (1 Pet 1:1), provinces for the most part evangelized by Paul himself or his colleagues.

10. Certainly, not all those who are nominally Christian will be brought back to the practice of their faith. Yet the way the community practices its Sunday and paschal demands can have a great impact on the forces of de-Christianization. Hence the need for what might be called a "second evangelization," a new missionary impulse among those Christian communities which find themselves isolated in countries that used to be Christian.

11. "Call not alliance what this people calls alliance, and fear not, nor stand in awe of what they fear. But with the Lord of hosts make your alliance—for him be your fear and your awe" (Isa 8:12-13).

The psalms often appeal to God's holiness, recalling that he is the Most High, the Rock, etc., and asking him not to let the wicked blaspheme his name by acting as if he counted for nothing.

12. In the "Our Father," we ask first: "Hallowed be thy name." The other petitions flow from this: "Thy kingdom come, thy will be done . . . deliver us from evil." "For the kingdom, the power and the glory are yours, now and forever."

13. Legendary stories, on the other hand, often put injurious and insulting words in the mouths of the accused.

14. *Martyre de saint Polycarpe*, X, in *Sources chrétiennes* 10 (Paris: Cerf, 1951) 257.

Polycarp, bishop of Smyrna, was martyred on February 23, 155, at age 86.

It was in the stadium to which he had been taken that he confessed his faith before the proconsul Statius Quadratus, in the midst of an unruly crowd that had come to watch the games with the wild animals. One can understand why he would have held these people to be unworthy to hear his defense. Unable to be touched by the flames of the pyre, he was killed with a sword, his body then being tossed on the fire.

15. John 14:15, 21, 23; 15:10, 12, 17.

16. The expression "on that day," particularly used by the prophets—Isa 2:17; 4:1-2; 7:18, 20, 21, 23; Jer 4:9; Zech 2:15; 12:4, 6, 8, 9, 11; 13:1; etc.—in some way points toward the end of the time of hope inspired by such and such an oracle. Faith today in the presence of the Lord Jesus is also turned toward his manifestation on the day of his coming.

17. Bernard (1090-1153), *Sermon sur le Cantique des cantique*, 74, 6, in *Oeuvres mystiques de saint Bernard* (translation A. Beguin), (Paris: Seuil, 1953) 766-67.

18. Eucharistic Prayer II.

Year B: The Love of the Lord Fills the Universe—Pages 184-191

1. The very length of the story (Acts 10:1-48) shows how much importance the author accords to it. Peter, in order to justify his conduct to the community in Jerusalem, tells them what happened (Acts 11:1-18). He also recalls it briefly during the discussion of the Council of Jerusalem (Acts 15:7-11).

2. Lydda is 11 miles southeast of Tel-Aviv, 22 miles from Jerusalem.

3. Joppa (or Jaffa) is 16 miles from Lydda, on the Mediterranean.

4. He was an officer of the "Italica" cohort (Acts 10:1), whose composition was mostly Italian.

5. "Proselytes" were the non-Jews who, after their conversion, were circumcised.

6. "To fear God" and "to act uprightly," i.e., to obey the prescriptions of the Law, was the ruling principle among those who "feared God."

7. Certain non-Christians will sometimes say: "I am more Christian than you are." So too will the nonpracticing often speak to those who regularly attend Mass. But the first will not tolerate an attempt to make them "anonymous Christians," because they regard this as an attempt at being incorporated.

8. Passion can make one commit actions that remain crimes, however extenuated by circumstances.

Without going so far, what can one not do under the pretext that "everything is permitted when one loves" or "when one is loved"?

9. Augustine (354-430), *Confessions*, III, I, 1, in *Oeuvres de saint Augustin* 13, Bibliothèque augustinienne (Bruges: Desclée de Brouwer, 1962) 363-65.

10. *Commentaire de la Première épître de saint Jean*, treatise VII, 8, (P. Agaesse) in *Sources chrétiennes* 75 (Paris: Cerf, 1961) 329.

11. "This text has often been abused by being understood in a permissive sense, as if the perfect were freed from all law. Augustine means something quite different. Relying on the gospel and on the letters of Paul and John, he professes that the whole Law may be summarized in the double precept of love, not because love can dispense with following the other commandments, but because it expresses their fullness and assures their fulfillment. True freedom does not consist in following one's caprices and instincts, but in being freed by grace from the tyranny of the passions and depending only on God, as Augustine expresses in this other concise formula: *Eris liber, si fueris servus: liber peccati, servus justitiae* ("You will be free, if you make yourself a slave: free from sin, slave to justice") in *Joan. Evang.*, XLI, 8 (*Patrologie latine*, vol. 35, col. 1696). Moreover, as we have noted in our introduction (pp. 80–81), the formula, understood in its context, far from encouraging an excessive indulgence, justifies the rigors and demands of true love" (P. Agaesse, ibid., 328–29, n. 1).

12. *Commentaire de la Première épître de saint Jean*, treatise X, 7, ibid., 427.

13. Augustine (354–430), *Homélie sur l'Ancien Testament*, 34 in *La Liturgie des Heures*, vol. 2, Temps pascal, Tuesday III, p. 546.

14. John 15:1-8: Gospel for the Fifth Sunday.

15. "As the Father has loved me": the verb is not in the present tense. It is not therefore a question of the eternal love the Father has for his Son, but the love the Father bears him for what he has done at a particular time.

16. Gregory the Great (pope from 590 to 604), *Homélie* 27, 1, in S. Bouquet, *L'Evangile selon saint jean explique par les Pères*, Les pères dans la foi (Paris: Desclée de Brouwer, 1985) 119–20.

17. Matt 20:26-27; 23:11; Mark 9:35; 10:43-44; Luke 22:26.

18. Benedict (d. ca. 547), *Rule*, chapter four.

19. B.-M. Chevignard, *La doctrine spirituelle de l'Evangile*, Foi vivante 4 (Paris: Cerf, 1965) 100.

20. Vatican II, Dogmatic Constitution on the Church (*Lumen Gentium*), no. 11.

21. Vatican II, Constitution on the Sacred Liturgy (*Sacrosanctum concilium*), no. 47.

22. Commission Francophone Cistercienne, *Tropaires des dimanches*, Le Livre d'Heures d'En-Calcat (Dourgne, 1980) 41.

Year C: The Church of the Risen Lord
and the Life of the Spirit—Pages 192–202

1. Acts 10:34-38.
2. Acts 11:1-8.
3. See n. 6, p. 343.
4. Acts 13:44-51.
5. See n. 3., p. 340.
6. See Gal 2:12; Acts 15:5, 24.
7. Luke simplifies his presentation of the facts. If one refers to what Paul says, he made two visits to Jerusalem: one, three years after his conversion, the other fourteen years later. He emphasizes that nothing was added to the decision of the "council" (Gal 2:1-10). In Acts, by a literary artifice that serves the author's overall project, Paul's first visit seems to be very close to his conversion (Acts 9:27). As for the Council of Jerusalem, it concludes with a decree regarding Paul himself (Acts 15:22-29), whereas he seems to be ignorant of

its existence when later on James speaks to him of it (Acts 21:25). In fact, Luke addresses two distinct controversies at the same time. The first took place in Jerusalem: should the new converts be held to the observance of the Law or not (Gal 2:1-10)? The second, at Antioch, concerned the relations between Christians who came from Judaism and converts from paganism (Gal 2:11-14).

8. One seems to be listening to Paul: Gal 2:15-21; 3:22-26; Rom 11:32; Eph 2:1-10.

9. This question about meat offered to idols (idolothytes) and then sold in the market divided the Corinthians. Paul tells them that, theoretically, there is nothing to forbid them from eating it. But, if some members of the community are scandalized by others who do in fact eat it, charity demands that the latter abstain (1 Cor 8:1-13).

10. This prohibition is found in chapter 17 of Leviticus.

11. A. de Saint-Exupéry, Lettre à un otage, in Oeuvres, Bibliothèque de la Pléiade (Paris: Gallimard, 1965) 404.

12. Acts 21:20-25; Rom 3:21-31; 7:1-6; 14; 1 Cor 8; 10:23-33; Gal 2:11-21; 5:1-12; etc.

13. The pope's formula for promulgating the texts drawn up by Vatican II: "The whole and each of the points which have been enacted in this Constitution (Decree, Declaration) have been pleasing to the Fathers of the council. And by virtue of the apostolic power we hold from Christ, in union with the venerable Fathers, we approve and decree them in the Holy Spirit, and we ordain that what has been established in council may be promulgated for the glory of God."

14. "Christians cherish a feeling of deep solidarity wih the human race and its history" (Vatican II, Pastoral Constitution on the Church in the Modern World, Gaudium et spes, no. 1).

"The sacred council has set out to impart an ever-increasing vigor to the Christian life of the faithful; to adapt more closely to the needs of our age those institutions which are subject to change; to foster whatever can promote union among all who believe in Christ; to strengthen whatever can help to call all mankind into the Church's fold. Accordingly it sees particularly cogent reasons for undertaking the reform and promotion of the liturgy" (Constitution on the Sacred Liturgy, no. 1).

15. Vv. 15-21, omitted in the liturgy, concern the dimensions of the city and the materials—various precious stones—that form the seven foundations of its ramparts and its gates. The symbolism here is obscure; therefore the Lectionary has not retained these verses.

16. Since Sinai (Exod 19), the mountain is the symbolic place of encounters with God and important revelations.

17. Commission Francophone Cistercienne, Tropaires des dimanches, Le Livre d'Heures d'En-Calcat (Dourgne: 1980) 151 (Fiche de chant K 145).

18. The first two parts are read on the Fifth and Sixth Sundays of Easter, Year A: John 14:1-12; 14:15-21.

19. Chapter 14 of John's Gospel is structured around three questions, posed successively by Thomas ("Master, we do not know where you are going; how can we know the way?": v. 5), Philip ("Master," show us the Father": v. 8), and Judas ("Master . . . what happened that you will reveal yourself to us and not to the world?" v. 22). To Thomas, Jesus responds: "I am the way and the truth and the life"; to Philip: "Whoever has seen me has seen the Father." Now it is in response to Judas' question that he is speaking.

20. F. Mauriac, Journal, t. 3 (Paris: Grasset, 1940) 45.

21. Isa 9:5-6; Mic 5:4; Zech 9:10; Ps 72:3, 7. "Peace" is even one of God's names: Judg 6:24. See Vocabulaire de théologie biblique (Paris: Cerf, 1970) col. 878–84.

22. John 13:19; 16:4.

23. J. H. Newman, Parochial and Plain Sermons, t. 4, sermon 11 (London: Revingtons, 1869) 168–69.

24. Matt 4:13; Luke 4:43.

25. See n. 14, above.

26. Commission Francophone Cistercienne, *Tropaires des dimanches*, Le Livre d'Heures d'En-Calcat (Dourgne: 1980) 42.

The Ascension of the Lord—Pages 203–209

1. Nicene Creed.

2. Fiche de chant A 191 (Text and music: Chambarand).

3. Since this name means "lover of God," one might think that it refers not to a particular person, but to all the "lovers of God" who read the book. But Luke qualifies it with a term (*kratiste* in Greek), which means "eminent." Thus we are rather inclined to regard "Theophilus" as a person, a Christian of high rank, member of the Church of Antioch, and considered to be a qualified representative of the Greek communities to which Luke dedicates each of the two halves of his work.

4. For Luke (Luke 1:1-2), as for Mark (Mark 1:1), the Gospel begins with the preaching of John the Baptist and Jesus' baptism in the waters of the Jordan. Matthew has Jesus' preaching begin after the arrest of John the Baptist (Matt 4:12-17). And John gives particular importance to the testimony of the precursor who inspired the call of the first disciples (John 1:29-51) following, "on the third day," the sign of Cana, the first that Jesus performed (John 2:1-12). Thus each of the four evangelists places, in his own way, the beginning of the Gospel in relation to the ministry of John the Baptist.

5. In Acts, the Holy Spirit is mentioned 56 times; 49 times in the Gospels (Matt: 11; Mark: 7; Luke: 17; John: 14) and 126 times in the other apostolic writings; in all, 231 times in the whole of the New Testament.

6. See *Days of the Lord*, vol. 6, pp. 106–107. The account of this "journey to Jerusalem" is read from the Thirteenth to the Thirty-first Sunday of Ordinary Time, Year C.

7. John 14:16; 15:26; 16:7-15.

8. See among others: Acts 2:33; 5:31; 7:55; Luke 24:52; 1 Tim 3:16.

9. C. M. Martini, "L'Ascension de Jésus," in *Assemblées du Seigneur*, 2nd series, no. 28 (Paris: Publication de Saint-André—Cerf, 1969) 9.

10. See: 2 Kgs 2:1-12; Dan 7:13; Matt 24:30; 26:64; Mark 13:26; 14:62; Luke 21:27; 1 Thess 4:17; Rev 1:7; 14:14-16.

11. Matt 17:4; Mark 9:5.

12. Matt 17:5; Mark 9:7.

13. Moses and Elijah spoke of Jesus' departure. Moreover, Matt (17:12), Mark (9:12), and Luke (9:44) place the second announcement of the passion after the transfiguration.

14. The women saw the two men who appeared to them at the tomb as angels (Luke 24:23). Matt (28:2, 5) says: "an angel of the Lord"; Mark (16:5): "a young man . . . clothed in a white robe"; John (20:12): "two angels in white . . . ."

15. The New Testament often speaks of the Lord's return: the sayings on vigilance (Matt 24:43-51; 25:1-13; Luke 12:25-48; 13:24-30). See also: Matt 25:31-46; John 14:28; Col 3:4; Rev 3:11; 22:7, 12, 20; etc.

16. The prayers composed by these men and women who have "retired" from the world testify to this. Thus the texts of the monks and nuns in Commission Francophone Cistercienne, often cited in *Days of the Lord*.

17. Vatican II, Constitution on the Sacred Liturgy (*Sacrosanctum concilium*), no. 10.

18. The statement made by Cardinal C. M. Martini at the end of the *VIIe Symposium des évêques européens* (Rome, October 12–17, 1989), is entitled precisely: "Habiter la Galilée des nations," in *La documentation catholique*, 86 (1989), 1013-20.

Year A: Christ Raised to Heaven, Present in the Church—Pages 210–215

1. Along with those addressed to the Colossians and to Philemon, in whose home the Colossian community gathered, the Letter to the Ephesians was written during the two years Paul spent in captivity in Rome, as Acts tells us (28:16, 30-31). The apostle was living under guard, but with a certain freedom of action: he could receive guests into his house, preach, teach, receive news of the Churches and write to them. Thus it was a propitious time for him for reflection, prayer, and contemplation.

Acts ends with Paul's captivity in Rome, saying nothing of the outcome of the trial, for which he had appealed to the emperor: was he acquitted or condemned? Did Luke finish writing his book before the sentencing, ca. 62–63? This is not likely, since one would then have to place Luke's Gospel—and even more Mark's—at a very early date, which modern scholarship will not accept. It would seem that the author was not interested in the trial. The important thing for him is Paul's preaching in Rome.

2. The best study is still that of J. Dupont, *Gnosis. La connaissance religieuse dans les épîtres de saint Paul* (Bruges-Paris: Desclée de Brouwer, 1949). See also the article "Connaître," in *Vocabulaire de théologie biblique* (Paris: Cerf, 1970) col. 203–04.

3. J. Dupont, o.c., p. 540.

4. G. Bachelard, *La flamme d'une chandelle* (Paris: Presses universitaires de France, 1961) 56–57.

5. In Col 1:24, Paul speaks in the same way about the passion: ". . . and in my flesh I am filling up what is lacking in the afflictions of Christ on behalf of his body."

6. Except for that reported by Mark (16:14-15), all the Easter appearances are scenes of recognition that end by Jesus sending the disciples out on a mission.

7. "Luke only speaks of prostration after the resurrection (24:52). John notes it only once, in the case of the man born blind, after his healing (9:38). Mark speaks of two prostrations, both of them omitted by Matthew: that of the Gerasene demoniac before his healing, while he was still under the influence of the demons (Mark 5:6), and that of the Roman soldiers who bowed down in mockery of the king of the Jews (Mark 15:19). Matthew mentions acts of homage ten times: in the episode of the magi (three times: 2:2, 8, 11) and after the resurrection (twice: 28:9, 17); by the leper (8:2), the synagogue leader (9:18) and the Canaanite woman (15:25), who beg for healing; when the mother of Zebedee's sons asks that they receive the first place (20:20); and finally, after the tempest died down, the disciples prostrated themselves before Jesus while saying: 'Beyond doubt you are the Son of God!' (14:33)" (J. Dupont, "L'évangile de saint Matthieu: quelques clés de lecture," in *Communautés et liturgies* 57 (1975), p. 10).

8. God's manifestations—"theophanies"—are not so obvious that they dismiss all doubts: Gen 18:12; Judg 6:11-24; Mark 16:8; Luke 24:11, 25-37; John 20:25.

9. Like Matthew, Mark (16:7) says that the risen Jesus made a rendezvous with the apostles in Galilee. According to Luke (Luke 24:50; Acts 1:12), it was at Bethany, near Jerusalem, that Jesus left them. John's Gospel speaks of appearances both in Jerusalem (20:19-29) and on the shore of the sea of Tiberias in Galilee (21:1-14). The testimony of tradition is very plain: after his resurrection, Jesus showed himself several times to the apostles and to the other disciples in order to prove to them that he, who was crucified, was alive (1 Cor 15:5-7). But neither the evangelists nor the author of Acts (nor Paul) wanted to make out a list of where each of the appearances occurred. On the basis of the traditions that were passed on to them—the gospel was preached before it was written down—Matthew, Mark, Luke, and John fashioned a truthful but personal presentation of the good news (Luke 1:1-4). None of them pretended to report all of Jesus' sayings and miracles, or all that he did. This has been acknowledged from the beginning (John 21:25). It would be a mistake to amalgamate the Four Gospels to try to create a complete account of Jesus' life . . . and the ap-

pearances of the resurrected. The intention and the literary genre of Acts from the election of Matthias on (Acts 1:15) are different. In the second part of his work, Luke made a chronicle of the life of the primitive Church and especially Paul's missionary action. One can follow the stages of his missionary journeys on a map, which cannot be done with the long "journey to Jerusalem," the literary and theological framework of the second part of Luke's Gospel (9:51–19:27): see *Days of the Lord*. vol. 6, pp. 125–26.

10. Isa 8:23, quoted in Matt 4:15.

11. Matt 8:20; 9:6; 10:23; 11:19; 12:8; 12:32, 40; 13:37, 41; 16:13, 27-28; 17:9, 12, 22; 19:28; 20:18, 28; 24:27, 30, 37, 39, 44; 25:31; 26:2, 24, 45, 63-64; 28:19.

12. The others said that Jesus held his power from "Beelzebul, the prince of demons" (Matt 12:24; see also 10:25).

13. This explicit mention of the three persons of the Trinity does not allow us to infer that it was part of the baptismal formula from the beginning. It seems more likely that baptism first occurred with the formula: "I baptize you in the name of the Lord Jesus" (Acts 8:16; 10:48; 19:5).

14. On the true disciple of Jesus according to Matthew, see J. Dupont, o.c. note 7, 25-32.

15. On Jesus as the "master" who teaches, see ibid., 32-37 and 40.

16. The pope and the bishops do not exercise this magisterium in an isolated manner. In the document mentioned in n. 18, p. 346, Cardinal C. M. Martini says: "The bishops feel themselves to be in solidarity with the theologians, whose task seems particularly difficult and urgent in Europe today. Let us then encourage all those theologians, preachers and catechists who are involved in a task much like the introduction of faith into Europe. The Holy Spirit who teaches, corrects, animates and directs, will never be far from the efforts of those who proclaim what 'eye has not seen, ear has not heard,' but what 'God has prepared for those who love him' and what has been 'revealed to us through the Spirit' (cf. 1 Cor 2:9-10)."

And Cardinal G. Danneels: "In these demanding conditions—seriousness and competence in research, reception of the Word in faith, respect of one's proper role without absolutizing it, deep-seated respect for people such as they are—exegesis will be a service and a richness for the Church. Let us add that in its very austerity, exegetical work will thus be an authentic spiritual journey, in humble and trusting hearing of the Other of whom the biblical Word speaks" ("Exégèse et service de l'Eglise auiourd'hui," in *A cause de l'Evangile. Mélanges offerts à Dom Jacque Dupont* [Paris: Publications de Saint-André—Cerf, 1985] 14).

Vatican II, at which there were many such people, highlighted the indispensable role of theologians and exegetes: Dogmatic Constitution on Divine Revelation (*Dei Verbum*), no. 23; Pastoral Constitution on the Church in the Modern World (*Gaudium et spes*), nos. 44, 62.

17. In the Old Testament, God constantly promises his people that he will be with them, that he will not abandon them to their own powers. See, e.g.: Isa 7:14; 8:8, 10.

18. Augustine (354–430), *Traité sur saint Jean*, X, 9, cited in *Assemblées du Seigneur*, 2nd series, no. 28 (Paris: Publications de Saint-André—Cerf, 1969) 12.

19. D. Rimaud—C. Geoffray (Fiche de chant J 1).

Year B: *Christ Raised to Heaven, and the Church, His Body—* Pages 216–220

1. See above, n. 1, p. 347.

2. Ps 68:19ab: "You have ascended on high, taken captives, received men as gifts—even rebels." Paul writes: "and gave gifts to men," using, doubtlessly, a Jewish interpretation that attributes the text to Moses going up onto the mountain to receive the gift of the Law.

In the old *Bréviaire*, one response for the ascension said: *Ascendens Christus in altum, alleluia, captivam, duxit captivitatem, alleluia!* ("Christ goes up, leading his captives"). In *La Liturgie des Heures*, Ps 68 is introduced in the Office of Readings by the following antiphon: "The Lord God ascended on high; he has led captivity captive, alleluia."

3. It is typical, and one might say even necessary, that the liturgy "unfolds the whole mystery of Christ from the incarnation and nativity to the ascension, to Pentecost and the expectation of the blessed hope of the coming of the Lord" (Vatican II, Constitution on the Sacred Liturgy, no. 102). It would be a mistake to take this unfolding as a dividing of the mystery, claiming that each celebration actualizes one part, since it would ignore underlying unity, which is often referred to in the celebration itself.

4. The analogy with the body and its members is developed in the 1 Cor (12:12-30).

5. In Greek (*kephale*), as in English, the head signifies the superior part of the body, a leader, someone who is above others.

6. Commission Francophone Cistercienne, *Tropaires des dimanches*, Le Livre d'Heures d'En-Calcat (Dourgne 1980) 43 (Fiche de chant J LH 107).

7. Mark 16:1-8: Easter Vigil, Year B.

8. On the distinction between canonicity—to which inspiration is tied—and authenticity, see n. 2, p. 321.

9. Mark 1:1, 14; 10:29; 13:10; 14.

10. This is what is already suggested in the superscription "Here begins the gospel of Jesus Christ, the Son of God" (Mark 1:1).

11. The reference is to the judgment on the last day: Acts 3:20; 10:42; 17:30; Rom 5:10; 8:24; 13:11; Phil 3:20.

12. The faith by which one receives the Lord—"the good news"—is often explicitly linked with baptism: Acts 2:41; 8:12, 36; 11:20; 14:1; 15:7; 16:33; 17:11, 34; Rom 10:14.

13. Regarding these hesitancies: Acts 15; Gal 2.

14. Mark 3:7; 4:35; 5:1; 7:24, 31. "He withdrew," "He returned," are common expressions in Mark's Gospel. It is difficult to follow Jesus' movements, and sometimes even to understand how he could have passed from one locale to another. The evangelist seems not to be interested in enlightening his readers on this point. Rather, he wants to show that Jesus went everywhere, that he was always on the move. Paul did the same. But he went ever farther, to Rome.

15. Matt 10:8; Mark 3:15; 6:13; Luke 9:1; 10:9.

16. Acts 2:3-11; 10:44-46; 19:6; 1 Cor 14.

17. Acts 3:1-10, 4.12-16, 9.32-43, 13.5-12; 14:6-10; 19:11-17; 20:7-12.

18. Maximus of Turin (d. between 408 and 423), *Homélie sur l'Ascension*, quoted in *Assemblées du Seigneur*, 2nd series, no. 28 (Paris: Publication de Saint-André—Cerf, 1969) 48.

19. D. Hameline, in *La Liturgie des Heures*, vol. 2, p. 715 (Fiche de chant I 262).

Year C: Christ, Our Hope, Raised to Heaven—Pages 221-225

1. The believer is not a "theist" who professes a "philosophical doctrine (independent of all positive religion) that admits the existence of one, personal God, distinct from the world but having power over it" (*Dictionnaire alphabétique et analogique de la langue française*, by P. Robert, tome 6 [Paris, 1977]). The believer believes that God has revealed himself and saved the world. The Christian knows, through faith, that this revelation has reached its peak in Jesus Christ, through whom salvation has been achieved. One speaks not of "one God," but of "God the Father of Jesus Christ through whom the Holy Spirit has been revealed and communicated."

2. Despite its common title, Hebrews is not written like a letter. But it ends with a personal message (Heb 13:22-25) in the form of "a word of encouragement."

3. This is Yom Kippur. The description of the ritual to be performed in the Temple is described in Leviticus (16:2-34). See Heb 9:1-7.

4. Two goats were offered, and lots were drawn to select one "for the Lord" and one "for Azazel" (probably the name of a demon). The first was sacrificed and its blood was used in the purification rites. The other was driven out into the desert, with the sins of the people laid on it by the imposition of hands. The Greek and the Vulgate translations refer to it as the "scapegoat."

5. Preceded by one or more days of fasting, Yom Kippur is wholly consecrated, even today, to awaiting forgiveness from God. In Jerusalem, the ordinary activities of life come to a halt at sundown. Even the international airport at Lod is closed. In the evening, in front of the Western Wall of the Temple, where a huge crowd of the faithful is gathered, when the signal is given by the sound of the shofar, there are dances, songs, acclamations, all in indescribable atmosphere, where each person shares the joy of forgiveness.

6. Ephraim, deacon (ca. 306-73), *Hymne de la liturgie syrienne pour la fête de l'Ascension*, quoted in *Assemblées du Seigneur*, 2nd series, no. 28 (Paris: Publications de Saint-André—Cerf, 1969) 37.

7. Luke 9:22, 44; 17:25; 18:31-33; 22:37; 24:25-27.

8. Some legends make Luke the physician into a painter who, most notably, had made a portrait of the Virgin.

9. Augustine (354-430), *Homélie pour l'Ascension. Sermon "Mai."* 98, 1-2, in *Patroloïe latine. Supplement*, t. 2, col. 234. Quoted in *La Liturgie des Heures*, vol. 2, pp. 713-14.

10. Luke's iconographic emblem is the bull, the sacrificial animal, because his Gospel begins with the vision of the priest Zechariah, the father of John the Baptist, in the Temple of Jerusalem.

11. Leo the Great (pope 440-61), *Sermon pour la Fête de l'Ascension*, 2, in *Sources chrétiennes* 74 (Paris: Cerf, 1961) 139-41; in *La Liturgie des Heures*, vol. 2, pp. 726-27.

12. Memorial acclamation.

13. P. Teilhard de Chardin, *Le milieu divin. Essai de vie intérieure*, in *Oeuvres*, vol. 4 (Paris: Seuil, 1957) 197.

14. Cl. Bernard, Hymne pour l'Office du soir le jour de l'Ascension, in *La Liturgie des Heures*, vol. 2, p. 720 (Fiche de chant J 36-2).

Seventh Sunday of Easter

Year A: Thanksgiving Prayer of Christ and the Church—Pages 226–232

1. Acts 2:42-47; 4:32-35; 5:12-16. These three pictures are usually called the "summaries" of Acts. They are read on the Second Sunday of Easter, Years A, B, and C respectively. See text, pp. 91-93; 97-99; 103-105.

2. "A sabbath's journey away." The Law prescribed: "On the seventh day everyone is to stay home and no one is to go out" (Exod 16:29). This prescription is related to the law of sabbath rest that forbids all work, even domestic, and journeys to procure food. On the sixth day, in the desert, one received a double portion of bread (Exod 16:21, 29). In line with this, it was determined that on the sabbath one could travel no more than 2,000 cubits, about three-tenths of a mile. Acts calculates the distance between Mount Olivet and the place the apostles were staying in reference to this traditional measure.

3. "The house" would have been known to the first readers of the book, much as we know what is meant by the reference "the church." We might wish to identify this house with the one in which Jesus celebrated the Last Supper, but we cannot be sure of this. Instead, Luke speaks of "the house of Mary the mother of John (also known as Mark)," where Peter went after his miraculous deliverance from prison, "where many others were gathered in prayer" (Acts 12:22).

4. On Easter morning, the women who discovered the empty tomb knew where to find the disciples to share with them what they had seen (Matt 28:8; Mark 16:10; Luke 24:9; John 20:18). The risen Jesus appeared to the disciples gathered in a house (Luke 24:21; John 20:19, 26), to the Eleven "as they were at table" (Mark 16:14).

5. The tradition of an appearance on the shore of the Sea of Tiberias (John 21:1-19) does not mean that the apostles had really dispersed, each going back to his own home and former occupation.

6. A list of the apostles is given by each of the first three evangelists: Matt 10:2-4; Mark 3:16-18; Luke 6:13-16. Peter is always named first, and Judas—of whom Acts never speaks after the first chapter—is always last. There are differences though, especially in the order in which the others are named. John (21:2) does not give a complete list.

7. The presence of women in Jesus' entourage is confirmed by Matt (27:55) and Mark (15:41). This was quite exceptional in the culture of Palestine (see John 4:27).

8. The "memorial" of the Virgin Mary, mother of God, in the Eucharistic Prayer and at the end of the Prayer of the Hours recalls this.

9. Acts 15:13; 21:18; Gal 2:9.

James "the brother of Jesus" (Mark 6:3; Gal 1:19) also known as James "the minor," son of Clopas and Mary (Mark 15:40; John 19:25), brother of Joseph (Matt 27:56), originally from Nazareth, must not be confused with James "the major," one of the Twelve and the brother of John (Matt 4:21; 10:2; Acts 1:13), nor with James the "son of Alphaeus" (Matt 10:3; Acts 1:13).

10. H. Kahlau, in *Traces de Dieu*, Introduction et présentation des textes par J.-P. Bagot, A. Mandouze, E. Mathiot, Langage des hommes/Parole de Dieu 4 (Paris: Droguet et Ardant—Cerf, 1975) 29-30.

11. Acts 2:42-46; 4:32; 5:12.

12. Second Sunday of Easter, Year A, text pp. 91–94. See also: Acts 3:1.

13. The problem in representing Christ on the cross lies in the need to evoke both his suffering and his glorification.

14. The name "Christian" was first given to the disciples at Antioch in A.D. 40 (Acts 11:26). At first it was a nickname. But the disciples quickly adopted it and bore it with pride. It would be impossible to find a better title for those who follow Christ.

15. Cyprian (d. 258), *Correspondance*, tome 1, lettre 31 (Paris: Les Belles Lettres, 1925) 78–79.

16. See also: Rom 8:17; 2 Cor 1:5; 4:10; 1 Thess 1:1; Heb 11:26; 13:13-14.

17. Likewise: Mark 6:41; 7:34; John 11:41-42.

18. See C. Vagaggini, *Initiation théologique à la liturgie*, vol. 1, (translation-adaptation Ph. Rouillard) (Bruges: Apostolat liturgique, 1959) 29 and 135–74; vol 2, translation-adaptation R. Gantoy (Bruges-Paris: Publications de Saint-André, 1963) 153. "All good comes to us from the Father, through Jesus Christ his incarnate Son, by means of the presence of the Holy Spirit within us and, likewise, it is by the presence of the Spirit in us and through Christ that everything returns to the Father" (vol. 1, p. 139).

19. It is related to the first page of John's Gospel (1:1-18), which presents the mystery of the incarnation from a similar theological and mystical height.

20. The two other parts are read on the Seventh Sunday, Years B (John 17:11b-19) and C (John 17:20-25).

21. John 2:11, 23; 6:14; 7:31; 9:16; 10:25, 37-38; 11:47; 12:18; 14:11; 20:30-31.

22. Matt 9:8; Mark 2:12; Luke 5:25-26; 7:16; 13:13; 17:15; 18:43; 23:47.

23. One finds here what the ''prologue'' of John's Gospel said about the Word who was ''in the beginning'' ''present to God,'' who ''was God'' and ''became flesh'' (John 1:1-5, 14)

24. From the Greek word *anamnesis* which means ''recollection, memory.'' We call that portion of the Eucharistic Prayer which follows the consecration and recalls the various stages of the paschal mystery of Christ the ''anamnesis.''

25. J. H. Newman, *Lectures on Justification,* IX (London: Rivington, 1838) 251.

26. Commission Francophone Cistercienne, *Tropaire des dimanches,* Le Livre d'Heures d'En-Calcat (Dourgne, 1980) 44 (Fiche de chant K 146-1).

Year B: The Lord Dwells with His Own—Pages 233–239

1. This story seems to have been inserted at a later date.

2. The liturgical version omits two whole verses (18-19) and part of a third (20b). Vv. 18-19 are a parenthesis in Peter's speech: ''[Judas] bought a parcel of land with the wages of his iniquity, and falling headlong, he burst open in the middle, and all his insides spilled out. This became known to everyone who lived in Jerusalem, so that the parcel of land was called in their language 'Akeldama,' that is, Field of Blood.'' This does not fully agree with what is found in Matt 27:3-10, where it is said that the field was bought by the priests, and that Judas hanged himself. Luke was writing for foreigners (when speaking of the inhabitants of Jerusalem he says: ''their language''). The circumstances of Judas' death were a source for many popular traditions, all of which harkened back to a brutal and ignominious death in an ill-named place: ''Akeldama, the Field of Blood.''

Verse 20 cites Ps 69:26 (''Let their encampment become desolate; in their tents let there be no one to dwell'') and part of Ps 109:8 (''May his days be few; may another take his office''). These two psalms are speaking of people who harm a just man.

3. See text, p. 226.

4. Ibid., n. 6, p. 351.

5. Matt 27:34, 48: ''In my thirst they gave me vinegar to drink'' (Ps 69:22b); John 15:25: ''Too many for my strength are they who wrongfully are my enemies'' (Ps 69:5b); Rom 15:3: ''The insults of those who blaspheme you fall upon me'' (Ps 69:10b). To which should be added John 2:17: ''Zeal for your house consumes me'' (Ps 69:10a).

6. One might also appeal to the symbolic value of the number twelve in Scripture: the twelve tribes of Israel; the twelve thrones on which Jesus had said that the apostles would sit in judgment over the twelve tribes of Israel (Matt 19:28; Luke 22:30); the twelve thousand chosen from each of the twelve tribes (Rev 7:4-8).

7. This is an undebatable point in Luke's theology: Luke 24:48; Acts 1:8, 22; 2:32; 5:32; 10:39, 41; 13:31.

8. Only the bishop of Rome is the personal successor of a specific apostle—Peter—and thus is the head of the episcopal college.

9. Paul's case is an exception, but it does not refute the principle. He never knew, nor *a fortiori* followed Jesus during his earthly life; he was not one of the Twelve. And yet he was acknowledged as an apostle and a witness of the resurrected because he had seen the Lord on the road to Damascus (Acts 22:15; 26:16).

10. The term ''vocation'' has a double meaning: the inner call felt by an individual and the call of the Church. The first is not in itself a right: it must be ratified by the Church.

11. Some authors attribute to him a certain number of non-verifiable details. Thus Clement of Alexandria (born ca. 150) identifies him with Zacchaeus.

12. Vatican II, Dogmatic Constitution on the Church (*Lumen Gentium*), no. 22.

13. The beginning (1 John 4:7-10) is read on the Sixth Sunday.

14. This spiral development is characteristic of John. It appears in the great discourses of his Gospel: chapters 6 and 14-17 in particular.

15. Fr. Varillon, *Prière avec l'Eglise*, I (Paris: Bloud et Gay, 1945) 75.

16. John 14:21, 28.

17. Bossuet, "Oraison funèbre d'Anne de Gonzague de Clèves, Princesse Palatine," in *Oeuvres de Bossuet*, t. 2 (Paris: Firmin-Didot, 1879) 50.

18. See text, p. 107.

19. R. Guardini, *Le Seigneur. Méditation sur la personne et la vie de Jésus Christ*, vol. 2 (Paris: Alsatia, 1945) 88.

20. See 1 Pet 4:13-16: second reading for the Seventh Sunday of Easter, Year A.

21. L. Deiss, from Rom 8:35-39 (Fiche de chant M 19).

22. In the Bible's vocabulary, "to consecrate" means "to put aside for sacrifice": Exod 13:2; 28:31; 29:1, 21, 27; 40:9; Lev 16:6; Deut 15:19.

23. See Eucharistic Prayer III.

24. Commission Francophone Cistercienne, *Tropaire des dimanches*, Le Livre d'Heures d'En-Calcat (Dourgne: 1980) 45.

Year C: Behold Christ, Standing at the Right Hand of God— Pages 240-248

1. Acts 6:8-8:1: a total of 69 verses.

2. The word "martyr" comes from the Greek *martus*, (*marturos*), which means "witness."

3. It is worth the trouble to read this story from its beginning, or at least to be aware of it. Stephen's activity is summarized in a significant way: "Now Stephen, filled with grace and power, was working great wonders and signs among the people" (Acts 6:8). The elders of a synagogue, scandalized by this "foreigner" and unable to argue effectively with him, bribe witnesses to accuse him of having uttered blasphemy against Moses, against God, and against the Temple, saying that Jesus would destroy the Temple and alter the laws given by Moses (6:9-15). Brought before the Sanhedrin, Stephen embarks on a long, accusatory speech: "You always oppose the holy Spirit . . . Which of the prophets did your ancestors not persecute? They put to death those who foretold the coming of the righteous one, whose betrayers and murderers you have now become" (7:1-50). Finally comes the reading for this Sunday.

Stephen has always been a very popular saint. Countless churches are dedicated to him. In France 68 villages and townships are called Saint-Etienne. His feast is December 26.

4. He speaks of Jesus' "passage" to Jerusalem (Luke 9:31); his "entering" into glory (Luke 24:26); his being "taken up" to heaven (Acts 1:2, 11, 12; 2:34); his "sitting" at the right hand of God (Luke 20:42; 22:69; Acts 2:34); and his "coming" in glory (Luke 9:26; 12:36-39; 18:8; 19:23; 21:37; Acts 1:11; 12:36).

5. Matt 13:19-20 and Mark 13:11 report the same promise, but attribute this assistance to the Holy Spirit.

In Rev 5:6, the sacrificial lamb who intercedes for the saints is also "standing."

6. Matt 24:29-31; Mark 13:24-27.

7. Ignatius of Antioch (martyred in 107), "Lettre aux Romains," IV, 2, *Lettres*, in *Sources chrétiennes* 10 (Paris: Cerf, 1951) 131.

8. Ibid., V, 3, p. 133.

9. "Lettre aux Ephésiens," 1, 2, ibid., 69; III, 1, ibid., 71; "Lettre aux Tralliens," V, 2, ibid., 115–17.

10. Ignatius of Antioch, "Lettre aux Romains," IV, 1, in o.c., p. 131. And also: "Do nothing for me besides ensuring that I may be offered as a libation to God, when the altar is ready" (ibid., II, 2, 129).

11. Eusebius of Caesarea (ca. 265–338), *Histoire ecclésiastique*, IV, 15, 33-35, in *Sources chrétiennes* 31 (Paris: Cerf, 1952) 187.

12. Acts 6:8-16: Matt 26:59-61; Mark 14:55-59.

13. Acts 7:57: Matt 26:65; Mark 14:63.

14. Acts 7:58: Matt 27:33; Mark 15:22; Luke 23:33; John 19:17.

15. Acts 7:60: Luke 23:34.

16. Acts 7:59-60: Luke 23:46; Matt 27:50; Mark 15:37.

17. Acts 7:60: John 19:30.

18. The Greek name for the book is *apocalupsis*, ''Apocalypse.'' The term is used to denote a writing that reveals what will happen in a near or distant future.

19. In similar terms: Matt 4:17. According to Luke (4:16-22), on the occasion of his first preaching in the synagogue at Nazareth, Jesus proclaimed that the prophecies—especially those of Isa 61:1-2 and 58:6—were fulfilled in him.

20. Alpha and Omega are respectively the first and last letters of the Greek alphabet.

21. The liturgical version omits v. 15: ''Outside are the dogs, the sorcerors, the unchaste, the murderers, the idol-worshipers, and all who love and practice deceit.'' This is a terrible saying. But the parable of the talents ends with a no less fearful sentence on the ''worthless servant'': ''And throw this useless servant into the darkness outside, where there will be wailing and grinding of teeth'' (Matt 25:30).

22. See Rev 3:4-5, 18; 6:11; 7:9, 14. In all these texts, he speaks of the ''white robe'' worn by the chosen. The last (7:14) says more specifically that they have ''washed their robes and made them white in the blood of the Lamb.''

23. John 8:24, 28. See also John 6:48, 51; 8:12, 28; 10:9, 11, 14; 11:25; 14:6.

24. Bernard (1090–1153), *Sermon 67 sur le Cantique des cantique*, 3, in *Oeuvres mystiques*, translation A. Beguin (Paris: Seuil, 1967) 589-91.

25. The story of creation, particularly that of man and woman (Gen 2:23-24) is clearly underlying this whole passage.

26. *Marana tha* is an Aramean liturgical formula common in the first Christian assemblies.

27. *La Doctrine des Douze Apôtres* (*Didachè*), 10, 2-6, in *Sources chrétiennes* 248 (Paris: Cerf, 1978) 179-83.

28. The first two parts are read in Years A (John 17:1-11a) and B (John 17:11b-19).

29. Eucharistic Prayer II.

30. Vatican II, Decree on Ecumenism (*Unitatis redintegratio*), no. 1.

31. Commission Francophone Cistercienne, *Tropaires des dimanches*, Le Livre d'Heures d'En-Calcat (Dourgne: 1980) 46.

Pentecost—Pages 249–250

1. From the Greek *pentecoste* which means ''fiftieth.'' Under the name *Chavout*, this is a Jewish feast celebrated fifty days after Passover (*Pessah*). At first an agricultural feast of the harvest or ''of Weeks'' (Exod 23:16; 34:22; Tob 2:1; 2 Macc 12:32), it became, at an undetermined time, a feast ''of oaths'' that commemorated the covenant at Sinai (a change in vowels, thus in pronunciation, allowed it to move from ''weeks'' to ''oaths''). It certainly had this significance by 300 B.C. The meaning of the Jewish Pentecost is important for the understanding of the Christian Pentecost. See the article ''Pentecôte,'' in *Dictionnaire encyclopédique de la Bible* (Paris: Brepols, 1987) 1003-04.

2. See text, pp. 77-78.

3. Vatican II, Dogmatic Constitution on the Church (*Lumen Gentium*), no. 4.
The formula in quotation marks comes from Cyprian (d. 258), *Traité sur l'oraison dominicale*,

23; Augustine (354–430), *Sermons* 71, 20, 33; John Damascene (ca. 650–750), *Traité contre les iconoclastes*, 12.

4. To "commemorate" signifies, in the language of the Christian liturgy—as already in the Jewish liturgy—recalling the past, whose benefits (graces) are renewed today. "Memorial" and "actualization" go hand in hand.

A "mystery" is an event contained within a time, but is not closed upon itself. Accomplished once and for all time by God, it is a stage of salvation history and, consequently, has an eternal dimension. It is always today that the power of salvation strikes us, the salvation that God has once taken the initiative to unfold.

5. Until the reform of Holy Week promulgated by Pius XII on November 27, 1955, a vigil similar to the Easter Vigil was celebrated on Saturday morning, complete with Liturgy of the Word (six readings from the Old Testament), blessing of the baptismal water, and litany of the saints, followed by a Mass with two readings. In the reform, the Vigil was suppressed, retaining only the Mass with its two readings. The formulary of our present Mass dates from 1969.

6. In parish churches on Saturday evening, it is usually the Mass for Sunday that is celebrated.

7. This, since the promulgation of the second edition of the *Ordo lectionum missae*, January 21, 1981. It is true that one may always use the texts chosen for Year A. However, the readers of *Days of the Lord* will certainly not wish to be deprived of the benefit of meditating on the texts proposed for each year.

Vigil Mass—Pages 251–267

1. Commission Francophone Cistercienne, *La nuit, le jour* (Paris, Desclée, 1973) 105 (Fiche de chant K 161). Proposed as a hymn after the the First Vespers of Pentecost in *La Liturgie des Heures*, vol. 2, p. 783.

2. The story of Babel is placed at the end of these eleven chapters that are a prelude to the whole Bible, inserted here as a result of a long literary process.

3. Inserted between the "Table of the Nations" (Gen 10) and the genealogy of Shem, which ends with Abraham (Gen 11:10-32), the episode of Babel serves as a transition between the account of the beginnings marked by sin and that of the covenant which involves the process of redemption.

4. Excavations in Mesopotamia witness to a period where colossal monuments and huge pyramid-like towers were built. (One of these towers was destroyed in Iran, during its war with Iraq.)

The biblical story speaks of building with "bricks for stone" and "bitumen for mortar." Might not these new techniques—previously unknown in Palestine—have made people eager to exploit them, even so far as to attempt to dominate matter and defy time and space?

Later on, the prophetic tradition concerning Babylon will play an important role in the interpretation of Babel. Thus Babel will be Babylon, the great city of Mesopotamia, representative of measureless pride, and whose fall is prophesied many times (Isa 14:4-21; 47; Jer 51; Ps 137:8-9).

5. See H. Cox, *La cité séculière. Essai théologique sur la sécularisation et l'urbanisation* (Paris: Casterman, 1968). In this work, the author—who has since altered his optimistic position—believes that one can find in the Bible itself the origin of secularization. He has been accused of illustrating his thesis by the Bible, rather than proving it.

6. Because of its enigmatic character, Babel opens up the possibility of many meanings and interpretations.

7. The narrative cycle of the Flood has its own interpretation of the separation of peoples and the multiplicity of languages.

8. "The only part of it (the text) that allows for a universal interpretation is found in v. 6: 'This is their first attempt, and now nothing they imagine will be impossible for them.' The divine act of dispersion and confusion arises from a diagnosis (reflection on the city and the tower) and a prognosis (the unbounded horizon of human possibilities). The text does not allow one to speak of a curse or a blessing. A proper characterization of the divine action lies in a more neutral word, one with less religious connotation: we will call it *prophylactic*" (H. Bost, o.c., note 2, 84).

9. The Church would be remiss in the performance of its prophetic duty if it did not recall at both convenient and inconvenient times the absolute primacy of such values as life, the dignity of every human person, peace, etc. The way it does so may indeed be a source of dispute and discussion. But it is undoubtedly necessary that some voices be raised to awaken the human conscience and lead people to reflect seriously on the means and ends of their endeavors and the exercise of their power, which grows ever greater. The Church is one of these voices: this is its mission.

10. Augustine (354–430), *La cité de Dieu*, XVI, 4–11, in *Oeuvres*, 36, Bibliothèque augustinienne (Paris: Desclée de Brouwer, 1960) 194–226, devotes a great deal of space to a commentary on Gen 11, and to a meditation on the origin of languages. He takes from other Fathers of the Church the idea that Hebrew was the primitive language of humanity (safeguarded by the children of Eber: Gen 10:21-30), and that there were 72 languages among the peoples who were dispersed after the Flood (Gen 10:31-32). In several of his *Sermons sur la Pentecôte*, he draws from the event of the gift of languages (Acts 2:4) the conclusion that there no longer is a sacred language, that all languages may henceforth bear the Spirit.

11. See: Deut 32:8; Acts 2:1-12.

12. G. Gusdorf, *La Parole*, Initiation philosophique 3 (Paris: Presses universitaires de France, 1956) 15–16.

13. Nersès Snorhali (1102–73), *Jésus, Fils unique de Père*, in *Sources chrétiennes* 203 (Paris: Cerf, 1973) 49–50.

14. Vv. 8b-15, omitted by the Lectionary, recount the purification of the people, in which Moses proceeded as God had ordered him.

15. See: Deut 1:31; 32:1; and also: Hos 11:3-4; Isa 46:3-4; 63:9.

16. It is one of the leitmotifs of the second and third parts of Isaiah: Isa 41:8-9; 42:19; 43:10; 44:1-2, 21; 45:4; 48:20; 49:3; 54:17; 56:6; 61:6; 63:17; 65:8-9, 13, 15; 66:14.

17. "Holy nation" is an uncommon expression, only found in very few texts: Deut 7:6; 14:2, 21; 28:9. It is more common to speak of Israel as a nation holy or sacred "to God" (e.g., Jer 2:3).

18. Preface of Sundays I.

19. See: Deut 4:11-12.

20. Ps 18:8-15; 29:3-8; 46:7; 68:34; 83:15-16; Isa 29:6.

21. Deut 4:15. When the theophany of Sinai is presented, for instance in a movie, it is accompanied by images created by technology that, far from evoking the solemn grandeur of the scene, almost always provoke laughter because of their absurdity. It is an undeniable fact that certain religious realities ought not to be objectified or theatricalized.

22. Fiche de chant K 24. Text and music by L. Deiss.

23. Symeon the New Theologian (949–1022), *Hymnes* III, in *Sources chrétiennes* 196 (Paris: Cerf, 1973) 217, 233–35.

24. This sort of coercion is typical in the psalms. It expresses a profound trust in God's justice, to which familiar appeal is made: Ps 6:6; 35:22-26; 69:7-8; 86:14; 88:11-13; 109:21; 143:11-12.

25. Ezek 17:24; 20:12; 36:36; 37:28.

26. This formula occurs 54 times in Ezek. For God is revealed by what he does, whether he chastises or forgives and restores life to his people.

27. This is also an epiclesis (a Greek word meaning "invocation") of the Spirit that the priest pronounces at Mass over the bread and wine, so that these offerings "may become the Body and Blood of our Lord, Jesus Christ."

28. "Spirit" without the article denotes the breath that comes from God and animates all living things. It is personalized when one speaks of "the Spirit."

29. Hymn "*Veni, creator Spiritus,*" in *La Liturgie des Heures*, vol. 2, pp. 406–07.

30. The conjunction of the themes "creation" and "word," along with that of "exodus," dominate the second part of Isaiah: 40:26; 41:4; 43:1-4, 7, 15, 21; 44:1, 21, 24; 46:3; 48:12; 51:13.

31. *Les odes de Salomon*, 22, Quand vous prièrez (Paris: Desclée de Brouwer, 1981) 44. These poems were composed in the 2nd c., but we cannot be sure either of their author or their geographical origin, for we do not know in what language they were originally written.

32. This is what one does in a "biblical circle." The marginal references to other parallel or complementary texts provided in many modern Bibles can serve as a point of departure for a reading that takes account of the context of the whole Bible, or at least all of one book.

33. "As directly as possible," because the Christian meaning of a biblical text rests on a proper perception of the meaning it has in itself. This cannot be a license to take a text as a pretext for concluding any number of things that are utterly foreign to it.

34. This orientation is presented in two ways: first by the choice of readings, particularly during Advent, Lent, and for feasts and solemnities; then by the selection of verses, thereby not beginning and ending the reading on the basis of exegetical criteria, and not including all the verses within a particular section. This practice is entirely legitimate, and does not constitute a censoring of the text, provided that its meaning is not twisted. Indeed, Scripture itself cites Scripture in this way.

35. Isa 58:6; 61:1-2, cited by Jesus during his first preaching at the synagogue in Nazareth (Luke 4:18-19).

36. One need not distinguish between "dreams" and "visions." Both are terms that evoke a revelation, an illumination. See the article "Songes" in *Vocabulaire de théologie biblique* (Paris: Cerf, 1970) col. 1245-47.

37. Rom 7:14-24; Eph 4:22-24; Col 3:9-10.

38. We have been created, Paul says, so that what is corruptible in us may be swallowed up into life. And he adds: "Now the one who has prepared us for this very thing is God, who has given us the Spirit as a first installment" (2 Cor 5:5).

39. Elsewhere, Paul puts more emphasis on the present reality of God's gift (1 Cor 1:18, 21; 15:2; 2 Cor 2:15; Eph 2:5-8; 2 Tim 1:9; Titus 3:5; etc.). But he is concerned that some people may think that they have nothing then for which to wait (1 Cor 15:12; 2 Tim 2:18). This is why he puts the accent here on the fact that the Christian lives in waiting: *homo viator* (man on the way).

40. S. Lyonnet, *Les étapes du mystère du salut selon l'Epître aux Romains*, Bibliothèque oecuménique 8 (Paris: Cerf, 1969) 212.

See: Vatican II, Pastoral Constitution on the Church in the Modern World (*Gaudium et spes*), nos. 35, 38, 77, 78, 92, 93.

41. On the origin and evolution of this feast, see the article "Tentes (Fête des)," in *Dictionnaire encyclopédique de la bible* (Paris: Brepols, 1987) 1251–53.

42. Ibid., 5, 1.

43. *Sukkoth* is celebrated Oct. 12–13 in 1992, Sept. 30–Oct. 1 in 1993, Sept. 20–21 in 1994, etc. These same years the first day of the year (Rosh Hashanna) occurs on Sept. 20–21, Sept. 9–10, Sept. 28–29, Sept. 16–17, Sept. 6–7. Jewish feasts last from one sundown till the next.

44. Even today, during this feast, many Israelis build a booth in their garden or, more

modestly, on the balcony of their apartment. In certain places there are large booths: in the garden of a synagogue, especially on the esplanade of the eastern wall. Typically, people do not live in them, but they stay there during the day and it is there that they receive their friends. Some of them are very ornate, especially as decorated with branches of trees from which hang bunches of fruit, most of all oranges and citrons. Outside, one can see pious Jews who ceremoniously carry a *lulab* in their right hands, a bouquet composed of a palm and three branches (myrrh, willow and citron) carefully selected to ensure that they are faultless.

45. This oracle may be found in the liturgy of Easter Vigil (seventh reading). The prayer of blessing of the water for aspersion before the Sunday Mass, and the traditional song allude, during Eastertime, to this oracle.

46. Most modern Bibles have adopted the most ancient punctuation. It is from Jesus' heart that "rivers of living water" shall flow. One tradition, however, divides it in the following manner: "Let anyone who thirsts come to me and drink. Whoever believes in me, as scripture says, 'Rivers of living water will flow from within him.'" This second reading—which attributes the saying not to Jesus but to the believer—corresponds less well with John's style and context. Yet sermons are often based on this latter reading.

47. Exod 17:1-8; Num 20:2-11; Ps 78:15-16; 105:41.

48. See: *Days of the Lord*, vol. 2, Third Sunday in Lent, Year A.

49. When the priest drew forth water from the fountain of Siloam, this verse was sung: "With joy you will draw water at the fountain of salvation" (Isa 12:3).

50. Cyril of Alexandria (ca. 380–444), *Commentaire sur saint Jean*, V, 2, in *L'Evangile selon saint Jean expliqué par les Pères*, Les Pères dans la foi (Paris: Desclée de Brouwer, 1985) 86.

51. Eucharistic Prayer III.

52. Commission Francophone Cistercienne, *La nuit, le jour* (Paris: Desclée, 1973) 96 (Fiche de chant I 132).

Sunday Mass—Pentecost—Pages 268–269

1. Matt 3:16; Mark 1:10; Luke 3:22; John 1:32.
2. Gospel for Mass on Saturday evening.
3. Gospel of the Ascension, Year C.
4. Gospel for Pentecost Sunday, Year A.
5. First Reading, Years A, B, C.
6. Orthodox Judaism in Jesus' day seems to have been ignorant of this interpretation of the feast: it only appears in the rabbinic writings from the 2nd c. on. But the *Book of Jubilees* —an apocryphal writing of the Old Testament written in Hebrew two centuries before Jesus Christ—mentions it explicitly. See *Dictionnaire encyclopédique de la bible* (Paris: Brepols, 1987), articles "Pentecôte," 1003-04, and "Apocryphes de l'Ancien Testament, 50, Livre des Jubilés," 105.
7. One possible entrance antiphon for the Mass (Rom 5:5; 8:11).
8. Another possible entrance antiphon (Wis 1:7).
9. P. de la Tour du Pin (Fiche de chant K 72).

Years A, B, C: The Spirit Makes One People of All Nations— Pages 270–274

1. Luke 4:14–9:50.
2. Luke 9:51–19:27.

3. Luke 19:28–21:38. The respective length of these three parts of the Gospel of Luke is itself significant: Galilean ministry, 265 verses; journey to Jerusalem, 345 verses; last ministry in the city, 106 verses.

4. Luke 22:1-23, 56.

5. Luke 24:44-49.

6. Luke 24:50-52.

7. Luke 24:49; Acts 1:6.

8. Acts 1:8; Luke 24:47.

9. There is no doubt that it is easier to comprehend the significance of such an event from the past when it is placed within a well-constructed scene, judiciously highlighted and edited. We know very well that there are many such possible scenes that would legitimately attest to historical truth. With respect to the Gospels, there are different presentations of the same ministry, teaching, and history of Jesus according to Matthew, Mark, Luke and John: one Gospel in four gospels, not four copies. A simple historical chronicle—"on this day, at this hour, in this place, this was done, this was said," etc.—a record of events or a travelogue are very valuable for history, but as documents, as keys to the reconstruction of the interior framework of events that allow their meaning to be determined through the proper connections, each relegated to its proper place and perspective: and this is the work of the historian. His work is not to cavil, but to give some details more attention than the mere chronicler would have. Ultimately, "having carefully traced the sequence of events from the beginning," he forms them as they have been passed on from reliable witnesses into "a narrative" (Luke 1:1-3). Someone else will present them differently, though with the same historical rigorousness. We should add, though, that the Gospels, though historically based, are above all else announcements of Jesus Christ and his message.

10. See text, p. 268.

11. Luke 24:49; Acts 1:4, 5, 8, 12-14.

12. Exod 19:16-25; Deut 4:36.

13. Num 11:25-29; 1 Sam 10:5-6, 10-13; 19:20-24; 1 Kgs 22:10; Joel 3:1 is also cited by Peter when he addresses the crowd (Acts 2:17).

14. Acts 10:46: the beneficiaries were Cornelius and his family and friends; this has been called the "Pentecost of the Gentiles" (cf. Acts 19:6).

15. One should read 1 Cor 12–14, the remarkable short treatise on discernment of charisms, especially the gift of tongues. For Paul, the supreme and certain criterion is love. Yet the apostle cannot be denied a certain spiritualist or mystic character, as we see when he speaks of the revelations that he has received. Note that it is precisely in these chapters of 1 Cor, devoted to charisms, that we find the great hymn to love: "If I speak in human and angelic tongues, but do not have love . . . " (1 Cor 13:1-3).

16. "Similarly, if you, because of speaking in tongues, do not utter intelligible speech, how will anyone know what is being said? For you will be talking to the air" (1 Cor 14:9).

17. To answer that the apostle, through the Spirit, spoke in strange tongues which each person present understood in his or her own language, is to say that these people received the "gift of interpretation" to which Paul alludes (1 Cor 14:13); or, to recapture his image, that the instrument gives forth only clanging sounds, but the ear perceives the voice of the flute, the harp, or the trumpet (1 Cor 14:7-8).

Yet without suddenly becoming true polyglots, one could suppose that the apostles proclaimed God's praises—his "wonders"—in several languages.

18. First of the readings suggested for the Vigil Mass.

19. To impose one language—always one's own—as a universal language is a form of hegemony and colonialism, not only of a cultural order. Mutual respect, rather, consists in making the necessary effort to understand and speak the language of the other. How-

ever necessary it may be, recourse to an interpreter is always a last resort. Evangelization must occur, as soon as possible, in the language of those who are its object.

20. *Homélie africaine du VIe siècle pour la Pentecôte*, in *La Liturgie des Heures*, vol. 2, p. 779.

21. Gen 10 draws up a list of 70 peoples who came from the sons of Noah after the Flood. Paul, though, does not know why there are "different languages" in the world (1 Cor 14:10).

22. This is a quote of Isa 40:5, according to the Greek version of the Old Testament.

23. Irenaeus (ca. 135–202), *Contre les hérésies*, 3, 17, 2, in *Sources chrétiennes* 211 (Paris: Cerf, 1974) 331.

24. Vatican II, Pastoral Constitution on the Church in the Modern World (*Gaudium et spes*), n. 40, 2.

25. See the Eucharistic Prayer, prayer of epiclesis—invocation—of the Spirit, and consecration.

26. Closing doxology of the Eucharistic Prayer.

Year A: Gift of the Risen Christ, the Spirit for the Common Good—
Pages 275–280

1. By nature and definition, God has no face. Any material representation is at best hazardous; in any case, one must take to it with reserve, fully aware that God is not as one represents or imagines him. Because of the danger of illusion and idolatry, the Old Testament absolutely forbids all representation of God: "The idols of the nations are silver and gold, the handiwork of men. They have mouths but speak not; they have eyes but see not . . ." (Ps 135:15-17). Islam, too, forbids all representation of God, and even all figurative painting in mosques. Jesus, the Son of God, had a human face that could have been painted. As for God, we call him Father: although his face cannot be known, this appellation has a very definite meaning. But as for the Spirit . . . One can only evoke it in symbols: fire or dove, as the Gospels say (Matt 3:16; Mark 1:10; Luke 3:22; John 1:32).

2. This was the case in Corinth. Many "mystery" religions flourished in this cosmopolitan city. Initiates alone could participate in the secret rites, which came from agricultural cults centered around the celebration of the great rhythms of natural fertility; they were supposed to enable the initiate to participate in the death and rebirth of a god, as in the mysteries of Eleusis (near Athens, center of a cult in honor of Demeter, personification of the earth), Serapis (an Egyptian god), Mithra (an Indo-Iranian deity), etc. These religions could be extremely good or extremely bad. They could be characterized by ecstatic manifestations, trances, convulsions, etc., or an atmosphere of joy and exaltation, though they sometimes led to all sorts of disorders: paintings and drawings discovered in certain sanctuaries illustrate this at length. Doubtlessly, these religions were much in fashion, and very fascinating. The search for a symbolic identification through rites with the life and fate of a god, particularly his death and resurrection: is this not a profound human aspiration? The aberrant, even licentious, character of certain rites, in certain religions of this kind—they still exist today—is one thing. But is there no truth hidden under this exterior? O. Casel (1886–1948), *Le mystère du culte dans le christianisme*, 2nd French edition, Lex orandi 38 (Paris: Cerf 1964), (German original *Das Christliche Kultmysterium* [Regensburg: F. Pustet, 1932]) pursued this intuition. Fr. Casel's teaching, freed from what is perhaps overly systematic about it, is better understood today. We can acknowledge that the work of the liturgist of Maria-Laach has been of great benefit to the liturgy.

3. Discernment of the gifts of the Spirit occurs at all times. It is particularly indispensable—though not always in evidence—in "charismatic" groups.

4. The Church and spiritual masters know well that it is better not to be too quick to declare that a particular experience, a "mystical" phenomenon, an undertaking, etc., or

even a vocation, truly comes from the Spirit. It is usually easier to recognize what does not come from it. "Therefore I tell you that nobody speaking by the spirit of God says, 'Jesus be accursed,' " Paul writes (1 Cor 12:3a: the beginning of this verse is omitted in the liturgical version).

5. Gal 5:16-25 is read for Year B.

6. See also 1 Cor 13:4-7; 2 Cor 6:6; 2 Pet 1:5-7.

7. Among these are peace, kindness, humility, and joy. It can happen that one suffers sorrowful moments of anguish, even of doubts about the faith. But, however long they last, they cannot touch the profound peace that ends up triumphing over such temptations. The popular saying captures this well: "A sad saint is a bad saint." We may also think of the anecdote about St. Philip Neri (1515–95). Known for his spirit of discernment, he was once asked to come to a convent in order to give his advice on a nun's "mystical" (?) states. He received her in the parlor and, without preamble, asked her: "Are you holy?" Her response—"Yes, Father"—was enough.

8. Rom 5:5; 8:14-16; Gal 4:5.

9. John Chrysostom (ca. 350–407), *Homélie 30 sur 1 Co 3*, trans. in *Jean Chrysostome commente saint Paul*, Les Pères dans la foi (Paris: Desclée de Brouwer, 1988) 289.

10. This typical teaching of Paul runs through many of his letters: Rom 12:5; 1 Cor 6:15; 10:17; 12:12, 27; Eph 1:23; 2:16; 4:4, 12, 16; 5:23, 30; Col 1:18, 24; 2:19; 3:15.

11. John Chrysostom, o.c., p. 291.

12. We reprise here a part of the Gospel for the Second Sunday of Easter (John 20:19-31). There, the account of this resurrection appearance, followed by what happened "a week later," was read for its teaching on faith: to believe without having seen. On Pentecost, we stop at v. 23 to focus on the gift of the Holy Spirit, which Jesus bestowed on the disciples. Likewise, in Year C, we reprise part of the Gospel read on the Sixth Sunday of Easter.

13. Rom 1:7; 1 Cor 1:3; 2 Cor 1:2; Gal 1:3; Eph 1:2; Phil 1:2; Col 1:2; 1 Thess 1:1; 2 Thess 1:2; 1 Tim 1:2; 2 Tim 1:2; Titus 1:4; Phil 1:3; 1 Pet 1:2; 2 Pet 1:2; Jude 2.

14. The Greek words employed by John to express "flesh," "eating," are so realistic that they cannot be taken in a purely spiritual sense.

When Jesus said "I am the bread that came down from heaven" (John 6:41), greater than manna, "so that one may eat it and not die" (John 6:49-50), his words were a cause for scandal (John 6:52, 60-61). And the rest of the discourse insists (John 6:53-59): Yes, it is of my "flesh" that I am speaking, and it must really be "eaten."

15. See also John 3:5; 4:14; 6:51-55; 7:38-39.

16. See the note in the *Bible de Jérusalem* (I, p. 1560)

17. John 6:47; 19:35.

18. They were "incredulous for joy and were amazed" (Luke 24:41).

19. John insists on this point: Jesus is "the One sent by God": John 3:34; 4:34; 5:23-24, 36-38; 6:29, 38-39, 44, 57; 6:57; 7:18, 28-29, 33; 8:16, 18, 26, 29, 42; 9:4; 10:36; 11:42; 12:44-45, 49; 13:16, 20; 14:24; 15:21; 16:5; 17:8, 18, 23, 25.

20. John 3:17; 12:47.

21. John 7:37-39 is read in the Vigil Mass.

22. This oracle is also read during the Vigil.

23. Matt 9:2; Mark 2:5-9; Luke 5:20; 7:47-48.

24. ". . . whoever believes in me will do the works that I do, and will do greater ones than these, because I am going to the Father" (John 14:12).

25. Eucharistic Prayer III.

26. Ibid.

27. Eucharistic Prayer II.

28. Nersès Snorhali (1102–73), *Jésus, Fils unique du Père*, in *Sources chrétiennes* 203 (Paris: Cerf, 1973) nos. 771-74, 189.

Year B: *Witnesses of Christ with the Holy Spirit—*
Pages 281–286

1. The occasion for this letter was provided by the confusion produced in the young Christian communities of Galatia when some people preached a return to the ancient Jewish customs: without them, they said, there is no salvation. Paul reacted with a very forceful letter: only the cross of Christ can save us; only it can free us from sin and the agonies of life (Gal 5:1-12). In reading the text selected today, one would not imagine that it comes from a letter that is clearly polemical. However, if it has been chosen, it is because it has a value even beyond this context.

2. Doubtlessly inspired by the lists of vices that circulated in pagan and Jewish literature at the time. Hence the diversity of the lists found in Paul's letters: Rom 1:29-31; 13:13; 1 Cor 5:10-11; 6:9-10; 2 Cor 12:20; Eph 4:31; 5:3-5; Col 3:5-8; 1 Tim 1:9-10; 6:4; 2 Tim 3:2-5; Titus 3:3. See also: Matt 15:19; Mark 7:21-22; 1 Pet 4:3; Rev 21:8; 22:15.

3. Other lists: 1 Cor 13:4-7; 2 Cor 6:6; Eph 5:9; 1 Tim 6:11; 1 Pet 1:5-7.

4. Symeon the New Theologian (949–1022), *Hymnes* I, in *Sources chrétiennes* 156 (Paris, Cerf, 1969) 151–53.

5. Acts 5:31-39. Paul, in one of his defense speeches, says that he was educated "at the feet of Gamaliel" (Acts 22:3).

6. A. George, "Les temoins de Jésus devant le monde (Jn 15, 26–16:4)," in *Assemblées du Seigneur*, 1st series, no. 50 (Bruges: Publications de Saint-André, 1966) 32.

7. John is the only one to use this term: 14:16, 26; 15:26; 16:7; 1 John 2:1.

8. A. George, a.c., p. 32, n. 1.

9. In John, this term most often denotes everything, marked by sin, that is opposed to God, Christ, the light, the truth, etc.

10. The verb "to witness" occurs 12 times in John (21 times in the whole New Testament), and the term "testimony" 44 times (103 in the whole New Testament).

11. Matt 11:27; Luke 10:22.

12. See text, p. 275.

13. Matt 10:18; Mark 13:9; Luke 21:13.

14. "Martyr" means witness.

15. John 7:17-18. Christ likewise only announced what the Father had taught him and what he had heard from him: John 7:17-18; 8:28, 38; 12:49-50; 14:10.

16. *Anaggelein*, the Greek verb which occurs three times in two verses, and which the Lectionary translates as "to tell about" has a very strong sense in apocalyptic literature. Thus in the Greek translation of Daniel, where it is applied to the interpretation of dreams: Dan 2:2, 4, 7, 9, 11, 16, 24, 27; 5:12, 15; 9:23; 10:21; 11:2. So one can understand the "explanation" of the parables reserved by Jesus for his disciples: Matt 13:36 especially; also: "When the Messiah comes, he will tell us everything" (John 4:25).

17. Cyril of Jerusalem (ca. 315–86), *Catéchèses*, X, 16, in *Les écrits des saints* (Namur: Editions du Soleil levant, 1952) 373.

18. Basil of Caesarea (329–79), *Traité du Saint-Esprit*, XV, 36, in *Sources chrétiennes* 17 (Paris: Cerf, 1947) 171–72.

Year C: *The Spirit of the Father in the Lord's Prayer—*Pages 287–292

1. "It is [Christ] whom we proclaim, admonishing everyone and teaching everyone with all wisdom, that we may present everyone perfect in Christ" (Col 1:28).

2. See: Eucharistic Prayer III, intercession for Masses for the dead.

3. Paul goes so far as to say: "Now the Lord is the Spirit . . . " (2 Cor 3:17). This does not mean that there is a personal identity between Son and Spirit, but that the risen one will henceforth act through the Spirit.

4. Hesychius (beginning of the 4th c.) in *Les plus beaux textes sur le Saint-Esprit* collected by Y. Arsène-Henry, new edition (Paris: Lethielleux, 1968) 198.

5. Eph 3:6; 2 Tim 1:1; Titus 1:2; Gal 3:22, 26.

6. 1 Cor 6:9-10; Gal 5:21; Eph 5:5.

7. Rom 5:2; 8:18; Eph 1:18.

8. Rom 6:22-23; Gal 6:8; Titus 1:2.

9. Irenaeus (ca. 135–202), *Contre les hérésies*, V, 8, 1, in *Sources chrétiennes* 152 (Paris: Cerf, 1969) 95–97.

10. Canticle for Mass on Pentecost Sunday.

11. On the Sixth Sunday of Easter, Year C we read John 14:23-29. Likewise, on the Second Sunday of Easter we read, John 20:19-31, of which a portion (John 20:19-23) is reprised on Pentecost, Year A.

12. This discourse is structured around three questions posed successively by Philip, Judas, and Thomas: see n. 19, p. 345.

The selection made by the Lectionary does not do violence to the text. The second part of John 14 concerns "the promise of the Spirit." It is introduced by vv. 15 16: "If you love me, you will keep my commandments. And I will ask the Father, and he will give you another Advocate to be with you always." This is what is dealt with till the end of the chapter (v. 31). But John's thought does not proceed in a direct manner. He meditates on the themes, not one after another, but by constantly moving between them. To grasp the coherence of this pattern, one must follow the evangelist's meandering meditations. However, without forcing his text into a new structure, one can stop it at a particular junction, in order to feed oneself with its "daily bread," without pretending to grasp its full richness. John's fluidity invites us to read him in this manner, with the help of the Spirit that directed him when he wrote.

13. Love for Jesus is mentioned especially in the later writings of the New Testament: John 8:42; 14:15, 23; 16:27; 21:15-17; Eph 6:24; 1 Pet 1:8. However, see Matt 10:37 (Mark 8:34-35; Luke 14:26): "Whoever loves father or mother more than me . . ."

14. See: John 15:10; 1 John 5:2-4; 2 John 6; Rev 12:17; 14:12.

15. Acts 2:38; 8:20; 10:45; 11:17.

16. Augustine (354–430), *Traité sur saint Jean*, LXXVI, 2, in J.-P. Migne, *Patrologie latine* 35, col. 1831: "Dilection sanctos discernit a mundo."

17. These words recur like a refrain: John 15:11; 16:1, 4, 5, 25, 33.

18. Hilary, bishop of Poitiers (ca. 315–67), *Traité sur la Trinité*, 10, 73, in *La Liturgie des Heures*, vol. 2, p. 773.

19. Augustine (354–430), *Commentaire de la Première lettre de saint Jean*, IV, 1, trans. P. Camelot, in *La vie spirituelle*, 75 (1946), pp. 362-363, reprised in Y. Arsène-Henry, *Les plus beaux textes sur le Saint-Esprit*, new edition (Paris: Lethielleux, 1968) 193.

20. J. H. Newman, *Douze sermons sur le Christ* (Paris: Egloff, 1943) 208.

Everyday Pentecost—Pages 293–295

1. Irenaeus (ca. 135–202), *Contre les hérésies*, III, 17, 1, in *Sources chrétiennes* 211 (Paris: Cerf, 1974) 329-331.

2. Matt 3:13; 4:17, 23-25; Mark 1:9, 14; John 1:29, 35, 43.

3. Acts 1:21-22; 10:37-38.

4. D. Rimaud, *Les arbres dans la mer* (Paris: Desclée, 1975) 145 (Fiche de chant K 79).

From Bethlehem to Emmaus—Pages 296–303

1. Third Sunday of Easter, Year A.

2. This is what the name means in Hebrew.

3. Midnight Mass for Christmas. See *Days of the Lord*, vol. 1, pp. 200–208.

4. This quote from the prophet (from the Greek text) is found in Matt 1:23, read at the evening Mass on Christmas Eve.

5. *General Norms for the Liturgical Year*, n. 22. See text, pp. 77–78.

6. Gregory of Nyssa (ca. 335–95), *Sermon sur la naissance de Jésus Christ* in J.-P. Migne, *Patrologie grecque*, vol. 46, col. 1148, cited in *Le mystère de Noël*, texts collected by A. Hamman and Fr. Quéré-Jaulnes, Lettres chrétiennes 8 (Paris: Grasset, 1963) 172–73.

7. Prayer after the first reading (Gen 1:1–2:2) at the Easter Vigil.

8. Gregory Nazianzen (329–89), *Sermon 38 pour la Théophanie bu la Nativité du Sauveur*, (given at Constantinople in 380), in J.-P. Migne, *Patrologie grecque*, vol. 36, col. 334, cited in *Le mystère de Noël*, o.c. (n. 6), p. 156.

9. Bernard (1090–1153), *Sermon pour l'Epiphanie*, 1, 1-2, in J.-P. Migne, *Patrologie latine*, vol. 183, col. 143, trans. in *La Liturgie des Heures*, vol. 1, p. 268.

10. Entrance antiphon for Mass on the Second Sunday after Christmas. (This mass is never celebrated in those places where Epiphany occurs on the Sunday after January 1.) This same text is found in *La Liturgie des Heures*, vol. 1, p. 259; as the antiphon of the *Magnificat*, December 26, but in another translation: "While earth was rapt in silence and night only half through its course, your almighty Word, O Lord, came down from his royal throne."

11. The shepherds (Luke 2:11, 19), the magi (Matt 2:11), Mary Magdalene (John 20:16), the apostles (Luke 24:32).

12. See: H. Urs von Balthasar, *Jesus nous connaît-il? Le connaissons-nous?*, trans. from the German by J. Minery (Paris: Centurion, 1980) 75–77.

13. See text cited from Augustine, p. 292.

14. See A. Gelin, *Les pauvres de Yahvé*, Temoins de Dieu 14, 3rd edition revue (Paris: Cerf, 1962).

15. Matt 5:3-12; Luke 6:20-25.

16. Commission Francophone Cistercienne, *Sur la trace de Dieu* (Paris: Desclée, 1979) 12–13 (Fiche de chant I 258).